ARISTOTLE'S ETHICS

ARISTOTLE'S

ETHICS

WRITINGS FROM THE
COMPLETE WORKS

Revised, edited, and with an introduction by

JONATHAN BARNES

and

ANTHONY KENNY

PRINCETON UNIVERSITY PRESS

Princeton and Oxford

Published by Princeton University Press, 41 William
Street, Princeton, New Jersey 08540
In the United Kingdom: Princeton University Press, 6
Oxford Street, Woodstock, Oxfordshire OX20 1TW

press.princeton.edu

Jacket design by Jason Alejandro

Library of Congress Cataloging-in-Publication Data

Aristotle.
[Works. Selections. English. 2014]
Aristotle's ethics : the complete writings / edited by
Jonathan Barnes and Anthony Kenny.
pages cm
Includes indexes.
ISBN 978-0-691-15846-4 (pbk. : alk. paper) 1. Ethics—Early works to
1800. I. Barnes, Jonathan, 1942–editor of compilation. II. Kenny,
Anthony, 1931–editor of compilation. III. Title.

B407.B37 2014
171'.3—dc23   2013030226

British Library Cataloging-in-Publication Data is available

This book has been composed in MVB Verdigris
Pro, Lydian MT, and Syntax LT Std.

Printed on acid-free paper.

Printed in the United States of America

5 7 9 10 8 6 4

CONTENTS

ARISTOTLE'S ETHICS

INTRODUCTION

ARISTOTLE WAS BORN IN 384 IN THE SMALL TOWNSHIP OF Stagira, in north-eastern Greece. His father, Nicomachus, was a physician attached to the Macedonian court. At the age of seventeen he moved south to Athens, and joined the Academy, that brilliant band of philosophers, scientists, mathematicians, and politicians which gathered in Athens under Plato's leadership. For twenty years he remained as Plato's pupil and colleague, and made a name for himself as an industrious student, a vigorous polemicist, and an independent thinker, with an early interest in rhetoric, logic, metaphysics, and ethics.

In 359 King Philip II succeeded to the throne of Macedon. He adopted an expansionist policy, waged war on a number of Greek city-states, and made himself master of Greece. It cannot have been an easy time for a Macedonian in Athens, though Aristotle remained on the warmest terms with Plato, whom on his death in 347 he described as the best and happiest of mortals 'whom it is not right for evil men even to praise'.

Once Plato was dead, however, Aristotle found it prudent to emigrate. He settled in the eastern Aegean, first at Atarneus, then at Assos. Hermias, the ruler of Atarneus, was a graduate of the Academy, and offered an intellectual home to Aristotle and a few fellow-exiles. Aristotle later married his adopted daughter.

During his period in Assos, and during the next few years when he lived at Mytilene on the island of Lesbos, Aristotle carried out extensive scientific research, particularly in zoology and marine biology, whose results remained unrivalled for two millennia. Here Aristotle first worked with Theophrastus, who was to become his successor and greatest pupil.

In 343 Aristotle was summoned to the Macedonian capital by King Philip as tutor to his thirteen year old son, the future Alexander the Great. We know nothing of the content of his instruction, though forgers later concocted correspondence between the monarch and the philosopher. Within ten years of succeeding his father, Alexander had made himself master of an empire that stretched from the Danube to the Indus and included Libya and Egypt. While Alexander was conquering Asia, Aristotle was back in Athens, where in 335 he established his own school in the Lyceum, a gymnasium just outside the city boundary. Now fifty, he built up a substantial library, and collected around him a group of research students, called 'peripatetics' because they walked up and down while discussing philosophy. And for a decade he explored and expounded and taught the entire field of human knowledge—logic, metaphysics, theology, history, politics, ethics, aesthetics, psychology, anatomy, biology, zoology, botany, astronomy, meteorology, and the ancient equivalents of physics and chemistry.

Aristotle's anatomical and zoological studies gave a new and definitive turn to his philosophy. Though he retained a lifelong interest in metaphysics, his mature philosophy constantly interlocks with empirical science, and his thinking takes on a biological cast. Most of the works that have come down to us, with the exception of the zoological treatises, probably belong to this second Athenian sojourn. There is no certainty about their chronological order, and indeed in the form in which they have survived it is possible to detect evidence of different layers of composition, though no consensus has been reached about the identification or dating of these strata.

In 323 Alexander died in Babylon. When the news reached Athens, Aristotle, unwilling to share the fate of Socrates, left the city lest the Athenians put a second philosopher to death. He went to Chalcis, where he died a few months later. His will, which has survived, is a happy and humane document.

ARISTOTLE LEFT BEHIND A SUBSTANTIAL CORPUS OF PHIL-
osophical writing: although most of it has long been lost, the
items which have survived fill two thousand or more modern
pages, and they cover almost the whole range of Aristotle's
extensive intellectual interests.

In his major works Aristotle's style is very different from
that of Plato. The prose he wrote is commonly neither lucid
nor polished, though he could write passages of moving elo-
quence when he chose. His treatises, as we have them, are
thought to derive from the lecture courses which he gave
during his long teaching career—they are, so to speak, his
lecture notes. The notes were not used once and then filed
away: rather, they were taken up, year in year out, as the exi-
gencies of lecturing dictated; and they were subject to a series of additions, corrections and refinements. They were
later prepared for public circulation; and although the ancient editors doubtless indulged in some ordering and pol-
ishing, what we now have before us is essentially what Aristotle had on the lectern in front of him when he addressed
his pupils. If we look for a modern parallel for the composition and editing of the treatises, we might think of a twentieth century posthumous publication: *Sense and Sensibilia*, by
the Oxford philosopher J. L. Austin, was published after his
death by a colleague who put together a text from Austin's
own lecture notes which had evolved over the years.

Everything Aristotle wrote is fertile with ideas and full of
energy; every sentence is packed with intellectual punch.
But effort is needed to decode the message of his jagged
clauses: what has been delivered to us from Aristotle across
the centuries is a set of telegrams rather than epistles.

HUMAN KNOWLEDGE, ACCORDING TO ARISTOTLE, DIVIDES
into disciplines or 'sciences'. These sciences group under
three main heads: the contemplative, the practical, and the
productive. The major divisions of contemplative science are
theology, mathematics, and 'physics' or natural science; and
the majority of Aristotle's surviving works, being concerned

3

with natural science, fall therefore under the heading of contemplation. Productive sciences are, naturally enough, sciences that have a product. They include weaving and architecture, with products such as garments and houses, but also disciplines such as strategy and rhetoric, where the product is something less concrete, such as victory on the battlefield or in the law-courts. Aristotle's ethical treatises are works of practical science. What that means is that the characteristic aim of studying ethics is not the acquisition of knowledge about action but action itself—we study ethics, according to Aristotle, not in order to know what good men are like, but in order to act as good men act.

Ethics is only one of the practical sciences. Another is politics. The two sciences are continuous with each other, and Aristotle's *Politics* is in a manner a complement to his ethical writings. The practical sciences cannot easily be studied in isolation, either from one another or from the theoretical sciences: a student of ethics is unlikely to discover how a good man will act unless he has some knowledge of the general capacities and characteristics of human beings. One of the most familiar utterances of Aristotelian anthropology is the claim that man is a 'political animal': distinctively human activity is carried on in a political setting.

Aristotle often addressed ethical topics, but much of what he wrote is lost or survives only in fragments. The standard corpus of his works contains three substantial treatises of moral philosophy: the *Nicomachean Ethics* (NE), the *Eudemian Ethics* (EE), and the *Magna Moralia* (MM). In addition there is a pamphlet *On Virtues and Vices* (VV). The titles of the first two treatises have been variously interpreted. In antiquity the adjectives 'Nicomachean' and 'Eudemian' were taken to refer either to the authors of the works or to their dedicatees (though one does not normally dedicate one's lecture notes). French scholars refer to the *Éthique à Nicomaque* and the *Éthique à Eudème*; but the adjectives are generally taken to indicate that the former work was edited by Aristotle's son Nicomachus and the latter by his pupil Eudemus.

As for the *Magna Moralia* or *Large Ethics*, which is in fact by far the smallest of the three treatises, the commonest explanation of the title invokes the fact that the two 'books' into which it is divided are each much larger than any of the 'books' of the other two treatises.

The status of the three treatises and the relationship among them is complex and controverted. Between Aristotle's death and the second century AD a dozen authors cite Aristotle's ethical writings: all but one of them take their quotations from books that form part of the *Eudemian Ethics*. But this early primacy of the Eudemian over the Nicomachean treatise comes to an abrupt end in the second century AD with the work of Aspasius, who wrote a line-by-line commentary on several books of the *Nicomachean Ethics*. Since that time it has been almost universally agreed that the NE is not only a genuine work but also the most important of the three treatises. In the nineteenth century, indeed, the EE was treated as spurious, and published under the name of Aristotle's pupil, Eudemus of Rhodes. In the twentieth century scholars came to regard it as a genuine but immature work, superseded by an NE written in the Lyceum period. Throughout the Middle Ages, and since the revival of classical scholarship, it is the NE that has been treated as *the* Ethics of Aristotle, and it is indeed the most generally popular of all his surviving works.

But there is a twist to the story. The EE—in the modern editions—has a large gap in the middle: it contains nothing corresponding to Books 5, 6, and 7 of the NE. But at the end of Book III of the EE, the mediaeval manuscripts indicate that Books IV, V, and VI have not been copied out since they are the same as the three Nicomachean books. It has become clear, on both stylistic and philosophical grounds, that the three 'common' books began their career in the EE and were later added to fill a gap in the NE. (The most obvious sign of this is that modern editions of the NE contain two distinct accounts of pleasure in Books 7 and 10—the transplantation created an otherwise inexplicable duplication.)

Once the common books are restored to the EE the case for regarding the EE as an immature and inferior work collapses: nothing remains, for example, of the argument that the EE is closer to Plato, and therefore earlier, than the NE. Moreover, internal historical allusions suggest that the disputed books, and therefore the EE also, belong to the Lyceum period. But the similarities and dissimilarities between the two treatises are perhaps to be explained not by any simple chronological hypothesis, but rather by differences in audience and editorship.

What of the MM? Both style and content make it most unlikely to be an authentic work of Aristotle, and internal historical references have been taken to suggest a date in the late fourth century. However, it never explicitly discusses Aristotle in the third person, and its author appears to refer to Aristotle's works as his own. In general the MM follows closely the line of thought of the EE, but it contains a number of misunderstandings of its doctrine. Some scholars regard it as an independent construction of the time of Theophrastus; others surmise that it consists of notes made by a student at the Lyceum during Aristotle's delivery of a course of lectures resembling the EE. In the latter case, a modern parallel may be found in the posthumous publications by pupils of Wittgenstein of their notes of his Cambridge lectures.

As for VV, it is a trifle, and if it is Aristotelian in its ultimate inspiration, rare is the scholar who has ever thought that it came from Aristotle's own hand.

THE TEACHING OF THE THREE ETHICAL TREATISES IS, IN general, very similar. The ground covered by them overlaps with that covered by Plato's *Republic*, though Aristotle's rejection of the Theory of Ideas makes for substantial differences between the moral teaching of the two philosophers. The Idea of good, Aristotle says, cannot be the chief good of which ethics treats, if only because ethics is a practical science, about what is within human power to achieve, whereas

an everlasting and unchanging Idea of good could only be of
theoretical interest.

In place of the Idea of good Aristotle offers happiness (in
Greek, *eudaimonia*) as the supreme good with which ethics is
concerned; for, like Plato, he sees an intimate connection
between living virtuously and living happily. In all the ethical
treatises a happy life is a life of virtuous activity, and each of
them offers an analysis of the concept of virtue and a classification of virtues of different types. One class is that of the
virtues of character, or the 'moral' virtues, such as courage
and temperance, that constantly appeared in Plato's ethical
discussions. The other class is that of intellectual virtues:
here Aristotle makes a much sharper distinction than Plato
ever did between the intellectual virtue of wisdom, which
governs ethical behaviour, and the intellectual virtue of understanding, which is expressed in theoretical endeavour
and contemplation. The principal difference between the
NE and the EE is that in the former Aristotle regards perfect
happiness as constituted solely by the exercise of a single intellectual virtue in the activity of theoretical contemplation,
whereas in the latter it consists of the harmonious exercise
of all the virtues, both intellectual and moral.

At the beginning of each of his treatises Aristotle reduces
the possible answers to the question 'What is a good life?' to
a short-list of three: wisdom, virtue, and pleasure. All thinkers, he says, connect happiness with one or other of three
forms of life, the philosophical, the political, and the hedo-
nistic. This triad provides the key to his own ethical inquiry.
All the treatises contain detailed analyses of the concepts of
virtue, wisdom and pleasure. And when Aristotle comes to
present his own account of happiness, he can claim that it
incorporates the attractions of all three of the traditional
forms of life.

A crucial step towards achieving this is to apply the distinction between layers of potentiality and actuality that is
ubiquitous in Aristotle's thought. The most relevant layer
in this ethical area is that between a state and its use or

exercise. Virtue and wisdom are both states, whereas happiness, Aristotle claims, is an activity, and therefore cannot be simply identified with either of them. The activity that constitutes happiness is, however, a use or exercise of virtue or virtues.

In each treatise, to fill out this conclusion takes many pages of analysis and argument—and analysis and argument of a particular kind. Aristotle warns us that the method of ethics is not the same as that of the contemplative or productive sciences. The sciences, he emphasizes, cannot all aspire to an equal degree of 'precision' or *akribeia*: different subject matters make different demands, and the subject matter of ethics in particular allows only a modest amount of precision. This notion remains somewhat obscure; but one important feature of it seems to be that of generality as opposed to universality: ethical judgements, like other judgements about sublunary matters, are lacking in precision because they hold 'only for the most part'. This does not mean that Aristotle held that there are no absolutely valid moral rules: he tells us that there are—for instance there is no such thing as committing adultery with the right person at the right time in the right way, because adultery is always wrong. However, the observance of such absolute prohibitions will not get one very far towards the good life, and Aristotle, unlike his later Christian disciples, does not spend much time on them.

In any event, Aristotle does not attempt to establish rules which determine what is to be done in any specific concrete situation. Among the contemplative sciences mathematics offers precise measurement in every case; and the movement of the heavens can in principle be determined accurately. That is not so with the productive sciences, of which Aristotle's favourite example is medicine: medical science alone will not determine the treatment to be given to an individual patient in a particular case—there is need of the judgement of the practised and practising doctor. Moreover, the reasoning that lies behind the doctor's judgement will use the formal rules of deduction in a different manner from the contemplative sciences, arguing not from axiomatic principles to theoretical conclusions, but from the end to be achieved to the action to be undertaken. Ethics, in its turn, is one stage further removed from the contemplative sciences: the action to be done on a particular occasion will only be an expression of virtue if it springs from the experience and judgement of the individual moral agent.

Any work of practical philosophy is liable to contain judgements of two different sorts. It will contain, on the one hand, substantive moral judgements, to the effect that certain men or types of men, or actions or types of action, et cetera, are (at least for the most part) good or bad, right or wrong, virtuous or vicious, obligatory or impermissible, and so on. On the other hand, a work of moral philosophy will contain judgements about such substantive moral judgements, to the effect that they are or are not factual or objective or prescriptive, et cetera; that the concepts they use are to be elucidated in such and such a way; that they are logically interrelated in such and such a manner, and so on. In short, it will contain adversions on what is sometimes called the 'logic' of moral discourse.

Aristotle does not draw a distinction between these two kinds of judgement (termed by some modern philosophers 'ethical' vs. 'meta-ethical' judgements). Nor is it easy to apply the distinction to individual propositions in his treatises. Perhaps indeed it is not always helpful to try to do so, since what he is up to often cuts across the distinction. To illustrate this, consider the famous doctrine of the virtuous mean.

The doctrine in fact has two parts or aspects. First, the actions and emotions which express moral virtue will, Aristotle tells us, avoid excess and defect. A temperate person, for instance, will avoid eating or drinking too much; but he will also avoid eating or drinking too little. Virtue chooses the mean, or middle ground, between excess and defect: eating and drinking the right amount. Aristotle goes through a long list of virtues, beginning with the traditional ones of courage and temperance, but including others such as liberality, candour, dignity, and conviviality, and sketches how each of them is concerned with a mean. It should be stressed that this part of the doctrine of the mean is not intended as a recipe for mediocrity or an injunction to stay in the middle of the herd. Aristotle warns us that what constitutes the right amount to drink, the right amount to give away, the right amount of talking to do, may differ from person to person, in the way that the amount of food fit for an Olympic champion may not suit a novice athlete.

Secondly, the virtues, besides being concerned with middle amounts of action and emotion, are themselves means in the sense that they occupy a middle ground between two contrary vices. Thus courage is in the middle, flanked on one side by over-confidence and on the other by cowardice; generosity treads the narrow path between miserliness and prodigality. But while there is a mean of action and passion, there is no mean of virtue itself: there cannot be too much of a virtue in the way that there can be too much of a particular kind of action or emotion.

Aristotle's account of virtue as a mean seems to many readers to be truistic in its first aspect and false in its second. After all, Aristotle himself allows that, in some cases at least, the virtuous mean is surrounded by more than a pair of vices; and in addition he says that it is 'true but unilluminating' to state that a temperate man will drink neither too much nor too little. Nonetheless, the doctrine of the virtuous mean is part of a distinctive ethical theory which contrasts with other influential systems of various kinds. Religious ethical theories, such as traditional Jewish or Christian doctrine, give the concept of a moral law (natural or revealed) a central role. Because most of the Ten Commandments begin with 'thou shalt not', this led historically to an emphasis on the prohibitive aspect of morality. Aristotle does believe that there are some actions that are altogether ruled out, as we saw earlier; but he stresses not the minimum necessary for moral decency but rather the conditions of achieving moral excellence. Nor is it only religious systems that contrast with Aristotle's account. For a utilitarian, or any kind of consequentialist, there is no class of actions to be ruled out in advance. Since the morality of an action, on this view, is to be judged by its consequences there can, in a particular case, be the right amount of adultery or murder.

Aristotle's teaching on the mean thus contains both ethical and meta-ethical elements. On the one hand he offers specific ethical injunctions, while on the other he sketches out the general structure of a moral system, which is a meta-ethical activity.

ARISTOTLE'S ETHICAL SYSTEM HAS HAD A PROFOUND AND lasting effect: by later philosophers it has been warmly embraced and hotly repudiated, never coldly ignored; and in various ways it has helped to mould the common moral consciousness. Thus modern readers who take up the ethical works for the first time will find themselves already familiar, at least to some degree, with several of its leading notions. They will also find much of it surprising—the dozens of pages on friendship, with scarcely a word about sex; or the appearance of pride and conviviality as virtues, and humility and diffidence as vices. Moreover, it can actually be questioned whether his ethical writings are works of moral philosophy at all, in the sense in which the word 'moral' was understood by later philosophers such as Jeremy Bentham, Immanuel Kant, and John Stuart Mill.

Certainly, one of Aristotle's aims is to help us understand what it is to be a good human being. But do his treatises examine the *morally* good man? This is not explicit in Aristotle's texts, which introduce the moral virtues at a later stage in the argument—and when he speaks of moral virtue the adjective is to be understood in a mildly archaic sense and means 'to do with character'. If we drop the assumption, we might suppose that Aristotle is dealing, primarily, not with moral goodness but with human expertise, or the technique of being a good man. A good man, according to Aristotle's initial suppositions, is a man who does well the things that are the uniquely characteristic activities of human beings. Moral conduct is part, but only a part, of such activities.

To see the difference between Aristotle's ethical system and the moral systems of later philosophers we should focus on the role played by happiness. Aristotle holds that happiness or *eudaimonia* is the supreme end of life. He does not maintain that happiness is the immediate aim of every action, but rather that it is the ultimate aim. What this amounts to may be put, dramatically, as follows: Suppose you are doing X. I ask you why, and you reply 'In order to achieve Y'. I then ask you why you are aiming at Y, and you say 'In order to achieve Z'. Our conversation may go on as long as you please; but, Aristotle argues, if your doing X is a purposeful action and not a pointless frivolity, then there must eventually come a point at which you reject my questioning and say: 'I am not aiming at that in order to achieve any further aim— that is my ultimate aim'. Aristotle also maintains that your penultimate line in any complete dialogue of this sort must be 'In order to achieve my own happiness'.

At different points in his ethical treatises, Aristotle presents two theses about happiness. One is that every considered human action does, as a matter of fact, aim at the agent's happiness. The other is that every considered human action ought, if it is to be rational, aim at the agent's happiness. (It is not clear whether he ever held these two propositions simultaneously.) Both these theses appear to be false. A woman may well map out her life in the service of others—staying in an unhappy marriage, perhaps, for the sake of her children; and surely in some cases she may be rational to do so.

Nevertheless, the belief that one's own happiness is and ought to be the ultimate end of one's actions was dominant throughout antiquity and survived into the Christian era. Augustine and Aquinas, no less than Aristotle, thought of individual happiness as the supreme good: however, according to them it could only be fully realised in an afterlife, and it was not to be achieved by one's own actions but was in the gift of God.

The thesis that happiness is as a matter of fact the aim of every fully human action was called into question in the middle ages by Anselm and Duns Scotus. Scotus agreed that human beings have a natural tendency to pursue happiness; but in addition he postulated another natural tendency—the tendency to pursue justice, no matter what the consequences may be for our own welfare.

The thesis that one's own happiness ought rationally to be the aim of every action was called into question in the age of enlightenment. Thus Jeremy Bentham maintained that the real standard of morality was the greatest happiness of the greatest number, and Immanuel Kant dethroned happiness itself from the central position it had held since Plato and Aristotle. Like Scotus, Kant thought that morality needed a different basis: he called it the sense of duty. But where Scotus had placed the appetite for justice on equal terms with the pursuit of happiness, Kant regarded duty as the supreme motive which must trump every other.

Earlier the question was raised whether Aristotle, Bentham, and Kant were all engaged in the same activity of moral philosophy. The answer is yes, if moral philosophy is the study of the ultimate reasons determining what we ought and ought not to do. The supreme position is assigned by Kant to duty, and by Aristotle to individual happiness, and by Bentham to general happiness. But were Aristotle and Bentham talking about the same thing? Bentham equated happiness with pleasure, which was a single indefinable feeling—produced, no doubt, in many different ways—and this feeling was the one thing that was good in itself and was the point of doing anything whatever. Aristotle on the other hand made a sharp distinction between the two concepts. Indeed, he thought it unhelpful to talk about pleasure in the abstract: there were pleasurable experiences and pleasurable activities, and the evaluation of a pleasure depended simply on the evaluation of the activity or experience enjoyed.

In everyday modern English, the sense of the word 'happiness' seems closer to Bentham than to Aristotle: it means a mental or emotional state or attitude. *Eudaimonia*, on the other hand, is not simply a mental state. To call a man *eudaimon* is to say something about how he lives and what he does. The notion of *eudaimonia* is closely tied, in a way in which the notion of happiness is not, to success. It would indeed be a mistake to replace 'happiness' by 'success' as a translation of the Greek word, since the success which *'eudaimonia'* denotes is a very specific project, that of living a good life. But these considerations mean that the traditional English translation is not a perfect fit to Aristotle's concept.

Happiness, Aristotle tells us early in each of his treatises, is activity of soul in accordance with virtue, in a complete life. Given that 'activity of soul in accordance with virtue' means the excellent performance of whatever activities are typical of living creatures, we can paraphrase Aristotle's definition of human happiness as follows: A man is happy if and only if, over some considerable period of time, he frequently performs with some success the most perfect of typically human tasks.

Well, what, if anything, is typical of humans? The Aristotelian answer is that man is a rational animal and that his typical task is therefore rational activity. According to Aristotle, men may be said to be rational on two counts, and the notion of rational action is correspondingly twofold: I act rationally either in so far as I base my actions in some way upon reasoning, or in so far as I indulge in some sort of ratiocinative exercises. Selling my shares in the expectation of a drop in the market, and following out the Euclidean proof of Pythagoras' theorem, are both rational acts, but rational in different ways; in the first case I might be said to be following or obeying my reason, in the second case simply to be exercising it.

Aristotle's account of the moral virtues provides a description of rational activities of the first kind. He sums up his account of moral virtue by saying that it is a state of character expressed in choice, lying in the appropriate mean, determined by the prescription that a wise person would lay down. The role of reason appears in this definition in the reference to the prescription of the wise person. In order to complete this account, Aristotle has to explain what wisdom is, and how the wise person's prescriptions are reached. This he does in a book in which he treats of the intellectual virtues, whose exercises exhibit rationality of the second kind.

The two principal intellectual virtues are wisdom (or *phronesis*) and understanding (*sophia*): the first is the virtue of practical reason, concerned with human affairs, and the second is the virtue of theoretical reason, concerned with unchanging and eternal truths. The intellectual virtue of practical reason is inseparably linked with the moral virtues of the non-rational part of the soul. It is impossible, Aristotle tells us, to be really good without wisdom, or to be really wise without moral virtue. Virtuous action must be based on virtuous purpose. Purpose is reasoned desire, so that if purpose is to be good both the reasoning and the desire must be good. It is wisdom that makes the reasoning good, and moral virtue that makes the desire good. Aristotle admits the possibility of correct reasoning in the absence of moral virtue: this he calls 'cleverness'. He also admits the possibility of right desire in the absence of correct reasoning: such are the naturally virtuous impulses of children. But it is only when correct reasoning and right desire come together that we get truly virtuous action.

Readers of Aristotle are sometimes puzzled by this. If we have to acquire virtue in order to become wise, and we cannot become wise without virtue, how can we ever become wise or virtuous? The difficulty is spurious. It is as if one were to ask 'How can one become a husband? To be a husband you need to have a wife, but a woman can't be a wife unless she has a husband'. Just as a single union makes a man a husband and a woman a wife, the wedding of wisdom and virtue makes intelligence into wisdom and natural virtue into moral virtue.

In both of Aristotle's ethical treatises the virtue of theoretical reasoning takes higher rank than the virtue of practical reasoning. Indeed, in the NE happiness itself is identified with the exercise of understanding. Happiness, it has been stated, is the activity of soul in accordance with virtue, and if there are several virtues, in accordance with the best and most perfect virtue. We have, in the course of the treatise, learnt that there are both moral and intellectual virtues, and that the latter are superior; and among the intellectual virtues, understanding, which concerns eternal truths, is superior to wisdom, which concerns human affairs. Supreme happiness, therefore, is activity in accordance with understanding, an activity which Aristotle calls 'contemplation'.

What is contemplation? Aristotle does not offer any wholly satisfactory answer to this question, but two things are clear. First, an Aristotelian contemplator is no ascetic, denying the body for the good of his mind: Aristotle insists that a moderate supply of 'external goods' is a precondition of 'happy' intellectual activity. Secondly, Aristotelian contemplation is not, as we might be tempted to imagine, an exercise in discursive reasoning: it is not a matter of intellectual questing or research. As an argument for the thesis that a contemplator enjoys himself Aristotle observes that 'it stands to reason that those who possess knowledge pass their time more pleasantly than those who are still in pursuit of it'. Looking at a painting and listening to a piece of music, rather than producing a landscape or composing a sonata, are analogues of whatever it is that Aristotle has in mind.

In the EE happiness is identified not with the exercise of a single dominant virtue but with the exercise of all the virtues. Nonetheless, contemplation has a dominant position in the life of the happy person. For Aristotle says that the standard for measuring virtuous choices is set by their relationship to contemplation: 'What choice or possession of natural goods . . . will most conduce to the contemplation of god is best, and this is the noblest standard'.

Activity in accordance with the virtues is pleasant, and so the truly happy man will also have the most pleasant life. For a virtuous person will find things pleasant if and only if they are actually good: if goodness and pleasantness do not thus coincide then a person is not virtuous but is in an inferior state which Aristotle calls 'continence'. The bringing about of this coincidence is the task of ethics. The EE ideal of happiness, therefore, given the role it assigns to contemplation, to the moral virtues, and to pleasure, can claim, as Aristotle promised, to combine the features of the traditional three lives, the life of the philosopher, the life of the politician, and the life of the pleasure-seeker. The happy man will value contemplation above all, but part of his happy life will be the exercise of political virtues and the enjoyment in moderation of natural human pleasures of body as well as of soul.

AN ETHICAL SYSTEM LIKE ARISTOTLE'S, WHICH MAKES the agent's happiness the ultimate aim of his actions, must appear impossibly self-centred; and the attempt to make one's own happiness the foundation stone of ethics is surely a fundamental defect in the Aristotelian theory. Within this egocentric framework Aristotle did devote much careful thought to the individual's relationships to others. His reflections on these matters are to be found primarily in the chapters on justice and on friendship in each of the ethical treatises. In addition, a number of the other virtues are essentially social—for example, generosity and conviviality. But the ultimate point of these virtues—and indeed of justice itself—is the agent's own happiness.

Aristotle makes a distinction between universal and particular justice. Universal justice, he tells us, is complete virtue, considered not in the abstract but in relation to one's neighbour. Each of the virtues he has considered in the earlier books is incomplete unless this relation to others is incorporated in it. Many people can exercise virtue in their own affairs, but not in relation to their neighbour.

Particular justice is a specific virtue in its own right. Among other things, it concerns the matters that would nowadays be the province of the criminal and civil courts. Aristotle offers us several subdivisions: there is distributive justice (governing the allotment of the proceeds of military or commercial ventures, for instance) and rectificatory justice (the compensation for losses incurred either through defaults on contracts or as the result of crimes). Distributive justice involves taking into account the worth of the individuals between whom the goods are to be distributed—though it is not clear whether a person's 'worth' depends on his original contribution to the project or on his social status within a particular constitution. The consideration of distributive justice leads Aristotle into a disquisition on the nature of money and the purposes of commercial exchange. He adumbrates theses that later developed into the mediaeval doctrine of the just price, the economists' concept of the free market, and the Marxist labour theory of value. In treating of rectificatory justice Aristotle does not offer any theory to justify the institution of punishment, but devotes his attention to methods of restoring the *status quo* between wrongdoer and victim. In treating of political justice, he endeavours to sort out the relation between the natural and conventional elements in the constitution of a just society.

For Aristotle, justice and friendship are closely connected. His word for friendship also covers love, and his discussions of friendship treat of many kinds of loving relationships: those between husband and wife and between parents and children as well as those with comrades and business partners. In the relationship between husband and wife the husband is always presented as the superior partner, and commonly as the clear master of the household. Children, in Aristotle's view, should be seen and not heard, and not even seen too often: there can be friendship between father and son, but the two cannot be friends. Among the relationships which are more normally thought of as friendships Aristotle distinguished three different kinds: those based on virtue, those based on utility, and those based on pleasure. At times this tripartite division seems to operate as a strait-jacket confining his empirical observations, and it leads to a complex and implausible account of why a virtuous man has any need for friends at all. But the books are full of psychological insights on such matters as the factors that put a strain on relationships of different kinds and lead to their break-up.

THE TEXTS CONTAINED IN THIS VOLUME ARE NOT NEW translations of the Aristotelian ethical treatises. They are revised versions of the translations contained in the *The Complete Works of Aristotle* published by Princeton University Press in 1984, which was in its turn a revision, by Jonathan Barnes, of the eleven volumes of the Oxford Translation of Aristotle which had been published between 1908 and 1954. The Oxford Translation was undertaken under the auspices of the Jowett Copyright Trustees, a body set up under the will of Benjamin Jowett, Master of Balliol College, Oxford, from 1870 to 1893. The original Oxford translation of the NE was made by W. D. Ross, and later lightly revised by J. O. Urmson. The translation of the MM was by St G. Stock, and that of the EE and the VV by J. Solomon. The translations were made on the basis of Bywater's Greek text of the NE (and the common books), which was first published as an Oxford Classical Text in 1894, and of Susemihl's Teubner editions of the EE, the MM, and the VV, which were printed in Leipzig in 1883 and 1884. The translations presented here use the same editions of the Greek texts: in those few places in which we have preferred a different reading the fact is signalled in a footnote.

Innovations in the present revision are of various kinds. First, a few plain mistakes of translation have been corrected. Secondly—following a principle enunciated by Ross in the preface to his version of the NE—, we have imposed a greater homogeneity in the translation of several key words.

Thirdly, one or two of the earlier translations of technical or semi-technical terms have been altered (the new versions are all noted in the Glossary).

A few examples may indicate where we have replaced the earlier versions of technical terms. For '*arete*' we have reverted to the traditional 'virtue' in place of the 'excellence' introduced by Barnes in the Revised Oxford Translation. We have preferred 'correct reasoning' to 'right reason' for '*orthos logos*'. As for '*phronesis*' and '*sophia*', for centuries the standard translations were 'prudence' and 'wisdom'. But 'prudence' now means something like 'caution', and the expert knowledge of scientists and philologists is no longer called 'wisdom', which has acquired an overwhelmingly practical sense. So we have opted for 'wisdom' for '*phronesis*' and 'understanding' for '*sophia*'. It goes without saying that neither of those two translations is an exact fit—not even for the most part or in the majority of cases. The same is true of 'virtue' and '*arete*', of 'happiness' and '*eudaimonia*', and of any number of other pairings.

There are several cases where it is not possible to render a single Greek word by a single English counterpart—not even for the most part. Two salient examples are '*arche*' and '*ergon*'. The first of these can mean 'beginning', 'source', 'origin', 'axiom', 'principle', and also 'rule' or 'office'. For the second, different sentences call for 'function', 'task', 'job', 'work', 'output', 'product', 'deed', . . . In such cases, where it would be absurd to insist on homogeneity of translation, we have tried to reduce to a minimum the number of English equivalents.

As a result of the changes that have been mentioned, the revised translations differ from the original ones in something like twenty places a page. Nonetheless, the general style has not been greatly modified and the present version is recognizably the Oxford Translation.

It differs more visibly from the original Oxford Translation in two further respects. First, and unlike almost all other translations of Aristotle, it presents in the correct form the EE and what remains of the NE: that is to say, the 'common books' are printed in the EE and it is the NE which has a gap in it. Secondly, and again unlike almost all other translations of Aristotle, we have abandoned the traditional division of the texts into 'books' and 'chapters': the chapters were invented in the Renaissance, and have nothing to recommend them; the books are ancient, but they are primarily determined not by the content of the text but by its length. Thus in the NE the account of friendship fills Book 8 and Book 9 (it was too long to fit into a single ancient book-roll), and conversely Book 7 contains two quite distinct discussions, of incontinence and of pleasure. The revised translation divides the text into modern chapters, which are fixed by their content—the division being based, often enough, on explicit indications in Aristotle's text.

The loss of book and chapter divisions should not hamper reference to particular passages, since nowadays citations are invariably made by reference to the page, column, and line of the edition by Immanuel Bekker. The present version sets the relevant Bekker indications in the margins of the text.

EUDEMIAN ETHICS

FIRST OXFORD TRANSLATION:

Books ΑΒΓΗΘ
J. Solomon
Books ΔΕΖ
W. D. Ross

GREEK TEXT:

Books ΑΒΓΗΘ
F. Susemihl, Teubner
Books ΔΕΖ
I. Bywater, OCT

CONTENTS

3: ACTION

INTRODUCTION

THE MAN WHO STATED HIS OPINION IN THE GOD'S PRE-　
cinct in Delos made an inscription on the propylaeum to the
temple of Leto, in which he separated from one another the
good, the noble and the pleasant as not all properties of the
same thing. He wrote:

> Most noble is what is most just, but best is health,　　　　5
> and pleasantest the getting what one longs for.

Let us disagree with him; for happiness is at once the most
noble and best of all things and also the pleasantest.

About each thing and kind there are many considerations
that raise problems and need investigation. Of these some　10
concern knowledge only, some the acquisition of things and
the performance of acts as well. About those which involve
contemplative philosophy only we must when occasion
arises say what is appropriate to that study. But first we must　15
consider in what the good life consists and how it is to be acquired, whether all who receive the epithet 'happy' are so by
nature (as we are tall, short, or of different complexions), or
by learning (happiness being a kind of knowledge), or by
some sort of training—for men acquire many qualities neither by nature nor by learning but by habituation, base quali-　20
ties if they are habituated to the base, good if to the good. Or
do men become happy in none of these ways, but either—
like those possessed by nymphs or deities—through a sort of
divine influence, being as it were inspired, or by fortune? For　25
many declare happiness to be identical with good fortune.

That men, then, possess happiness through all or some or
one of these causes is not obscure; for practically all events
can be traced back to these originating principles; for all acts
arising from thought may be included among acts that arise

30   from knowledge. Now to be happy and to live blissfully and nobly must consist mainly in three things, which seem most desirable; for some say wisdom is the greatest good, some virtue, and some pleasure. Some also dispute about the magnitude of the contribution made by each of these to happiness, declaring the contribution of one to be greater than that of another—some regarding wisdom as a greater good than virtue, some the opposite, and others regarding pleasure as a greater good than both. And some consider the happy life to be compounded of all these, some of two, and others hold it to consist in one.

1214b

5

First then about these things we must enjoin everyone that has the power to live according to his own choice to set up for himself some object for a noble life to aim at (whether honour or reputation or riches or education), with reference to which he will then do all his acts, since not to have one's life organized in view of some end is an indication of much folly. Then above all he must first define for himself neither impetuously nor carelessly in which of our belongings the good life is lodged, and what are the indispensable conditions of its attainment. For health is not the same as the indispensable conditions of health; and so it is with many other things, so that the noble life and its indispensable conditions are not identical. Of such things some are not peculiar to health or even to life, but common to pretty well all states and actions—for instance, without breathing or being awake or having the power of movement we could have neither good things nor bad; but some are peculiar to each kind of thing, and these it is important to observe: for instance, the eating of meat and walking after meals are not appropriate in the same way as the things mentioned above with regard to being in a good condition. For herein is the cause of the disputes about happiness, its nature and causes; for some take to be parts of happiness what are its indispensable conditions.

10

15

20

25

To examine all the beliefs about it is superfluous; for children, sick people, and the insane all have views, but no

30

intelligent person would raise problems about them; for such persons need not reasons but years in which they may change, or else medical or political chastisement—for medicine, no less than whipping, is a chastisement. Similarly we have not to consider the views of the multitude (for they talk at random about practically everything, and especially about happiness); for it is absurd to apply reason to those who need not reason but experience. But since every study has its own problems, plainly there are such relating to the best life and the best existence: it is well to examine these beliefs; for a disputant's refutation of the arguments contrary to his own is a demonstration of the argument itself.

Further, it pays not to neglect these considerations, especially with a view to that at which all inquiry should be directed, namely the causes that enable us to share in the good and noble life—if anyone finds it invidious to call it the blessed life—and with a view to the hope people have of attaining what is upright. For if the noble life consists in what is due to fortune or to nature, it would be something that many cannot hope for, since its acquisition is not in their power, nor attainable by their care or activity; but if it depends on the individual and his personal acts being of a certain character, then the good would be both more general and more divine, more general because more would be able to possess it, more divine because happiness would then be open to those who make themselves and their acts of a certain character.

Most of the doubts and problems raised will become evident if we define well what we ought to think happiness to be—whether it consists merely in having a soul of a certain character (as some of the older philosophers thought) or whether the man must indeed be of a certain character but it is even more necessary that his actions should be of a certain character.

If we make a division of the kinds of life, some do not even pretend to this sort of well-being, their business being done for the sake of what is necessary—for instance, those

1215a

5

10

15

20

25

concerned with vulgar crafts, or with commercial or servile
occupations (by vulgar I mean crafts pursued only with a
view to reputation, by servile those which are sedentary and
wage-earning, by commercial those connected with markets
and selling in shops). But there are three things directed to a
happy employment of life, those which we have above called
the three greatest of human goods: virtue, wisdom, and
pleasure. We thus see that there are three lives which all
those choose who have power: the lives of the political man,
of the philosopher, and of the voluptuary. For of these the
philosopher intends to occupy himself with wisdom and
contemplation of truth, the political man with noble acts
(which are those springing from virtue), the voluptuary with
bodily pleasures. Therefore each calls a different person
happy, as was indeed said before. Anaxagoras of Clazo-
menae, being asked who was the happiest of men, said:
'None of those you suppose, but one who would appear an
absurd being to you'. He answered in this way because he
saw that the questioner assumed that it was impossible for
one not great and beautiful or rich to deserve the epithet
'happy', while he himself perhaps thought that the man who
lived painlessly and pure of injustice or else engaged in some
divine contemplation was, as far as a man may be, blessed.

In many other cases it is difficult to assess things well, but
most difficult where it seems to all to be easiest and knowledge to be in the power of any man—namely, the question of
what of all that is found in living is desirable, and what, if attained, would satisfy our appetite. For there are many con-
tingencies that make men fling away life, such as disease, excessive pain, storms, so that it is plain that, if one were given
the power of choice, not to be born at all would, as far at
least as these reasons go, have been desirable. Further, the
life we lead as children is not desirable;[1] for no one in his
senses would face returning to this. Further, many incidents

---

1 Omitting τις (an addition to the received text proposed by Casaubon
and printed by Susemihl: 'Further, what is the life we lead as children?').

involving neither pleasure nor pain or involving pleasure but 25
not of a noble kind are such that non-existence is preferable
to life. And generally, if one were to bring together all that all
men do and experience but not voluntarily because not for
its own sake, and were to add to this an infinity of time, one
would none the more choose on account of these experi- 30
ences to live than not to live. But further, neither for the
pleasure of eating or that of sex, if all the other pleasures
were removed that knowing or seeing or any other sense
provides men with, would any man value life, unless he were
utterly servile; for it is plain that to the man making this 35
choice there would be no difference between being born a
brute and a man: at any rate the ox in Egypt, which they hon- 1216a
our as Apis, in most of such matters has more power than
many monarchs. We may say the same of the pleasure of
sleeping. For what is the difference between sleeping an un-
broken sleep from one's first day to one's last, for a thousand 5
or any number of years, and living the life of a plant? Plants
at any rate seem to possess this sort of life, and similarly children; for children, too, have a continuous natural life from
their first coming into being in their mother's womb, but
sleep the entire time. It is plain then from these considerations that men, though they look, fail to see what is well- 10
being and what the good in life.

They say that Anaxagoras answered a man who was raising problems of this sort and asking why one should choose
to be born rather than not by saying: 'For the sake of contemplating the heavens and the whole order of the universe'.
He, then, thought the choice of life for the sake of some sort 15
of knowledge to be valuable. Those who felicitate Sardanapallus or Smindyrides the Sybarite or any other of those who
live the voluptuary's life, these evidently all place happiness
in the feeling of delight. Others would rather choose virtu- 20
ous actions than wisdom or bodily pleasures—at any rate
some choose these not only for the sake of reputation but
even when they are not going to win credit by them. But
most political men are not truly so called: they are not in

25   truth political; for the political man is one who chooses
noble acts for their own sake, while most take up the political life for the sake of wealth and from covetousness.

   From what has been said, then, it is evident that all connect happiness with three lives, the political, the philosophi-
30   cal, and the voluptuous. Now among these the nature and
quality and sources of the pleasure of the body and sensual
enjoyment are plain, so that we have to inquire not what
such pleasures are but whether they tend to happiness or not
and how they tend, and whether—supposing one should attach to the noble life certain pleasures—one should attach
35   these, or whether some other sort of engagement in these is
a necessity but the pleasures through which men reasonably
think the happy man to live pleasantly and not merely painlessly are different.

   About that let us inquire later. First let us consider virtue
and wisdom, the nature of each, and whether they are parts
of the good life either in themselves or through the actions
1216b   that arise from them, since everyone—or at least everyone
worth considering—connects them to happiness.

   Socrates the elder thought knowledge of virtue to be the
5   end, and he used to inquire what justice is, what courage and
each of the parts of virtue; and it was reasonable for him to
do so, for he thought all the virtues to be kinds of knowledge.
So to know justice and to be just come simultaneously; for
the moment that we have learned geometry or building we
10   are builders and geometers. Therefore he inquired what virtue is, not how or from what it arises. This is right with regard to the contemplative sciences; for there is no other part
of astronomy or physics or geometry except knowing and
contemplating the nature of the things which are the sub-
15   jects of those sciences—though nothing prevents them from
being coincidentally useful to us for much that we cannot do
without. But the end of the productive sciences is something
different from science and knowledge—for instance, health
is different from medicine, law and order (or something of
the sort) from political science. Now to know anything that

is noble is itself noble; but regarding virtue, at least, it is not 20
to know what it is but to recognize out of what it arises that
is most valuable. For we do not want to know what courage
is but to be courageous, nor what justice is but to be just—as
we want to be in health rather than to know what being in
health is, and to be in good condition rather than to know 25
what being in good condition is.

About all these matters we must try to get conviction by
arguments, using people's perceptions as evidence and illustration. It would be best that all men should clearly concur
with what we are going to say, but if not, then that all should
do so in a sort of way at least—and this if converted they will 30
do. For every man has some contribution to make to the
truth, and it is on this basis that we must give some sort of
proof about these matters. For by advancing from true but
unilluminating judgements we shall arrive at illuminating
ones, always exchanging the usual confused statements for
more perspicuous ones. 35

In every inquiry there is a difference between philosophical and unphilosophical remarks: therefore we should not
think even in political inquiry that the sort of consideration
which makes not only the nature of the thing evident but
also its cause is superfluous; for such consideration is in
every inquiry philosophical. But this needs much caution.
For there are some who, through thinking it to be the mark 1217a
of a philosopher to make no random statement but always to
give a reason, often unawares give reasons foreign to the
subject and empty—this they do sometimes from ignorance,
sometimes because they are boasters—by which reasons
even men experienced and able to act are trapped by those 5
who neither have nor are capable of having practical and
constructive thought. This happens to them from want of
education; for inability in regard to each matter to assess
which reasons are appropriate to the subject and which are
foreign to it is want of education. And it is right to assess 10
separately the explanation and the conclusion both because
of what has just been said (namely, that one should attend

not merely to what is inferred by argument but often more to people's perceptions—whereas now when men are unable to answer the argument they are compelled to believe what has been said), and also because often that which seems to have been shown by argument is true indeed but not for the cause which the argument assigns; for one may prove truth by means of falsehood, as is plain from the *Analytics*.

I

HAPPINESS AND THE HUMAN GOOD

AFTER THESE PREFATORY REMARKS LET US FIRST START from what we have called the first unilluminating judgements, seeking to discover in an illuminating manner what happiness is. Now this is admitted to be the greatest and best of human goods—we say human, because there might perhaps be a happiness peculiar to some superior being (say, a god); for of the other animals, which are inferior in their nature to men, none share the epithet 'happy': no horse, bird, or fish is happy, nor anything the name of which does not imply some share of a divine element in its nature; rather, it is in virtue of some other sort of participation in good things that some have a better life and some a worse.

We must examine later whether this is so. At present we say that of goods some are matters of human action, some not; and this we say because some things—and therefore also some good things—do not change, yet these are perhaps as to their nature the best. Some things, again, are matters of action, but only to beings superior to us. Things are said to be matters action in two ways; for both that for the sake of which we act and the things we do for its sake are matters of action—for instance, we put among matters of action health and riches and also the acts done for the sake of them (namely, healthy practices and business affairs). So it is plain that we must regard happiness as the best of what are matters of human action.

We must then examine what is the chief good, and in how many ways we speak of it. The answer seems principally to be contained in three beliefs. For men say that goodness itself is

the best of all things, goodness itself being that whose property is to be the primary good and the cause by its presence in
other things of their being good. They say that both belong
to the Idea of good (I mean by 'both', being the primary good
and being the cause of other things' being good by its presence in them). For it is especially of this that the good is
predicated truly (other things being good by participation in
and likeness to this); and this is the primary good—for the
destruction of that which is participated in involves also the
destruction of that which participates in the Idea and is
named from its participation. But this is the relation of the
primary to the later, so that the Idea of good is goodness itself—for it is (they say) separable from what participates in
it, like all other Ideas.

The consideration of this belief belongs necessarily to another inquiry and one more general; for arguments that are
at once destructive and general belong to no other science.
But if we must speak briefly about these matters, we say first
that it is speaking generally and emptily to say that there is
an Idea whether of good or of anything else—this has been
considered in many ways both in our public and in our philosophical discussions. Next, however much there are Ideas
and in particular an Idea of good, they are perhaps useless
with a view to a good life and to action. For things are said to
be good in as many ways as they are said to be. Being, as we
have divided it in other works, indicates now quiddity, now
quality, now quantity, now time, and again some of it consists in being changed and in changing; and the good is
found in each of these modes: in substance as intelligence
and god, in quality as justice, in quantity as appropriateness,
in time as opportunity, while as examples of it in change, we
have that which teaches and that which is being taught. As
then being is not one in all the cases we have mentioned, so
neither is goodness; nor is there one science either of being
or of goodness.

Not even things named good in the same form are matters
for a single science—for instance, opportunity or appropri-

42

ateness. Rather, one science considers one kind of opportunity or appropriateness, and another another: for instance,
opportunity and appropriateness in regard to food are studied by medicine and gymnastics, in military actions by generalship, and similarly with other sorts of action, so that it can   1218a
hardly be the province of one science to consider goodness
itself.

Further, in things having a prior and posterior, there is no
common element apart from them and separable. For then
there would be something prior to the first; for the common
and separable element would be prior, because with its destruction the first would be destroyed as well: for instance, if   5
the double is the first of the multiples, then the multiple
which is predicable in common cannot be separable, for it
would be prior to the double. ***[1] if the common element
turns out to be the Idea: for instance, if one made the common element separable. For if justice is good, and so also is   10
courage, there is then, they say, goodness itself—for which
they add 'itself' to the common definition. But what could
this mean except that it is eternal and separable? Yet what is
white for many days is no whiter than that which is white for
a single day; so the good will not be more good by being eternal. Hence the common good is not identical with the Idea;   15
for the common good belongs to all.

We should show the nature of goodness itself in the opposite way to that now used. For now from what is not agreed
to possess the good they show to be good the things admitted to be good—for instance, from numbers they show that
justice and health are goods, for they are arrangements and
numbers, and it is supposed that goodness is a property of   20
numbers and units because unity is goodness itself. But they
ought, from what are admitted to be goods (for instance,
health, strength, and temperance), to show that nobility is
present even more in the changeless; for all these things are
order and rest. If so, then the changeless is still more noble;

1 Susemihl marks a lacuna.

43

for it has these attributes still more. And it is a bold way to
demonstrate that unity is goodness itself on the grounds
that numbers have desire; for they do not make it evident
how they desire but speak in altogether too abstract a way.
And how can one assume that there is desire where there is
no life? One should think seriously about this and not suppose without reasons what it is not easy to be convinced of
even with reasons. And to say that all existing things desire
some one good is not true; for each seeks its own special
good—the eye vision, the body health, and so on.

There are then these problems in the way of there being
goodness itself. Further, it would be useless to political science, which, like all others, has its proper good—as, for instance, gymnastics has good bodily condition.[2] And similarly, neither is the common good either goodness itself (for
it might belong even to a small good) or a matter of action
(for medicine does not consider how to procure an attribute
that may be an attribute of *anything*, but how to procure
health; and so each of the other crafts). But goodness is mani-
fold, and one part of it is nobility, and part is a matter of action and part not. The sort of good that is a matter of action
is an object aimed at, but the good in things unchanging is
not like that.

It is evident, then, that neither the Idea of good nor the
common good is the goodness itself that we are looking for;
for the one is unchanging and not a matter of action, and the
other, though changing, is not a matter of action either. But
the object aimed at as end is best, and the cause of all that
comes under it, and primary in relation to all goods. This
then will be goodness itself: the end of matters of human action. And this is what comes under the craft that is authoritative over all others, which is politics and economics and

2 In the manuscripts there follow two sentences which Susemihl, after
Cook Wilson, deletes: 'Further, there is what is written in the argument—
that the Idea itself of good is useful to no craft, or to all crafts in the same
way. Further, it is not a matter of action.'

wisdom. For these disciplines differ from the others by their   15
being of this nature; whether they differ from one another
must be stated later. And that the end is the cause of what
comes under it, the method of teaching makes plain; for the
teacher first defines the end and thence shows of each of the
other things that it is good; for the end aimed at is the cause.
For instance, since to be in health is such-and-such, such-
and-such must needs be what is advantageous for it. The   20
healthy is the moving cause of health and yet[3] only of its existence: it is not the cause of health's being good. Further, no
one shows that health is good (unless he is a sophist and no
doctor but someone who produces sophistical arguments
that are foreign to the subject), any more than he proves any
other originating principle.

We must now consider, making a fresh start, in how many
ways the good as the end of man and the best thing among   25
matters of action, is the best of all, since it is best.

After this, then, let us make a new start and speak about   Book B
what comes next. All goods are either outside or in the soul,
and of these those in the soul are more desirable (this distinction we make in our public discussions). For wisdom,
virtue, and pleasure are in the soul, and some or all of these   35
seem to all to be the end. But internal to the soul some items
are states or capacities, others activities and movements.

Let this then be supposed, and also that virtue is the best
condition or state or capacity of all things that have a use or a   1219a
task. This is plain from an induction; for in all cases we lay
this down: for instance, a garment has a virtue, for it does
something and is used, and the best state of the garment is
its virtue; so too with a boat, a house, and the like. So too,   5
therefore, with the soul—for it has a task. And let us suppose
that the better the state, the better the task; and as the states
are to one another, so let us suppose the corresponding tasks
to be to one another. And the task of anything is its end. It is
evident, therefore, from this that the task is better than the

3 Reading καίτοι (Ross) for καὶ τότε ('and at that time . . .').

45

10   state; for the end is best, as being an end; for we supposed
the best, the ultimate item, to be the end which everything
else is for the sake of. That the task, then, is better than the
state or condition is plain.

There are two ways in which we speak of tasks: in some
cases, the task is something in addition to the use—for instance, in housebuilding it is the house and not just the act of
15   building, and in medicine it is health and not just the curing
and restoring to health; while the task of other things is the
use—for instance, of vision it is seeing, and of mathematical
science contemplation. Hence, necessarily, where the task is
the use, the use is better than the state.

Having made these distinctions, we say that the task of a
20   thing is the same as the task of its virtue, only not in the same
way. For instance, the task both of the craft of cobbling and
of the action of cobbling is a shoe: if, then, the craft of cobbling and the good cobbler have a virtue, their task is a good
shoe. And similarly with other cases.

Further, let the task of the soul be to produce life, that is
25   to say[4] the exercise of life while awake—for slumber is a sort
of idleness and rest. Therefore, since the task must be one
and the same both for the soul and for its virtue, the task of
the virtue of the soul will be a virtuous life. This, then, is the
final good, which (as we saw) is happiness. And it is plain
from our suppositions (namely, that happiness is the chief
30   good, that ends and the best goods are in the soul, and that[5]
happiness itself is either a state or an activity), that since an
activity is better than the corresponding state, and the best
activity than the best state, and since virtue is the best state,
the activity of the virtue of the soul is the chief good. But
happiness, we saw, is the chief good. Therefore happiness is
35   the activity of a good soul. But since happiness is something
complete, and life is either complete or incomplete and so

4 Reading τοῦτο (Cook Wilson) for τοῦ and κατ' ἐγρήγορσιν (Spengel) for
καὶ ἐγρήγορσις.

5 Here Susemihl marks a lacuna.

also virtue—total or partial—and the activity of what is incomplete is itself incomplete, happiness will be the activity of a complete life in accordance with complete virtue.

That we have rightly stated its genus and definition common opinions bear witness. For to do well and to live well are held to be identical with being happy, and each of these—living and doing—is a use or activity; for the life of action is one of use: the smith produces a bridle, the good horseman uses it.

It is also held that one cannot be happy for just a single day, or while a child, or for any single stage of life: that is why Solon's advice holds good, never to call a man happy when living, but only when his life is ended. For nothing incomplete is happy, not being whole.

Further, to virtue praise is given, because of its deeds; and to the deeds, encomia: we crown the winners, not those who have the capacity to win but do not win. Further, the character of a man is assessed by his deeds. Further, why is happiness not praised? Surely because other things are praised owing to this, either by their having reference to it or by their being parts of it. That is why felicitation, praise, and encomia differ; for encomia address the particular deed, praise the general character,[6] and felicitation the end.

This makes plain the problem that is sometimes raised—why for half their lives are the good no better than the base? For all are alike when asleep. The cause is that sleep is an idleness, not an activity of the soul. That is why, even if there is some other part of the soul (for instance, the nutritive part), its virtue is not a part of entire virtue, any more than the virtue of the body is; for in sleep the nutritive part is more active, while the perceptual and the desiderative are incomplete in sleep. But as far as they do partake of some sort of movement, even the dreams of the virtuous are better than those of the bad, unless they are caused by disease or maiming.

6 Inserting τοῦ before τοιοῦτον (Bonitz).

2

VIRTUE

AFTER THIS WE MUST CONSIDER THE SOUL. FOR VIRTUE belongs to the soul and not coincidentally. But since we are investigating human virtue, let it be supposed that the parts of the soul partaking of reason are two, but that they partake
30 not in the same way, but the one by its natural tendency to command, the other by its natural tendency to obey and listen. (If there is a part that is non-rational in some other way, let it be disregarded.) It makes no difference whether the soul is divisible or indivisible, so long as it has different capacities, namely those mentioned above, just as in a curve it is not possible to separate the concave from the convex, or, again,
35 the straight from the white, although the straight is not white except coincidentally and is not the same in substance.[1]

We also neglect any other part of the soul that there may be, for instance the vegetative. For the above-mentioned parts are peculiar to the human soul. (That is why the virtues of the nutritive part and that concerned with growth are not
40 those of man.) For *qua* man[2] he must have the power of calculating, of originating things,[3] and of action. But calcula-
1220a tion governs not calculation but desire and the emotions: he must then have these parts. And just as good condition of the body is compounded of the partial virtues, so also is the virtue of the soul, *qua* end.
5 Of virtue there are two species, the moral and the intellectual. For we praise not only the just but also the judicious

---

1 Reading οὐσίᾳ τὸ αὐτό (Bonitz) for οὐσία τοῦ αὐτοῦ.

2 Omitting εἰ (Ross).

3 Retaining the καί which Susemihl deletes.

and men of understanding. For we supposed that what is praiseworthy is either the virtue or what it does, and these are not activities but have activities. Since the intellectual virtues involve reason, they belong to that rational part of the soul which gives commands by its possession of reason, while the moral belong to the part which is irrational but by its nature obedient to the part possessing reason; for we describe the character of a man by saying not that he is a man of understanding or clever but that he is good-tempered or over-confident.

After this we must first consider moral virtue, its quiddity, its parts—for our inquiry has come round to this—and how it is produced. We must inquire as everyone does in other things: we inquire having something to start from, so that by way of true but unilluminating judgements, we always try to grasp what is true and illuminating. For we are now in the same position as if we knew[4] that health is the best condition of the body, or that Coriscus is the darkest man in the market-place: we do not know what either of these is, but for the attainment of knowledge of what either is it is helpful to be in this condition.

First, then, let it be laid down that the best condition is produced by the best things, and that with regard to everything the best is done from the virtue of that thing (for instance, the exertions and the food are best which produce a good bodily condition, and from such a condition men best exert themselves). Further, every condition is produced and destroyed by some sort of application of the same things—for instance, health from food, exertion, and the weather. This is plain from an induction. Virtue too, then, is that sort of condition which is produced by the best movements in the soul, and from which are produced the soul's best deeds and emotions; and by the same things, if they happen in one way, it is produced, and if in another, it is destroyed. The use of virtue is relative to the things by which it is increased and

4 Adding ἔχοιμεν (Dirlmeier)—Susemihl marks a lacuna.

destroyed, and it puts us in the best condition towards them.
An indication that both virtue and vice are concerned with
the pleasant and the painful is that punishment, being a
therapy and operating through contraries (as therapies do in
everything else), operates through these.

THAT MORAL VIRTUE, THEN, IS CONCERNED WITH THE
pleasant and the painful is plain. Character, being as its
name indicates something that grows by habit[5]—and that
which is under guidance other than innate is trained to a
habit by frequent movement of a particular kind—is the active principle present after this process. (In inanimate things
we do not see this; for even if you throw a stone upwards ten
thousand times, it will never go upward except by force.)
Consider, then, character to be this: a quality in accordance
with commanding reason belonging to the irrational part of
the soul which is able to obey reason.

We have to state in respect of what part of the soul we
have character of this or that kind.[6] It is in respect of the capacities for emotion that men are called emotional, and in
respect of the states that men are called[7] susceptible or un-
susceptible to the emotions. After this comes the division
made in ***[8] into emotions, capacities, and states. By emotions I mean such as rage, fear, shame, appetite—in general,
all that is usually followed of itself by sensuous pleasure or
pain. The quality does not depend on these—they are merely
experienced—but on the capacities. By capacity I mean that
in virtue of which men who exercise their emotions are
called after them: for instance, irascible, insensate, amorous, bashful, shameless. And states of character are the
causes through which these belong to us either according to

5 Aristotle connects ἦθος ('character') with ἔθος ('habit').

6 Reading ποῖ' ἄττα with the manuscripts (Susemihl prints Spengel's correction: ποιότης τά).

7 Omitting τῷ (Russell).

8 The received text is corrupt, and no satisfactory correction has been
proposed.

reason or contrariwise: for instance, courage, temperance, cowardice, self-indulgence.   20

After these distinctions we must grasp that in everything continuous and divisible there is excess, deficiency and a middle state, and these in relation to one another or in relation to us—for instance in gymnastics, medicine, building, navigation, and in any sort of action, alike scientific and non-   25
scientific, craftsmanlike and non-craftsmanlike. For motion is continuous, and action is motion. In all cases the middle state in relation to us is the best; for this is as knowledge and reason direct. And this everywhere also makes the best state of character. This is plain both by induction and by reason-   30
ing. For contraries destroy one another, and extremes are contrary both to one another and to the middle; for the middle is in relation to either extreme the other extreme: for instance, the equal is greater than the less but less than the greater. Therefore moral virtue must have to do with things in the middle and be a sort of mean. We must then grasp   35
what sort of mean virtue is and about what sort of middle states; let each be taken from the list by way of illustration and considered:

irascibility	insensitivity	good temper	
over-confidence	cowardice	courage	
shamelessness	bashfulness	modesty	1221a
self-indulgence	insensibility	temperance	
envy	(unnamed)	indignation	
profit	loss	the just	
prodigality	illiberality	liberality	5
boastfulness	self-deprecation	candour	
flattery	surliness	friendliness	
obsequiousness	churlishness	dignity[9]	
vanity	diffidence	pride	10
extravagance	shabbiness	magnificence[10]	

9 After this trio the manuscripts offer: 'luxuriousness—submission to evils—endurance', which (after Fritzsche) Susemihl deletes.

10 After this trio the manuscripts offer 'villainy—simplicity—wisdom', which (after Spengel) Susemihl deletes.

These and the like are the phenomena in the soul. They receive their names some from being excesses and the rest from being deficiencies. For the irascible is one who is angry more than he ought to be, and more quickly, and with more people than he ought: the insensitive is deficient in regard to persons, occasions, and manner. The man who fears neither what nor when nor as he ought is over-confident: the man who fears what he ought not and when he ought not and as he ought not is cowardly. ***[11] Similarly, self-indulgent ***[11] one prone to appetite and exceeding in all possible ways: while he who is deficient and does not feel appetite even so far as is good and in accordance with nature but is as much without emotion as a stone, is insensible. The man who covets things from any source is a profiteer: the man who makes it from none, or perhaps few, is a loser. The boaster is one who pretends to more than he possesses: the self-deprecator is one who pretends to less. The man who is more ready than is proper to join in praise is a flatterer: the man who is less ready is surly. To do too much to give pleasure is obsequiousness: to give pleasure seldom and reluctantly is churlishness.[12] The vain man is he who thinks himself worthy of more than he is: the diffident thinks himself worthy of less. Further, the prodigal is he who exceeds in every sort of expenditure: the illiberal is he who is deficient in every sort. Similar are the shabby and the ostentatious: the latter exceeds what is fitting, the former falls short of it.[13] A man is envious when he feels pain at the sight of prosperity more often than he ought; for even those who deserve prosperity cause when prosperous pain to the envious: the contrary

11 Susemihl (after Spengel and Fritzsche) marks two lacunas.

12 Here Susemihl (after Fritzsche) deletes a passage which reads: 'Further, one who can face no pain, even if it is good for him, is luxurious: one who can face all pain alike has broadly speaking no name but by extension is called hard, patient, or ready of submission.'

13 Here Susemihl (after Spengel) deletes a sentence which reads: 'The villain covets in every way and from every source: the simpleton not even whence he should'.

character has not so definite a name—he is one who shows
excess in not grieving even at the prosperity of the undeserv-
ing but welcomes it all, as gluttons welcome food, while his
opposite is vexed through envy.

It is superfluous to add to the definition that the particular relations to each thing should not be coincidental; for no   5
science, contemplative or productive, uses such additions to
its definitions in speech or action: the addition is directed
against logical chicanery. Take the above then, as abstract definitions, which will be made more precise when we speak of
the contrasting states of character.

Of these phenomena themselves there are species differ-   10
ently named according as the excess is in time, in degree, or
in the object producing the emotion: for instance, one is
quick-tempered through feeling anger quicker than one
ought, hard and passionate through feeling it more, bitter
through tending to retain one's anger, violent and abusive
through the punishments one inflicts from anger ***[14] Gour-   15
mands, gluttons, and drunkards are so named from having
an emotional capacity to enjoy against reason one or the
other kind of nutriment.

Nor must we forget that some of the things mentioned
cannot be taken to depend on the manner of action, if manner means excess of emotion: for instance, the adulterer is   20
not so called because he sleeps with married women more
than he should—for there is no such thing. Rather, the act is
in itself depraved: both the emotion and its character are expressed in the same word. Similarly with outrage. That is
why men dispute: they say that they had intercourse but did
not commit adultery (for they acted in ignorance or by com-   25
pulsion), or that they gave a blow but committed no outrage;
and similarly in other such cases.

Having said this, we must next say that, since there are
two parts of the soul, the virtues are divided correspondingly: those of the rational part are intellectual, whose task is

14 Susemihl marks a lacuna.

53

truth whether about a thing's nature or how it comes about,
while the others belong to the part irrational but desider-
30 ative—for not any and every part of the soul, supposing it to
be divisible, is desiderative. Necessarily, then, the character
must be base or virtuous by its pursuit or avoidance of certain pleasures and pains. This is plain from our classification
35 of the emotions, capacities, and states; for the capacities and
states are capacities and states of the emotions, and the emotions are distinguished by pain and pleasure. So for these
reasons and also because of our previous propositions every
moral virtue has to do with pleasures and pains. For by what-
40 ever things any soul naturally becomes better or worse, it is
with regard to and in relation to these things that it finds
1222a pleasure. We say men are base through pleasures and pains
by pursuing and avoiding those one ought not to or as one
ought not to. That is why all readily define the virtues as insensibility or immobility as regards pleasures and pains, and
5 vices as constituted by their contraries.

Since we have supposed that virtue is that sort of state
from which men have a tendency to do the best actions and
through which they are in the best disposition towards what
is best, and best is what is in accordance with correct reasoning, and this is the mid-point between excess and deficiency
10 relative to us, it follows that moral virtue is a mean in each
case and is concerned with certain mid-points in pleasures
and pains and[15] in the pleasant and the painful. The mean
will sometimes be in pleasures (for there too is excess and
deficiency), sometimes in pains, sometimes in both. For he
15 who is excessive in his feeling of delight exceeds in the pleasant, and he who exceeds in his feeling of pain, in its contrary—and this either *tout court* or with reference to some
standard: for instance, when he differs from the majority of
men. The good man, however, feels as he ought. Since there

15 Omitting αὐτόν (Spengel).

is no state[16] in consequence of which its possessor will in some cases admit the excess and in others the deficiency of the same thing, it follows that just as these acts are contrary   20
to one another and to the middle, so the states will also be contrary to one another and to virtue.

It happens that sometimes all these contrarieties are evident enough, sometimes those on the side of excess, sometimes those on the side of deficiency. And the reason for the contrariety is that the inequality or likeness to the middle state is not always of the same kind: rather, in one case one   25
might change to the middle state more quickly from the excess and in another case from the deficiency, and the person further distant seems more contrary: for instance, in regard to the body excess in exertion is healthier than deficiency   30
and nearer to the middle state, but in food deficiency is healthier than excess. And so the states of choice which apply to physical training will favour health more according to each of the two choices: now those which opt for great exertions, now those which prefer abstemiousness; and he who is contrary to the appropriate and the reasonable will be now the man who avoids exertion and not both things, and   35
now the voluptuary and not the man who starves himself. This happens because from the start our nature does not diverge in the same way from the mid-point as regards all things: rather, we are less inclined to exert ourselves and more inclined to be voluptuaries. So it is too with regard to the soul.

We regard, then, as the state contrary to the middle, that   40
towards which both ourselves and men in general are more inclined to err—the other extreme, as though not existent, escapes notice, being unperceived because of its rarity. Thus we oppose anger to good temper, and the irascible to the good-tempered. Yet there is also excess in the direction of   1222b

16 Reading ἐπεὶ δὲ <οὐκ> ἐστί (Dodds). The received text gives: 'Since there is a state...'.

good temper and readiness to be reconciled, and the repression of anger when one is struck. But the men prone to this are few, and all incline more to the opposite extreme: that is why rage is no flatterer.

5 And since we have made a list of the states in regard to the several emotions, with their excesses and deficiencies,[17] and the contrary states in which men are as correct reasoning directs them to be (what correct reasoning is, and with an eye to what standard we are to fix the mid-point, must be considered later) it is evident that all the moral virtues and vices 10 have to do with excesses and deficiences of pleasures and pains, and that pleasures and pains arise from the above-mentioned states and emotions. But the best state in respect of each class of things is the one in the middle. It is plain then that all, or at least some, of the virtues will be connected with means.

17 The text is uncertain.

3

ACTION

LET US, THEN, TAKE ANOTHER STARTING-POINT FOR THE
succeeding inquiry. Every substance is by nature a sort of
originating principle: that is why each can produce many
things similar to itself—for instance, man man, animals in
general animals, and plants plants. But in addition to this
man alone of animals is also an origin of actions of a kind;   20
for action is ascribed to no other animal. Of originating
principles, those which are primary sources of movement
are said to be controlling, and most properly so those that
have necessary results: god is doubtless an origin of this
kind. There is no such thing as control among originating
principles without movement (for instance, those of mathematics), though by analogy we use the name there also. For   25
there, too, if the originating principle should move, practically all that is proved from it would change; but these consequences do not themselves change, one being destroyed by
another, except by destroying the supposition and proving
by way of that. Man is the originating principle of a kind of
movement; for action is movement. Since, as elsewhere, the   30
originating principle is the cause of all that exists or arises
through it, we must take the same view as in demonstrations. For if, supposing the triangle to have its angles equal
to two right angles, the quadrilateral must have them equal
to four right angles, it is evident that the cause of this is that
the triangle has them equal to two right angles. If the triangle changes, then so must the quadrilateral—for instance,   35
having six right angles if the triangle has three, and eight if it
has four. But if the triangle does not change but remains as it
was before, so too must the quadrilateral.

The necessity of what we are endeavouring to show is plain from the *Analytics*; at present we can neither affirm nor deny anything with precision except just this: supposing there were no other cause for the triangle's being as it is, then the triangle would be a sort of principle or cause of all that comes later. So if some of the things that exist can be in a contrary state, then so of necessity can its principles. For what results from the necessary is necessary; but the results from these can be the contrary. What depends on men forms a great portion of things of this kind , and of such things men themselves are the originating principles. So it is evident that all the actions which a man controls and of which he is the origin can either happen or not happen, and that their happening or not happening—those at least for whose existence or non-existence he is authoritative—is in his power. But for what it is in his power to do or not to do, he is himself responsible; and what he is responsible for is in his power. And since virtue and vice and the deeds to which they give rise are praiseworthy or blameworthy—for we do not blame or praise what is due to necessity or to fortune or to nature, but what we ourselves are responsible for; for what another is responsible for, for that he bears the blame or praise—it is plain that both virtue and vice have to do with matters where the man himself is the responsible origin of his actions.

We must then grasp of what actions he is himself the responsible origin. We all admit that for acts that are voluntary and done from the choice of each man he is responsible but for involuntary acts he is not himself responsible. All that he does from choice he plainly does voluntarily. It is plain then that virtue and vice have to do with voluntary acts.

We must then grasp what is the voluntary and the involuntary, and what is choice, since by these virtue and vice are defined. First we must consider the voluntary and involuntary. Of three things it would seem to be one: what is in accordance with either desire or choice or thought—the voluntary being what is in accordance with and the involuntary what goes against one of these. But desire is divided into three sorts, will or wanting, passion, and appetite. We have, then, to distinguish these, and first to consider the case of appetite.

All that is in accordance with appetite would seem to be voluntary; for all the involuntary seems to be enforced, and what is enforced is painful, and so is all that men do and suffer from compulsion—as Evenus says, 'All to which we are compelled is unpleasant'. So that if something is painful it is enforced, and if enforced painful. But all that is against appetite is painful—for appetite is for the pleasant—and therefore enforced and involuntary. So what is in accordance with appetite is voluntary; for they are contraries.

Further, all depravity makes one more unjust, and incontinence seems to be depravity, the incontinent being the sort of man that acts in accordance with his appetite and against his calculation, and shows his incontinence when he is active in accordance with it. But to act unjustly is voluntary: he will therefore act voluntarily, and what is done in accordance with appetite is voluntary. Hence the incontinent will act unjustly by acting in accordance with his appetite. Indeed, it would be absurd that those who become incontinent should be more just.

From these considerations, then, what is in accordance with appetite would seem voluntary—but from the following the contrary. What a man does voluntarily he wants to do, and what he wants to do he does voluntarily. But no one wants what he thinks to be bad. But surely the man who acts incontinently does not do what he wants, for to act incontinently is to act through appetite against what the man thinks best. Hence it will result that the same man acts at the same time both voluntarily and involuntarily; but this is impossible.

Further, the continent will act justly, and more so than incontinence; for continence is a virtue, and virtue makes men more just. One acts continently whenever he acts against his appetite in accordance with his calculation. So that if to act justly is voluntary, as to act unjustly is—for both these seem to be voluntary, and if the one is voluntary, so must the other be—but action against appetite is involuntary, then the same man will at the same time do the same thing voluntarily and involuntarily.

The same argument may be applied to passion. For there is thought to be an incontinence and a continence of passion
20 just as there is of appetite; and what is against passion is painful, and the repression is enforced, so that if the enforced is involuntary, everything in accordance with passion is voluntary. Heraclitus seems to be regarding the strength of passion when he says that the restraint of it is painful: 'It is hard', he says, 'to fight passion; for it buys with its life'. But if
25 it is impossible for a man voluntarily and involuntarily to do the same thing[1] at the same time in regard to[2] the same part of the act, then what is in accordance with will is more voluntary than what is in accordance with appetite or passion; and evidence of this is that we do many things voluntarily without anger or appetite.

It remains then to consider whether what is wanted and
30 what is voluntary are identical. But this too is evidently impossible. For we supposed, and it is held, that depravity makes men more unjust, and incontinence seems a kind of depravity. But the contrary will result; for although no one wants what he thinks bad, he does it when he becomes incontinent. If, then, to commit injustice is voluntary, and the voluntary is what is in accordance with will, then when a
35 man becomes incontinent he will no longer act unjustly—rather, he will be more just than before he became incontinent. But this is impossible.

That the voluntary then is not action in accordance with desire, nor the involuntary action against desire, is plain.

Again, that the voluntary is not the same as what is in accordance with choice is evident from the following considerations. It has been demonstrated that what is in accor-

---

1 Reading αὐτό, with half the tradition, for αὐτόν.
2 Omitting τό after ἅμα (Russell).

dance with will is not involuntary but rather that all that   1224a
one wants is voluntary—though it has only been shown that
one can do voluntarily what one does not want. But many
things we want we do suddenly, but no one chooses an act
suddenly.

If, as we saw, the voluntary must be one of these three—   5
action according either to desire or to choice or to thought—
and it is not two of these, it remains that the voluntary consists in action with some kind of thinking.

Advancing the argument a little further, let us finish our
definition of the voluntary and the involuntary. To act perforce or not perforce seems connected with these terms; for   10
we say that the enforced is involuntary and all the involuntary enforced. So first we must consider actions done perforce, their nature and their relation to the voluntary and the
involuntary. Now the enforced and the compelled, and force
and compulsion, seem opposed to the voluntary and to persuasion in the case of actions done. Generally, we speak of   15
force and compulsion even in the case of inanimate things;
for we say that a stone moves upwards and fire downwards
by force and compulsion; but when they move according to
their natural internal impulse, we do not speak of force; nor
do we call it voluntary either: rather, there is no name for   20
this antithesis. When they move against this impulse, then
we say they move perforce. So too among animate things
and among animals we often see things being acted on and
acting from force, when something from without moves
them against their own internal impulse. Now in the inanimate the originating principle is simple, but in the animate
there is more than one; for desire and reason do not always
agree. And so with the other animals what is enforced is sim-   25
ple (just as in the inanimate), for they have not desire and
reason contrary to one another, but live by desire; but men
have both—or do so at a certain age, namely the age at which
we ascribe actions to them. For we do not say that children
act or that brutes do, but only men who have come to act
from calculation.

30   The enforced seems always painful, and no one does
something perforce and yet with delight. That is why there
arises much dispute about the continent and incontinent;
for each of them acts with two impulses mutually contrary,
so that (as they say) the continent man forcibly drags himself
35   from the pleasant appetites (for he feels pain in dragging
himself away against the resistance of desire), while the incontinent suffers force against his calculation. But the latter
seems less to be in pain; for appetite is for the pleasant, and
this he follows with delight. So the incontinent rather acts
voluntarily and not from force, because he acts without pain.
But persuasion is opposed to force and compulsion, and the
1224b   continent goes towards what he is persuaded of, and so proceeds not perforce but voluntarily. But appetite leads without persuading, being devoid of reason.

We have, then, shown that these alone seem to act perforce and voluntarily,[3] and why they seem to—namely from
a certain likeness to the enforced action, in virtue of which
5   we attribute enforced action also to the inanimate. Yet if we
add the addition made in our definition, there also the problem is solved. For it is when something external moves a
thing or brings it to rest, against its own internal impulse,
that we say this happens perforce; and when it does not, we
do not say that it happens perforce. But in the continent and
the incontinent it is the present internal impulse that leads
10   them—for they have both impulses. So that neither acts perforce, but, as far at least as the above goes, voluntarily and
not by compulsion. For the external originating principle
that hinders or moves in opposition to the internal impulse
is what we call compulsion—for instance, when we strike
someone with the hand of one whose will and appetite alike
resist; but when the origin is within, there is no force.
15   Further, there is both pleasure and pain in both; for the
continent feels pain now in acting against his appetite, and
he has the pleasure of hope that he will be later benefited, or

3 Reading ἕκοντες (Allan) for ἄκοντες ('involuntarily').

else he is already being benefited because he is in health; while the incontinent is pleased at getting through his incontinency the object of his appetite, but he has a pain of expectation, thinking that he is doing something bad. So to say that both act perforce is not without reason, the one sometimes acting involuntarily because of his desire, the other because of his calculation; for these two items, being separated, are thrust out by one another. Hence men extend what they say to the soul as a whole, because they see something of the sort in the elements of the soul. Now of the parts of the soul this may be said; but the soul as a whole acts voluntarily, both in the continent man and in the incontinent, neither of whom acts perforce—rather, one of the elements in them does, since by nature we have both. For reason is there by nature, because if development is permitted and not maimed, it will be there; and appetite, because it accompanies and is present from birth. But these are practically the two marks by which we define the natural: it is either that which accompanies all of us as soon as we are born, or that which comes to us if development is allowed to proceed regularly—for instance, grey hair, old age, and so on. So each acts against nature, and yet in the abstract each acts according to nature—but not the same nature. The problems then about the continent and incontinent are these—do both, or one of them, act perforce, so that they act either involuntarily or else at the same time both perforce and voluntarily, and if force is involuntary, both voluntarily and involuntarily? And it is pretty plain from what has been said how these problems are to be met.

In another way, too, men are said to act by force and compulsion without any disagreement between reason and desire, namely when they do what they assume to be both painful and base but are threatened with whipping, imprisonment, or death if they do not do it. Such acts they say they were compelled to do. Or shall we deny this, and say that all do what they do voluntarily? For they have the power not to do it, and to face the suffering.

Again perhaps one might say that some such cases were voluntary and some not. For where it is in the agent's power whether a situation should obtain or not the acts that he does but does not want to do he always does voluntarily and not perforce; but those in which he has not this power, he does perforce in a way (but not *tout court*) because he does not choose the very thing he does but the end for which it is done, since there is a difference, too, in this. For if a man were to murder another so as not to be caught at blind man's buff he would be laughed at if he were to say that he acted perforce and on compulsion: there ought to be some greater and more painful evil that he would suffer if he did not do what he did. For then he will act on compulsion and perforce, or at least not by nature, when he does something bad for the sake of something good or for release from something worse—and involuntarily, for such acts are not in his power.

That is why many regard love, rage in some cases, and natural conditions as involuntary, as being too strong for nature: we sympathize with them inasmuch as these things exert a force upon their nature. A man would more seem to act perforce and involuntarily if he acted to escape violent than if to escape gentle pain, and generally if to escape pain than if to get pleasure. For that which is in his power—and all turns on this—is what his nature is able to bear; and what it is not, and what is not under the control of his natural desire or his calculation, that is not in his power. That is why those who are inspired and prophesy, though what they do is the product of thought, we still say have it not in their power either to say what they said, or to do what they did. Nor is it a result of appetite. So that some thoughts and emotions are not within our power, nor the acts[4] following such thoughts and calculations—rather, as Philolaus said, some reasons are too strong for us.

So if the voluntary and involuntary have to be considered in reference to the presence of force, let this be our account.

4 Reading καὶ πράξεις (Richards) for ἢ πράξεις.

Nothing obscures the idea of the voluntary so much as arguing that people can act from force and yet voluntarily.[5]

Since we have reached this conclusion, and the voluntary
has been defined neither by desire nor by choice, it remains   1225b
to define it as that which is in accordance with thought. The
voluntary seems contrary to the involuntary; and to act with
knowledge of the person acted on, instrument and end (for
sometimes one knows who one is acting on (for instance,
one's father), but not to what end (for instance, to kill, not to
save, as in the case of Pelias' daughters), or one knows the object to be a drink but takes it to be a philtre or wine when it   5
was really hemlock) seems contrary to action in ignorance of
the person, instrument, or thing, if the ignorance is not coincidental. All that is done owing to ignorance, whether of person, instrument, or thing, is involuntary; the contrary therefore is voluntary. All, then, that a man does—it being in his
power not to do it—not in ignorance and on his own initiative must needs be voluntary; and this is what voluntariness   10
is. But all that he does in ignorance and owing to his ignorance, he does involuntarily. Since knowledge or awareness
is of two sorts, one the possession and the other the use of
knowledge, the man who has but does not use knowledge
may in one way be justly called ignorant, but in another way
not justly—for instance, if he had not used his knowledge
owing to carelessness. Similarly, one might be blamed for   15
not having the knowledge, if it were something easy or necessary and he does not have it because of carelessness or
pleasure or pain. This, then, we must add to our definition.

Such, then, is our definition of the voluntary and the
involuntary.

LET US NEXT SPEAK ABOUT CHOICE, FIRST RAISING VARIOUS
problems about it. For one might doubt to what genus it be-   20
longs and in which kind to place it, and whether the voluntary and the chosen are or are not the same. Some insist that

5 The text is uncertain.

choice is either belief or desire, and the inquirer might think that it is one or the other—for both accompany it. Now that it is not desire is evident; for then it would be either will or appetite or passion—for no one desires without having experienced one of these feelings. But passion and appetite belong also to the brutes while choice does not; further, even those who have both of these often choose without either passion or appetite; and when they are under the influence of their passions they do not choose but endure. Further, passion and appetite always involve pain, but we often choose without pain. But neither are will and choice the same; for we often want what we know is impossible (for example, to rule all mankind or to be immortal), but no one chooses such things unless ignorant of the impossibility, nor, generally, does he choose what is possible if he does not think it in his power to do or not to do it. So it is evident that the object of choice must be one of the things in our power.

Similarly, choice is plainly not belief nor simply what one thinks; for the object of choice was something in one's power and many things may be believed that are not in our power (for instance, that the diagonal is commensurable). Further, choice is not either true or false. Nor yet is choice belief about matters of action which are in our power, as when we think that we ought to do or not to do something. The following point applies to will as well as to belief: no one chooses an end but rather things that contribute to an end— for instance, no one chooses to be in health but to walk or to sit for the purpose of keeping well; no one chooses to be happy but to make money or run risks for the purpose of being happy. And in general, in choosing we make plain both what we choose and for what we choose it, the latter being that for which we choose something else, the former that which we choose for something else. But it is the end that we specially want, and we believe we ought to be healthy and happy. So it is evident from this that choice is different both from belief and from will; for will and belief pertain especially to the end, but choice does not.

It is plain, then, that choice is not will, nor belief, nor assumption *tout court*. But in what does it differ from these?
And how is it related to the voluntary? The answer to these
questions will also make it plain what choice is. Of things   20
that can either be or not be, then, there are some such that
we can deliberate about them, while about others we cannot.
For some things can either be or not be, but bringing them
about is not in our power: rather, they are due some to nature and others to other causes; and about these no one   25
would attempt to deliberate except in ignorance. But about
others, not only is being and not being possible, but so too[6]
is human deliberation; these are things the doing or not
doing of which is in our power. That is why we do not deliberate about the affairs of India nor how the circle may be
squared; for the first are not in our power, and the second is   30
not a matter of action at all (by which it is plain that choice is
not belief *tout court*). Matters of choice and action belong to
the class of things in our power; but we do not deliberate
about all matters of action that are in our power.

That is why one might then raise the problem: Why do
doctors deliberate about matters within their science but not   35
grammarians? The reason is that error may occur in two
ways (either in calculation or in sense-perception when we
are engaged in the very act), and in medicine one may go
wrong in both ways, but in grammar one can do so only in
respect of the perception and action, and if they inquired   1226b
about this there would be no end to their inquiries.

Since then choice is[7] neither belief nor will singly nor yet
both together (for no one chooses suddenly, though on a
sudden a man believes he ought to act and wants to act), it
must be compounded of both—for both are found in a man   5
choosing. But we must ask how it is compounded out of
these. The very name in a way makes it plain. For choice is

6 Susemihl marks a lacuna here.
7 Omitting ἔστι (Bonitz).

not simply picking but picking one thing before another;[8] and this is impossible without consideration and deliberation: that is why choice arises out of deliberative belief.

Now about the end no one deliberates (this being fixed for all), but about that which tends to it—whether this or that tends to it, and—supposing that resolved on—how it is to be brought about. We all deliberate about this till we have brought the process to an originating principle within ourselves. If then, no one chooses without preparation and deliberation about what is better or worse, and if of the things which contribute to an end and which may or may not come about, we deliberate about those that are in our power, then it is plain that choice is a deliberative desire for something in our power. For we all deliberate about what we choose, though we do not choose all the things we deliberate about. I call a desire deliberative when deliberation is its origin and cause, and the man desires because of the deliberation.

That is why in the other animals choice does not exist, nor in man at every age or in every condition. For there is no deliberation or assumption about why to act. But nothing prevents many people from having a belief about whether a thing is to be done or not, but not through calculation. For the deliberating part of the soul is that which considers a cause of some sort; for the end is one of the causes: a cause is that owing to which a thing is or comes about, and the end of a thing's being or coming about we call its cause (for instance, of walking, the fetching of things, if this is the purpose for which one walks). That is why those who have no aim fixed have no inclination to deliberate.

So if a man of himself and not through ignorance does or abstains from that which is in his power to do or not do, he acts or abstains voluntarily; but we do many such things without deliberation or forethought: it follows that all that

8 'Choice' is προαίρεσις, a compound of αἵρεσις ('choice') and πρό ('before', 'in preference to').

has been chosen is voluntary, but not all the voluntary is chosen, and that all that is according to choice is voluntary, but   35
not all that is voluntary is according to choice.[9] And at the
same time it is evident from this that those legislators define
well who enact that some phenomena are to be considered
voluntary, some involuntary, and some done aforethought;
for if they are not thoroughly precise, at least they touch on   1227a
the truth. But about this we will speak in our investigation of
justice. It is plain that choice is not simply will or simply belief but belief and desire together when they are drawn from   5
deliberation.

Since in deliberating one always deliberates for the sake
of something, and he who deliberates has always an aim by
reference to which he judges what is advantageous, no one
deliberates about the end: rather, this is the originating principle and supposition, like the suppositions in the contemplative sciences (we have spoken about this briefly at the   10
start and more precisely in the *Analytics*). Everyone's inquiry,
whether made with or without craftsmanship, is about what
tends to the end—for instance, whether they shall go to war
or not, when this is what they are deliberating about. But the
reason or purpose will come first—for instance, riches, plea-   15
sure, or anything else of the sort that happens to be our purpose. For the man deliberating deliberates if, starting from
the end, he has considered what[10] conduces to bringing the
end within his own action, or what he can do towards the
end. But the end is always something good by nature, and
men deliberate about it in particular—for instance, the doctor whether he is to give a drug, or the general where he is to   20
pitch his camp. To them there is a good end, which is the
thing that in the abstract is best. But against nature and by
perversion[11] not the good but the apparent good is the end.

9 Reading ἑκούσια (Susemihl's ἀκούσια is a misprint).
10 Omitting the ἤ which Susemihl adds.
11 Reading διαστροφῇ (Fritzsche) for διαστροφήν.

The reason is that some things cannot be used for anything
but what their nature determines—for instance, sight; for
one can see nothing but what is visible, nor hear anything
but what is audible. But a science enables us to do what does
not belong to that science; for the same science is not similarly related to health and disease, but naturally to the former and unnaturally to the latter. Similarly will is of the good
naturally but of the bad unnaturally; and by nature one
wants the good but against nature and by perversion[12] the
bad as well.

But further, the corruption and perversion of a thing does
not tend to anything whatever but to the contrary or the intermediate. For out of this province one cannot go, since
mistake leads not to anything whatever but to the contrary
where there is a contrary, and to that contrary which is contrary with regard to the science. Therefore, both the mistake
and the choice must deviate from the middle towards the
contrary—and the more and the less are contrary to the middle. The cause is pleasantness or painfulness; for we are so
constituted that the pleasant appears good to the soul and
the more pleasant better, while the painful appears bad and
the more painful worse. So from this also it is plain that virtue and vice have to do with pleasures and pains; for they
have to do with objects of choice, and choice has to do with
the good and bad or what appears such, and pleasure and
pain naturally seem such.

It follows then, since moral virtue is a mean and is always
concerned with pleasures and pains, whereas vice lies in excess or deficiency and is concerned with the same matters as
virtue, that moral virtue is a state tending to choose the
mean in relation to us in things pleasant and painful, in regard to which, according as one is pleased or pained, men
are said to have a definite sort of character—for one is not
said to have a special sort of character for loving what is
sweet or what is bitter.

12 Reading διαστροφῇ (Fritzsche) for διαστροφήν.

THESE DISTINCTIONS HAVING BEEN MADE, LET US SAY
whether virtue makes the choice unerring and the end correct so that a man chooses for the end he ought, or whether
(as some say) it makes the reasoning so. But what does this is   15
continence; for this does not destroy the reason. And virtue
and continence differ. We must speak later about them, since
those who think that virtue makes the reasoning correct, do
so for this cause—namely, that continence is of this nature
and continence is one of the things we praise.

Now that we have discussed the problems let us state our
view.[13] It is possible for the aim to be correct but for a man to   20
go wrong in what contributes to that aim; and again the aim
may be mistaken while the things leading to it are correct; or
both may be mistaken. Does then virtue make the aim correct or rather the things that contribute to the aim? We say
the aim, because this is not attained by deduction or reasoning but is to be supposed as an origin or principle. For the   25
doctor does not inquire whether one ought to be in health or
not but whether one ought to walk or not; nor does the
trainer ask whether one ought to be in good condition or not
but whether one ought to wrestle or not; nor does any other
craft inquire about the end. For as in the contemplative sciences the suppositions are principles, so in the productive
the end is a principle and a supposition. For instance, since   30
this body is to be made healthy, therefore so and so must be
found in it if health is to be had—just as there: if the angles
of the triangle are equal to two right angles, then so and so
must be the case. The end aimed at is, then, the principle of
the thinking, and the end of the thinking is the principle of
the action.

If of all correctness either reason or virtue is the cause,
then if reason is not the cause, then the end (but not the   35
things contributing to it) must owe its correctness to virtue.
The end is the purpose; for all choice is of something and for
the sake of something. The purpose, then, is the mid-point,

13 Reading λέγωμεν (a mediaeval correction) for λέγομεν ('we state . . .').

and virtue is the cause of this by choosing the purpose. Still choice is not of this but of the things done for the sake of this. To hit on these things—namely, what ought to be done for the sake of the end—belongs to another capacity but of the correctness of the end of the choice the cause is virtue. And that is why it is from a man's choice that we assess his character—that is, from the purpose for which he acts, not from the act itself. Similarly, vice brings it about that we choose for contrary purposes. If, then, a man, having it in his power to do noble things and abstain from ignoble, does the contrary, it is plain that this man is not virtuous. Hence it follows that both vice and virtue are voluntary; for there is no compulsion to do what is depraved. Therefore vice is blameworthy and virtue praiseworthy. For the involuntary if ignoble and bad is not blameworthy and if good is not praiseworthy: rather, the voluntary is. Further, we praise and blame all men with regard to their choice rather than their deeds (though the exercise of virtue is more desirable than virtue), because men do base acts under compulsion, but no one chooses them so. Further, it is because it is not easy to see the nature of a man's choice that we are compelled to assess his character by his deeds. The exercise then is more desirable but the choice is more praiseworthy. And this both follows from our suppositions and is in agreement with people's perceptions.

4

THE MORAL VIRTUES

THAT THE VIRTUES ARE MEANS,[1] AND THAT THESE ARE
states of choice, and that the contrary states are vices and
what these are, has been stated in general terms. But let us
take them individually and speak of them in order; and first
let us speak of courage. Practically everyone is agreed that
the courageous man is concerned with fears and that courage is one of the virtues; and in the table we distinguished
confidence and fear as contraries—for in a way they are opposed to one another. Plainly, then, those named after these
states will be similarly opposed to one another—that is, the
coward (for he is so called from fearing more than he ought
and being less confident than he ought) and the over-
confident man (who is so called for fearing less than he
ought and being more confident than he ought). That is why
they have names cognate to those of the qualities: for instance, 'over-confident' is cognate to 'over-confidence'. So
that since courage is the best state in regard to fear and confidence, and one should be neither like the over-confident
(who are deficient in one way, excessive in another) nor like
cowards (of whom the same may be said, only not about the
same objects, but contrariwise—for they are deficient in
confidence and excessive in fear), it is plain that the middle
state between over-confidence and cowardice is courage; for
this is the best.

The courageous man seems to be for the most part fearless, the coward prone to fear: the latter fears many things

1 Reading αἱ ἀρεταί (Fritzsche) for ἐν ταῖς ἀρεταῖς ('That among the
virtues...').

and few, great things and small, and intensely and quickly, while the former, on the contrary, fears either not at all or slightly and reluctantly and seldom, and great things, and he faces even what is intensely frightening, whereas the coward does not face even what is slightly frightening. What, then, does the courageous man face? First, is it the things that are frightening to himself or to another? If the latter, his courage would be nothing much. But if it is the things that he himself fears, then he must find many things frightening—frightening things[2] being things that cause fear to those who find them frightening, powerful fear if intensely frightening, weak fear if slightly frightening. Then it follows that the courageous man feels much and serious fear; but, on the contrary, courage seemed to make a man fearless, fearlessness consisting in fearing few things if any, and in fearing slightly and with reluctance.

But perhaps things are called frightening—like pleasant and good—in two ways. Some things are pleasant or good in the abstract, others are so to a particular person and not in the abstract but rather the contrary—base and not pleasant (for instance, what is beneficial to the vicious or pleasant to children as such). Similarly the frightening is either in the abstract such or such to a particular person. What, then, a coward as such fears is not frightening to anyone or but slightly so; but what is frightening to the majority of men or to human nature, that we call frightening *tout court*. The courageous man shows himself fearless towards these and faces such things, which are frightening to him in one way but not in another—frightening to him *qua* man, but not frightening to him except slightly so, or not at all, *qua* courageous. These things, however, are frightening; for they are so to the majority of men. This is why the state of the courageous man is praised: his condition is like that of the strong or healthy.

---

2 Omitting μεγάλα καί and reading φοβερά· <τὰ δὲ φοβερὰ> φόβου (Bonitz). Susemihl retains μεγάλα καί ('find great things and many things frightening') and marks a lacuna after φοβερά.

For these are what they are, not because in the case of the one no exertion and in the case of the other no excess crushes them, but because they are either unaffected *tout court* or affected only to a slight extent by the things that affect the many or the majority. The diseased, then, and the 35 weak and the cowardly are affected by the common emotions as well, only more quickly and to a greater extent than the many, ***[3] Again, by the things that affect the many they are wholly unaffected or but slightly affected.

The problem is raised that if nothing is frightening to the courageous man, he would not have any fears. Or perhaps 1229a nothing prevents him in the way above mentioned? For courage consists in following reason, and reason bids one choose the noble. That is why the man who faces the frightening from any other cause than this is either out of his wits or foolhardy; but the man who does so for the sake of the noble is alone fearless and courageous. The coward, then, fears even what he ought not and the over-confident man is 5 confident even when he ought not to be; the courageous man both fears and is confident when he ought to be and is in this way in a middle state—for he is confident or fears as reason bids him. But reason does not bid a man to face what is very painful or destructive unless it is noble: the over-confident man is confident about such things even if reason does not bid him be so; the coward is not confident even if it 10 does; and the courageous man alone is confident about them if reason bids him.

There are five kinds of courage, so named for a certain similarity; for they all face the same things but not for the same reasons. One is a political courage, due to the sense of shame. Another is military, due to experience and knowl- 15 edge, not (as Socrates said[4]) of what is fearful but of the resources one has to meet what is fearful. The third kind is due to inexperience and ignorance: it is that of children and

3 Susemihl marks a lacuna.
4 See Plato, *Protagoras* 360D.

madmen which makes the latter face whatever comes and
the former take hold of snakes. Another kind is due to hope,
which makes those who have often been fortunate face dangers—and also those who are drunk, for wine makes them
optimistic. Another kind is due to irrational feeling—for instance, love or rage; for a man in love is over-confident
rather than cowardly and faces many dangers, like the man
who slew the tyrant in Metapontum or the man of whom
stories are told in Crete. Similar is the action of anger or
rage; for rage puts a man out of his wits. That is why wild
boars are thought to be courageous though they are not really so; for they behave as such when beside themselves, but
at other times are unpredictable like over-confident men.
Nevertheless, the courage due to rage is above all natural (for
rage is invincible—and that is why children are excellent
fighters), but political courage is the effect of custom. But in
truth none of these is courage, though all are useful for encouragement in danger.

So far we have spoken of the frightening generally; but it
is well to distinguish further. In general, then, whatever is
productive of fear is called frightening, and this is all that is
apparently going to cause destructive pain. For those who
expect some other pain may perhaps have another pain and
another emotion but not fear—for instance, if a man fore-
sees that he will suffer the pain which the envious suffer or
the jealous or the ashamed. Rather, fear only occurs on the
appearance of such pains whose nature is to be destructive to
life. That is why men who are very soft as to some things are
courageous, and some who are hard and enduring are cowards. Indeed, it is thought pretty much a property of courage
to take up a certain attitude towards death and the pain of it.
For if a man were so constituted as to face as reason requires
heat and cold and similar not dangerous pains, but to be soft
and fearful about death, not for any other emotion but just
because it means destruction, while another was soft in regard to these but unaffected in regard to death, the former

would seem cowardly, the latter courageous; for we speak of danger only in regard to such objects of fear as bring near to us that which will cause such destruction: it is when this is apparently close that danger appears.

The frightening things, then, in regard to which we call a man courageous are, as we have said, those which are apparently capable of causing destructive pain, and these when they appear near and not far off, and are of such magnitude, real or apparent, as is not out of proportion to man—for some things must appear frightening and must disturb any man. For, just as things hot and cold and certain other powers are too strong for us and for the conditions of the human body, nothing prevents it from being so too with regard to the emotions of the soul.

The cowardly, then, and the over-confident are deceived by their characters; for to the coward what is not frightening seems frightening, and what is slightly frightening intensely so, while in the contrary way, to the over-confident man the frightening seems safe and the intensely frightening but slightly so; but the courageous man thinks things what they truly are. Therefore, if a man faces the frightening through ignorance (for instance, if a man faces in the transport of madness the attack of a thunderbolt), he is not courageous; nor yet if, knowing the magnitude of the danger, he faces it through rage—as the Celts take up their arms and meet the waves (in general, all the courage of foreigners involves rage). Some face danger for pleasure—for rage is not without a certain pleasure, involving as it does the hope of vengeance. But still, whether a man faces death for this or some other pleasure or to avoid greater evils, he would not justly be called courageous. For if dying were pleasant, the self-indulgent would have often died because of their incontinence, just as now—since what causes death is pleasant though not death itself—many knowingly incur death through their incontinence, but none of them would be thought courageous even if they do it with perfect readiness to die. Nor is a man courageous if he seeks death to avoid exertions, as many do; to use Agathon's words:

1230a   Base men too weak for exertion long for death.

And so the poets narrate that Chiron, because of the pain of his wound, prayed for death although he was immortal. Similarly all who face dangers owing to experience, as practically all soldiers do. For the truth is the very contrary of what Socrates thought. He thought that courage was knowledge. But those who know how to ascend masts are confident not because they know what is frightening but because they know how to help themselves in fearful circumstances. Nor is all that makes men fight more confidently courage; for then, as Theognis puts it, strength and riches would be courage—'Every man' (he says) 'is daunted by poverty'. Evidently some, though cowards, face dangers because of their experience, and do so because they do not think them dangers, as they know how to help themselves. An indication of this is the fact that, when they think they can get no help and the danger is close at hand, they do not face it. But of all courageous men of this sort, it is those who face danger because of shame who most seem to be courageous, as Homer says Hector faced the danger from Achilles: 'And shame seized Hector'; and : 'Polydamas will be the first to taunt me'.[5] Such courage is political.

The true courage is neither this nor any of the others, but like them, as is also that of brutes which from rage run to meet the blow. For a man ought to hold his ground though frightened, not because he will incur disrepute, nor through anger, nor because he does not expect to be killed or has the capacity to protect himself (for in that case he will not even think that there is anything to be feared). Rather, since all virtue implies choice (we have said before what this means—that it makes a man choose everything for the sake of some end, and that the end is the noble), it is plain that courage,

5 Homer, *Iliad* XXII 100.

because it is a virtue, will make a man face what is frighten- 30
ing for some end, so that he does it neither through ignorance (for his virtue rather makes him assess things correctly), nor for pleasure but because the act is noble—since,
if it is not noble but frantic, he does not face the danger, for
that would be ignoble. In regard, then, to what things courage is a mean state, between what, and why, and the meaning 35
of the frightening, we have now spoken pretty adequately for
our present purpose.

AFTER THIS WE MUST TRY TO DRAW CERTAIN DISTINC-
tions regarding self-indulgence and temperance. We talk of
self-indulgence in more ways than one. A man is self-
indulgent when he has not been chastised or cured (just as
what has not been cut is uncut), and of such men, some are   1230b
capable, others incapable of chastisement (just as the uncut
includes both what cannot be cut and what can be but has
not been cut). So too with the self-indulgent[6]. For it is both
that which by its nature refuses chastisement, and that which
is of a nature to accept but has not yet received chastisement 5
for the errors in regard to which the temperate man acts correctly—for instance, children, who are called self-indulgent
in this sense. And again, in another sense we give the name
to those hard to cure and to those it is quite impossible to
cure through chastisement. Self-indulgence, then, being
spoken of in several ways, it is evident that it has to do with
certain pleasures and pains, and that the forms differ from   10
one another and from other states by the kind of attitude towards these. We have already stated how we apply 'self-
indulgence' to various states by extension. As to those who
from insensibility are unmoved by these same pleasures,
some call them insensible, while others describe them as such 15
by other names; but this phenomenon is not very familiar or

6 'Self-indulgent' is ἀκόλαστος, which comes from κολάζειν ('chastise')
and a negative prefix—just as 'uncut' is ἄτμητος, from τέμνειν ('cut') and a
negative prefix.

common because all rather err in the opposite direction, and it is congenital to all to be overcome by and to be sensible to such pleasures. It is the state chiefly of such as the boors introduced on the stage by comic writers, who will not go near
20   even moderate and necessary pleasures.

Since temperance has to do with pleasures, it must also have to do with certain appetites: we must, then, ascertain which. For the temperate man does not exhibit his temperance in regard to all appetites and all pleasures but rather (so
25   it is believed) about the objects of two senses, taste and touch—and in truth about those of touch alone. For his temperance is shown not in regard to visual pleasure in the beautiful (so long as it is unaccompanied by sexual appetite) or pain at the ugly; nor, again, in regard to the pleasure or pain of the ear at harmony or discord; nor, again, in regard to olfactory pleasure or pain at pleasant or disagreeable smells—
30   a man is not called self-indulgent for feeling or want of feeling in regard to such matters. For instance, if one sees a beautiful statue, or horse, or human being, or hears singing, without wanting to eat or drink or have sex but only to contemplate the beautiful and to hear the singers, he would not
35   be thought self-indulgent any more than those who were charmed by the Sirens.

Rather, temperance and self-indulgence have to do with those two senses whose objects alone are felt by and give delight and pain to brutes as well; and these are the senses of
1231a   taste and touch: the brutes seem insensible to the pleasures of all the other senses in pretty much the same way—for instance, harmony or beauty; for they obviously have no feeling worth considering at the mere contemplation of the beautiful or the hearing of the harmonious, except, perhaps, in some miraculous instances. And with regard to pleasant
5   and disagreeable smells it is the same, though all their senses are sharper. They do, indeed, feel delight in certain smells; but these gladden them coincidentally and not of their own nature. By not of their own nature I mean those that delight us owing to expectation and memory—for instance, food

and drink; for these we delight in because of a different pleasure, that of eating or drinking. The smells enjoyed for their   10
own nature are for instance those of flowers (that is why
Stratonicus neatly remarked that some things smell beautiful and others pleasant[7]). Brutes are not excited over every
pleasure connected with taste—not over those which are
sensed at the tip of the tongue but only over those sensed in
the gullet, the experience being more like touch than taste.   15
That is why gourmands pray not for a long tongue but for the
gullet of a crane, as did Philoxenus, the son of Eryxis. So we
should regard self-indulgence as concerned, broadly speaking, with objects of touch. Similarly it is with such pleasures
that the self-indulgent man is concerned. For sottishness,
gluttony, lecherousness, gourmandizing, and all such things   20
are concerned with the above-mentioned senses; and these
are the parts into which we divide self-indulgence. But in regard to the pleasures of sight, hearing, and smell, no one is
called self-indulgent if he is in excess: rather, we blame such
faults without reproaching them—and so in general all in
regard to which we do not speak of men as continent, the incontinent being neither self-indulgent nor temperate.   25

The man, then, so constituted as to be deficient in the
pleasures in which all for the most part must share and delight is insensible (or whatever else we ought to call him);
and the man in excess is self-indulgent. For all naturally take
delight in these objects and conceive appetites for them, and
they neither are nor are called self-indulgent (for they nei-   30
ther exceed by delighting more than they ought when they
get them, nor by feeling greater pain than they ought when
they miss them); nor are they insensitive (for they are not deficient in feeling delight or pain but rather in excess).

Since there is excess and deficiency in regard to these   35
things, there is plainly also a mean, and this state is the best
and contrary to both of the others. So if the best state about

7 Reading τὰ... τὰ... (Casaubon) for the received τὰς... τὰς... ('some
smells smell...').

81

the objects with which the self-indulgent is concerned is temperance, temperance will be the mean in regard to the above-mentioned sensuous pleasures, being a mean between self-indulgence and insensibility. The excess is self-

1231b   indulgence and the deficiency either nameless or expressed by the names we have suggested. More precise distinctions about the class of pleasures will be drawn in what is said later about continence and incontinence.

5   IN THE SAME WAY WE MUST ASCERTAIN WHAT IS GOOD temper and bad temper. For we see that the good-tempered man is concerned with the pain that arises from rage, being characterized by a certain attitude towards this. In our diagram we have opposed to the irascible, to the bad-tempered, and to the savage (all such being names for the same state)

10   the slavish and the unintelligent. For these are pretty much the names which people especially apply to those whose rage is not moved even when it ought to be, but who take insults easily and are humble in the face of disdain—for slowness in

15   that feeling of pain which we call rage is opposed to quickness, intensity to mildness, short duration to long. And since there is here, as we have said there is elsewhere, excess and deficiency—for the bad-tempered is one that feels anger more quickly, to a greater degree, and for a longer time, and when he ought not, and at what he ought not, and frequently,

20   while the slavish is the contrary—it is plain that there is a middle to this inequality. Since, then, both the above-mentioned states are mistaken, it is clear that the middle state between them is upright; for he is neither too soon nor too late, and does not feel anger when he ought not, nor feel no anger when he ought. So since in regard to these emo-

25   tions the best condition is good temper, good temper will be a mean, and the good-tempered person midway between the bad-tempered and the slavish.

PRIDE, MAGNIFICENCE, AND LIBERALITY ARE ALSO MEANS— liberality being shown in the acquisition or expenditure of

wealth. For the man who is more delighted than he ought to   30
be with every acquisition and more pained than he ought to
be at every expenditure is illiberal; he who feels less of both
than he ought is prodigal; and he who feels both as he ought
is liberal. (By 'as he ought', both in this and in the other cases,
I mean 'as correct reasoning directs'.) Since the two former
lie in excess and deficiency, and where there are extremes   35
there is also a middle which is best, and there is a single best
for each kind of action, it follows that liberality is the mean
between prodigality and illiberality in regard to the acquisition and expenditure of wealth.

We talk of wealth and business affairs in two ways: one
may use one's property in its own right (for instance, a shoe   1232a
or a coat), and one may use it coincidentally—not the use of
a shoe for a weight but (for instance) the selling of it or letting it out for money, which is a use of a shoe. Now the lover
of money is a man eager for money: for him the possession   5
of money is more important than its coincidental use. An illiberal man may even be prodigal in the coincidental use of
wealth—for it is in the natural use of it that he aims at increase. The prodigal runs short of necessaries. The liberal
man gives his superfluities.   10

There are also species of these which exceed or fall short
as regards parts—for instance, the miserly, the stingy, the
avaricious, are all illiberal: the miserly is characterized by
his refusal to spend, the avaricious by his readiness to accept anything, the stingy by his strong feeling over small
amounts, while the man who is illiberally unjust is a miscal-   15
culator and cheat. And similarly one sort of prodigal is a
waster by his disorderly expenditure, the other a non-
calculator who cannot face the pain of calculation.

AS TO PRIDE WE MUST DEFINE ITS SPECIFIC NATURE FROM   20
the qualities that we ascribe to the proud. For just as with
other things, in virtue of their nearness and likeness up to a
certain point, their divergence beyond that point escapes notice, so it is with pride. That is why sometimes men who are

contrary lay claim to the same character—for instance, the illiberal to that of the liberal, the churlish to that of the
25 dignified, the over-confident to that of the courageous. For they are concerned with the same things, and are up to a certain point contiguous, as the courageous man and the over-confident man are ready to face danger—but the former in one way, the latter in another; and these ways differ greatly.

Now, we assert that the proud man, as is indicated by the name we apply to him, is characterized by a certain greatness of soul and capacity;[8] and so he seems like the dignified and
30 the magnificent man, since[9] pride seems to accompany all the virtues. For to assess correctly great goods and small is praiseworthy. Now, those goods are thought great which are pursued by the man of the best character in regard to what
35 seem to be pleasures;[10] and pride is the best. But every virtue correctly assesses the greater and the less among its objects, as the wise man and virtue would direct, so that all the virtues seem to go with this one, or this with all the virtues.

Further, it seems characteristic of the proud man to be contemptuous. Each virtue makes one contemptuous of
1232b what is esteemed great contrary to reason (for instance, courage is contemptuous of dangers of this kind—for it considers it disgraceful to hold them great, and numbers are not always frightening;[11] and the temperate is contemptuous of many great pleasures, and the liberal of wealth). This characteristic seems to belong to the proud man because he busies
5 himself about few things, and those great, and not because someone else thinks them so—the proud man would consider rather what one virtuous man thinks than what many ordinary men do, as Antiphon after his condemnation said to Agathon when he praised his defence of himself. Disdain

8 'Pride' is μεγαλοψυχία, a compound from μέγας ('great') and ψυχή ('soul').

9 Reading ὅτι (a suggestion of Susemihl) for ὅτε ('when').

10 Reading δοκοῦντα (Fritzsche) for τοιαῦτα.

11 The text of these two clauses is uncertain.

seems to be the emotion particularly characteristic of the 10
proud man. Again, as regards honour, life, and riches—
about which men seem to busy themselves—he thinks nothing of them except honour. He would be pained if denied
honour, and if ruled by someone unworthy. He delights
most of all when he obtains honour.

In this way he would seem to be inconsistent; for it is inconsistent to be[12] concerned above all with honour, and yet 15
to be contemptuous of the multitude and[13] of reputation. So
we must first distinguish. For honour, great or small, is of
two kinds: it may be given by a crowd of ordinary men or by
those worth considering; and, again, there is a difference according to the ground on which honour is given. For it is
made great not merely by the number of those who give the 20
honour or by their quality, but also by its being honourable;
and in truth, office and all other goods are honourable and
worth pursuing only if they are truly great, so that there is no
virtue without greatness. That is why every virtue, as we have
said, makes a man proud in regard to the object with which
that virtue is concerned. But still there is a single virtue, 25
pride, alongside of the other virtues, and he who has this
must be called in a special sense proud. Since some goods
are honourable and some as we distinguished earlier, and of
such goods some are in truth great and some small, and of
these some men are worthy and think themselves so, among 30
these we must look for the proud man.

We must distinguish four different kinds of men. For a
man may be worthy of great goods and think himself worthy
of them, and again there may be small goods and a man worthy of them and thinking himself worthy; and we may have
the opposites in regard to either kind of goods: there may be
a man worthy of small who thinks himself worthy of great 35
and honourable goods; and, again, one worthy of great but
thinking himself worthy of small. He then who is worthy of

12 Reading τό for τῷ (with half the tradition).
13 Retaining the καί which Susemihl deletes.

the small but thinks himself worthy of the great is blameworthy; for it is unintelligent and not noble that he should
obtain out of proportion to his worth. The man also is
blameworthy who, being worthy of great goods and possess-
1233a   ing them does not think himself worthy to share in them.
There remains then the contrary of these two—the man who
is worthy of great goods and thinks himself worthy of them
and is such as to think himself worthy of them. He is praiseworthy and in the middle between the other two.

5   Since, then, in respect of the choice and use of honour
and the other honourable goods, the best condition is pride,
and we define the proud man as being this and not as being
concerned with things useful, and since the[14] mean is the
most praiseworthy state, it is plain that pride is a mean. Of
the contraries, as shown in our diagram, the condition con-
10   sisting in thinking oneself worthy of great goods when not
worthy is vanity (for we give the name of vain to those who
think themselves worthy of great things though they are
not); and the condition of not thinking oneself worthy of
great things though one is, we call diffidence (for it is held to
be the mark of the diffident not to think himself worthy of
anything great though he possesses that for which he would
15   justly be deemed worthy of it): hence, it follows that pride is
a mean between vanity and diffidence.

The fourth of the sorts of men we have distinguished is
neither wholly blameworthy nor yet proud, not having to do
with anything that possesses greatness. He neither is worthy
nor thinks himself worthy of great goods: that is why he is
not contrary to the proud man. Yet to be worthy and think
20   oneself worthy of small goods might seem contrary to being
worthy and thinking oneself worthy of great ones. But such
a man is not contrary to the proud, for he is not blameworthy (his state being what reason directs): he is, in fact,
the same in nature as the proud man (for both think themselves worthy of what they are worthy of), and he might

14 Deleting αὕτη (Rackham).

become proud—for of whatever he is worthy of he will think himself worthy. But the diffident man who possesses great 25 and honourable things and does not think himself worthy of them—what would he do if he was worthy of small things? Either[15] he would think himself worthy of great things and thus be vain, or else of still smaller. That is why no one would call a man diffident if, being an alien in a city, he does not think himself worthy of ruling but rather submits, but only if 30 he is well born and thinks office a great thing.

THE MAGNIFICENT MAN IS NOT CONCERNED WITH ANY and every action or choice but with expenditure (unless we use the name in an extended sense): without expense there cannot be magnificence. It is what is fitting in ornament, and ornament is not to be got by ordinary expenditure but 35 consists in exceeding what is necessary. The man, then, who tends to choose in great expenditure the fitting magnitude, and desires this sort of mean, and with a view to this sort of pleasure, is magnificent. The man whose inclination is to something larger but out of harmony has no name, though he is near to those called by some tasteless and ostentatious. 1233b For instance, if a rich man, spending money on the marriage of his beloved, thinks it fitting to make such arrangements as one makes to entertain those who are only there to raise a glass, he is shabby; while one who receives guests of this sort in the way suited to a marriage feast resembles the ostenta- tious man, if he does it neither for the sake of reputation nor 5 to gain power; but he who entertains worthily and as reason directs, is magnificent; for what is fitting is worthy, and nothing unworthy is fitting. And what one does should be fit- ting ∗∗∗[16] For in what is fitting is involved the worth of the object[17] (for instance, one thing is fitting for a servant's,

15 Reading ἤ for εἰ (with half the tradition), and rejecting Susemihl's lacuna.

16 Susemihl marks a lacuna.

17 The text is uncertain.

10 another for a lover's wedding) and the worth of the enter-
tainer both in extent and kind—for instance, people thought
that the entertainment offered by Themistocles at the Olympic games was not fitting to him because of his previous
humble station but would have been to Cimon. The man
who is indifferent to questions of worth is in none of the
above classes. Similarly with liberality; for a man may be nei-
15 ther liberal nor illiberal.

IN PRETTY WELL ALL THE OTHER BLAMEWORTHY OR
praiseworthy qualities of character there are excesses, deficiencies, and means of the emotions: for instance, the envious man and the spiteful man. For, to consider the states of
character to which they owe their names, envy is pain felt at
20 deserved good fortune, while the emotion of the spiteful
man has itself no name[18]—but such a man makes plain his
nature by[19] delighting in undeserved ill fortune. Midway between them is the man inclined to indignation, the name
given by the ancients to pain felt at either good or bad for-
25 tune if undeserved, and to delight felt at them if deserved.
That is why they think that indignation or Nemesis is a god.

  Modesty is a mean between shamelessness and bashfulness; for the man who cares for no one's opinion is shameless, he who cares for everyone's alike is bashful, he who
cares for that of manifestly upright men is modest.

30 Friendliness is a mean between hostility and flattery; for
the man who readily keeps company with another in all his
appetites is a flatterer; the man who opposes him in all is
prone to hostility; and the man who does not keep company
in all pleasure (nor resists all) but rather in what seems to be
best is friendly.

  Dignity is a mean between churlishness and obsequious-
35 ness. For the contemptuous man who lives with no consider-

18 Omitting ἐπὶ τό.

19 Reading ἐστι τῷ for ἐπὶ τό (Casaubon). 'Spiteful' is ἐπιχαιρέκακος, 'delight in' is χαίρειν.

ation for another is churlish; the man who adapts his whole life to another and is submissive to everybody is obsequious; and he who acts thus in certain cases but not in others, and to those worthy, is dignified.

The candid and simple man, whom they call straightforward, is midway between the self-deprecator and the boaster. For the man who knowingly and falsely underestimates himself is a self-deprecator; the man who exalts himself is a boaster; the man who represents himself as he is, is candid, and in the Homeric phrase genuine; in general the one loves truth, the other falsehood.

Conviviality also is a mean, the convivial man being midway between the antisocial boor and the buffoon. For just as where food is concerned the finicky differs from the omnivorous in that the one takes little or nothing and that with reluctance, while the other accepts everything readily, so is the boor related to the vulgar buffoon: the one finds it hard to accept a joke, the other accepts all easily and with pleasure. One ought to take neither attitude: rather, one ought to accept some things and not others, as reason directs—and the man who does this is convivial. The demonstration is the same: conviviality of this kind, supposing we do not use the word in some extended sense, is a most upright state, and the mean is praiseworthy and the extremes blameworthy. Conviviality is of two kinds, one being delight in a joke, even when directed against oneself, if it be funny (one case is mockery), the other being the capacity of producing such things. The two sorts differ from one another but both are means. For the man who can[20] produce what a good assessor will be pleased at, even if the joke is against himself, will be midway between the vulgar and the frigid man. This definition is better than that which requires the thing said to be not painful to the person mocked, no matter what sort of man he is: one ought rather to approve of the man who is in the mean—for he is a good assessor of things.

1234a

5

10

15

20

20 Reading ὁ δυνάμενος (Sylburg) for τὸν δυνάμενον.

All these means are praiseworthy, but they are not virtues,
nor are their contraries vices—for they do not involve choice.
All of them occur in the classifications of emotions; for each
is an emotion. Since they are natural, they contribute to the
natural virtues; for, as will be said later, each virtue is found
both naturally and also otherwise, including wisdom. Thus
envy contributes to injustice (for the acts arising from it affect another), indignation to justice, modesty to temperance—that is why some even put temperance into this
genus. The candid and the false are respectively sensible and
foolish.

The middle state is more contrary to the extremes than
these to one another, because the middle is found with neither, but the extremes often with one another and sometimes the same people are at once cowardly and over-
confident, or prodigal in some ways, illiberal in others, and
in general are lacking in uniformity in a bad sense—for if
they lack uniformity in a good sense, men of the mean type
are produced; since, in a way, the extremes are present in the
middle. The contrariety between the middle and the extremes does not seem to be alike in both cases: sometimes it
is that of the excessive extreme, sometimes that of the deficient, and the causes are the two first given—rarity (for instance, of those insensible to pleasures), and the fact that the
error to which we are most prone seems the more contrary.
There is a third reason: the more like seems less contrary—
for instance, over-confidence to courage, prodigality to
liberality.

We have, then, spoken sufficiently about the other praiseworthy virtues: we must now speak of justice.

5

JUSTICE *

WITH REGARD TO JUSTICE AND INJUSTICE WE MUST CON-
sider what kind of actions they are concerned with, what
sort of mean justice is, and between what the just is midway. 5
Our investigation should follow the same method as the preceding discussions.

We see that all men mean by justice that kind of state of
character which makes people disposed to do what is just
and makes them act justly and want what is just; and similarly by injustice that state which makes them act unjustly 10
and want what is unjust. Let us too, then, first lay this down
as a rough sketch. For the same is not true of the sciences
and the capacities as of states of character. For it seems that
whereas the same capacity or science deals with contraries, it
is contrary[1] states of character which deal with contraries—
for instance, as a result of health we do not produce contrar- 15
ies but what is healthy; for we say a man walks healthily,
when he walks as a healthy man would.

Now often one contrary state is recognized from its contrary, and often states are recognized from their subjects; for
if good condition is evident, bad condition also becomes evi- 20
dent; and good condition becomes evident from the things
that are wholesome, and they from it. If good condition is
firmness of flesh, it is necessary both that bad condition
should be flabbiness of flesh and that the wholesome should
be that which produces firmness in flesh.

* Chapters 5–8 of EE have usually been printed as Books EZH of NE (see
pp. 5 and 20): that is why the Bekker numbering changes.
1 Deleting οὐ ('it is not contrary states . . .').

And it follows for the most part that if one contrary is
spoken of in several ways, the other also will be spoken of in
several ways: for instance, if just things are so, then so too
are unjust things. Now justice and injustice seem to be spoken of in several ways, but because the ways are close to each
other the homonymy escapes notice and is not plain as it is,
comparatively, when the ways are far apart (for here the difference in outward form is great)—for instance, both the
collar-bone of an animal and the key with which we lock a
door are called *kleis*, homonymously. Let us then ascertain
the different ways in which a man may be said to be unjust.
Both the lawless man and the covetous and unfair man are
thought to be unjust, so that plainly both the law-abiding
and the fair man will be just. The just, then, is the lawful and
the fair, the unjust the unlawful and the unfair.

Since the unjust man is covetous, he must be concerned
with goods—not all goods but those with which good and
bad fortune have to do, which in the abstract are always good
but for a particular person not always. (Men pray for and
pursue these things; but they should not—rather, they
should pray that the things that are good in the abstract may
also be good for them, and should choose the things that are
good for them.) The unjust man does not always choose the
greater but also the lesser (in the case of things bad in the abstract); but because the lesser evil is itself thought to be in a
way good, and covetousness is directed at the good, therefore he is thought to be covetous. And he is unfair; for this
contains and is common to both.

Since the lawless man was seen to be unjust and the law-
abiding man just, plainly all lawful things are in a manner
just; for the things laid down by legislation are lawful, and
each of them, we say, is just. Now the laws pronounce on all
subjects, aiming at the common advantage either of all or of
the best or of those in control, or something of the sort; so
that in one way we call those things just that tend to produce and preserve happiness and its parts for the political

association. The law bids us do the deeds of a courageous   20
man (for instance, not to desert our post or take flight or
throw away our arms), and those of a temperate man (for
instance, not to commit adultery or violence), and those of
a good-tempered man (for instance, not to strike another or
slander him), and similarly with regard to the other virtues
and forms of depravity, commanding some acts and forbid-
ding others; and the correctly framed law does this cor-   25
rectly, and the hastily conceived one less well.

This form of justice, then is complete virtue—not in the
abstract, but in relation to others. And therefore justice is
often thought to be the greatest of virtues and neither evening nor morning star is so wonderful; and proverbially 'in
justice is every virtue comprehended'. And it is complete   30
virtue *par excellence*, because it is the use of complete virtue.
It is complete because he who possesses it can use his virtue
towards others too and not only by himself; for many men
can use virtue in their own affairs but not in their relations
with others. This is why the saying of Bias is thought to be   1130a
true: 'Rule will show the man'—for a ruler *ipso facto* stands
in a relation to other men and is a member of an association. For this same reason justice, alone of the virtues, is
thought to be another's good—because it is related to others; for it does what is advantageous to another, either a   5
ruler or an associate. Now the worst man is he who exercises his depravity both towards himself and towards his
friends, and the best man is not he who exercises his virtue
towards himself but he² who exercises it towards another;
for this is a difficult task. This kind of justice, then, is not
part of virtue but virtue entire, nor is the contrary injustice   10
a part of vice but vice entire. What the difference is between
virtue and this kind of justice is plain from what we have
said: they are the same state, but being virtuous is not the
same as being just—rather, what, as a relation to others, is

2 Reading ἀλλ᾽ ὁ (Rackham) for ἀλλά.

justice is, as a certain kind of state considered in the abstract, virtue.

WE ARE INVESTIGATING THE JUSTICE WHICH IS A PART OF
15   virtue; for there is a justice of this kind, as we maintain. Similarly it is with injustice of this particular sort that we are concerned.

That there is such a thing is indicated by the fact that while the man who exercises the other forms of depravity acts unjustly but not covetously (for instance, the man who throws away his shield through cowardice or speaks harshly through bad temper or fails to help a friend with his wealth
20   through illiberality), when a man acts covetously he often exhibits no one of these vices, let alone all of them, but certainly viciousness of some kind (for we blame him) and injustice. There is, then, another kind of injustice which is a part of the wider injustice, and something unjust which answers to a part of what is more widely unjust as contrary to the law. Again, if one man commits adultery for the sake of
25   profit and makes money by it, while another does so at the bidding of appetite though he loses money and is penalized for it, the latter would be held to be self-indulgent rather than covetous, while the former is unjust but not self-indulgent: plainly, therefore, he is unjust by reason of his profiting. Again, all other unjust acts are ascribed invariably to some particular kind of depravity—for instance adultery
30   to self-indulgence, the desertion of a comrade in battle to cowardice, physical violence to anger; but if a man profits, his action is ascribed to no form of depravity except injustice. Evidently, then, there is apart from the wider injustice another, particular, injustice which shares the name of the
1130b   first, because its definition falls within the same genus; for the sense of both involves a relation to others but the one is concerned with honour or wealth or safety—or that which includes all these, if we had a single name for it—and its motive is the pleasure that arises from profit; while the other is

concerned with all the objects with which the virtuous man ₅
is concerned.

It is plain, then, that there is more than one kind of justice,
and that there is one which is distinct from virtue entire: we
must try to grasp what and what sort of thing it is.

The unjust has been divided into the unlawful and the unfair, and the just into the lawful and the fair. To the unlawful
answers the aforementioned sort of injustice. But since the ₁₀
unfair and the unlawful are not the same but are different as
a part is from its whole (for all that is unfair is unlawful, but
not all that is unlawful is unfair), the unjust and injustice are
not the same as but different from the former kind, as part
from whole; for this injustice is a part of the wider kind of ₁₅
injustice, and similarly the one kind of justice is part of the
other. Therefore we must speak also about particular justice
and particular injustice, and similarly about the just and the
unjust.

The justice, then, which answers to the whole of virtue
and the corresponding injustice, one being the use towards
others of virtue as a whole and the other that of vice, we may ₂₀
leave on one side. How the just and the unjust which answer
to these are to be distinguished is evident; for practically the
majority of the acts commanded by the law are those which
are prescribed from the point of view of virtue taken as a
whole; for the law bids us practise every virtue and forbids us
to practise any depravity. And the things that tend to pro- ₂₅
duce virtue taken as a whole are those of the acts prescribed
by the law which have been prescribed with a view to education for the common good. But with regard to the education
of the individual as such, which makes him, considered in
the abstract, a good man, we must determine later whether
this is the business of politics or of another craft; for perhaps
it is not the same in every case to be a good man and a good
citizen.

Of particular justice and that which is just in the corre- ₃₀
sponding sense, one kind is that which is found in distribu-

tions of honour or wealth or the other things that fall to be divided among those who have a share in the constitution (for in these it is possible for one man to have a share either unequal or equal to that of another), and another kind is that

1131a which plays a rectifying part in interactions between individuals. Of this there are two divisions; for of interactions some are voluntary and others involuntary: voluntary such as sale, purchase, lending, pledging, borrowing, depositing, letting

5 (they are called voluntary because the originating principle of these interactions is voluntary); while of the involuntary some are clandestine, such as theft, adultery, poisoning, procuring, enticement of slaves, assassination, false witness, and others involve force, such as assault, chains, death, mugging, mutilation, abuse, insult.

10 SINCE THE UNJUST MAN AND AN UNJUST ACT ARE UNFAIR or unequal,[3] it is plain that there is also a midpoint between inequalities. And this is the equal; for in any kind of action in which there is a more and a less there is also an equal. If, then, the unjust be unfair or unequal, the just is fair or equal, as all men suppose it to be, even apart from argument. And since the equal is in the middle, the just will be in the mid-

15 dle. Now equality implies at least two things. The just, then, must be both midway and equal and relative to something and for certain persons: *qua* midway it must be between certain things (which are greater and less); *qua* equal, it involves two things; *qua* just, it is for certain people. The just, therefore, involves at least four terms; for the persons for whom it

20 is just are two, and the things in which it is found are two. And the same equality will exist between the persons and between the things concerned; for as the latter—the things concerned—are related, so are the former. If they are not equal, they will not have what is equal—hence the quarrels and complaints when either equals have and are awarded unequal shares or unequals equal shares. Further, this is plain

3 A single Greek word, ἴσος, corresponds both to 'fair' and to 'equal'.

from the fact that awards should be according to worth; for 25
all men agree that what is just in distribution must be according to worth, though they do not all specify the same
sort of worth—democrats identify it with the status of free-
man, supporters of oligarchy with riches (or with high birth),
and supporters of aristocracy with virtue.

The just, then, is something proportionate, proportion 30
being not a property only of the kind of number which consists of abstract units, but of number in general. For proportion is equality of ratios, and involves four terms at least.
(That discrete proportion involves four terms is plain. So too
does continuous proportion; for it uses one term as two and
mentions it twice: for instance, as the line A is to the line B, 1131b
so is B to C—B, then, has been mentioned twice, so that if B
is taken twice, the proportional terms will be four.) The just,
too, involves at least four terms, and the ratio is the same—
for there is a similar distinction between the persons and be- 5
tween the things. As the term A, then, is to B, so will C be to
D, and therefore, by permutation, as A is to C, B will be to D.
Hence the whole is in the same ratio to the whole; and this
coupling the distribution effects, and, if the terms are so
combined, effects justly. The coupling, then, of the term A 10
with C and of B with D is what is just in distribution, and this
species of the just is in the middle, and the unjust is what violates the proportion; for the proportional is in the middle,
and the just is proportional. (Mathematicians call this kind
of proportion geometrical; for it is in geometrical proportion that it follows that the whole is to the whole as either
part is to the corresponding part.) This proportion is not 15
continuous; for we cannot get a single term standing for a
person and a thing.

This, then, is what the just is—the proportional; the unjust is what violates the proportion. Hence one term becomes more, the other less, as indeed happens in fact; for the
man who acts unjustly has more, and the man who is unjustly treated less, of what is good. In the case of what is bad 20
the reverse is true; for the lesser evil is reckoned a good in

comparison with the greater evil, since the lesser evil is more desirable than the greater, and what is desirable is good, and what is more so is a greater good.

This, then, is one species of the just.

25 THE REMAINING ONE IS THE RECTIFICATORY, WHICH IS found in interactions both voluntary and involuntary. This form of the just has a different specific character from the former. For the justice which distributes common funds is always in accordance with the kind of proportion mentioned above (for in the case in which the distribution is made from 30 common funds it will be according to the same ratio which the funds put into the business bear to one another); and the injustice opposed to this kind of justice is that which violates the proportion. But the justice in interactions is a sort of 1132a equality indeed, and the injustice a sort of inequality: not according to that kind of proportion, however, but according to arithmetical proportion. For it makes no difference whether an upright man has defrauded a base man or a base man an upright one, nor whether it is an upright or a base man that has committed adultery: the law looks only to the 5 distinctive character of the harm, and treats the parties as equal, if one acts unjustly and the other is unjustly treated, and if one inflicted harm and the other received it.

Therefore, this kind of injustice being an inequality, the judge tries to equalize it; for in the case in which one has received and the other has inflicted a wound, or one has killed and the other been killed, the suffering and the action have been unequally distributed; but the judge tries to equalize 10 things by means of a loss,[4] taking away from the profit of the assailant. For the term 'profit' is applied broadly to such cases, even if it be not a term appropriate to certain cases (for instance, to the person who inflicts a wound), and 'loss' to the sufferer. When the suffering has been measured, the one

---

4 'Loss' translates ζημία, which normally means 'fine' or (more generally) 'penalty'.

98

is called loss and the other profit. Therefore the equal is midway between the more and the less, but the profit and the   15
loss are more and less in contrary ways—more of the good
and less of the evil are profit, and the contrary is loss. Midway between them is, as we saw, the equal, which we say is
just; hence corrective justice will be in the middle between
loss and profit. This is why, when people dispute, they take   20
refuge in the judge: to go to the judge is to go to justice; for
the nature of the judge is to be a sort of animate justice. They
look for the judge as a person in the middle, and in some
States they call judges mediators, supposing that if they get
what is in the middle they will get what is just. The just, then,
is in the middle, since the judge is so.

The judge restores equality: it is as though there were a   25
line divided into unequal parts, and he took away that by
which the greater segment exceeds the half, and added it to
the smaller segment. And when the whole has been divided
in two, then they say they have their own when they have got
what is equal. It is for this reason also that in Greek the just   30
is called '*dikaios*'—because it is a division into two parts or
dicha (as if one were to call it *dichaion*) and the judge or *di-
kastês* is a bisector or *dichastês*. The equal is midway between
the greater and the lesser according to arithmetical proportion.[5] For when something is subtracted from one of two
equals and added to the other, the other exceeds it by these
two; for if what was taken from the one had not been added
to the other, the latter would have exceeded it by one only. It   1132b
therefore exceeds the midpoint by one, and the midpoint exceeds by one that from which something was taken. By this,
then, we shall recognize both what we must subtract from
that which has more, and what we must add to that which
has less: we must add to the latter that by which the mid-
point exceeds it, and subtract from the greatest that by   5
which it exceeds the midpoint. Let the lines AA, BB, CC be

5 In the manuscripts, the sentence 'The equal . . . proportion' follows ' . . .
what is equal' in 1132a29: we translate Rassow's transposition.

equal to one another. From AA subtract AE, and to CC add CD, so that the whole line DCC exceeds EA by CD and CF;

10 therefore it exceeds BB by CD.[6]

These names, both loss and profit, have come from voluntary exchange; for to have more than one's own is called profiting, and to have less than one's original share is called los-

15 ing, for instance in buying and selling and in all other matters in which the law has left people free to make their own terms. When they get neither more nor less but make a fair exchange,[7] they say that they have their own and that they neither lose nor profit.

There the just is midway between a sort of profit and a sort of loss, namely those which are involuntary: it consists

20 in having an equal amount before and after.

SOME THINK THAT RECIPROCITY IS JUSTICE IN THE ABstract, as the Pythagoreans said; for they defined justice in the abstract as reciprocity. Now reciprocity fits neither dis-

25 tributive nor rectificatory justice—yet people want even the justice of Rhadamanthus to mean this:

> Should a man suffer what he did, straight justice would be done

—for in many cases they are not in accord: for instance, if an official has struck someone, he should not be struck in return, and if someone has struck an official, he ought not to

30 be struck only but punished in addition. Further, there is a great difference between what is voluntary and what is involuntary. But in associations for exchange this sort of justice does hold men together—reciprocity in accordance with a proportion and not on the basis of equality. For it is by

6 At this point the manuscripts have the following sentence: 'And this is

10 true of the crafts also; for they would have been destroyed if what the patient suffered had not been just what the agent did, and of the same amount and kind'. The sentence recurs word for word at 1133a14–16, where it seems slightly less out of place: Muretus deleted it here.

7 The text is obscure, but this must be the general sense.

proportionate requital that the State holds together. Men look to return either evil for evil—and if they cannot do so, think their position slavery—or good for good—and if they cannot do so there is no exchange, but it is by exchange that they hold together. This is why they give a prominent place to the temple of the Graces—to promote the requital of services; for this is characteristic of grace—we should serve in return one who has shown grace to us, and should another time take the initiative in showing it.

Proportionate requital is secured by cross-coupling. Let A be a builder, B a shoemaker, C a house, D a shoe. The builder, then, must get from the shoemaker the latter's product, and must himself give him in return his own. If, then, first there is proportionate equality of goods, and then reciprocal action takes place, the result we mention will be effected. If not, it is not equal, and does not hold together; for there is nothing to prevent the product of the one being better than that of the other, and they must therefore be equalized. (And this is true of the crafts also; for they would have been destroyed if what the patient suffered had not been what the agent did, and of the same amount and kind.) For it is not two doctors that form an association but a doctor and a farmer, or in general people who are different and unequal; and they must be equalized.

This is why all things that are exchanged must be somehow commensurable. It is for this end that money has been introduced, and it becomes in a way a middle term; for it measures all things, and therefore both the excess and the defect—how many shoes are equal to a house or to a given amount of food. The number of shoes exchanged for a house (or for a given amount of food) must therefore correspond to the ratio of builder to shoemaker. For if this be not so, there will be no exchange and no association. And this proportion will not be effected unless the goods are somehow equal. All goods must therefore be measured by some one thing, as we said before. Now this unit is in truth need, which holds all things together (for if men did not need anything,

1133a

5

10

15

20

25

or did not have similar needs, there would be either no exchange or not the same exchange); but money has become
30   by compact a sort of representative of need. This is why it has
the name '*nomisma*' in Greek—because it exists not by nature
but by *nomos* or convention and it is in our power to change it
and make it useless.

There will, then, be reciprocity when the terms have been
equalized so that as farmer is to shoemaker, the shoemaker's
1133b product is to that of the farmer. But we must not bring them
into a figure of proportion when they have already exchanged (otherwise one extreme will have both excesses),
but when they still have their own goods. Thus they are
equals and associates just because this equality can be ef-
5   fected in their case. Let A be a farmer, C food, B a shoemaker, D his product which has been equalized. If it had not
been possible for reciprocity to be thus effected, there would
have been no association.

That need holds things together as a single unit is made
plain by the fact that when men do not need one another—
when neither needs the other or one does not need the
other—they do not exchange, as we do when someone wants
what one has oneself: for instance, when people permit the
10   exportation of corn in exchange for wine. This equality
therefore must be established. And for the future exchange—that if we do not need a thing now we shall have it if
ever we do need it—money is as it were our surety; for it
must be possible for us to get what we want by bringing the
money. Now the same thing happens to money: it is not always worth the same; yet it tends to be steadier. This is why
15   all goods must have a value set on them; for then there will
always be exchange, and if so, association.

Money, then, acting as a measure, makes goods commensurate and equalizes them; for neither would there have been
association if there were not exchange, nor exchange if there
were not equality, nor equality if there were not commensura-
bility. Now in truth it is impossible that things differing so
much should become commensurate, but with reference to

need they may become so sufficiently. There must, then, be a   20
unit, and that fixed by agreement (that is why it is called
money[8]); for it is this that makes all things commensurate,
since all things are measured by money. Let A be a house, B
ten minae, C a bed. A is half of B, if the house is worth five
minae or equal to them; the bed, C, is a tenth of B: it is plain,
then, how many beds are equal to a house, namely five. That   25
exchange took place before there was money is plain; for it
makes no difference whether it is five beds that exchange for a
house, or the money value of five beds.

We have now said what the unjust is and what the just.
These having been defined, it is plain that just action is mid-   30
way between acting unjustly and being unjustly treated; for
the one is to have more and the other to have less. Justice is a
kind of mean—not in the same way as the other virtues, but
rather because it relates to the middle, while injustice relates   1134a
to the extremes. And justice is that in virtue of which the just
man is said to do by choice that which is just, and to distribute either between himself and another or between two others not so as to give more of what is desirable to himself and   5
less to his neighbour (and conversely with what is harmful),
but so as to give what is equal in accordance with proportion; and similarly in distributing between two other persons. Injustice, on the contrary, is related to the unjust,
which is excess and deficiency, contrary to proportion, of the
beneficial or harmful. That is why injustice is excess and deficiency—because it is related to excess and deficiency, in   10
one's own case excess of what is in the abstract beneficial and
deficiency of what is hurtful, while in the case of others it is
as a whole similar but proportion may be violated in either
direction. In the case of unjust action to have less is to be unjustly treated, to have more is to act unjustly.

Let this be taken as our account of the nature of justice   15
and injustice, and similarly of the just and the unjust in
general.

8 See above, 1133a30–31.

SINCE ONE MAY ACT UNJUSTLY WITHOUT THEREBY BEING unjust, we must ask what sort of unjust acts imply that the doer is thereby unjust with respect to each type of injustice, for instance a thief, an adulterer, or a brigand. Or does that make no difference? For a man might even lie with a woman knowing who she was, but the origin of the act might be not choice but emotion. He acts unjustly, then, but is not unjust—for instance, a man is not a thief, yet he stole, nor an adulterer, yet he committed adultery; and similarly in other cases.

We have previously stated how the reciprocal is related to the just; but we must not forget that what we are looking for is not only what is just in the abstract but also political justice. This is found among men who share their life with a view to self-sufficiency, men who are free and either proportionately or arithmetically equal, so that between those who do not fulfil this condition there is no political justice but something similar to justice. For justice exists only between men who share a law; and law exists for men between whom there is injustice; for legal judgement is the assessment of the just and the unjust. And between men between whom there is injustice there is also unjust action (though there is not injustice between all between whom there is unjust action), and this is assigning more to oneself of things good in the abstract and less of things bad in the abstract. This is why we do not allow a man to rule, but rather reason, because a man behaves thus in his own interests and becomes a tyrant.

The ruler is the guardian of justice, and, if of justice, then of equality also. And since he is thought to have no more than his share, if he is just (for he does not assign to himself more of what is good in the abstract, unless it is proportional to his merits—so that it is for others that he labours, and that is why men, as we stated previously, say that justice is another's good), therefore a reward must be given him, and this is honour, and privilege; but those for whom such things are not enough become tyrants.

The justice of a master and that of a father are not the same as the above kinds, though they are like them; for there can be no injustice in the abstract towards things that are one's own, but a man's possessions, and his child until it reaches a certain age and sets up for itself, are as it were part of himself, and no one chooses to harm himself (that is why there can be no injustice towards oneself). Therefore there is no political justice or injustice here; for political justice is, as we saw, according to law, and between people naturally subject to law, and these, as we saw, are people who have an equal share in ruling and being ruled. That is why justice occurs rather towards a wife than towards children and possessions—it is household justice, and it is different from political justice.

OF POLITICAL JUSTICE PART IS NATURAL, PART LEGAL OR conventional—natural, that which everywhere has the same sense and does not exist by people's thinking this or that; conventional, that which is originally indifferent, but when it has been laid down is not indifferent: for instance, that a ransom shall be a mina, or that a goat and not two sheep shall be sacrificed, and again all the laws that are passed for particular cases: for instance, that sacrifice shall be made in honour of Brasidas, and the provisions of decrees. Some think that all justice is of this sort because that which is by nature is unchangeable and has everywhere the same sense (as fire burns both here and in Persia), while they see change in the things which are just. This, however, is not altogether true, but true up to a point. Or rather, with the gods it is perhaps not true at all, while with us there is something that is just by nature, yet all of it is changeable—and nevertheless some is by nature, some not by nature. It is plain which sort of thing, among things capable of being otherwise, is by nature, and which is not but is conventional and by compact, given that both are equally changeable. And in other things the same distinction will apply: by nature the right hand is stronger, yet it is possible that all men should come to be ambidextrous.

1135a The things which are just by virtue of a compact and of advantage are like measures; for wine and corn measures are not everywhere equal, but larger in wholesale and smaller in retail markets. Similarly, the things which are just not by nature but by human enactment are not everywhere the same,

5 since constitutions also are not the same, though there is but one which is everywhere by nature the best.

Of things just by convention each is related as the universal to its particulars: the things that are done are many, but each of them is one, since it is universal.

There is a difference between an act of injustice and what is unjust, and between an act of justice and what is just; for a

10 thing is unjust by nature or by enactment; and this very thing, when it has been done, is an act of injustice, whereas before it is done is not yet one but it is unjust. So, too, with an act of justice. (The general term is rather 'just action', an act of justice being the correction of an act of injustice.)

Each of these must later be examined separately with re-

15 gard to the nature and number of its species and the nature of the things with which it is concerned.

THE JUST AND THE UNJUST BEING AS WE HAVE DESCRIBED them, a man acts unjustly or justly whenever he does such things voluntarily: when involuntarily, he acts neither unjustly nor justly except coincidentally, as when people do things which happen to be just or unjust. Acts of injustice

20 and of justice are determined by voluntariness or involuntariness; for when it is voluntary it is blamed, and at the same time it is then an act of injustice; so that there will be things that are unjust but not yet acts of injustice, if voluntariness be not present as well.

By the voluntary I mean, as has been said before, any of the things in a man's own power which he does with knowledge

25 and not in ignorance either of the person acted on or of the instrument or of the end (for instance, whom he is

striking, with what, and to what end), each such act being
done not coincidentally nor perforce (for instance, if you take
my hand and strike someone else with it, I do not act voluntarily; for the act was not in my power). The person struck
may be the striker's father, and the striker may know that it is
a man or one of the persons present but not know that it is his   30
father; a similar distinction may be made in the case of the
end, and with regard to the whole action. Therefore that
which is done in ignorance, or though not done in ignorance
is not in the agent's power, or is done perforce, is involuntary.
(Many natural processes, we knowingly both do and undergo,   1135b
none of which is either voluntary or involuntary: for instance,
growing old or dying.) In the case of unjust and just acts alike
the injustice or justice may be only coincidental; for a man
might return a deposit unwillingly and from fear, and then he
must not be said either to do what is just or to act justly, ex-   5
cept coincidentally. Similarly the man who under compulsion
and involuntarily fails to return the deposit must be said to act
unjustly, and to do what is unjust, only coincidentally.

Of voluntary acts we do some by choice, others not by
choice: by choice those which we do after deliberation, not   10
by choice those which we do without previous deliberation.
Thus there are three kinds of harm in associations: those
done in ignorance are mistakes when the person acted on,
the act, the instrument, or the end is other than the agent
assumed—he thought either that he was not throwing anything or not this missile or not at this person or not to this
end, but it turned out that the end was not what he thought
it would be (for instance, he threw not in order to wound   15
but to prick), or the person hit or the missile was other than
he supposed. Now when the harm is done against reasonable expectation, it is a misfortune. When it is not contrary
to reasonable expectation but does not imply vice, it is an
error (for a man errs when the ignorance[9] originates in him,

9 Reading ἀγνοίας (Jackson) for the received αἰτίας ('the cause originates
in him').

but he is the victim of misfortune when its origin lies out-
20 side him). When he acts with knowledge but not after deliberation, it is an act of injustice—for instance, the acts due to
rage or to other emotions necessary or natural to man; for
when men do such harmful and erroneous acts they act unjustly, and the acts are acts of injustice, but this does not
imply that the doers are unjust or vicious; for the harm is
25 not due to depravity. But when a man acts from choice, he is
unjust and depraved.

That is why acts proceeding from rage are rightly judged
not to be done from forethought; for it is not the man who
acts from rage but he who angered him who is the origin.
Again, the matter in dispute is not whether the thing happened or not, but its justice; for it is apparent injustice that
30 occasions anger. For they do not dispute about the occur-
rence of the act—as in transactions where one of the two
parties must be depraved—unless they do so owing to forgetfulness; but, agreeing about the fact, they dispute on
which side justice lies (whereas a man who has plotted cannot be ignorant that he has done so), so that the one thinks
he is being treated unjustly and the other disagrees.

1136a   If a man harms another by choice, he acts unjustly; and
these are the acts of injustice which imply that the doer is an
unjust man, provided that the act violates proportion or
equality. Similarly, a man is just when he acts justly by choice;
but he acts justly if he merely acts voluntarily.

5   Of involuntary acts some deserve sympathy, others do
not. For the errors which men make not only in ignorance
but also from ignorance deserve sympathy, while those
which men do not from ignorance but (though they do them
in ignorance) owing to an emotion which is neither natural
nor human do not deserve sympathy.

10 SUPPOSING THAT WE HAVE SUFFICIENTLY DEFINED WHAT
it is to be unjustly treated and what to act unjustly, we may
raise the problem of whether there is any truth in Euripides'
absurd remark:

—I slew my mother, that's my tale in brief.
—Were you both willing, or unwilling both?

Is it truly possible to be voluntarily treated unjustly, or is it   15
always involuntary, as all unjust action is voluntary? And is it
always of the latter kind or else always of the former, or is it
sometimes voluntary, sometimes involuntary? So, too, with
being justly treated: all just action is voluntary, so that it is
reasonable that there should be a similar opposition in ei-   20
ther case—that both being unjustly and being justly treated
should be either voluntary or involuntary. It would be
thought absurd even in the case of being justly treated, if it
were always voluntary; for some are non-voluntarily treated
justly. One might also raise the problem of whether everyone
who has suffered what is unjust is being unjustly treated, or
it is with suffering as with acting: in both it is possible to par-   25
take of justice coincidentally. Similarly (it is plain) for injustice; for to do what is unjust is not the same as to act unjustly,
nor to suffer what is unjust as to be treated unjustly. And
similarly in the case of acting justly and being justly treated;
for it is impossible to be unjustly treated if the other does not   30
act unjustly, or justly treated unless he acts justly.

If to act unjustly is simply to harm someone voluntarily,
if 'voluntarily' means 'knowing the person acted on, the instrument, and the manner of one's acting', and if the incontinent man voluntarily harms himself, then he will voluntarily be unjustly treated and it will be possible to treat
oneself unjustly. (This also is one of the problems—whether   1136b
a man can treat himself unjustly.) Again, a man may voluntarily, owing to incontinence, be harmed by another who
acts voluntarily, so that it would be possible to be voluntarily treated unjustly.

Or is our definition incorrect? Must we to 'harming another, knowing the person acted on, the instrument, and
the manner of one's acting' add 'against his will'? Then a
man may be voluntarily harmed and voluntarily suffer what   5
is unjust, but no one is voluntarily treated unjustly; for no

one wants to be unjustly treated, not even the incontinent man. Rather, he acts against his will; for no one wants what he does not think to be good, but the incontinent man does things that he thinks he ought not to do. Again, one who gives what is his own, as Homer says Glaucus gave Diomedes

armour of gold for brazen, the price of a hundred beeves for nine,[10]

is not unjustly treated; for though to give is in his power, to be unjustly treated is not in his power—rather, the unjust agent must be present. It is plain, then, that to be unjustly treated is not voluntary.

Of the questions we intended to discuss two still remain: whether it is the man who has assigned to another more than he is worth who acts unjustly, or he who gets it; and whether it is possible to treat oneself unjustly. If the former alternative is possible and the distributor acts unjustly and not the man who gets it, then if a man assigns more to another than to himself, knowingly and voluntarily, he treats himself unjustly; which is what moderate people seem to do, since the upright man tends to take less. Or does this statement too need qualification? For he perhaps gets more than his share of some other good, for instance of reputation or of what is in the abstract noble. Again, the question is solved by applying the distinction we applied to unjust action; for he suffers nothing against his own will, so that he is not unjustly treated as far as this goes, but at most only suffers harm.

It is evident too that the distributor acts unjustly, and not always the man who gets more. For it is not he to whom what is unjust happens that acts unjustly, but he who happens to do an unjust act voluntarily, or the person in whom lies the originating principle of the action, and this lies in the distributor, not in the receiver. Again, since we speak in different ways of doing things, and there is a way in which inanimate

10 *Iliad* VI 236.

things and a hand and a servant who obeys an order kill, he does not act unjustly though he does what is unjust.

Again, if the distributor made his assessment in ignorance, he does not act unjustly in respect of conventional justice, and his assessment is not unjust in this way—but in a way it is unjust (for conventional justice and primary justice are different); but if with knowledge he assessed unjustly, he is himself covetous either for gratitude or for revenge. As much, then, as if he were to share in the unjust act, the man who has made an unjust assessment for these reasons has got more; for, assessing the land on that condition, he received not land but money.

Men think that acting unjustly is in their power, and therefore that being just is easy. But it is not: to lie with one's neighbour's wife, to strike one's neighbour, to offer a bribe, is easy and in our power, but to do these things from a certain state of character is neither easy nor in our power. Similarly to know what is just and what is unjust requires, men think, no great understanding, because it is not hard to comprehend the matters dealt with by the laws (though these are not the things that are just, except coincidentally); but to know how actions must be done and distributions effected in order to be just is a greater task than knowing what is good for the health; though even there, while it is easy to know what honey, wine, hellebore, cautery, and surgery are, to know how, to whom, and when they should be applied with a view to producing health, is no less a task than that of being a doctor.

Men think that acting unjustly is no less characteristic of the just man because he would be not less but even more capable of doing each of these acts: he could lie with a woman or strike someone; and the courageous man could throw away his shield or turn and flee in this direction or in that. But to play the coward or to act unjustly consists not in doing these things, except coincidentally, but in doing them from of a certain state of character, just as to practise medicine and to heal consists not in applying or not applying the

1137a

5

10

15

20

111

25   knife, in using or not using drugs, but in doing so in a certain way.

Just acts occur between people who participate in things good in the abstract and can have an excess or deficiency of them; for some beings (for instance, presumably the gods) cannot have an excess of them, and to others, those who are incurably bad, not even the smallest share in them is beneficial but all are harmful, while to others they are beneficial

30   up to a point; therefore justice is something particularly human.

OUR NEXT SUBJECT IS UPRIGHTNESS OR EQUITY AND THE upright or the equitable, and the relation of equity to justice and of the equitable to the just. For on examination they appear to be neither the same *tout court* nor generically differ-

35   ent; and while we sometimes praise what is equitable and the equitable man (so that we extend the name by way of praise

1137b   even to instances of the other virtues in the sense of 'good', meaning by 'more equitable'[11] that a thing is better), at other times, when we reason it out, it seems absurd if the equitable, being something different from the just, is yet praiseworthy; for either the just is not virtuous or the equitable is

5   not just, if they are different; or, if both are virtuous, they are the same.

These, then, are pretty much the considerations that give rise to the problem about the equitable. They are all in a way correct and not contrary to one another; for the equitable, though it is better than one kind of justice, yet is just, and it is not as being a different class of thing that it is better than the

10   just. The same thing, then, is just and equitable, and while both are virtuous the equitable is superior. What creates the problem is that the equitable is just, but not the legally just but rather a correction of legal justice. The reason is that all law is universal but about some things it is not possible to make a universal statement which will be correct. In those

11 Reading τῷ (Ross) for the received τό.

cases, then, in which it is necessary to speak universally but   15
not possible to do so correctly, the law takes what holds for
the most part, though it is not ignorant of the error. And it is
nonetheless correct; for the error is not in the law nor in the
legislator but in the nature of the thing, since the stuff of matters of action is of this kind from the start.

When the law speaks universally, then, and a case arises   20
which conflicts with the universal statement, then it is correct, when the legislator fails us and has erred by speaking in
the abstract, to supply what is missing—to say what the legislator himself would have said had he been present, and
would have put into his law if he had known. That is why the
equitable is just, and is better than one kind of justice—not
better than justice in the abstract, but better than the error   25
that arises from speaking in the abstract. And this is the nature of the equitable: it is a correction of law where the law is
defective owing to its universality. The reason why all things
are not determined by law is that about some things it is impossible to lay down a law, so that a decree is needed. For
when the thing is indefinite the rule also is indefinite, like
the lead rule used by builders on Lesbos: the rule adapts it-   30
self to the shape of the stone and is not rigid, and so too the
decree is adapted to the facts.

It is plain, then, what the equitable is, and that it is just
and is better than one kind of justice. It is evident also from
this who the equitable man is: the man who chooses and
does such acts, and is no stickler for justice in a bad sense but
tends to take less though he has the law on his side, is equi-   1138a
table, and this state of character is equity, which is a sort of
justice, and not a different state.

WHETHER A MAN CAN TREAT HIMSELF UNJUSTLY OR NOT,
is evident from what has been said. For one class of just acts   5
are those in accordance with any virtue which are prescribed
by the law: for instance, the law commands a man not to kill
himself, and what it commands him not to do it forbids.
Again, when a man in violation of the law harms another

voluntarily and not in retaliation he acts unjustly, and a voluntary agent is one who knows both the person he is affect-
10   ing and the instrument; and he who through anger voluntarily stabs himself does this contrary to correct reasoning,
and this the law does not allow; therefore he is acting unjustly. But towards whom? Surely towards the State, not towards himself. For he suffers voluntarily, and no one is voluntarily treated unjustly. This is also why the State punishes,
and a certain dishonour attaches to the man who destroys
himself, on the ground that he is treating the State unjustly.
15   Further, in the sense in which the man who acts unjustly
is unjust only and not base all round, it is not possible to
treat oneself unjustly (this is different from the previous
case: this kind of unjust man is vicious in a particular way
just as the coward is, not as being vicious all round, so that
his unjust act does not manifest all-round viciousness). For
that would imply the possibility of the same thing's having
been subtracted from and added to the same thing at the
20   same time; but this is impossible—the just and the unjust always involve more than one person. Further, unjust action is
voluntary and done by choice, and comes first (for the man
who because he has suffered does the same in return is not
thought to act unjustly); but if a man harms himself he suffers and does the same thing at the same time. Further, it
would mean that a man could be voluntarily treated unjustly.
Besides, no one acts unjustly without committing particular
25   acts of injustice; but no one commits adultery with his own
wife or burgles his own house or steals his own property.
        In general, the question 'Can a man treat himself un-
justly?' is solved also by the distinction we applied to the
question 'Can a man be voluntarily treated unjustly?'
        It is evident too that both are base, being unjustly treated
30   and acting unjustly; for the one means having less and the
other having more than the middle amount, which is like the
healthy in medicine and good condition in physical training.
But still acting unjustly is the worse; for acting unjustly involves vice and is blameworthy—it involves either complete

vice and vice *tout court* or else something close to it (for not all voluntary unjust action implies injustice). But being unjustly treated does not involve vice and injustice. In itself, then, being unjustly treated is less base, but there is nothing to prevent its being coincidentally a greater evil. But the art of medicine cares nothing for this: it calls pleurisy a more serious mischief than a stumble; yet the latter may sometimes be coincidentally the more serious, if a man falls because he stumbles and so is taken prisoner or put to death by the enemy.

1138b

In an extended sense and in virtue of a resemblance there is a justice, not indeed between a man and himself but between certain parts of him—not every kind of justice but that of a master or of a householder. For these are the relationships in which the part of the soul that has reason stands to the irrational part; and it is with a view to these parts that people think a man can be unjust to himself, because these parts are liable to suffer something against their desires; there is therefore thought to be a mutual justice between them as between ruler and ruled.

5

10

Let this be taken as our account of justice and of the other moral virtues.

6

THE INTELLECTUAL VIRTUES

Book E SINCE WE HAVE PREVIOUSLY SAID THAT ONE OUGHT TO choose the middle, not the excess nor the deficiency, and
20 that the middle is what is prescribed by correct reasoning, let us refine this. In all the states of character we have mentioned, as in all other matters, there is a mark to which the man who possesses reason looks, and heightens or relaxes his activity accordingly, and there is a standard which determines the mean states which we say are intermediate between excess and deficiency, being in accordance with cor-
25 rect reasoning. But such a statement, though true, is by no means illuminating; for in all other pursuits which are objects of knowledge it is true to say that we must not exert ourselves nor relax too much or too little but to a middling amount and in accordance with correct reasoning; but if a
30 man had only this he would be none the wiser—for instance, he would not know what to apply to the body if someone were to say 'What medicine prescribes, and as one who possesses the art prescribes'. That is why, with regard to the states of the soul too, not only must what we have said be truly said—in addition, it must be determined what correct reasoning is and what is the standard that fixes it.

We divided the virtues of the soul and said that some are
1139a virtues of character and others of intellect. We have discussed the moral virtues: with regard to the others let us express our view as follows, beginning with some remarks about the soul. It was said earlier that there are two parts of the soul—that which possesses reason and that which is ir-
5 rational. Let us now draw a similar distinction within the

part which possesses reason, and let it be assumed that there are two parts which possess reason—one by which we contemplate the kind of things whose originating principles cannot be otherwise, and one which concerns what can be otherwise; for where objects differ in kind the part of the soul answering to each is different in kind, since it is in virtue   10
of a certain likeness and relationship with their objects that they have the knowledge they have. Let one of these parts be called the scientific and the other the calculative; for to deliberate and to calculate are the same thing, but no one deliberates about what cannot be otherwise. Hence the calculative is one part of that which possesses reason. We must, then,   15
grasp what is the best state of each of these two parts; for this is the virtue of each, and the virtue of each thing is relative to its proper task.

THERE ARE THREE THINGS IN THE SOUL WHICH CONTROL action and truth—sense-perception, intelligence, desire. Of these perception originates no action: this is plain from the fact that brutes have perception but no share in action.   20

What affirmation and negation are in thinking, pursuit and avoidance are in desire; so that since moral virtue is a state concerned with choice, and choice is deliberative desire, the reasoning must be true and the desire correct if the choice is to be virtuous, and the latter must pursue just what   25
the former asserts. This kind of thought and of truth is practical. Of thought that is contemplative and neither practical nor productive, the good and the bad are truth and falsity (for this is the task of everything intellectual); while of the part which is practical and intellectual the good is truth in   30
agreement with correct desire.

The origin of action—that from which the movement starts, not that for the sake of which—is choice, and that of choice is desire and reasoning with a view to an end. This is why choice cannot exist either without intelligence and thought or without a moral state of character; for good

35   action and its contrary cannot exist without thought and
character. Thought as such, however, moves nothing, but
1139b   only that which aims at an end and is practical; for this rules
the productive intellect as well, since everyone who makes
makes for an end, and it is not matters of production which
are ends *tout court* (though they may be ends for something
and of someone) but rather matters of action. For good action is an end, and desire aims at this. That is why choice is
5   either desiderative intelligence or intellectual desire, and
such an origin of action is a man. (Nothing that is past is an
object of choice—for instance, no one chooses to have
sacked Troy; for no one deliberates about what is past but
about what will be and can be otherwise, while what is past
cannot not have taken place. That is why Agathon is correct
when he says:

10   For this alone is lacking even to God,
To make undone things that have once been done.)

The product of both the intellectual parts, then, is truth.
Therefore the states in respect of which each of these parts
will best reach truth are the virtues of the two parts.

LET US START, THEN, FROM A DIFFERENT LEVEL, AND DIS-
15   cuss these states once more. Let it be assumed that the states
by virtue of which the soul possesses truth by way of affirmation or denial are five in number—they are craftsmanship,
knowledge, wisdom, understanding, intelligence (for assumption and belief may be mistaken).
Now what knowledge is, if we are to speak precisely and
not follow similarities, is evident from what follows. We all
20   assume that what we know cannot be otherwise: of things
that can be otherwise we do not know, when they have
passed outside our consideration, whether they are or are
not. Therefore the object of knowledge is of necessity. Therefore it is eternal; for things that are of necessity *tout court*
are all eternal; and things that are eternal are ungenerated

and imperishable. Again, all knowledge is thought to be ca-   25
pable of being taught, and its object of being learned. And all
teaching starts from what is already known, as we say in the
Analytics;[1] for it proceeds sometimes through induction and
sometimes by deduction. Now induction is the origin of the
universal and deduction proceeds from universals. There are   30
therefore originating principles on which deduction depends
which are not reached by deduction: so it is by induction that
they are acquired. Knowledge, then, is a state capable of
demonstrating things, and it has the other characteristics
which we specify in the *Analytics*; for it is when a man believes in a certain way and the principles are known to him
that he has knowledge, since if they are not better known   35
to him than the conclusion, he will have his knowledge
coincidentally.

Let this, then, be taken as our account of knowledge.

Among things that can be otherwise are included both   1140a
matters of production and matters of action: producing and
acting are different (as to what they are, we rely on the public
discussions). Hence the reasoned state concerned with action is different from the reasoned state concerned with production. That is why they are not included one in the other;   5
for neither is acting producing nor is producing acting. Now
since housebuilding is a craft and is essentially a reasoned
state concerning production, and there is neither any craft
that is not such a state nor any such state that is not a craft,
craftsmanship is identical with a state concerning produc-   10
tion, involving true reasoning. Every craft is concerned with
coming into being and with crafting and considering how
something may come into being which can be or not be, and
whose origin is in the producer and not in the product; for
crafts are concerned neither with things that are or come into   15
being by necessity, nor with things that do so in accordance
with nature (since these have their origin in themselves).

1 See *Posterior Analytics* A, 71a1–11.

Producing and acting being different, craftsmanship must be a matter of producing, not of acting. And in a manner fortune and craftsmanship are concerned with the same objects: as Agathon says,

> craftsmanhip loves fortune and fortune craftsmanship.

Craftsmanship, then, as has been said, is a state concerned with production and involving true reasoning, and lack of craftsmanship, its contrary, is a state concerned with production and involving false reasoning. Both are concerned with what can be otherwise.

REGARDING WISDOM WE SHALL GET AT THE TRUTH BY considering who are the persons we call wise. It is thought to be a mark of a wise man to be able to deliberate well about what is good and advantageous for himself, not in some particular respect (for instance, about what sorts of thing conduce to health or to strength), but about what sorts of thing conduce to the good life as a whole. An indication of this is the fact that we call people wise in some particular respect when they have calculated well with a view to some virtuous end which is not the object of any craft. Thus in general the man who is good at deliberating is wise. Now no one deliberates about things that cannot be otherwise nor about things that it is impossible for him to do. Therefore, since knowledge involves demonstration, and there is no demonstration of things whose originating principles can be otherwise (for all such things can be otherwise), and since it is impossible to deliberate about things that are of necessity, wisdom is not knowledge or craftsmanship—not knowledge because matters of action can be otherwise, not craftsmanship because action and production are different kinds of thing. It remains, then, that it is a true and reasoned state concerned with action with regard to the things that are good or bad for man. For while producing has an end other than itself, action cannot; for good action itself is its end. We think Pericles and men like him are wise because they can consider

what is good for themselves and what is good for men in general: we think that those can do this who manage households 10
or States.

This is why we call temperance by this name: we imply
that it preserves wisdom.[2] Now what it preserves is an assumption of the kind we have described. For it is not just any
assumption that pleasant and painful objects destroy and
pervert (for instance, that the triangle has or has not its an- 15
gles equal to two right angles) but those about matters of action. For the originating principles of matters of action are
the ends of action; but the man who has been destroyed by
pleasure or pain fails outright to see any such principle—to
see that for the sake of this or because of that he ought to
choose and do whatever he chooses and does: vice is destructive of the originating principle.

Wisdom, then, must be a reasoned and true state con- 20
cerned with action with regard to human goods. Further,
while there is such a thing as virtue in the crafts, there is no
such thing as virtue in wisdom; and in the crafts he who errs
voluntarily is preferable, but in wisdom, as in the virtues, it is
the reverse. Plainly, then, wisdom is a virtue and not a craft.
There being two parts of the soul that possess reason, it must 25
be the virtue of one of the two, and of the believing part; for
belief is about what can be otherwise, and so is wisdom. But
yet it is not only a reasoned state: an indication of this is the
fact that a state of that sort may be forgotten but wisdom
cannot. 30

KNOWLEDGE IS AN ASSUMPTION ABOUT THINGS THAT ARE
universal and necessary, and there are originating principles
of everything that is demonstrated and of all knowledge (for
knowledge involves reasoning). This being so, the principle
of what is known cannot be an object of knowledge, of
craftsmanship, or of wisdom; for that which can be known

---

2 'Temperance' is σωφροσύνη, which Aristotle etymologizes as σῴζειν τὴν
φρόνησιν.

1141a can be demonstrated, and art and wisdom deal with things that can be otherwise. Nor are principles the objects of understanding; for it is a mark of the man of understanding to have demonstrations about some things. If, then, the states by which we have truth and are never deceived about things
5 that cannot or that can be otherwise are knowledge, wisdom, understanding, and intelligence, and it cannot be any of the three (by the three I mean wisdom, knowledge, and understanding), it remains that it is intelligence which deals with principles.

UNDERSTANDING WE ASCRIBE, IN CONNECTION WITH THE
10 crafts, to the most precise craftsmen: we say of Phidias that he understands stone and of Polyclitus that he understands statues, indicating here by understanding nothing more than a virtue of craftsmanship. But we think that some people have a general understanding, not limited to some particular field or in any other respect, as Homer says in the *Margites*:

15   Him did the gods make neither a digger nor yet a ploughman
       Nor understanding in anything else.

So understanding must plainly be the most precise of the forms of knowledge. It follows that the man of understanding must not only know what follows from the principles but also possess truth about the principles. So understanding must be intelligence combined with knowledge, being knowledge of the most valuable things which has, as it were,
20 been crowned.

It would be absurd to think that the art of politics or wisdom is the most virtuous kind of knowledge, since man is not the best thing in the world. If what is healthy or good is different for men and for fish, but what is white or straight is always the same, everyone would say that understanding
25 is the same but that wisdom is different; for it is that which considers well the various matters concerning itself which they say is wise, and it is to this that one will entrust such

matters. This is why they say that some even of the brutes are wise, namely those which evidently have a power of forethought with regard to their own life. It is evident also that understanding and the art of politics cannot be the same; for if the state of mind concerned with a man's own interests is to be called understanding, there will be many sorts of understanding: there will not be one concerned with the good of all animals (any more than there is one art of medicine for all existing things), but a different one for each. If they say that man is the best of the animals, this makes no difference; for there are other things much more divine in their nature even than man—for instance, and most evidently, the things from which the world is constituted.

From what has been said it is plain, then, that understanding is knowledge combined with intelligence of the things that are by nature most valuable. This is why they say that Anaxagoras, Thales, and men like them have understanding but not wisdom when they see them ignorant of what is to their own advantage, and they say that they know things that are remarkable, admirable, difficult, and superhuman, but useless because it is not human goods that they look for.

Wisdom on the other hand is concerned with things human and things about which it is possible to deliberate; for we say that it is especially the task of a wise man to deliberate well. No one deliberates about things that cannot be otherwise, nor about things which have not an end and a good which is a matter of action. The man who is a good deliberator *tout court* is the man who is capable of aiming by calculation at what is best for man among matters of action. Nor is wisdom concerned with universals only—it must also recognize the particulars; for it is concerned with action and action is concerned with particulars. This is why some who do not know, and especially those who have experience, are more practical than others who know; for if a man knew that light meats are digestible and healthy, but did not know which sorts of meat are light, he would not produce health:

123

the man who knows that chicken is healthy is more likely to produce health. Wisdom is concerned with action; therefore one should have both, or the latter in preference to the former.

HERE, TOO, THERE MUST BE A MASTER KIND. THE ART OF politics and wisdom are the same disposition, but being a politician is not the same as being wise. So far as concerns

25 the State, the master kind is legislative, while that which is related to particulars has the general name of politics: this has to do with action and deliberation—for a decree is the ultimate item among matters of action. This is why these men are alone said to take part in politics; for they alone act in the way in which manual labourers act.

30 But wisdom is identified especially with that form of it which is concerned with a man himself—with the individual; and this is known by the general name of wisdom. Of the other kinds one is household management, another legislation, another politics, and of politics one part is deliberative and the other judicial. Knowing what is good for oneself will be one kind of knowledge, but it is very different: the

1142a man who knows and concerns himself with his own interests is thought to be wise, while politicians are thought to be busybodies. Hence Euripides:

> But how could I be wise, who might at ease,
> Numbered among the army's multitude,
> 5 Have had an equal share? . . .
> For those who aim too high and do too much . . .

They look for their own good, and think that one ought to do so. From this belief, then, has come the view that such men are wise; yet perhaps one's own good cannot exist without household management, nor without a form of government.

10 Further, how one should order one's own affairs is not plain and needs inquiry.

An indication of this is the fact that while young men become geometricians and mathematicians and gain understanding in matters like these, it is thought that none is wise. The cause is that such wisdom is concerned with particulars, which become familiar from experience, and a young man has no experience; for it is length of time that gives experience. One might also inquire why a boy may become a mathematician, but not a man of understanding or a natural scientist. Is it because the objects of mathematics exist by abstraction, while the originating principles of these other subjects come from experience, and because young men have no conviction about the latter but merely use the language, while the quiddity of mathematical objects is plain enough?

Further, error in deliberation is either about the universal or about the particular: we may fail to know either that all water that weighs heavy is poor, or that this particular water weighs heavy.

That wisdom is not knowledge is evident; for it is, as has been said, concerned with the ultimate, since matters of action are of this nature. It is contrasted then with intelligence; for intelligence concerns terms which are not the result of reasoning, while wisdom is concerned with the ultimate particular, which is the object not of knowledge but of perception—not the perception of qualities peculiar to one sense but a perception akin to that by which we perceive that the ultimate item is a triangle—for things stop there too. But this is rather perception than wisdom, though it is another kind of perception.

THERE IS A DIFFERENCE BETWEEN INQUIRY AND DELIBERATION; for deliberation is a particular kind of inquiry. We must grasp the nature of skill in deliberation as well—whether it is a form of knowledge, or belief, or perspicacity, or some other kind of thing. It is not knowledge: men do not inquire about the things they know, but skill in deliberation is a sort of deliberation, and he who deliberates inquires and calculates. Nor is it perspicacity; for this involves no reasoning and is quick, whereas men deliberate for a long time, and

5   say that one should carry out quickly the conclusions of one's deliberation, but deliberate slowly. Again, astuteness is different from skill in deliberation: it is a sort of perspicacity. Nor again is skill in deliberation belief of any sort.

Since the man who deliberates badly errs, while he who deliberates well does so correctly, skill in deliberation is plainly a kind of correctness—but neither of knowledge nor of belief. For there is no such thing as correctness of knowledge (since there is no such thing as error of knowledge), and correctness of belief is truth; and at the same time everything that is an object of belief is already determined. But again skill in deliberation involves reasoning. It remains, then, that it is a matter of thinking; for this is not yet assertion, since, while belief is not inquiry but already a sort of assertion, the man who is deliberating, whether he does so well or ill, is inquiring and calculating.

Skill in deliberation is a certain correctness of deliberation. That is why we must first inquire what deliberation is and what it is about. And, there being more than one kind of correctness, plainly skill in deliberation is not any and every kind; for the incontinent man and the base man, if he is clever,[3] will attain as a result of his calculation what he sets himself to do, so that although he will have deliberated correctly, he will have got for himself a great evil. But to have deliberated well is thought to be a good thing; for the kind of correctness of deliberation that is skill in deliberation is that which tends to attain what is good. But it is possible to attain what is good by a false deduction and to attain what one ought to do but not how one ought, the middle term being false; so that this too is not yet skill in deliberation—this state in virtue of which one attains what one ought but not how one ought. Again it is possible to attain it by long deliberation while another man attains it quickly. Therefore in the former case we have not yet got skill in deliberation, which is correctness with regard to what is beneficial in respect of

---

3 Reading εἰ δεινός (Ross) for ἰδεῖν (which Bywater prints between obeli).

what we ought to do and how and when. Further it is possible to have deliberated well either *tout court* or with reference
to a particular end. Skill in deliberation *tout court*, then, is   30
that which succeeds with reference to what is the end *tout
court*, and the other kind is that which succeeds relatively to a
particular end. If, then, it is characteristic of wise men to
have deliberated well, skill in deliberation will be correctness
about what is advantageous with regard to the end about
which wisdom makes a true assumption.

JUDGEMENT, AND GOOD JUDGEMENT, IN VIRTUE OF WHICH
we speak of people as being judicious and having good judge-   1143a
ment, are neither entirely the same as knowledge or belief
(for at that rate all men would be judicious), nor are they one
of the particular sciences, such as medicine, concerned with
what is healthy, or geometry, concerned with magnitudes.
For judgement is neither about things that are always and   5
are unchangeable, nor about any and every one of the things
that come into being; rather, it is about things about which
one might raise problems and deliberate. That is why it is
about the same objects as wisdom; but judgement and wisdom are not the same. For wisdom issues commands, since
its end is what ought to be done or not to be done; but judgement only assesses. (Judgement is identical with good judge-   10
ment, and judicious people are those who have good judgement.) Now judgement is neither the having nor the
acquiring of wisdom: rather, just as learning is called judging when it is a matter of using knowledge, so too when it is a
matter of using belief to assess[4] what someone else says
about matters with which wisdom is concerned (and assess-   15
ing soundly—'well' and 'soundly' are the same). And the
word 'judgement' as applied to men who are said to have
good judgement comes from the application of the word to
learning; for we often call learning judging.

4 Deleting ἐπί before τὸ κρίνειν (Thurot).

127

WHAT IS CALLED SENSE, IN VIRTUE OF WHICH MEN ARE
20   said to be sympathetic⁵ and to have sense, is the correct assessment of the equitable. An indication of this is the fact
that we say the equitable man is above all others a sympathetic man and identify equity with sympathy in certain matters. And sympathy is sense which correctly assesses what is
equitable; and correct sense is a sense of the true.

25   THESE STATES CONVERGE, AS MIGHT BE EXPECTED, ON
the same point; for when we speak of sense and judgement
and wisdom and intelligence we credit the same people with
possessing sense and intelligence and being wise and judicious. For all these capacities deal with ultimates or particulars; and being judicious, sensible, or sympathetic consists
30   in being able to assess the things with which the wise are
concerned; for the practice of equity is something common
to all good men in their dealings with others.⁶ Now all matters of action are particulars or ultimates; for not only must
the wise man know them, but judgement and sense are also
concerned with matters of action, and these are ultimates.
35   Intelligence is concerned with the ultimates in both directions; for both the primary terms and the ultimates are ob-
1143b   jects of intelligence and not of reason, and in demonstrations one sort of intelligence grasps the unchangeable and
primary terms, while in practical cases another sort grasps
what is ultimate and contingent and the other proposition.
For these are the originating principles of that for the sake
of which, since the universals are reached from the particu-
5   lars; of them therefore we must have perception, and this is
intelligence.

This is why these states are thought to be natural—why,
while no one is thought to have understanding by nature,
people are thought to have by nature sense and judgement
and intelligence. An indication of this is the fact that we

5 'Sympathy' is συγγνώμη and 'sense' is γνώμη.

6 The text of this sentence is uncertain and its sense is obscure.

think such things correspond to our time of life, and that a
particular age brings with it intelligence and sense, thereby
suggesting that nature is the cause.[7] So we ought to attend to   10
the undemonstrated sayings and beliefs of experienced and
older people or of wise people not less than to demonstrations; for because experience has given them an eye they see
correctly.

We have stated, then, what wisdom and understanding
are, and with what each of them is concerned, and we have   15
said that each is the virtue of a different part of the soul.

ONE MIGHT RAISE THE PROBLEM OF WHAT USE THEY ARE.
For understanding will contemplate none of the things that
will make a man happy (for it is not concerned with any com-   20
ing into being), and though wisdom has this merit, for what
purpose do we need it? Wisdom is the state concerned with
things just and noble and good for man, and these are the
things which it is the mark of a good man to do; but we are
none the more able to act for knowing them if the virtues are   25
states, just as we are none the better able to act for knowing
the things that are healthy and wholesome (in the sense not
of producing but of issuing from the state of health); for we
are none the more able to act for having mastered medicine
or gymnastics. But if we are to say that a man is wise for the
sake not of these things but for what he becomes, wisdom
will be of no use to those who are virtuous. But again it is of   30
no use to those who lack virtue; for it will make no difference
whether they have wisdom themselves or obey others who
have it, and it would be enough for us to do what we do in the
case of health: though we want to become healthy, nevertheless we do not learn medicine. Besides this, it would be
thought absurd if wisdom, being inferior to understanding,
were in control of it, as seems to be implied by the fact that

7 In the manuscripts there follows a sentence which Bywater thinks is out
of place: 'That is why intelligence is both an origin and an end; for demonstrations depend on and are about these things.'

the craft which produces anything rules and issues commands about that thing.

35   These, then, are the questions we must discuss: so far we
have only stated the problems.

1144a   First let us say that in themselves these states must be desirable because they are the virtues of the two parts of the
soul, even if neither of them produces anything. Secondly,
they do produce something—but not as medicine produces
health. Rather, as health produces health, so does under-
5   standing produce happiness; for, being a part of virtue entire,
by being possessed and exercised it makes a man happy.[8]
Again, the task of man is performed in accordance with wisdom and moral virtue; for virtue makes the aim correct, and
wisdom the things leading to it. (Of the fourth part of the
10   soul—the nutritive—there is no such virtue; for there is
nothing which it is in its power to do or not to do.)

With regard to our being none the more able because of
our wisdom to do what is noble and just, let us begin a little
further back, starting with the following principle. Just as we
say that some people who do just acts are not thereby just—
for instance, those who do the acts ordained by the laws ei-
15   ther involuntarily or owing to ignorance or for some other
reason and not for the sake of the acts themselves (though
they do what they should and all the things that the virtuous
man ought), so is it, it seems, that in order to be good one
must be in a certain state when one does the several acts—I
mean, for instance, one must do them as a result of choice
and for the sake of the acts themselves. Now while virtue
20   makes the choice correct, the question of what should naturally be done to carry it out belongs not to virtue but to another capacity.

We must devote our attention to these matters and give a
more illuminating statement about them. There is a capacity
which is called cleverness; and this is such as to be able to do
25   the things that tend towards the mark we have set before

8 Bywater prints the last clause between obeli.

ourselves, and to hit it. Now if the mark be noble, the cleverness is praiseworthy, but if the mark be base, it is villainy.
(That is why we call clever both wise men and villains.⁹) Wisdom is not the capacity, but it does not exist without this capacity. And this eye of the soul acquires its state not without
virtue as has been said and is plain. For deductions which   30
deal with matters of action have originating principles—
'Since the end and what is best, is of such and such a nature'
(whatever it may be: let it for the sake of argument be what
we please)—and they are not evident except to the good
man; for depravity perverts us and causes us to be deceived   35
about the principles of action. Hence it is evident that it is
impossible to be wise without being good.

WE MUST THEREFORE CONSIDER VIRTUE ONCE MORE; FOR   1144b
virtue involves a similar relationship: as wisdom is to cleverness—not the same, but like it—so natural virtue is to virtue
strictly speaking. For all men think that each type of character belongs to its possessors in a way by nature; for from the   5
very moment of birth we are just and inclined to temperance
and courageous and so on; but yet we look for something
else as that which is strictly speaking good—we seek the
presence of such qualities in another way. For children and
brutes have the natural dispositions, and without intelligence they are evidently harmful. But we seem to see this   10
much: just as a strong body which moves without sight may
stumble badly because of its lack of sight, so too here—but if
he acquires intelligence that makes a difference in action;
and his state, while still like what it was, will then be virtue
strictly speaking. Therefore, just as in the part which has beliefs there are two species, cleverness and wisdom, so too in   15
the moral part there are two, natural virtue and virtue strictly
speaking, and of these the latter involves wisdom.

This is why some say that all the virtues are forms of wisdom, and why Socrates in one respect was on the right track

9 Adding τούς before πανούργους (Allan).

20   while in another he went astray: in thinking that all the virtues were forms of wisdom he erred, but in saying that they cannot occur without wisdom he was right. An indication of this is the fact that now all men, when they define virtue, after naming the state and its objects add 'in accordance with 25   correct reasoning'—and the correct reasoning is that which is in accordance with wisdom. All men, then, seem somehow to divine that it is this kind of state that is virtue, namely that which is in accordance with wisdom. But we must go a little further. For it is not merely the state in accordance with correct reasoning, but the state that involves correct reasoning, that is virtue; and wisdom is correct reasoning about such matters. Socrates, then, thought the virtues were forms of reasoning (for he thought they were all forms of knowledge), 30   while we think they involve reason.

It is plain, then, from what has been said, that it is not possible to be good strictly speaking without wisdom, nor wise without moral virtue. In this way we may also refute the argument whereby it might be contended that the virtues are separate from each other: the same man, it might be said, is not best endowed by nature for all the virtues, so that he will 35   have already acquired one when he has not yet acquired another. This is possible in respect of the natural virtues, but 1145a   not in respect of those for which a man is called good *tout court*; for if one is present, namely wisdom, then all will be present. And it is plain that, even if it were of no practical use, we should need it because it is the virtue of a part, and that choice will not be correct without wisdom any more 5   than without virtue; for the one fixes the end and the other makes us do the things that lead to the end.

But it does not control understanding and the superior part of us, any more than medicine controls health; for it does not use it but sees to its coming into being: it issues or- 10   ders, then, for its sake, but not to it. Further, it would be like saying that politics rules the gods because it issues orders about all the affairs of the State.

7

CONTINENCE AND INCONTINENCE

LET US NOW MAKE A FRESH START AND POINT OUT THAT there are three kinds of character to be avoided—vice, incontinence, brutishness. The contraries of two of these are plain—one we call virtue, the other continence. To brutishness it would be most fitting to oppose superhuman virtue, something heroic and divine, as Homer has represented Priam saying of Hector that he was very good,

> For he seemed not, he,
> The child of a mortal man, but rather of a god.[1]

Therefore if, as they say, men become gods by excelling in virtue, of this kind must plainly be the state opposed to the brutish state; for as a brute has no vice or virtue, so neither has a god: his state is more honourable than virtue, and that of a brute is a different kind of state from vice. Since it is rarely that a godlike man is found—to use the epithet of the Spartans, who when they admire anyone highly call him a godlike man—so too the brutish type is rarely found among men. It is found chiefly among foreigners, and it is sometimes produced by disease or deformity. We also call by this evil name those who surpass men in vice.

Of this kind of disposition we must later make some mention, while we have discussed vice before: we must now discuss incontinence and softness and effeminacy, and also continence and endurance; for we must not assume either that the one is identical with virtue and the other with

---

1 *Iliad* XXIV 258.

depravity, or that they are a different genus. We must, as in all other cases, set out people's perceptions and, after first discussing the problems, go on to prove, if possible, the truth of all the reputable opinions about these phenomena

5 or, failing this, of the greatest number and the most authoritative; for if we both resolve the vexatious points and leave the reputable opinions undisturbed, we shall have proved the case sufficiently.

Both continence and endurance are thought to be included among things virtuous and praiseworthy, and both

10 incontinence and softness among things base and blameworthy; and the same man is thought to be continent and ready to abide by his calculations, or incontinent and ready to abandon them. The incontinent man, knowing that what he does is base, does it as a result of his emotions, while the continent man, knowing that his appetites are base, does not follow them because of his reason. The temperate man,

15 they say, is continent and disposed to endurance, while the continent man some maintain to be always temperate and others not; and some call the self-indulgent man incontinent and the incontinent man self-indulgent indiscriminately, while others distinguish them. The wise man, they sometimes say, cannot be incontinent, while sometimes they say that some who are wise and clever are incontinent. Again, men are said to be incontinent with respect to rage,

20 honour, and profit.

These, then, are the things that are said.

SOMEONE MIGHT RAISE THE PROBLEM OF WHAT KIND OF correct assumption is present in the man who behaves incontinently. That he should behave so when he has knowledge, some say is impossible; for it would be strange—so Socrates thought—if when knowledge was in a man some-

25 thing else could master it and drag it about like a slave. For Socrates was entirely opposed to the view in question, holding that there is no such thing as incontinence: no one, he said, acts against what is best, if he assumes it to be so, but by

reason of ignorance. Now this view contradicts people's clearest perceptions, and we must inquire about the phenomenon: if he acts by reason of ignorance, what is the manner of his ignorance? For that the man who behaves incontinently does not, before he is under the influence of the emotion, think he ought to act so, is evident. There are some who concede some parts but not others: that nothing is stronger than knowledge they admit, but they do not admit that no one acts against what he believes to be the better course, and therefore they say that the incontinent man has not knowledge when he is mastered by his pleasures, but rather belief. But if it is belief and not knowledge, and if it is not a strong assumption that resists but a weak one, as in men who are in two minds, we are sympathetic towards failure to stand by such assumptions in the face of strong appetites; but we are not sympathetic towards depravity, nor towards any of the other blameworthy states. Is it then wisdom whose resistance is mastered? That is the strongest of all states. But this is absurd: the same man will be at once wise and incontinent, but no one would say that it is the part of a wise man to do voluntarily the basest of things. Besides, it has been shown before that the wise man is a man of action (someone concerned with ultimates) and that he possesses the other virtues.

Further, if to be continent a man must have strong and base appetites, the temperate man will not be continent nor the continent man temperate; for a temperate man will have neither excessive nor base appetites. But they must be; for if the appetites are good, the state that restrains us from following them is base, so that not all continence will be virtuous; while if they are weak and not base, there is nothing dignified about resisting them, and if they are weak and base, there is nothing great.

Further, if continence makes a man ready to stand by just any belief, it is base—for instance, if it makes him stand even by a false belief; and if incontinence makes a man apt to abandon just any belief, there will be a virtuous sort of

20 incontinence, of which Sophocles' Neoptolemus in the *Philoctetes* will be an instance; for he is praiseworthy for not standing by what Odysseus persuaded him to do, because he is pained at telling a lie.

Further, the sophistic argument presents a problem; for, because they want to expose paradoxical results to show how clever they are when they succeed, the resulting deduction presents a problem (for thinking is tied up when it does
25 not want to stay with a conclusion it does not approve of, but cannot move forward because it cannot refute the argument). There is an argument from which it follows that folly coupled with incontinence is virtue; for by incontinence he does the contrary of what he assumes, and he assumes what
30 is good to be bad and something that he should not do, so that he will do what is good and not what is bad.

Further, he who by conviction does and pursues and chooses what is pleasant would be thought to be better than one who does so as a result not of calculation but of incontinence; for he is easier to cure since he may be convinced to change his mind. But to the incontinent man may be applied the proverb 'When water chokes, what is one to wash it down
1146b with?' If he had been convinced to do what he did, he would have desisted when he was convinced to change his mind; but as it is, he acts in spite of his being convinced of something quite different.

Further, if incontinence and continence are concerned with just any kind of object, who is it that is incontinent *tout court*? No one has all the forms of incontinence, but we say some people are incontinent *tout court*.

5 Of some such kind are the problems that arise. Some of the points must be refuted and the others left; for the resolution of a problem is a discovery.

WE MUST CONSIDER FIRST, THEN, WHETHER INCONTI-nent people act knowingly or not, and in what way knowingly; then with what sorts of objects the incontinent and the
10 continent man may be said to be concerned (I mean whether

with just any pleasure and pain or with certain determinate kinds), and whether the continent man and the man of endurance are the same or different; and similarly with regard to the other matters related to these considerations.

The origin of the investigation is the question whether the continent man and the incontinent are differentiated by their objects or by their attitude—I mean, whether the incontinent man is incontinent simply by being concerned with such and such objects, or, instead, by his attitude, or, instead of that, by both these things. Next, whether incontinence and continence are concerned with just any object or not. The man who is incontinent *tout court* is not concerned with just any object but with those with which the self-indulgent man is concerned, nor is he characterized simply by being related to these (for then his state would be the same as self-indulgence), but by being related to them in a certain way. For the one is led on in accordance with his own choice, thinking that he ought always to pursue the present pleasure; while the other does not think so, but pursues it.

As for the suggestion that it is true belief and not knowledge against which we act incontinently, that makes no difference to the argument; for some people when in a state of belief are not in two minds but think they know precisely. If, then, it is owing to their weak conviction those who have belief are more likely to act against their assumptions than those who know, there will be no difference between knowledge and belief; for some men are no less convinced of what they believe than others of what they know; as the case of Heraclitus makes plain. But since we speak in two ways of knowing something (for both the man who has knowledge but is not using it and he who is using it are said to know), it will make a difference whether, when a man does what he should not, he has the knowledge and is not considering it, or he is considering it; for the latter seems strange, but not if he is not considering it.

Further, since there are two kinds of proposition, there is nothing to prevent a man's having both and acting against his knowledge, provided that he is using the universal and not the particular; for it is particulars that are matters of action. And there are two kinds of universal: one with regard to the agent, the other to the object—for instance, that dry food is good for every man, and that I am a man, or that such and such food is dry. But whether this food is such and such, of this the incontinent man either has not or is not exercising the knowledge. There will, then, be an enormous difference between these manners of knowing, so that to know in one way would not seem at all absurd, while to know in the other way would be remarkable.

Further, men can have knowledge in another way than those just mentioned; for within the case of having knowledge but not using it we see a difference of state, so that someone has knowledge in a manner and yet does not have it—for instance, a man asleep or mad or drunk. But this is just the condition of men under the influence of their emotions; for outbursts of rage and sexual appetites and some other such things quite plainly alter our bodies, and in some men even produce fits of madness. It is plain, then, that incontinent people must be said to be in a similar condition to these. The fact that men use language expressive of the knowledge is no indication; for men under the influence of these emotions utter demonstrations and verses of Empedocles, and those who have just learned something can string together words but do not yet know—for it has to become part of themselves, and that takes time. So we must assume that men in an incontinent state speak as actors do.

Again, we may also view the cause as follows with reference to the facts of nature. The one belief is universal, the other is concerned with particulars where sense-perception is authoritative. When a single belief is produced from them, necessarily the soul thereupon affirms the conclusion, and if it is a practical matter immediately acts—for instance, if everything sweet ought to be tasted, and this (a particular sweetmeat) is sweet, a man who can act and is not restrained necessarily at the same time acts accordingly. When, then, a universal belief is present in us restraining us from tasting, and there is also the belief that everything sweet is pleasant and that this is sweet (and this is exercised), and appetite happens to be present in us, then the one tells us to avoid the object, but appetite leads us towards it (for each part of the soul can set us in motion). So it turns out that a man behaves incontinently under the influence (in a manner) of reason and belief—a belief contrary not in itself but coincidentally to correct reasoning (for the appetite is contrary, not the belief). Hence brutes are not incontinent because they make no universal assumptions but have imagination and memory of particulars.

1147b

5

The explanation of how the ignorance is dissolved and the incontinent man regains his knowledge is the same as in the case of the man drunk or asleep and is not peculiar to this condition: we must go to the students of natural science for it.

Since the last proposition is a belief about a perceptible object and also controls our actions, this a man either has not when he is in an emotional state, or has it in the way in which having knowledge does not mean knowing but only talking, as a drunken man may utter the verses of Empedocles. And because the last term does not seem to be universal nor equally an object of knowledge with the universal term, the position that Socrates looked to establish actually seems to result; for it is not in the presence of what is thought to be knowledge strictly speaking that the phenomenon occurs nor is it this that is dragged about as a result of the emotion—rather, perceptual knowledge is.

10

15

This must suffice as our answer to the question of whether or not men can act incontinently when they have knowledge, and in what way they have knowledge.

WE MUST NEXT DISCUSS WHETHER THERE IS ANYONE WHO is incontinent *tout court*, or all men who are incontinent are so in a particular respect; and if there is incontinence *tout court*, what its objects are.

20

That both continent persons and persons of endurance, and incontinent and soft persons, are concerned with pleasures and pains, is evident. Of the things that produce pleasure some are necessary while others are desirable in themselves but admit of excess, the bodily causes of pleasure being necessary (by such I mean those concerned with food and the need for sex, and the bodily matters with which we determined self-indulgence and temperance to be concerned)—while others are not necessary but desirable in themselves (for instance victory, honour, riches, and good and pleasant things of this sort). Those who go to excess with reference to the latter, against their own correct reasoning, we do not call incontinent *tout court*—we add the qualification 'in respect of wealth' or 'profit' or 'honour' or 'rage'— not incontinent *tout court*, on the ground that they are different from incontinent people and are called incontinent by reason of a resemblance. (Compare the case of Man, who won a contest at the Olympic games: in his case the general formula of man differed little from the one proper, but yet it was different.) An indication of this is the fact that incontinence, whether *tout court* or in a particular respect, is blamed not only as an error but also as a kind of vice, while none of the others is so blamed.

Of the people who are incontinent with respect to bodily enjoyments, with which we say the temperate and the self-indulgent man are concerned, he who pursues the excesses of things pleasant—and shuns those of things painful: of hunger and thirst and heat and cold and all the objects of touch and taste—not by choice but against his choice and his thinking, is called incontinent, not with the qualification 'in respect of this or that' (for example, 'of anger') but incontinent *tout court*. An indication of this is the fact that men are called soft with regard to these pleasures but not with regard to any of the others. And we group together the incontinent and the self-indulgent, the continent and the temperate man (but not any of these other types) because they are concerned somehow with the same pleasures and pains; but although they are concerned with the same objects, they are not similarly related to them, but some of them choose them while the others do not choose them.

This is why we should describe as self-indulgent rather the man who without appetite or with but a slight appetite pursues the excesses and avoids moderate pains, than the man who does so because of his strong appetites; for what would the former do, if he had in addition a vigorous appetite, and a strong pain at the lack of the necessary objects?

Of appetites and pleasures some belong to the class of things noble and virtuous—for some pleasant things are by nature desirable—while others are contrary to these, and others are intermediate, to adopt our previous distinction (for instance, wealth, profit, victory, honour). With reference to all objects whether of this or of the intermediate kind men are not blamed for being affected by them, for craving them, or for loving them, but for doing so in a certain way and for going to excess. (This is why all those who against reason either are mastered by or pursue one of the objects which are naturally noble and good, for instance those who busy themselves more than they ought about honour or about children and parents—for these are good things, and those who busy themselves about them are praised; but yet there is an excess even in them, if one were to fight against the gods like Niobe, or to be like Satyrus nicknamed 'the filial', who was thought to be extremely silly.) There is no depravity with regard to these objects, for the reason given—because each of them is by nature a thing desirable for its own sake. But excesses in respect of them are base and to be avoided. Similarly there is no incontinence with regard to them; for incontinence is not only to be avoided but is also blameworthy.

Owing to a similarity in the phenomenon people talk of incontinence, adding in each case what it is in respect of, as we may describe as a bad doctor or a bad actor one whom we should not call bad *tout court*. Just as in that case we do not apply the term without qualification because none of these

10 conditions is a vice but only analogous to one, so it is plain
that here too that alone must be assumed to be incontinence
and continence which is concerned with the same objects as
temperance and self-indulgence. We apply the term to rage
by virtue of a resemblance; and this is why we say with a qualification 'incontinent in respect of rage' just as we say 'of
honour', or 'of profit'.

15 SOME THINGS ARE PLEASANT BY NATURE, AND OF THESE
some are so in the abstract, and others are so for particular
classes either of animals or of men; while others are not
pleasant by nature, but some of them become pleasant by
reason of deformities, and others by reason of habits, and
others by reason of a depraved nature. It is possible with regard to each of the latter kinds to discern corresponding
states—I mean the brutish states, as in the case of the
20 woman who, they say, rips open pregnant women and de-
vours the infants, or of the things in which some of the sav-
ages about the Black Sea are said to delight (some in raw
meat, some in in human flesh, some lending their children
to one another to feast upon), or of the story of Phalaris.
25 These states are brutish. Others arise as a result of disease
(or, in some cases, of madness, as with the man who sacrificed and ate his mother, or with the slave who ate the liver of
his fellow), and others are diseased states resulting from
custom,[2] for instance the habit of pulling out your hair or of
biting your the nails, or again coals or earth, and in addition
to these sex with males; for these arise in some by nature and
in others from habit—as in those who have practised physi-
30 cal training[3] from childhood.

Those in whom nature is the cause no one would call incontinent, any more than one would apply the epithet to
women because they do not mount but are mounted; nor
would one apply it to those who are in a diseased condition

2 Omitting ἤ (with the Laurentian manuscript).
3 Reading γυμναζομένοις where Bywater prefers the variant ὑβριζομένοις
('who have been violated from childhood').

142

as a result of habit. To have these various types of habit is beyond the limits of vice, just as brutishness is; for a man who
has them, to master or be mastered by them is not incontinence *tout court* but that which is so by a similarity, just as
the man who is in this condition in respect of fits of rage is
to be called incontinent in respect of that feeling but not
incontinent.

For every excessive state, whether of folly, of cowardice,
of self-indulgence, or of bad temper, is either brutish or diseased: the man who is by nature apt to fear everything, even
the squeak of a mouse, is cowardly with a brutish cowardice,
while the man who feared a weasel did so in consequence of
disease; and of foolish people those who by nature do not
calculate and live by their senses alone are brutish, like some
races of the distant foreigners, while those who are so as a result of disease (for instance of epilepsy) or of madness are
diseased. Of these characteristics it is possible to have some
only at times and not to be mastered by them—for instance,
if Phalaris repressed his craving to eat a child, or deviant sexual pleasure; but it is also possible to be mastered, not merely
to have the feelings. Thus just as depravity which is on the
human level is called depravity *tout court* whereas other kinds
are so called with the qualification 'brutish' or 'diseased' but
not *tout court*, in the same way it is plain that some incontinence is brutish and some diseased, while only that which
corresponds to human self-indulgence is incontinence *tout
court*.

That incontinence and continence are concerned only
with the same objects as self-indulgence and temperance,
and that what is concerned with other objects is another species of incontinence and called incontinence not *tout court*
but by extension, is plain.

LET US CONSIDER WHETHER INCONTINENCE IN RESPECT
of rage is less ignoble than that in respect of the appetites.
Rage seems to listen to reason to some extent but to mishear
it, as do hasty servants who run out before they have heard
the whole of what one says, and then mistake the command,

or as dogs bark if there is but a knock at the door, before
30 looking to see if it is a friend: so rage by reason of the warmth
and hastiness of its nature, though it hears, does not hear an
order, and springs to take revenge. For reason or imagination makes it plain that we have been insulted or treated with
disdain, and rage, deducing as it were that anything like this
must be fought against, is angry at once; whereas appetite, if
reason or perception merely says that something is pleasant,
1149b springs to the enjoyment of it. Therefore rage obeys reason
in a manner, but appetite does not. It is therefore more ignoble; for the man who is incontinent in respect of rage is in
a sense defeated by reason, while the other is defeated by appetite and not by reason.

Further, we sympathize with people more easily for following natural appetites, since we sympathize with them
5 more easily for following such appetites as are common to
all men, and in so far as they are common. Now rage and bad
temper are more natural than the appetites for excess and
for unnecessary objects. Take for instance the man who defended himself on the charge of striking his father by saying
10 'Yes, but *he* struck *his* father, and *he* struck *his*, and' (pointing
to his child) 'this boy will strike *me* when he is a man—it runs
in the family'; or the man who when he was being dragged
along by his son bade him stop at the doorway, since he himself had dragged his father only as far as that.

Further, those who are more given to plotting are more
unjust. Now a man who rages is not given to plotting, nor is
15 rage itself—it is open. But appetite is—as they call Aphro-
dite 'guile-weaving daughter of Cyprus', and as Homer says
of her embroidered girdle:

Enchantment, that stole the wits even of the most sane.[4]

So if this form of incontinence is more unjust and ignoble
than that in respect of rage, it is both incontinence *tout court*
and in a manner vice.

4 *Iliad* XIV 214.

Further, no one commits outrage with a feeling of pain: everyone who acts in anger acts with pain, while the man who commits outrage acts with pleasure. If, then, those acts at which it is most just to be angry are more unjust, the incontinence which is due to appetite is the more unjust; for there is no outrage involved in rage.

Plainly, then, the incontinence concerned with appetite is more ignoble than that concerned with rage, and continence and incontinence are concerned with bodily appetites and pleasures; but we must grasp the differences among the latter themselves. For, as has been said at the beginning, some are human and natural both in kind and in magnitude, others are brutish, and others are due to deformities and diseases. Only with the first of these are temperance and self-indulgence concerned: this is why we call the brutes neither temperate nor self-indulgent except by extension, and only if some one kind[5] of animals exceeds another as a whole in outrage, destructiveness, and omnivorous greed; for they have no choice or calculation—rather, they are departures from what is natural as, among men, madmen are. Brutishness is less than vice, though more frightening; for it is not that the better part has been destroyed, as in man—they have no better part. Thus it is like comparing an inanimate thing with an animate in respect of badness; for the baseness of that which has no originating principle is always less destructive, and intelligence is a principle. Thus it is like comparing injustice with an unjust man. Each is in a way worse; for a bad man will do ten thousand times as many bad things as a brute.

WITH REGARD TO THE PLEASURES AND PAINS AND APPETITES and aversions arising through touch and taste, with which (as we have earlier determined) both self-indulgence and temperance are concerned, it is possible to be in such a state as to be defeated even by those of them which most

5 Reading τι (suggested by Bywater) for τινι.

people master, or to master even those by which most people are defeated; and among these possibilities, those relating to pleasures are incontinence and continence, those relating to
15 pains softness and endurance. The state of most people is intermediate, even if they lean more towards the worse states.

Since some pleasures are necessary while others are not, and are necessary up to a point while the excesses of them are not, nor the deficiencies, and similarly with appetites and pains, the man who pursues the excesses of things pleas-
20 ant, or pursues pleasant things to excess, and[6] does so by choice, for their own sake and not at all for the sake of any result distinct from them, is self-indulgent; for such a man is of necessity without regrets, and therefore incurable, since a man without regrets cannot be cured. The man who is deficient is the opposite. The man who is in the middle is temperate. Similarly, there is the man who avoids bodily pains
25 not because he is defeated by them but by choice. Of those who do not choose, one kind of man is led to them by pleasure, another because he avoids the pain arising from the appetite, so that these types differ from one another. Anyone would think worse of a man if with no appetite or with weak appetite he were to do something ignoble, than if he did it with an intense appetite, and worse of him if he struck a blow not in anger than if he did so in anger—for what would he have done if he had been under the influence of his emo-
30 tions? This is why the self-indulgent man is worse than the incontinent. Of the states named, then, one is rather a kind of softness, the other self-indulgence.

While to the incontinent man is opposed the continent, to the soft is opposed the man of endurance; for endurance consists in resisting, while continence consists in mastering, and resisting and mastering are different, just as not being defeated is different from winning. This is why continence
1150b is more desirable than endurance. Now the man who is

6 Reading καθ᾽ ὑπερβολὴν καί (with the Marcianus), where Bywater prints: †ἢ καθ᾽ ὑπερβολὰς† ἥ.

deficient in respect of resistance to the things which most men both can and do resist is soft and luxurious (for luxuriousness is a kind of softness): such a man trails his cloak to avoid the trouble of lifting it, and plays the invalid without thinking himself wretched, though that is what he is like.

The case is similar with regard to continence and incontinence. For if a man is defeated by strong and excessive pleasures or pains, there is nothing surprising in that—rather, we are ready to sympathize with him if he has resisted, as Theodectes' Philoctetes does when bitten by the snake, or Carcinus' Cercyon in the *Alope*, and as people who try to repress their laughter burst out in a guffaw, as happened to Xenophantus. But it is surprising if a man is defeated by and cannot resist pleasures or pains which most men can hold out against, when this is not due to heredity or disease, like the softness that is hereditary with the kings of the Scythians, or that which distinguishes the female sex from the male.

The lover of amusement, too, is thought to be self-indulgent, but is soft. For amusement is a relaxation, since it is a rest; and the lover of amusement is one of the people who go to excess in this.

Of incontinence one kind is impetuosity, another weakness. For some men after deliberating fail, owing to their emotions, to stand by the conclusions of their deliberation, others because they have not deliberated are led by their emotions; for—just as people who have once been tickled[7] are not tickled again—some people perceive beforehand and see ahead and rouse themselves and their calculative faculty in advance, and so are not defeated by their emotions, whether they are pleasant or painful. It is quick-tempered and atrabilious people that suffer especially from the impetuous form of incontinence: the former because of their quickness and the latter because of the intensity of their

---

7 Reading προγαργαλισθέντες (the better attested text) rather than προγαργαλίσαντες ('having once tickled').

feelings do not wait on reason because they are apt to follow their imagination.

THE SELF-INDULGENT MAN, AS WAS SAID, HAS NO RE-
30 grets; for he stands by his choice. But any incontinent man is
subject to regrets. This is why the position is not as it was
supposed in the formulation of the problem: rather, the self-
indulgent man is incurable and the incontinent man curable. For depravity is like a disease such as dropsy or con-
sumption, while incontinence is like epilepsy: the former is a
permanent, the latter an intermittent viciousness. And generally incontinence and vice are different in kind; vice is un-
conscious of itself, incontinence is not. Of incontinent men
1151a themselves, those who are carried away are better than those
who go through the reasoning but do not stand by it, since
they are defeated by a weaker emotion, and do not like the
others act without previous deliberation. The incontinent
man is like the people who get drunk quickly and on little
wine and on less than most people do.
5   Evidently, then, incontinence is not vice (though perhaps
it is so in a way); for incontinence goes against choice while
vice is in accordance with choice. Not but what they are similar in respect of the actions they lead to, as in the saying of
Demodocus about the Milesians: 'The Milesians are not
without sense, but they do the things that senseless people
do'. And incontinent people are not unjust but they will do
unjust acts.
       Since the incontinent man is apt to pursue, not from con-
10 viction, bodily pleasures that are excessive and against correct reasoning, while the self-indulgent man is convinced because he is the sort of man to pursue them, it is the former
that is easily convinced to change, while the latter is not. For
15 virtue and vice respectively preserve and destroy the originating principle, and in actions the purpose is the principle,
as the hypotheses are in mathematics: neither in that case is
it reason that teaches the principles, nor is it so here—virtue
either natural or produced by habituation is what teaches

correct belief about principles. Such a man as this, then, is temperate, and his contrary is self-indulgent.

There is a sort of man who is carried away by emotion against correct reasoning—a man whom emotion masters so that he does not act according to correct reasoning, but does not master to the extent of convincing him that one ought to pursue such pleasures without reserve. This is the incontinent man, who is better than the self-indulgent man, and not base *tout court*; for the best thing in him, the originating principle, is preserved. And contrary to him is another kind of man, he who stands fast and is not carried away, at least not by his emotions. It is evident from these considerations that the latter is a virtuous state and the former a base one.

IS THE MAN CONTINENT WHO STANDS BY JUST ANY REASONing and any choice or by correct choice, and is he incontinent who fails to stand by just any choice and reasoning or by reasoning that is not false and choice that is correct? This is a problem we posed earlier. Is it perhaps coincidentally any choice but *per se* true reasoning and correct choice by which the one stands and the other does not? If anyone chooses or pursues one thing for the sake of another, *per se* he pursues and chooses the latter but coincidentally the former. But when we speak in the abstract we mean what is *per se*. Therefore in a manner the one stands by and the other abandons any belief at all; but abstractly speaking, true belief.

There are some who are apt to stand by their beliefs and who are called strong-minded—those who are hard to convince and are not easily convinced to change. These have in them something like the continent man, just as the prodigal is in a way like the liberal man and the over-confident man like the confident man; but they are different in many respects. For it is emotion and appetite that do not change the continent man (since on occasion he will be easy to persuade), whereas it is reason that fails to change the others (for they hold on to their appetites) and many of them are led

by their pleasures. Now the people who are strong-minded
are the opinionated, the ignorant, and the boorish—the
opinionated being influenced by pleasure and pain; for they
15 delight in the victory they gain if they are not persuaded to
change, and are pained if their decisions lack authority, like
decrees. So that they are more like the incontinent than the
continent man.

There are some who fail to stand by their beliefs not as a
result of incontinence—for instance, Neoptolemus in
Sophocles' *Philoctetes*: true, it was for the sake of pleasure
that he did not stand fast—but a noble pleasure; for telling
20 the truth was noble to him, but he had been persuaded by
Odysseus to lie. For not everyone who does something for
the sake of pleasure is either self-indulgent or base or incontinent, but he who does it for an ignoble pleasure.

Since there is also a sort of man who takes less delight
than he should in bodily things and does not stand by rea-
25 son, he who is in the middle between him and the incontinent man is the continent man; for the incontinent man fails
to stand by reason because he delights too much, and this
man because he delights too little; while the continent man
stands fast and does not change on either account. If conti-
30 nence is something virtuous, both the contrary states must
be base, as they evidently are; but because the one is evident
in few people and seldom, then just as temperance is thought
to be contrary only to self-indulgence, so is continence to
incontinence.

Many things are called what they are called in virtue of a
resemblance, and the continence of the temperate man has
come about in virtue of a resemblance; for both the continent man and the temperate man are such as to do nothing
against reason for the sake of the bodily pleasures. But the
1152a former has and the latter has not base appetites, and the latter is such as not to feel pleasure against reason, while the
former is such as to feel pleasure but not to be led by it.
And the incontinent and the self-indulgent man are also
like one another: they are different, but both pursue bodily

pleasures—the latter, however, thinking that he ought to do   5
so, while the former does not think so.

NOR CAN THE SAME MAN BE WISE AND INCONTINENT AT
the same time; for it has been shown that a man is at the
same time wise and virtuous in respect of character. Further,
a man is wise not by knowing only but by also by being disposed to act; but the incontinent man is not disposed to act.
There is, however, nothing to prevent a clever man from   10
being incontinent (and this is why it is sometimes thought
that some people are wise but incontinent) because cleverness and wisdom differ in the way we have described in our
first discussions: they are near together in respect of their
reasoning, but differ in respect of their choice. The incontinent man is not like the man who knows and is considering
something, but like the man who is asleep or drunk. And he   15
acts voluntarily (for in a way he acts with knowledge both of
what he does and to what end), but he is not vicious since his
choice is upright—so that he is half-vicious. And he is not
unjust; for he does not plot: one type of incontinent man
does not stand by the conclusions of his deliberation, while
the atrabilious man does not deliberate at all. And thus the   20
incontinent man is like a city which passes all the decrees it
should and has virtuous laws but makes no use of them, as in
Anaxandrides' mocking remark,

The city willed it, that cares nought for laws.

But the vicious man is like a city that uses its laws but has vicious laws to use.

Incontinence and continence are concerned with that   25
which is in excess of the state characteristic of most men; for
the continent man stands fast more and the incontinent
man less than most men can.

Of the forms of incontinence, that of atrabilious people is
more curable than that of those who deliberate but do not
abide by their decisions, and those who are incontinent
through habituation are more curable than those in whom

30 incontinence is natural; for it is easier to change one's habit than one's nature. Even habit is hard to change just because it is like nature, as Evenus says:

> I say that habit's but long practice, friend,
> And this becomes men's nature in the end.

We have now stated what continence, incontinence, endur-
35 ance, and softness are, and how these states are related to each other.

8

PLEASURE

TO CONSIDER PLEASURE AND PAIN BELONGS TO THE PROV-
ince of the political philosopher; for he is the master-
craftsman of the end with a view to which we call one thing
bad and another good in the abstract. Further, it is one of
our necessary tasks to consider them; for we laid down that
moral virtue and vice are concerned with pains and plea-   5
sures, and most people say that happiness involves pleasure—this is why the blessed man is called by a name derived
from delight.[1]

Some think that no pleasure is a good, either in itself or
coincidentally, since the good and pleasure are not the same.
Others think that some pleasures are good but that most are   10
base. Again there is a third view, that even if all pleasures are
good, yet the chief good cannot be pleasure.

They hold that pleasure is not a good at all because every
pleasure is a perceptible process to a natural state, and no
process is of the same kind as its end—for instance, no process of building of the same kind as a house. Again, a tem-   15
perate man avoids pleasures. Again, a wise man pursues
what is free from pain, not what is pleasant. Again, pleasures
are a hindrance to thought, and the more so the more one
delights in them, for instance in sexual pleasure—for no one
could think of anything while absorbed in this. Again, there
is no craft of pleasure; but every good is the product of some
craft. Again, children and brutes pursue pleasures.   20

They say that not all pleasures are virtuous because there
are pleasures that are ignoble and objects of reproach, and

---

1 μακάριος ('blessed') from χαίρειν ('delight in').

because there are harmful pleasures (for some pleasant things are diseased).

They say that pleasure is not the chief good because pleasure is not an end but a process.

These are pretty much the things that are said.

25 That it does not follow from these grounds that pleasure is not a good, or even the chief good, is plain from the following considerations. First, since that which is good may be so in two ways (good in the abstract and good for a particular person), natures and states, and therefore also movements and processes, will be correspondingly divisible: of those which are thought to be base some will be base in the ab-

30 stract but not base for a particular person but desirable for him, and some will not be desirable even for a particular person but only at a particular time and for a short period, and not in the abstract; while others are not even pleasures but seem to be so, namely all those which involve pain and whose end is therapeutic—for instance, those of the sick.

Further, one kind of good being an activity and another being a state, the processes that restore us to our natural

35 state are coincidentally pleasant (the activity at work in the appetites concerns the remaining part of our state and na-

1153a ture); for there are pleasures that involve no pain or appetite (for instance, those of contemplation), nature in such a case not lacking anything. An indication of this is the fact that men do not delight in the same things[2] when their nature is being replenished as they do when it is in its restored state: in its restored state, they take delight in the things that are pleasant in the abstract, and when it is being replenished they enjoy the contraries of these as well—for then they

5 enjoy even sharp and bitter things, none of which is pleasant either by nature or in the abstract. Nor, then, are the pleasures; for as pleasant things differ from one another, so do the pleasures arising from them.

2 Omitting ἡδεῖ ('the same pleasant things').

154

Again, it is not necessary that there should be something else better than pleasure, as some say the end is better than the process; for pleasures are not processes nor do they all involve process: rather, they are activities and ends, and they attend not acquisition but use. Not all pleasures have an end different from themselves, but only the pleasures of persons who are being led to the completing of their nature. This is why it is not right to say that pleasure is a perceptible process: it should rather be called an exercise of the natural state, and instead of 'perceptible' 'unimpeded'. It is thought by some to be a process because they think it is good strictly speaking; for they think that an activity is a process—which it is not.

To say that pleasures are base because some pleasant things are diseased is like saying that healthy things are base because some healthy things are bad for business: both are base in the respect mentioned, but they are not for that reason base—indeed, contemplation itself sometimes harms health.

Neither wisdom nor any state of character is impeded by the pleasure arising from it: it is alien pleasures that impede; for the pleasures arising from contemplation and learning will make us contemplate and learn all the more.

The fact that no pleasure is the product of a craft arises reasonably enough: there is no craft of any other activity but of the capacities. (Though for that matter, the crafts of the perfumer and the patissier are thought to be crafts of pleasure.)

The arguments that the temperate man avoids pleasure and that the wise man pursues the painless life, and that children and brutes pursue pleasure, are all refuted by the same consideration. We have said how pleasures are good in the abstract and how they are not all good: both brutes and children pursue pleasures of the latter kind (and the wise man avoids their pains)—those which imply appetite and pain, and the bodily pleasures (which are of this nature) and the excesses of them, in respect of which the self-indulgent man is self-indulgent. This is why the temperate man avoids these pleasures; for he has pleasures of his own.

1153b   Further, it is agreed that pain is bad and to be avoided; for some pain is bad *tout court*, and other pain is bad because it is in some respect an impediment. Now the contrary of that which is to be avoided, *qua* something to be avoided and bad, is good. Pleasure, then, is necessarily a good. For the answer
5   of Speusippus, that it is just as the greater is contrary both to the less and to the equal, is not successful—for he would not say that pleasure is essentially something bad.

If certain pleasures are base, that does not prevent the chief good from being some pleasure—just as some knowledge might be, though certain kinds of knowledge are base. Perhaps it is even necessary, if each state has unimpeded ex-
10   ercises, that whether the exercise (if unimpeded) of all our states or of some one of them is happiness, this should be the most desirable—and this is a pleasure. Thus the chief good is some pleasure, though most pleasures are perhaps base in the abstract.

For this reason all men think that the happy life is pleas-
15   ant and weave pleasure into happiness—and reasonably too; for no activity is complete when it is impeded, and happiness is a complete thing: this is why the happy man needs the goods of the body and external goods and fortune—in order that he may not be impeded in these ways. Those who say that the victim on the rack or the man who falls into great
20   misfortunes is happy if he is good, are, whether voluntarily or involuntarily, talking nonsense. Because we need fortune, some people think good fortune the same thing as happiness; but it is not, for even good fortune itself when in excess is an impediment, and perhaps then is no longer justly called
25   good fortune; for its limit is fixed by reference to happiness.

The fact that all things, both brutes and men, pursue pleasure is an indication of its being somehow the chief good:

No voice is wholly lost that many peoples . . . [3]

3 Hesiod, *Works and Days* 763.

But since no one nature or state either is or is thought the best, all do not pursue the same pleasure—yet all pursue 30 pleasure. But perhaps they pursue not the pleasure they think they pursue nor that which they would say they pursue, but the same pleasure? For all things have by nature something divine in them. But the bodily pleasures have appropriated the name both because we most often steer our course for them and because all men share in them: thus because they alone are familiar, men think there are no others. 1154a

It is evident also that if pleasure and its exercise is not a good, it will not be the case that the happy man lives a pleasant life; for to what end should he need pleasure, if it is not a good? He may even live a painful life; for pain is neither bad 5 nor good if pleasure is not: why then should he avoid it? Nor will the life of the virtuous man be pleasanter, if his activities are not more pleasant.

WITH REGARD TO THE BODILY PLEASURES, THOSE WHO SAY that some pleasures are very desirable, namely the noble pleasures, but that the bodily pleasures and those with which 10 the self-indulgent man is concerned are not, must consider why[4] in that case the contrary pains are depraved. For the contrary of bad is good. Are the necessary pleasures good because that which is not bad is good? Or are they good up to a point? For in the case of states and processes where there is no excess of good, there is none of pleasure either, and where there is, there is of pleasure too. But there is an excess 15 of bodily goods, and the base man is base by virtue of pursuing the excess, not by virtue of pursuing the necessary pleasures (for all men in one way or another delight in fine food and wines and sexual intercourse—but not as they ought). Contrariwise with pain: he does not avoid the excess—he avoids it altogether; for pain is not the contrary to excess of 20 pleasure, except to the man who pursues this excess.

Since we should not only state the truth but also the cause of error—for this contributes towards producing conviction,

4 Placing a comma (rather than a full stop) after ἀκόλαστος.

since when a reasonable explanation is given of why what is
25   not true appears true, this convinces people the more of the
truth—so we must state why the bodily pleasures appear the
more desirable. First, then, it is because they expel pain; and
it is because of the excesses of pain that men pursue excessive pleasure, and in general bodily pleasure, supposing
pleasure to be a therapy. Now therapeutic pleasures are in-
30   tense—that is why they are pursued—because they show up
against their contrary. (Pleasure is thought not to be virtuous for two reasons, as has been said, namely because some
pleasures are actions of a base nature—either congenital, as
in the case of a brute, or due to habit, as those of base men;
1154b   while others are therapies of something lacking, and it is better to be in a state than to be getting into it, whereas these
arise during the process of being made complete and are
therefore coincidentally virtuous.) Further, they are pursued
because of their intensity by those who cannot take delight
in other pleasures. So some people[5] manufacture thirsts for
themselves. When these are harmless, there is nothing to
5   criticize; but when they are harmful, it is base. For they have
nothing else to enjoy, and a neutral state is painful to many
people because of their nature. For animals are always exert-
ing themselves, as the students of natural science testify, saying that sight and hearing are painful—but we have become
10   used to this, as they say. Similarly, in youth people, because
they are growing, are like drunken men, and youth is pleasant. Those of an atrabilious nature always need therapy; for
their body is ever irritated owing to its composition, and
they are always under the influence of intense desire. Pain is
driven out both by the contrary pleasure, and by any chance
pleasure if it be strong; and for these reasons they become
15   self-indulgent and base. But the pleasures that do not involve pains do not admit of excess; and these are among the
things pleasant by nature and not coincidentally. By things
pleasant coincidentally I mean those that are therapeutic

5   Reading τινές (Rackham) for τινάς.

(for because people are treated through some action of the
part that remains healthy, for this reason the process is
thought pleasant); and things naturally pleasant are those
that stimulate the action of the healthy nature.   20

There is nothing that is always pleasant, because our nature is not simple, but there is another element in us as well,
inasmuch as we are perishable, so that if the one element
does something, this is unnatural to the other nature, and
when the two elements are equalized, what is done seems
neither painful nor pleasant. For if the nature of anything   25
were simple, the same action would always be most pleasant
to it. This is why god always takes delight in a single and simple pleasure; for there is an exercise not only of movement
but also of immobility, and pleasure is found more in rest
than in movement. But 'change in all things is sweet', as the
poet says,[6] because of a certain viciousness; for as it is the
vicious man that is changeable, so the nature that needs   30
change is bad; for it is not simple nor upright.

We have discussed continence and incontinence, and
pleasure and pain, both what each is and in what way some
of them are good and others bad. Finally, we shall speak of
friendship.

6 Euripides, *Orestes* 234.

9

FRIENDSHIP

FRIENDSHIP, WHAT IT IS AND OF WHAT NATURE, WHO IS A
friend, and whether friendship is spoken of in one way or
20 many ways (and if many, how many), and, further, how one
should treat a friend, and what is justice in friendship—all
this must be examined not less than any of the things that
are noble and desirable in a character. For it is thought to be
25 the special task of politics to produce friendship, and men
say that virtue is useful because of this; for those who are unjustly treated by one another cannot be friends to one another. Further, we all say that justice and injustice are specially exhibited towards friends; the same man seems both
good and friendly, and friendship seems a sort of state of
character; and if one wants to stop men treating one another
unjustly, it is enough to[1] make them friends (for genuine
30 friends do not act unjustly). But neither will men act unjustly
if they are just; therefore justice and friendship are either the
same or not far different.

Further, we assume that a friend is among the greatest of
goods, and that friendlessness and solitude are most terrible, because all life and voluntary companionship is with
friends—for we spend our days with our family, kinsmen, or
1235a comrades, children, parents, or wife. It is only the private
justice practised to friends that is in our power, while justice
towards all others is determined by the laws and is not in our
power.

Many problems are raised about friendship. First, there
5 is the view of those who include extraneous matters and

---

1 Reading ἅλις (Jackson) for ἀλλ᾽ εἰς.

extend the term; for some think that like is friend to like, whence the sayings: 'How god ever draws like to like'; 'Birds of a feather'; 'Thief knows thief, and wolf wolf'. The natural philosophers even organize the whole of nature on the prin- 10 ciple that like goes to like—that is why Empedocles said that the dog sits on the tile because it most resembles it. Some, then, describe friendship thus. Others say that contraries are friends; for they say an object of love and of appetite is in every case a friend. But the dry does not crave the dry but the 15 moist—whence the sayings, 'Earth longs for the rain', and 'In all things change is pleasant' (change is change to a con- trary). And like hates like, for 'Two of a trade never agree', and animals nourished from the same source are enemies.

Such, then, is the discrepancy between these assumptions; 20 for some think the like a friend, and the contrary an enemy—

> The less is ever the enemy of the more,
> and begins a day of hate.

And, further, the places of contraries are separate, but friendship seems to bring together. But others think con- 25 traries are friends, and Heraclitus criticizes the poet who wrote

> May strife perish from among gods and men;

for (says he) there could not be harmony without the high and the low note, nor animals without female and male, which are contraries. There are, then, these two beliefs about friendship; and they are extremely general and very far apart. 30

There are other views that are nearer and more related to people's perceptions. Some think that base men cannot be friends but only good. Some think it absurd if mothers are not to love their own children (friendship is evidently pres- ent even among the brutes)—after all, they choose to die for 35 their children. Some think that only what is useful is a friend, an indication of this being the fact that all pursue the useful but the useless, even in themselves, they throw away (as old Socrates said, citing the case of our spittle, hairs, and nails),

and that we cast off useless parts, and in the end at death our
1235b body, the corpse being useless. (But those who have a use for
it preserve it, as in Egypt.) All these things seem contrary to
one another; for the like is useless to the like, and contrariety
5 is furthest removed from likeness, and the contrary is most
useless to its contrary—for contraries destroy one another.
Further, some think it easy to acquire a friend, others a very
rare thing to recognize one, and impossible without misfortune (for all want to seem friends to those who are doing
10 well). Others claim that we should distrust even those who
remain with us in misfortune, alleging that they are deceiv-
ing us and making pretence so that by giving their company
to us when we are in misfortune they may obtain our friendship when we return to good fortune.

We must, then, find an account[2] that will best explain the
beliefs held on these topics and also resolve the problems
and contrarieties. This will happen if the contrary views are
15 seen to be held reasonably; for such an account will be most
in harmony with people's perceptions; and the contrary
views stand, if what is said is true in one way but not in
another.

Another problem is whether the good or the pleasant is
20 what is loved. For if we love what we crave for—and being in
love is particularly like this, for 'None is a lover but one who
ever loves'—and if appetite is for the pleasant, in this way
what is loved is the pleasant. But if it is what we want, then it
is the good; and the good and the pleasant are different.

About all these and the other cognate matters we must at-
25 tempt to make distinctions, starting from the following
principle: the desired and the wanted are either the good or
the apparent good. This is why the pleasant is desired; for it
is an apparent good—for some think it such, and to some
it appears such though they do not think it so. For appearance and belief do not reside in the same part of the soul.

---

2 Reading λόγος (Casaubon): the manuscripts have λοιπός and Susemihl
prints τρόπος (Sylburg).

162

However that may be, it is plain that both the good and the pleasant are loved.

This being determined, we must make another supposi-   30
tion: of goods some are good *tout court*, some good to a particular man but not *tout court*; and the same things are at
once good *tout court* and pleasant *tout court*. For we say that
what is advantageous to a body in health is good *tout court* for
a body, but not what is good for a sick body, such as drugs   35
and surgery. Similarly, things pleasant *tout court* to a body are
those pleasant to a body that is healthy and sound in limb:
for instance, seeing in light, not in darkness, though the contrary is the case to one with ophthalmia; and the pleasanter
wine is not that which is so to one whose tongue has been
spoilt by inebriety (for they do not pass up[3] even bad wine),
but that which is pleasant to an uncorrupted sense. So too   1236a
with the soul: it is not what is so to children or to brutes but
what is so to adults—at least, when we remember both we
choose the latter. And as the child or brute is to the adult
man, so are the base and foolish to the upright and wise. To   5
these, things that suit their states of character are pleasant,
and those are things that are good and noble.

Since, then, things are good in more than one way (for
one thing we call good because its nature is such, and another because it is beneficial and useful), and further, the
pleasant is in part pleasant *tout court* and good *tout court*, and
in part pleasant to a particular individual and apparently   10
good, then just as in the case of inanimate things we may
choose and love a thing for either of these reasons, so in the
case of men—one because of his nature and his virtue, another because he is beneficial and useful, another because he
is pleasant, and for pleasure.

A man becomes someone's friend when he is loved and returns that love, and this does not somehow escape their no-   15
tice. There must, then, be three species of friendship, not all
being so named for one thing or as species of one genus nor

3 The text is uncertain.

yet as mere homonyms. For all are so called in relation to one of them which is the primary, just as is the case with the word 'medical'; for we speak of a medical soul, body, instru-
20 ment, or task, but strictly speaking the name belongs to that primarily so called. The primary is that of which the defini-tion is contained in the definition of all:[4] for instance, a med-ical instrument is one that a medical man would use, but the definition of the instrument is not contained in that of the medical man. Everywhere they look for what is primary. But because the universal is primary, they also take the primary
25 to be universal, and that is false. And so they are not able to do justice to all of people's perceptions about friendship; for since one definition will not fit all, they think the others are not friendships—but they are, only not in the same way. But finding that the primary friendship will not fit and supposing it would be universal if primary, they deny that the others even
30 are friendships. But there are many species of friendship. This was part of what we have already said, since we have dis-tinguished three ways in which friendship is spoken of: one based on virtue, another on utility, a third on pleasantness.

Of these the friendship based on utility is that of the ma-jority: men love one another because of their utility and to
35 the extent of this; so we have the proverb

Glaucus, a helper is a friend so long as[5] he fights,

And

The Athenians no longer know the Megarians.

The friendship based on pleasure is that of the young, for they are sensitive to pleasure. That is why their friendship easily changes; for with a change in their characters as they
1236b grow up there is also a change in their pleasures. The friend-ship based on virtue is that of the best men.

---

4 Reading πᾶσιν (Bonitz) for ἡμῖν.
5 Reading τόσσον φίλος (Fritzsche) for τὸν σοφὸν φίλον.

It is evident from this that the primary friendship, that of good men, is a mutual returning of love and choice. For he who is loved is a friend to him who loves him, and a man loving in return is a friend to the man loved.[6] This friendship, then, is peculiar to man; for he alone perceives choices. But the other friendships are found also among the brutes and utility is evidently in some degree present, both between tame animals and men, and between animals themselves— as Herodotus says that the sandpiper is useful to the crocodile, and as soothsayers speak of the coming together and parting of birds.

The base may be friends to one another on the ground both of utility and of pleasure. Some deny them to be friends because there is not the primary friendship between them; for a base man will treat a base man unjustly, and those who are unjustly treated by one another do not love one another. Yet they do love—but not with the primary friendship. Nothing prevents their loving with the other kinds; for owing to pleasure they put up with each other when they are harmed, just as if they were incontinent. Those whose love is based on pleasure do not seem to be friends either, when we investigate with precision, because their friendship is not of the primary kind. For that is firm whereas theirs is not. But as has been said, it is a friendship—not the primary kind but derived from it. To speak of friendship in that way only is to do violence to people's perceptions and makes one assert paradoxes. But it is impossible for all friendships to come under one definition. It remains that in a way only the primary sort is friendship; but in a way all are—not as as homonyms or as being related to one another by chance, nor yet as falling under one species, but rather as being related to some one thing.

Since the same thing is at the same time good *tout court* and pleasant *tout court* (if nothing interferes), and the genuine friend, the friend *tout court*, is the primary friend, and

6 The text of this sentence is uncertain.

such a man is desirable for himself (and he must be such; for
30 the man to whom[7] one wants good to happen for himself,
one must also desire to exist), the genuine friend is also
pleasant *tout court*. That is why any sort of friend is thought
pleasant.

Again, one ought rather to distinguish further; for it
needs reflection whether we love what is good for ourselves
35 or what is good in the abstract and whether the exercise of
friendship is attended with pleasure, so that the object loved
is pleasant, or not. For the two must be taken together. For
what is not good *tout court* (but perhaps[8] bad) is something to
avoid, and what is not good for oneself is nothing to one; but
what we are looking for is that what is good *tout court* should
1237a be good for the individual.[9] For what is good *tout court* is desirable, and what is so for the individual is desirable for him;
and these must agree. Virtue brings this about, and politics
exists to make them agree for those to whom as yet they do
not.[10] And one who is a human being is ready and on the
road for this (for by nature that which is good in the abstract
5 is good to him), and men rather than women, and those who
are naturally endowed rather than those who are not. The
road is through pleasure: what is noble must be pleasant.
When these[11] disagree a man cannot yet be perfectly virtuous, for incontinence may arise—for it is in the disagreement of the good with the pleasant in the emotions that incontinence occurs.

10 So since the primary friendship is grounded on virtue,
friends of this sort will be themselves good *tout court*, and
this not because they are useful but in another way. For good
to the individual and good *tout court* are two things, and as
with the beneficial so with states of character. For what is

7 Reading ᾧ (Spengel) for ὡς.
8 Reading ἄν πως (Jackson) for ἁπλῶς.
9 Reading αὐτῷ (Bekker) for οὕτως.
10 Here Susemihl marks a lacuna.
11 Reading ταῦτα (Bussemaker) for τοῦτο.

beneficial *tout court* differs from what is so to an individual, as[12] taking exercise does from taking drugs. So the state that constitutes human virtue is of two kinds: let us suppose that man is one of the things virtuous by nature; then the virtue of the naturally virtuous is good *tout court*, and the virtue of that which is not virtuous is good to it.

Similarly with the pleasant. For here one must pause and examine whether friendship can exist without pleasure, what difference it makes, and on which of the two loving is based—whether one loves a man because he is good even if he is pleasant[13] but not because he is. Now, loving being spoken of in two ways, does the exercise of friendship seem to involve pleasure because it is good? It is plain that just as in the case of knowledge what we have recently considered and learnt is most perceptible because of its pleasantness, so also is the recognition of the familiar, and the same account applies to both. By nature, at least, what is good *tout court* is pleasant *tout court*, and pleasant to those to whom it is good. That is why like at once delights in like, and nothing is so pleasant to man as man; and since this is so even before they are perfect, it is plain it must be so when they are perfect; and the virtuous man is perfect.

If the exercise of friendship is a mutual choice, with pleasure, of each other's acquaintance, it is plain in general the primary friendship is a mutual choice of the things that are good and pleasant *tout court* because they are good and pleasant; and this friendship is the state from which such choice springs. For its task is an activity, and this is not external but in the one who loves. But the task of every capacity is external; for it is in something different or in oneself *qua* different. That is why to love is to delight in but to be loved is not; for to be loved is not[14] the exercise of what is lovable, but to love is the exercise of friendship; and the one is found only in

12 Reading αὐτῷ οἷον (Bonitz) for καλὸν τοιοῦτον.

13 Deleting μή (Ross).

14 Inserting οὐ (Rackham).

the animate, the other also in the inanimate—for even inanimate things are loved.

Since the exercise of friendship is a matter of treating the
1237b   loved[15] *qua* loved, and the friend is loved by the friend *qua* friend and not *qua* musician or doctor, the pleasure coming from him *qua* himself is the pleasure of friendship. For he loves him for being himself and not someone else. So if he does not delight in him *qua* good the primary friendship does not exist. Nor should any of his coincidental qualities
5   hinder more than his goodness pleases. For if[16] a man has an unpleasant odour he is left alone: he must be content with benevolence without living together.[17]

This then is primary friendship, and all admit it to be friendship. It is through it that the others both seem to be friendships to some and are disputed. For friendship is
10   thought to be something firm, and this alone is firm. For a formed assessment is firm, and where we do not act quickly or easily, we make a correct assessment. There is no firm friendship without trust, and trust needs time. For one must make trial, as Theognis says:

15   You cannot know the mind of man or woman
till you have tried them as you would try an ox.

Nor is a friend made except through time: people do indeed want to be friends, and such a state is easily taken for friendship. For when men are eager to be friends, then because
20   they perform every friendly service to one another they think they not merely want to be but are friends. But it happens with friendship as with other things: as a man is not in health merely because he wants to be, neither are men already friends once they want to be friends. An indication of this is the fact that men in this condition, without having made
25   trial of one another, are easily made enemies: wherever each

15 Reading τῷ φιλουμένῳ (Fritzsche) for τὸ φιλούμενον.
16 Reading εἰ (Bekker) for τι.
17 Reading ἀγαπητὸν γὰρ τὸ εὐνοεῖν, συζῆν δὲ μή.

has allowed the other to test him, they are not easily made enemies; but where they have not, they will be convinced whenever those who try to break up the friendship produce evidence.

It is evident at the same time that this friendship does not exist between the base, for the base man feels distrust and is malignant to all, measuring others by himself. That is why the good are more easily deceived unless experience has taught them distrust. But the base prefer natural goods to a friend and none of them loves a man more than goods. So they are not friends. For with them, the goods of friends are not in common: the friend is made a part of goods, not the goods a part of the friend.

The primary friendship then is not found towards many because it is hard to test many men—one would have to live with each. Nor should one choose a friend like a garment. True, in all things it seems the mark of an intelligent man to choose the better of two alternatives; and if one has used the worse for a long time and not yet the better, the better is to be chosen—but not in place of an old friend, one of whom you do not know whether he is better. For a friend is not to be had without trial nor in a single day: there is need of time. That is why the bushel of salt has become proverbial. He must also be not merely good in the abstract but good for you, if the friend is to be a friend to you. For a man is good in the abstract by being good but is a friend by being good for another; and he is both good in the abstract and a friend when these two things agree so that what is good in the abstract is good for the other—and if not, then[18] abstractly good for the virtuous man and good to another because he is useful. Loving in itself prevents one from being at the same time a friend to many; for one cannot exercise friendship towards many at the same time.

From this it is plain that it is correctly said that friendship is a firm thing, just as happiness is a thing self-sufficient. It

18 Reading τοῦτο τῷ ἄλλῳ, εἰ δέ for τὸ τοῦτο ἄλλῳ εἰ καί.

has been correctly said: 'Nature is firm but wealth is not'—
but it is far better to say 'virtue' than 'nature'; and time is said
to show who is loved, and bad fortune rather than good fortune. For then it is plain that the goods of friends are common (for friends alone instead of things naturally good and
naturally bad—which are the matters with which good and
bad fortune are concerned—choose a man rather than the
existence of some of those things and the non-existence of
others). Misfortune makes it plain who are not really friends
but friends for some utility. Time makes both sorts plain; for
the useful man does not become plain quickly, as the pleasant man does—though the pleasant *tout court* is not plain
quickly either. For men are like wines and meats: the pleasantness of them quickly makes itself plain, but if it continues
longer it is unpleasant and not sweet. So it is with men. For
the pleasant *tout court* must be determined as such by its final
form and by time. Even the vulgar would admit this, judging
not[19] merely according to the outcome but in the way in
which, speaking of a drink, they call it sweeter. For a drink is
unpleasant not[20] for the outcome but from not being continuous, though it deceives us at the start.

The primary friendship then—by reason of which the
others get the name—is that based on virtue and due to the
pleasure of virtue, as has been said before. The other kinds
occur also in children, brutes, and base men: whence the sayings, 'Likeness in age delights' and 'The bad man is fused
into one with the bad by pleasure'. For the base may be pleasant to one another, not *qua* base or *qua* neither good or bad,
but (say) as both being singers, or the one fond of song and
the other a singer; and inasmuch as all have some good in
them, in this way they fit together with one another. Further,
they might be useful and beneficial to one another, not *tout
court* but in relation to their choice, or in virtue of some neutral characteristic.

19 Retaining οὐκ (Susemihl reads ὅτι, after Fritzsche).
20 Adding οὐ before διά.

An upright man may be a friend to a base man; for he may 1238b
be useful in relation to his choice—the base man being of
use to the virtuous in relation to the latter's current choice,
the upright man to the incontinent in relation to his current
choice and to the base in relation to his natural choice. And
he will want what is good, *tout court* what is good *tout court*, 5
and conditionally what is good for the friend, so far as poverty or illness is of advantage to him—and these for the sake
of the things that are good *tout court*: for instance, taking a
medicine—for that no one wants[21] but wants for some particular purpose. Again, they may be friends in the way in 10
which those not virtuous might be friends to one another.
For a man might be pleasant, not *qua* base but *qua* partaking
in some common property (for instance, *qua* musical).
Again, so far as there is something upright in all—that is
why some might be glad to keep company with a virtuous
man. Or in so far as they suit each individual; for all have
something of the good.

THESE THEN ARE THREE SPECIES OF FRIENDSHIP; AND IN
all of them the word friendship implies a kind of equality. 15
For even those who are friends through virtue are mutually
friends by a sort of equality of virtue.

Another variety is the friendship of superiority,[22] as the
virtue of a god is superior to that of a man. This is another
species of friendship (and so, in general, is that of ruler to 20
ruled)—as justice too is different, being here a proportional
and not an arithmetical equality. Into this class falls the relation of father to son and of benefactor to beneficiary; and
there are varieties of these again: for instance, there is a difference between the relation of father to son, and of husband to
wife, the latter being that of ruler to ruled, the former that of 25
benefactor to beneficiary. In these varieties there is not at all,
or not in equal degree, mutual love. For it would be ridiculous

21 Susemihl marks a lacuna here.
22 Reading ὑπεροχήν (Fritzsche) for ὑπερβολήν ('excess').

to accuse a god because the love he returns is not equal to the love he receives, or for the ruled to make the same complaint against his ruler. For the part of a ruler is to be loved, not to
30   love, or else to love in a different way. And the pleasure[23] that a self-sufficient man takes in his possessions or his child, and that which the indigent takes in what comes to him, are not the same. Similarly also with those who are friends through use or pleasure, some are on an equal footing and others on a basis of superiority. That is why those who think themselves
35   to be on the former footing complain if the other is not equally useful and does not treat them well; and similarly with regard to pleasure. This is plain in the case of lover and beloved; for this is frequently a cause of conflict between them. The lover does not perceive that the eagerness in each is not according to the same proportion. That is why Eunicus said[24] that

a beloved, not a lover, would speak thus.

They think that the proportion is the same for each.
1239a   There being, then, as has been said, three species of friendship—based on virtue, utility, and pleasantness— these again are subdivided each into two, one kind based on equality and the other on superiority. Both are friendships, but only those between whom there is equality are friends: it
5   would be absurd for a man to be the friend of a child, yet certainly he loves and is loved by him. Sometimes the superior ought to be loved, and if he loves, he is reproached for loving one unworthy; for measurement is made by the worth of the friends and a sort of equality. Some then, owing to deficiency
10   in age, are not worthy to receive an equal love, and others because of virtue or birth or some other such superiority. The superior ought to[25] claim either to love less or not to love at all, whether in the friendship of utility, pleasure, or virtue. Where the superiority is small, disputes naturally arise; for

23 Omitting οὐδέν (Spengel).
24 Reading εἴρηκεν Εὔνικος (Russell) for εὑρηκέναι νεῖκος.
25 Reading δεῖ (Spengel) for ἀεί.

the small is in some cases of no account—for instance, in weighing wood, though not in weighing gold. But men are bad at assessing what is small; for their own good by its near- 15 ness seems great, that of another by its distance small. When the difference is excessive, then not even those affected seek to make out that their love should be returned or equally re- turned—for instance, as if a man were to claim this from a god. It is evident then that men are friends when on an 20 equality with each other, but that they may have mutual love without being friends.

It is plain why men look for the friendship of superiority rather than that of equality; for in the former they obtain both love and superiority. That is why with some the flatterer is more honoured than the friend; for he procures the ap- 25 pearance of both for the object of his flattery. The ambitious are especially of this kind; for to be an object of admiration involves superiority. By nature some are born affectionate and others ambitious. He who delights rather in loving than in being loved is affectionate, and the other tends to be ambi- tious. He, then, who delights in being admired and loved 30 loves superiority: the other, the affectionate, loves the plea- sure of loving.[26] This by his activity he must have;[27] for to be loved is coincidental—one may be loved without knowing it but not love. Loving, rather than being loved, depends on the lover: being loved rather depends on the object of love. 35 An indication of this is the fact that the friend would choose, if both were not possible, rather to know than to be known, as we see women do when allowing others to adopt their children (for instance, Antiphon's Andromache). For want- ing to be known seems to be felt on one's own account and in order to get, not to do, some good; but wanting to know in order to do good and to love. That is why we praise those 1239b

<hr/>

26 Reading τῆς... ἡδονῆς with the manuscripts (Susemihl follows Spen- gel and prints a dative).

27 Reading ἀνάγκῃ ἐνεργοῦντι for ἀνάγκη ἐνεργοῦντα.

who persist in their love towards the dead; for they know but
are not known.

That, then, there are several sorts of friendship, that they
are three in number, and what are the differences between
5   being loved and having love returned, and between friends
on a basis of equality and friends on a basis of superiority,
has now been stated.

SINCE 'FRIENDLY' IS ALSO USED MORE GENERALLY (AS WAS
indeed said at the start) by those who take in extraneous
considerations—some saying that the like is friendly, and
some that the contrary is—we must speak also of the relation of these things to the friendships we have described. The
10   like is brought both under the pleasant and under the good.
For the good is simple but the bad multiform; and the good
man is ever like himself and does not change in character,
whereas the base and the foolish are quite different in the
evening from what they were in the morning. That is why unless the base come to some agreement, they are not friends
15   to one another but distance themselves; and unfirm friendship is not friendship. So in this way the like is friendly, because the good is like. But in a way also because of pleasure;
for those like one another have the same pleasures, and
everything too is by nature pleasant to itself. That is why the
voices, characters, and company of those of the same kind
20   are pleasantest to each other, even in the animals other than
man; and in this way it is possible for even the base to love
one another:

The bad man is fused into one with the bad by pleasure.

Contraries are friendly through utility; for the like is useless to itself. That is why master needs slave, and slave mas-
25   ter, and why man and woman need one another. And the
contrary is pleasant and craved for as something useful, not
as included in the end but as contributing towards it. For
when a thing has obtained what it craves, it has attained its
end and does not crave its contrary—for instance, the hot

does not desire the cold, nor the dry the wet. Yet in a manner   30
the love of the contrary is love of the good; for the contraries
desire one another because of the middle: they desire one
another like tallies because thus out of the two arises a single
thing midway between them. Further, the love is coincidentally of the contrary but *per se* of the mean; for contraries desire not one another but what is in the middle: if over-chilled
they return to the middle by being warmed, and if over-   35
warmed by being chilled; and so with everything else. Otherwise they are ever in a state of appetite, never in the middle
states. But that which is in the middle delights without appetite in what is naturally pleasant, while the others delight in
all that puts them out of their natural state. This species then
is found also among inanimate things; but love occurs when
it is found among the animate. That is why some delight in   1240a
what is unlike themselves, the austere in the convivial, the
energetic in the lazy; for they bring each other back to the
middle state. Coincidentally, then, as has been said, contraries are friendly, because of the good.

The number then of species of friendship, and the differ-   5
ent ways in which we speak of friends and of persons as loving and being loved, both where this constitutes friendship
and where it does not, have now been stated.

THE QUESTION WHETHER A MAN IS A FRIEND TO HIMSELF
or not requires much inquiry. For some think that each man
is above all a friend to himself, and they use this friendship as   10
a standard by which to assess his friendship to all other
friends. But if we look to argument and to the properties
usually thought characteristic of friends, then things are in
some respects contrary and in others evidently alike. For this
friendship is not friendship *tout court*, but has a certain analogy to it. For loving and being loved require two separate in-   15
dividuals. Therefore a man is a friend to himself rather as we
have described the incontinent and continent as voluntary
or involuntary, namely that the parts of his soul are in a certain relation to each other; and all things of this sort are

similar—for instance, whether a man can be a friend or enemy to himself, and whether a man can treat himself un- justly. For all these relations require two separate individu- als: in so far then as the soul is in a way two, these relations can in a way belong to it; but in so far as they are not sepa- rate, they cannot.

It is by a man's attitude to himself that the other modes under which we are accustomed to consider friendship in our discussions are determined. For a man seems to be a friend who wants good things—or what he thinks to be good things—for someone, not on his own account but for the sake of that person. In another way, if he wants someone's existence on that person's account and not on his own— even if he is not bestowing goods,[28]—he would seem most of all to love him. In another way if he desires to live with him for the sake of his company and for no other reason, as fa- thers want existence for their children but live with others. Now all these things conflict. For some think they are not loved unless it is for themselves that he wants the things, some unless he wants their existence, others unless he wants to live with them. Further, we shall take it as a mark of cher- ishing someone that one grieves with the grieving—not for some other reason, as when slaves grieve with their masters because their masters when grieving are cruel—but for their own sake,[29] as mothers feel towards their children, and birds that share one another's pains. For the friend wants most of all not to feel pain along with his friend but to feel the same pain (for instance, to feel thirsty when he is thirsty), if that can be—and if not, something as close as possible.[30] The same account is applicable to delight, which, if felt for no other reason than that the other feels delight, is a sign of friendship. Further, we say about friendship such things as

28 Deleting μὴ τῷ τὸ εἶναι.

29 Reading ἀλλά for ἀλλ' οὐ.

30 Reading εἰ δὲ μή, ὅτι ἐγγύτατα (after Fritzsche) for ὅτι μὴ ἐγγύτατα. (Susemihl, following another suggestion of Fritzsche's, deletes μή.)

that friendship is equality, and true friends a single soul. All such phrases are applicable to the single individual; for a man wants good for himself[31] in this fashion—no one does good to himself for some further reason or to gain favour.[32] Nor, as a single individual, does he boast of what he has done; for he who makes it plain that he loves seems to want to be loved, not to love. And especially existence, living together, sharing delight and grief, being a single soul, finding it impossible to live without one another rather than dying together—all these are characteristic of a single individual, who is perhaps his own companion.

All these things we find in the relation of the good man to himself. In the vicious man, as in the incontinent, things disagree, and for this reason it seems possible for a man to be his own enemy; but so far as he is single and indivisible, he is an object of desire to himself. Such is the good man and the man whose friendship is based on virtue; for the depraved man is not one but many, in the same day other than himself and fickle. So that a man's friendship for himself is reduced to the friendship of the good; for because a man is in a manner like himself, single, and good for himself, so far he is a friend and object of desire to himself. And this is natural to man; and the vicious man is unnatural. The good man never reproaches himself at the moment of his act, like the incontinent, nor the later with the earlier man, like one who regrets, nor the earlier with the later, like the liar. Generally, if it is necessary to distinguish as the sophists do, he is related to himself as Coriscus to virtuous Coriscus; for it is plain that the amount of virtuousness in the two is one and the same. When they complain about themselves, they kill themselves; yet every one seems good to himself.

The man that is good *tout court* looks to be a friend to himself, as has been said, since he has within him two parts which by nature want to be friends and which it is impossible

---

31 Reading αὐτῷ (Bekker) rather than αὑτῷ.

32 Adding ἕνεκα after χάριτος (Robinson).

30   to tear apart. That is why in the case of man each is thought
to be the friend of himself, but not so with the other animals:
for instance, the horse does not seem good to himself[33] and
is therefore not a friend. Nor are children, till they have attained the power of choice; for then their intelligence disagrees with their appetite. One's friendship to oneself re-
35   sembles the friendship arising from kinship; for neither
bond can be dissolved by one's own power: even if they quarrel, kinsmen remain kinsmen, and a man remains one man
so long as he lives.

The various ways in which we speak of loving, and how all
friendships reduce to the primary kind, is plain from what
has been said.

1241a   IT IS APPROPRIATE TO THE INQUIRY TO CONSIDER CON-
cord and benevolence; for some identify these, and others
think they cannot exist apart from one another. Benevolence is not altogether different from friendship nor yet the
same; for when we distinguish friendship according to its
5   three sorts, benevolence is found neither in the friendship of
utility nor in that of pleasure. For if one wishes well to the
other because that is useful to oneself, one would be so wish-
ing not for the other's sake, but for one's own; but benevolence seems like friendship[34] to be focussed not on him who
feels the benevolence but him towards whom it is felt. Now
if benevolence existed in the friendship based on pleasure,
then men would feel benevolence towards things inanimate.
10   So it is plain that benevolence is concerned with the friendship that depends on character; but benevolence shows itself
in merely wanting, friendship in also doing what one wants.
For benevolence is an origin of friendship: every friend is benevolent but not every benevolent person is a friend. He
who is benevolent only is like a man at the beginning, and
that is why it is the origin of friendship, not friendship itself.

33 Adding οὐ δοκεῖ ἀγαθός after αὑτῷ (Ross).
34 Adding καὶ ἡ φιλία after ὥσπερ (Fritzsche). Susemihl marks a lacuna.

***[35] For friends seem to be in concord and those who are   15
in concord seem to be friends. Friendly concord is not about
all things but about matters of action for those in concord
and about what relates to their common life. Nor is it agreement merely in thought or desire (for it is possible to think
one thing and crave the contrary,[36] as in the incontinent
there is this disagreement), nor if[37] a man concords with an-   20
other in choice, does he necessarily do so in appetite. Concord is found in the case of good men—at least, base men
when they choose and crave the same things[38] harm one another. Concord seems to be spoken of in more than one
way, like friendship. In its primary and natural form it is virtuous. That is why the base cannot be in concord. The other   25
form is the concord of the base, when they choose and crave
the same things. They must so desire the same thing that it
is possible for both to get what they desire; for if they desire
that which cannot belong to both, they will quarrel, and
those in concord will not quarrel. There is concord when   30
the two parties make the same choice as to who is to rule
and who to be ruled—not that each one should choose himself, but that both should choose the same person. Concord
is political friendship. So much then about concord and
benevolence.

THE PROBLEM IS RAISED OF WHY THOSE WHO HAVE   35
treated someone well have more love for those who have
been well treated than the latter for the former. The contrary
seems to be just. One might assume that it happens from
consideration of utility and what is beneficial to oneself; for
the one has a debt due to him, while the other has a debt to
repay. This, however, is not all: there is also something natural—activity is more desirable. The relation is the same as   1241b

---

35 Susemihl marks a lacuna.

36 Reading νοεῖν καί (Richards) for τὸ κινοῦν.

37 Reading οὐδ᾽ εἰ (with one manuscript) for οὐ δεῖ.

38 Reading ταὐτά for ταῦτα.

that between a product and an activity, and he who is well done by is as it were the product of him who does him well. That is why in animals there is a strong feeling for offspring both in begetting them and in preserving them afterwards. So fathers love their children—and mothers more than fathers—more than they are loved by them. And they love their own children more than their parents, because nothing is so good as activity; and mothers love more than fathers because they think the children to be more their own product; for a product is measured by difficulty, and the mother suffers more pain in birth.

So much then for friendship towards oneself and among several people.

JUSTICE SEEMS TO BE A SORT OF EQUALITY AND FRIEND-ship also involves equality, if the saying is not wrong that love is equality. Constitutions are all of them particular forms of justice; for a constitution is an association, and every association is held together by justice, so that whatever be the number of species of friendship, there are the same of justice and association; and they all border on one another and have similar differences. Since there is the same relation between soul and body, craftsman and tool, and master and slave, between them there is no association; for they are not two: rather, the first is one and the second belongs to the one. Nor is the good to be divided between the two: rather, that of both belongs to the one for the sake of which they exist. For the body is a natural tool, and the slave is as it were a part and detachable tool of the master, a tool being a sort of inanimate slave.

The other forms of association are parts of the political associations—for instance, fraternities and priestly colleges[39] or business associations.[40] All constitutions are found together in the household,[41] both the correct and the deviant

39 Reading ὀργεών (Dietsch) for ὀργίων.
40 Deleting ἔτι πολιτεῖαι (Fritzsche).
41 Reading οἰκίαις (Fritzsche) for οἰκείοις.

forms (for the same thing is true of constitutions as of harmonies). The government of the children by the father is mo- 30
narchic, the relation of husband and wife aristocratic, the relation of brothers that of a commonwealth; the corruptions
of these are tyranny, oligarchy, and democracy. The forms of
justice then are also so many in number.

Since equality is either arithmetical or proportional, there
will be various species of justice, friendship, and association:
on arithmetical equality rests the democratic association, 35
and the friendship of comrades—both being measured by
the same standard; on proportional the aristocratic[42] and
the monarchic. For the same thing is not just for the superior and the inferior: rather, what is proportional is just.
Such is the friendship between father and child; and the
same thing may be found in associations.

WE SPEAK OF FRIENDSHIPS OF KINSMEN, COMRADES, AND   1242a
associates, and of so-called political friendship. That of kinsmen has more than one species: that of brothers and that of
father and sons. One is proportional—that of the father;
and one arithmetical—that of brothers (which resembles the 5
friendship of comrades since here too age gives certain privileges). Political friendship has been established mainly in accordance with utility; for men seem to have come together
because they are not self-sufficient—though they would have
come together anyhow for the sake of living together. Political friendship alone and its corresponding deviation are not
simply friendships: in addition, they associate as friends. 10
The others rest on superiority. The justice belonging to the
friendship of the useful is pre-eminently justice; for it is political justice.

It is different when a saw and the craft that uses it come
together: they do so not for some common end—like a tool
and a soul—but for the sake of the user. It is true that the 15
tool itself[43] receives the attention that its task requires; for it

42 Deleting ἀρίστη (Bussemaker).
43 Reading αὐτος τό (Bonitz) for τοῦτο.

exists for the sake of its task. ***[44] And the essence of a gim-
let is twofold, but more strictly speaking it is its exercise,
namely boring holes. In this class come the body and a slave,
as has been said before.

20 To inquire, then, how one ought to keep company with a
friend is to look for a kind of justice; for generally all justice
is in relation to a friend. For justice involves a number of individuals who are associates, and the friend is an associate
either in family or in one's scheme of life. For man is not
merely a political but also a domestic animal, and his cou-
plings are not, like those of the other animals, confined to
certain times and formed with any chance partner, whether
25 male or female; nor is a man a solitary animal but one with[45]
a special tendency to association with those to whom he is by
nature akin. There would, then, be association and a kind of
justice, even if there were no State; and the household is a
kind of friendship.

The relation of master and slave is that of a craft and its
30 tools, and of a soul and its body; and these are not friendships, nor forms of justice but something analogous—just as
what is healthy is not justice but something analogous. The
friendship of man and wife is a friendship based on utility
and an association; that of father and son is the same as that
of god to man, of one who does well to him who is well done
by, and in general of the natural ruler to the naturally ruled.
35 That of brothers to one another is eminently that of comrades, inasmuch as it involves equality[46]—

For I was not declared a bastard brother to him;
but the same was called the father of both of us,
Zeus, my ruler.

For this is the language of men that look for equality. That is
1242b why in the household first we have the origins and springs of
friendship, of political organization, and of justice.

---

44 Susemihl marks a lacuna.
45 Reading ἰδίᾳ οὐ μοναυλικόν (Spengel) for διὰ δύμον αὐλικόν.
46 Reading ᾗ for ἡ before κατ᾽ ἰσότητα.

Since there are three sorts of friendship, based on virtue, utility, and pleasure, and two varieties of each of these—for each of them may imply either superiority or equality—and the justice involved in these is plain from the debates that have been held on it, in a friendship of superiority proportion is claimed—but not in the same way: rather, the superior claims an inverse proportion (as he is to the inferior, so should what he receives from the inferior be to what the inferior receives from him), he being in the position of ruler to ruled; and if he cannot get that, he claims at least arithmetical equality. For so it is in the other forms of association, the two members enjoying sometimes an arithmetical equality and sometimes a proportional one. For if they contributed arithmetically equal sums of money, they take an equal share; and if not equal, then proportional. Contrariwise, the inferior inverts this proportion and joins crosswise. But in this way the superior would seem to come off the worse, and friendship and association to be a service. Equality must then be achieved and proportion created by some other means; and this means is honour, which by nature belongs to a ruler or god in relation to the ruled. The profit and the honour must be equated.

The friendship that rests on equality is political: it is based on utility; and just as States are friends to one another, so in the like way are citizens. And just as 'the Athenians no longer know the Megarians', so citizens do not know one another when they are no longer useful to one another, and the friendship is on the basis of immediate payment. There is here, too, the relation of ruler and ruled which is neither the natural relation, nor that involved in monarchy: each is ruler and ruled in turn. Nor is it either's purpose to act with the beneficence of a god: rather, he aims to share equally in the good and in the service. Political friendship, then, claims to be one based on equality. Of the friendship of utility there are two species, the legal and the moral. Political friendship looks to equality and to the object as sellers and buyers do—hence the proverb 'A wage for a friend'. When, then, this political friendship is based on an agreement, it is of the legal kind; but when they leave things up to one another, we have the moral friendship and that of comrades. That is why complaints are very frequent in this sort of friendship; and the reason is that it is unnatural. For friendships based on utility and based on virtue are different; but these want to have both together, keeping company together for the sake of utility, but representing their friendship as moral, like that

1243a of upright men: that is why, as if trusting one another, they make a non-legal friendship.

For in general there are more complaints in the useful friendship than in either of the other two (for virtue is not an object of complaint, and pleasant friends having got what they wanted and given what they had, are done with it; but

5 useful friends do not dissolve their friendship at once, if their relations are not legal but those of comrades). Still the legal form of useful friendship is not an object of complaint. The legal relation is dissolved by a money-payment (for it measures equality in money), but the moral is dissolved voluntarily. That is why in some places the law forbids lawsuits for voluntary interactions between those who keep company

10 thus as friends—and correctly; for good men do not have bonds of justice with one another; and such as these have dealings with one another as good and trustworthy men. In this kind of friendship complaints on either side are dubious: how can either complain, seeing that they trust each other not in a legal but a moral way?

It is a further problem on which of two grounds we are to

15 assess what is just, whether by looking to the amount of service rendered, or to what was its value to the recipient; for, to borrow the language of Theognis, the service may be 'small to thee, O goddess, but great to me'. Or the contrary may hap-

20 pen, as in the saying: 'This is amusement to you but death to me'. Hence, as we have said,[47] come complaints. For the one claims a return on the ground of having done a great service, because he has done it at the request of the other, or with

47 Adding ὥσπερ before εἴρηται (Fritzsche).

some other plea, saying how much it was to the advantage of the other and not what it meant to himself; while the other, contrariwise, insists on its value to the other and not on its value to himself. Sometimes the receiver inverts the position: 25 he says how little has accrued to him, while the other insists on its great magnitude to *him*: for instance, if at some risk one has benefited another to the extent of a drachma, the one insists on the size of the risk, the other on that of the money, just as in the repayment of money—for there the dispute is on this point: the one claims its value then, the other its value 30 now (unless they have fixed the terms).

Political friendship, then, looks to the agreement and the thing, moral friendship to the choice: here then we have more justice, and a friendly justice. The cause of conflict is that moral friendship is more noble, but useful 35 friendship more necessary. They start, then, by proposing to be moral friends and friends through virtue; but as soon as some private interest arises, they show plainly that they were not so. For the multitude aim at the noble only when they have plenty of everything else—and at the nobler friendship similarly.

So it is evident what distinctions should be drawn in these 1243b matters. If they are moral friends, they should see if the choice of each is equal, and then nothing more should be claimed by either from the other. But if their friendship is of the useful or political kind, they agree to the extent that it is expedient. And if one declares that they are friends on one basis and the other on the other, it is not noble, when one 5 ought to do something in return, to use noble words. So too, in the other case; but since they have not fixed the terms, someone must assess them morally and neither must cheat the other by a false pretence—so each must put up with his fortune.[48]

That moral friendship is based on choice is plain, since 10 even if after receiving great benefits one does not repay them

48 The text is uncertain.

through inability but repays only what he can, he acts nobly; and a god is satisfied at getting sacrifices as good as we can offer. But a seller will not be satisfied if the buyer says he cannot pay more; nor will a lender.

15   Complaints are common in friendships which are not on a level, and it is not easy to see what is just. For it is hard to measure by a single unit things that are not on a level, as happens in the case of lovers. For there the one pursues the other as a pleasant person, in order to live with him, while the latter seeks the other in some cases for his utility. When

20   the love is over, one changes as the other changes. Then they calculate the *quid pro quo*.[49] Thus Python and Pammenes quarrelled; and so do teacher and pupil (for knowledge and wealth have no common measure); so Herodicus the doctor quarrelled with a patient who paid him only a small fee; such too was the case of the king and the lyre-player: the former

25   regarded the latter as pleasant, the latter the former as useful; and so the king, when it was time to give something in return, chose to regard himself as a pleasant companion, and said that just as the player had given him pleasure by singing, so he had given the player pleasure by his promise.

      Nevertheless, it is evident here too how one should decide: the measurement must be by a single measure here too—not by a term but by a ratio; for we must measure by

30   proportion, just as one measures in the political communities. For how is a cobbler to associate with a farmer unless one equates the product of the two by proportion? To all whose exchanges are not on a level proportion is the measure: for instance, if the one complains that he has given understanding, and the other that he has given money, we must measure the ratio of understanding to wealth, and then what

35   has been given for each. For if the one gives half of the lesser, and the other does not give a small fraction of the greater object, it is plain that the latter does injustice. Here, too, there may be a dispute at the start, if one party says they have come

49 Reading τί ἀντὶ τίνος for παντί τινος.

together for utility, and the other denies this and says that it is some other kind of friendship.

As REGARDS THE GOOD MAN WHO IS A FRIEND ON THE   1244a
basis of virtue, we must consider whether it is he to whom
one ought to render useful services and help, or rather one
who makes a return and has power. This is the same question
as whether we ought rather to do good to a friend or to a virtuous man. If the friend is also virtuous, there is perhaps no   5
great difficulty, if one does not exaggerate the one quality
and minimize the other, making him very much of a friend
but moderately upright. But in other cases many questions
arise—for instance, if the one has been but will no longer remain so, and the other will be but is not yet, or the one was
but is not, and the other is but has not been and will not be
***[50] The other is harder. For perhaps there is something in   10
what Euripides says: 'A word is your just pay for a word, but
a deed for him who has given deeds'. And one must not do
everything for one's father, but there are some things one
should do for one's mother, though a father is the better. For,
indeed, even to Zeus we do not sacrifice all things, nor does
he have all honours but only some. Perhaps, then, there are   15
things which should be rendered to the useful friend and others to the good one: for instance, because a man gives you
food and what is necessary, you need not live together; nor
need you give the man with whom you are ready to live that
which not he but the useful friend gives. Those who doing this
give all to their beloved when they ought not are worthless.

The definitions of friendship that we give in our discus-   20
sions all belong to friendship in some manner but not to the
same friendship. To the useful friend applies the fact that
one wants what is good for him, and to one who has done
well by us, and in fact to any kind of friend[51]—for this definition does not distinguish the class of friendship. For another

---

50 Susemihl marks a lacuna.
51 Reading ὁποίῳ δή for ὁποῖος δεῖ.

we want existence. For another, to live together. For the
25 friend on the basis of pleasure, sharing grief and delight. All
these definitions are appropriate to some friendship, but
there is none of which all are true. That is why there are many
definitions, and each appears to belong to a unique friendship though it does not. For instance, the choice of existence: the superior friend who has done good wants[52] the existence of his own product, and to him who has given
30 existence one ought to give in return—but not live together
with him but rather with the pleasant friend.

    Some friends treat one another unjustly: they love rather
the things than the possessor of them; and that is why they
love the persons much as they choose wine because it is pleasant, or riches because they are useful. For riches are more
useful than their owner, and that is why the owner should be[53]
resentful, as having been chosen in return for something in-
35 ferior. And they complain; for they now look for a good man,
when before they looked for one pleasant or useful.[54]

1244b WE MUST ALSO CONSIDER SELF-SUFFICIENCY AND FRIEND-
SHIP, and the relations they have to one another. For one
might raise a problem whether, if a man be in all respects
self-sufficient, he will have a friend, if one seeks a friend
from want and the good man is perfectly self-sufficient.[55] If
5 the possessor of virtue is happy, why should he need a friend?
For the self-sufficient man neither needs useful people nor
people to cheer him, nor to live with—his own company is
enough for him. This is most evident in the case of a god; for
it is plain that, needing nothing, he will not need a friend,
nor have one, supposing that he does not need one.[56] So the
happiest man will least need a friend, and only as far as it is

52 Susemihl marks a lacuna here.
53 Not adding οὐ as Susemihl does.
54 The text of the last two sentences is uncertain.
55 Susemihl marks a lacuna here.
56 Reading μηθενὸς δεομένῳ for οὔτε μηθὲν δεσπότου (after Casaubon).

impossible for him to be self-sufficient. Therefore the man   10
who lives the best life must have fewest friends, and they
must always be becoming fewer, and he must not busy himself that men become his friends but disdain not merely the
useful but even men desirable to live with. But surely this
makes it evident that a friend is not for utility or advantage: 15
rather, the friend on the basis of virtue[57] is the only friend.
For when we need nothing, then we all seek others to share
our enjoyment and to whom we may do good rather than receive good from. We assess things better when self-sufficient
than when in want, and most of all[58] we then seek friends   20
worthy to live with.

As to this problem, we must see if we have not been partially right, and partially missed the truth owing to our comparison. It will be plain if we ascertain what is life as activity
and as end. Evidently, it is perception and knowledge, so   25
that living together is perceiving together and knowing together. Self-perception and self-knowledge are most desirable to every one, and hence the desire of living is natural in
all; for living must be regarded as a kind of knowing. If then
we were to cut something off, and take knowledge on its own   30
and not attach it to ourselves[59]—this passes unnoticed as it is
written down, but in fact need not remain unnoticed[60]—
there would be no difference between this and another's
knowing instead of oneself; and this is like another's living
instead of oneself. Now reasonably enough, the perception
and knowledge of oneself is more desirable. For we must put
together two things in the argument: that life is desirable   35
and also that the good is, and thence that such a nature be-   1245a
longs to one and the same person.[61] If, then, of such a pair of

---

57 Reading ἀλλ' ὁ (Aldine) for the received ἀλλ' οὐ. Susemihl prints
Spengel's ἀλλά.

58 Reading μάλιστά τε (Sylburg) for ὅτε μάλιστα.

59 Adding τὸ αὑτόν (Robinson). Susemihl marks a lacuna.

60 The text and the sense of these sentences are uncertain.

61 Reading τῷ αὐτῷ for τὸ αὐτὸ τοῖς.

corresponding series there is always one series of the desirable, and the known and the perceived are, broadly speaking, constituted by their sharing in the nature of the determined so that to want to perceive oneself is to want oneself
5 to be of a certain definite characteristic—since, then, we are not possessed of each of such characteristics in ourselves but only by participation in these capacities in perceiving and knowing—for the perceiver becomes perceived in the way and in the respect in which he first perceives, and according to how and what he perceives; and the knower becomes
10 known in the same way—therefore one always wants to live because one always wants to know, and that because one wants oneself to be the object known.

The choice to live with others might seem, when considered in a certain way, silly. First, in the case of things common also to the other animals (for instance, eating together, drinking together); for what is the difference between doing these things in the neighbourhood of others or apart from them, if you take away speech? But even to share in speech of
15 a casual kind does not make the case different. Further, for friends who are self-sufficient neither teaching nor learning is possible; for if one learns, he is not as he should be, and if he teaches, his friend is not—but likeness is friendship. But
20 surely it is evident, and all of us find greater pleasure in sharing good things with friends as far as these come to each and are the best one can share: to some it falls to share in bodily pleasures, to others in artistic contemplation, to others in philosophy. And the friend must be present too: that is why they say[62] 'Distant friends are a burden'—so men must not be at a distance from one another when there is friendship between them. Hence sexual love seems like friendship; for
25 the lover longs to live with his beloved—but not as ideally he ought, but in a sensuous way.

That is what the argument says in raising the problem; but the facts are evidently different, so that it is clear that the

62 Reading φασι for φησι.

poser of the problem is in a way misleading us. We must see the truth from what follows. A friend wants to be, in the words of the proverb, another Heracles, another self. Humanity is scattered, and hard to bring together.[63] But though a friend is by nature what is most akin to his friend, one man is like another in body, and another like him in soul, and of them one like him in one part and another in another. But nonetheless a friend is meant to be, as it were, a separate self. Therefore, to perceive a friend must be in a way to perceive oneself and to know a friend to know oneself. So to share vulgar pleasures and to live together with a friend are, reasonably enough, pleasant (for perception of the friend always takes place at the same time), but still more to share in the diviner pleasures. The reason is that it is always pleasanter to contemplate oneself enjoying a superior good. This is sometimes an emotion, sometimes an action, sometimes something else. But if it is pleasant for a man himself to live well and also his friend, and to collaborate in living together, their association is above all in things included in the end.

That is why men should contemplate together and feast together—not for the pleasures of food or necessary pleasures (such companionship seems to be not[64] companionship but debauch). But the end which each can attain is that in which he wants to live with someone else—otherwise they desire to do good to and receive good from friends in preference to others.

Thus it is evident that they ought to live together, who want this above all things, and that the happiest and best man tends especially to do so. As to the fact that this was not evident in the argument, that too was reasonable since what was said was true. For it is because of the comparison, true though it is, that the solution is not found. For because a god is not such as to need a friend, we claim the same of the man

63 The text of this sentence is uncertain.

64 Adding γὰρ οὐχ after ὁμιλίαι (a suggestion of Susemihl—who in his text marks a lacuna).

who resembles a god. Yet by this reasoning the virtuous man will not even think; for the well-being of a god is not in this but in being superior to thinking of anything beside himself. The reason is that with us well-being involves something beyond us but a god is his own well-being.

As to our seeking and praying for many friends and at the same time saying that the man who has many friends has no friend, both are correct. For if it is possible to live with and share the perceptions of many at the same time, it is most desirable that these should be as many as possible; but since this is most difficult, the exercise of joint perception must take place among fewer. So it is not only hard to get many friends—for testing is necessary—but also to use them when you have got them.

Sometimes we want the object of our love to fare well away from us, sometimes to share the same fortune as ourselves, and to want to be together is characteristic of friendship. For if they can both be together and fare well, all choose this; but if they cannot be both, then they choose as the mother of Heracles might have chosen that her son should be a god rather than in her company but a serf to Eurystheus. One might say something like the mocking remark of the Spartan when some one bade him in a storm to summon the Dioscuri.

It appears to be the mark of a lover to keep the object of his love from sharing in hardships and of the beloved to want to share them: the conduct of both is reasonable. For nothing ought to be so painful to a friend as not to see his friend; but it seems that he ought not to choose what is for his own interest. That is why men keep their friends from sharing; for it is enough that they fare ill, so that they may not show themselves considering their own interest and choosing delight at the cost of a friend's pain, ***[65] Again, being relieved by not bearing their troubles alone. But since both well-

65 Susemihl marks a lacuna.

being and being together are desirable, it is plain that being together along with a smaller good is in a way more desirable than enjoying a greater good apart. But since the weight to be attached to being together is not clear, men differ: some[66] say that being together in all things is the mark of friendship—for instance, they say that it is more pleasant to dine together having the same food; others do not want that, since[67] if one takes extreme cases they agree that it is better to suffer intense adversity together than intense good fortune apart.[68]

There is something similar in the case of ill-fortune. For sometimes we want our friends to be absent and we want to give them no pain, when they are not going to be of any use to us; and sometimes we find it pleasantest for them to be present. But this contrariety is quite reasonable. For it happens in consequence of what we have said before: because in the abstract we avoid contemplating a friend in pain or in a poor state, as we should ourselves so placed; yet to see a friend is as pleasant as anything can be (for the reason we have stated), and to see him not ill if you are ill yourself. So whichever of these two is the pleasanter decides us whether to wish the friend present or not.

This also happens, for the same reason, in the case of the worse sort of men; for they are most ambitious that their friends should not fare well and not be absent if they themselves have to fare badly.[69] That is why sometimes they kill their beloved along with themselves. For they would perceive their own trouble the more, just as one who remembered that once he had fared well would feel it more than if he thought himself always to fare ill.

---

66 Reading οἱ μὲν καί (Spengel) for οἶον καί (Susemihl prints Casaubon's οἴονται).

67 Reading ἐπειδή (Rackham) for ἐπεὶ δέ.

68 The text of this sentence is uncertain: Susemihl marks two lacunas.

69 Reading ἀπεῖναι for εἶναι and ἂν ἀνάγκη for ἀνάγκαι (after Fritzsche).

10

VIRTUE IN GENERAL

ONE MIGHT RAISE THE PROBLEM WHETHER ONE CAN USE each thing both for its natural purpose and otherwise, and in the latter case either *qua* itself or coincidentally. For instance, one might use the eye for seeing, and also for misseeing by squinting, so that one thing appears as two. Both these uses are due to the eye being an eye; but it is possible to use the eye in another way—coincidentally (for instance, if one could sell or eat it).[1] Knowledge may be used similarly; it is possible to use it truly or to err: for instance, when a man voluntarily writes incorrectly, thus using knowledge as ignorance, like a person using his hand as a foot—dancing-girls sometimes use the foot as a hand and the hand as a foot.

If, then, all the virtues are kinds of knowledge, one might use justice also as injustice, and so one would be unjust and do unjust actions from justice, as ignorant things may be done from knowledge. If this is impossible, it is evident that the virtues are not kinds of knowledge. And even if ignorance cannot proceed from knowledge, but only error and the doing of the same things as proceed from ignorance, certainly from justice one will not act as from injustice.

Since wisdom is knowledge and something true, it may behave like knowledge: one might act foolishly out of wisdom, and commit the errors of the foolish. But if the use of each thing as such were single, then in so acting men would be acting wisely. Over other kinds of knowledge, then, there is something authoritative that diverts them; but how can

---

1 The text is uncertain.

there be any knowledge that diverts the most authoritative   10
of all? There is no longer any knowledge to do this. But it will
not be virtue, either, for wisdom uses that; for the virtue of
the ruler uses that of the ruled. Then what will it be?

Perhaps the situation is like that of incontinence, which is
said to be a vice of the irrational part of the soul, the incontinent man being a kind of self-indulgent man who retains his
intelligence. But if so, supposing appetite to be strong it will
twist him and he will calculate in the contrary way. Or is it   15
plain[2] that if there is virtue in this part but ignorance in the
reason, their roles will be reversed? So it will be possible to
use justice unjustly[3] and badly, and wisdom foolishly.

Hence the contraries of this will also be possible. For it is   20
absurd that depravity occurring sometimes in the irrational
part should twist virtue in the calculating part and make the
man ignorant, but that virtue in the irrational part, when ignorance is present in the rational,[4] should not twist the latter
and make the man assess things wisely and as he ought, and
again, that wisdom in the calculating part should not make
the self-indulgence in the irrational part act temperately.
(This is what continence seems to be.) And therefore it will   25
be possible to act wisely out of ignorance,

These consequences are absurd, especially that of acting
wisely out of ignorance; for we certainly do not see this in
any other case—for instance, self-indulgence does not twist
medical or grammatical knowledge; and virtue, if it is contrary, does not[5] twist ignorance; for it lacks the superiority.   30
Rather, virtue in general has this kind of relation to vice in
general. For whatever the just man can do, the unjust can do;
and in general the capacity to do something includes the
capacity not to do it. And so it is plain that wisdom goes

---

2 Reading ἢ ἔστι (Jackson) for ἡ σφι (Susemihl marks two lacunae).

3 Reading τ᾿ οὐ (Jackson) for τό.

4 The text of this sentence is uncertain (Susemihl marks two lacunae).

5 Reading οὐ for οὖν ὁ and inserting ἡ ἀρετή after ἄγνοιαν (Robinson).

together with those good states of the irrational part,[6] and the Socratic notion that nothing is stronger than wisdom is correct. But when he said knowledge, that was not correct. For wisdom is a virtue and not a sort of knowledge but another kind of cognition.[7]

6 Reading τοῦ ἀλόγου (Susemihl's suggestion) for ἄλλου.
7 Susemihl marks a lacuna here.

11

GOOD FORTUNE

SINCE NOT ONLY WISDOM AND VIRTUE PRODUCE WELL-
doing, but we say also that the fortunate do well, thus supposing that good fortune produces well-doing and the same   1247a
results as knowledge, we must inquire whether or not it is by
nature that one man is fortunate and another not, and what
is the truth about these things. For that there are fortunate
men we see: though foolish they are often successful in matters which fortune controls. Again, in matters involving   5
craftsmanship, fortune too largely enters—for instance,
generalship and navigation. So are they like this because of a
certain state of character, or is it not because of their own
qualities that they get fortunate results? At present men take
the former view, regarding some people as being so by nature: nature produces men with certain qualities so that they   10
differ from birth—just as some are blue-eyed and some
black-eyed ***,[1] so are some fortunate and others unfortunate. For that they do not succeed through wisdom is plain;
for wisdom is not irrational but can give a reason why it
acts as it does; but they cannot say why they succeed—that
would be craftsmanship. Further, it is evident that they are   15
foolish not about other things (that would not be in the least
absurd: for instance, Hippocrates was a geometer, but in
other respects was thought stupid and foolish, and once on a
voyage was robbed of much money by the customs-collectors
at Byzantium, owing to his simplicity, as we are told)—   20
rather, they are foolish in the very matters in which they are

---

1 The manuscripts here have some nonsensical words which defeat
emendation.

fortunate. For of ship-owners it is not the cleverest who are the most fortunate—rather, it is as in throwing dice, where one throws nothing and another throws a six,[2] according to his natural good fortune.

Or is it because they are loved, as they say, by a god, suc-
25 cess being something coming from without, as a badly built vessel often sails better, not owing to itself but because it has a good helmsman? So the fortunate man[3] has a good helms-man, namely, a spirit. But it is absurd that a god or a spirit should love such a man and not the best and most wise of men. If, then, success must be due either to nature or to in-
30 telligence or to some sort of protection, and the latter two are excluded, then the fortunate must be so by nature.

And yet nature is the cause of what is always or for the most part so, fortune of the contrary. If, then, it is thought that unexpected success is due to fortune—and that one is fortunate, if at all, then because of fortune—the cause is not
35 the sort that produces always or usually the same result.[4] Further, if a person succeeds or fails because he is a certain sort of man, just as a man sees badly because he is blue-eyed, then it is not fortune but nature that is the cause; and so he is not fortunate but rather naturally endowed. So we must say that the people we call fortunate are not so because of for-
1247b tune. Therefore they are not fortunate; for the fortunate are those whose[5] goods are caused by good fortune.

But if this is so, then does fortune not exist at all? Or does it exist but is not a cause? It must both exist and be a cause. It will, then, cause good things and bad things to certain peo-ple. But if it is to be wholly removed, and we ought to say that
5 nothing happens by fortune, and if we say that fortune is a

2 Adding ἐξ after βάλλει (Jackson). Susemihl prints πολύ ('much') after the Latin translation.

3 Omitting ἀλλά (Fritzsche), reading οὕτως (Fritzsche) for οὗτος, and add-ing ὁ before εὐτυχής (Susemihl's suggestion).

4 The text of this sentence is uncertain.

5 Reading εὐτυχεῖς... ὅσοις (Jackson) for τυχῆς... ὅσων.

cause because, though there is some other cause, we do not see it (that is why in defining fortune some make it a cause beyond human calculation, taking it to be a natural factor)—this would be another question.

Since we see people who are fortunate once only, why should they not succeed again and again for the same reason?[6] For the same cause produces the same effect.[7] Then this will not be a matter of fortune. Rather, when the same event follows from[8] indefinite and undetermined antecedents, it will be good or bad, but there will not be knowledge of it by experience,[9] since otherwise some would have learned to be fortunate, or even—as Socrates said—all types of knowledge would have been kinds of good fortune. What, then, prevents such things happening to a man often in succession, not because they must but as (say) one might continually throw a lucky number with the dice?

What then? Are there not in the soul impulses, some from calculation and others from irrational desire, the latter being the earlier? For if the desire arising from appetite for the pleasant is natural, everything would by nature march towards the good. If, then, some have a natural endowment (like singers[10] who have not learned how to sing), and if they do well by nature and move without the aid of reason in the direction[11] given them by nature, and crave for what they ought and when they ought and how they ought—such men will be successful, even if they are foolish and irrational, just as the others will sing[12] well though not able to teach

---

6 Omitting ἀλλά and reading τὸ αὐτὸ κατορθώσαιεν (Jackson) for τὸ ἀποκατορθῶσαι ἕν.

7 Reading τοῦ... αὐτοῦ τὸ αὐτό (Spengel) for τὸ... αὐτὸ τοῦτο.

8 Adding ἀπό before ἀπείρων (Jackson).

9 Reading ἐμπειρίαν (after the Latin translation) for ἀπειρίαν.

10 Reading ᾠδικοί (Sylburg) for ἄδικοι. (But the text of the whole sentence is uncertain.)

11 Adding ᾗ before ἡ φύσις (Jackson—Susemihl marks a lacuna).

12 Reading ᾄσονται (Sylburg) for ἔσονται.

singing. And those men are fortunate who for the most part succeed without the aid of reason. Men, then, who are fortunate will be so by nature.

Perhaps, however, good fortune is spoken of in several ways. For some things are done from impulse and are due to choice, and others not but rather the contrary; and if, in the former cases, they succeed where they seem to have calculated badly, we say that they have been fortunate; and again, in the latter cases, if they wanted a different or lesser good than they got.[13] The former may be fortunate by nature; for the impulse and the desire were for what they ought to be, and they succeeded, but the calculation was silly. People in this case, when their calculation seems incorrect and fortune is the cause of it, are saved by their desire, which is correct; but sometimes a man calculates again in this way owing to appetite and turns out unfortunate. But in the other cases how can the good fortune be due to a natural endowment in desire and appetite? Yet surely the good fortune here and in the other case is the same, or else there is more than one sort of good fortune and chance is of two kinds.[14]

Since we see some men fortunate against all knowledge and correct calculation, it is plain that the cause of good fortune must be something different. But is it good fortune or not by which[15] a man craves for what he ought and when he ought, though for him[16] human calculation could not lead to this? For that for which the appetite is natural[17] is not altogether uncalculating, though it is corrupted by something. A man, then, is thought to be fortunate, because fortune is the cause of things against reason, and this is against reason (for it is against knowledge and the universal). But probably it

---

13 The text of this sentence is uncertain.

14 Placing καὶ τυχὴ διττή after εὐτυχίαι (Spengel).

15 Reading ἤ (Sylburg) for ἡ.

16 Reading ᾧ (Jackson) for τό.

17 Reading οὐ γε (Jackson) for οὔτε (which Susemihl emends to οὐδέ).

does not spring from fortune, but seems so for the above reason. So this argument shows not that good fortune is due to nature, but that not all who seem to be fortunate are successful owing to fortune, but rather owing to nature; nor does it show that fortune is not the cause of anything—only not of all that it seems to be the cause of.   15

One might raise the problem whether fortune is the cause of someone's craving what he ought and when he ought. If so, will it not be the cause of everything, even of thought and deliberation? For one does not deliberate after previous deliberation which itself presupposed deliberation: rather, there is some originating principle. Nor does one think after   20 thinking previously to thinking, and so *ad infinitum*. Intelligence, then, is not the origin of thinking nor deliberation of deliberation. What, then, can be the origin except fortune? Thus everything will come from fortune.

Perhaps there is an origin with no other outside it, and this can act in this sort of way by being such as it is.[18] The object of our investigation is this: what is the origin of movement in the soul? The answer is plain: as in the universe, so in   25 the soul, it is god. For in a sense the divine element in us moves everything. The origin of reasoning is not reasoning but something greater. What could be greater even than knowledge and intelligence but god? For virtue is an instrument of intelligence. And for this reason, as I said earlier,[19] those are called fortunate who, whatever they start on,[20] suc-   30 ceed in it although they lack reason. And deliberation is of no advantage to them; for they have in them an originating principle that is better than intelligence and deliberation, while the others have reason but not this: they have inspiration but they cannot deliberate. For, though lacking reason,

18 With Walzer reading διὰ τό for διὰ τί (which Susemihl excises) and omitting τῷ.

19 Omitting οἱ (Jackson).

20 Adding ἅ after οἵ (Jackson).

they succeed, and, more than that of wise men and philosophers, their divination is speedy.[21] One might almost assume[22] that it is divination based on reasoning; but some of
them do it by experience, others by a habitual use of
reflection;[23] and these belong to the divine element,[24] which
sees well both the future and the present, even in those in
whom the reason is disengaged. That is why the atrabilious
dream well. For the originating principle seems to become
stronger when the reason is disengaged—just as the blind
remember better, being disengaged from the visible,[25] since
their memory is stronger.

    It is evident, then, that there are two kinds of good for-
tune, the one divine (that is why the fortunate seem to succeed owing to god) and the other natural. Men of this sort
succeed in accordance with their impulse, the others against
to their impulse, but both lack reason. And the one has per-
sistent good fortune, the other not.

21 The text of this sentence is uncertain.

22 Reading ὑπολαβεῖν (Ross) for ἀπολαβεῖν.

23 The text of this sentence is uncertain.

24 Reading θείῳ (Spengel) for the received θέῳ ('god').

25 The text is uncertain.

12

GENTLEMANLINESS

ABOUT EACH VIRTUE BY ITSELF WE HAVE ALREADY SPOKEN; and since we have distinguished their capacities separately, we must describe clearly the virtue that arises out of their combination, which we call[1] gentlemanliness. That he who truly receives this epithet must have the separate virtues is evident: it cannot be otherwise with anything else either— no one is healthy in his entire body and yet healthy in no part of it, but all the parts, or most and the most authoritative of them, must be in the same condition as the whole.

Goodness and gentlemanliness differ not only in name but also in themselves. For all goods have ends which are desirable for their own sake. Of them, those are noble which, existing all of them for their own sake, are praiseworthy. For these are those from which arise praiseworthy acts and which are themselves praiseworthy, such as justice itself and just acts, and also temperate acts[2] (for temperance is praiseworthy). But health is not praiseworthy, for its product is not; nor strenuous action, for strength is not. These are good but not praiseworthy. Induction makes this plain about the rest, too.

A good man is one for whom the natural goods are good. For the goods men fight for and think the greatest—honour, riches, bodily virtues, good fortune, and power—are naturally good but can be harmful to some because of their states of character. For neither the foolish nor the unjust nor the self-indulgent would get any good from the use of them, any

1 Reading καλοῦμεν (Jackson) for ἐκαλοῦμεν ('we called').
2 Reading αἱ (Richards) for οἱ before σώφρονες.

more than an invalid would from the food of a healthy man, or one weak and maimed from the equipment of one in health and sound in limb. A man is gentlemanly because those goods which are noble are possessed by him for them-

35 selves, and because he performs noble acts for their own sake, the noble being the virtues and the deeds which arise from virtue. There is also a political state of character, such as the Spartans have, or others like them might have. It is something like this: there are some who think one should have virtue but for the sake of the natural goods; and that is

1249a why such men are good (for the natural goods are good for them), but they do not have gentlemanliness. For they do not have the things that are noble for their own sake, which the gentlemanly choose[3]—and not only them but also those

5 which are not noble by nature but, being good by nature, are noble for them. For something is noble when that for the sake of which men act and desire it is noble—that is why[4] for the gentleman the naturally good is noble. What is just is noble, justice is proportion to worth, and he is worthy of these things. What is fitting is noble, and to him these

10 things—riches, high birth, and power—are fitting. So for the gentleman things advantageous are also noble; but for the many they do not coincide—for things good in the abstract are not good for them as they are for the good man. But for the gentleman they are also noble; for he does many

15 noble deeds by means of them. The man who thinks he ought to have the virtues for the sake of external goods performs noble acts coincidentally. Gentlemanliness, then, is complete virtue.

3 Adding ἅ after δι' αὐτά.
4 Reading διό (Solomon) for διότι.

13

CONCLUDING REMARKS

AS FOR PLEASURE, WE HAVE SAID WHAT IT IS AND IN WHAT way good—we have said that what is pleasant in the abstract is also noble, and what is good in the abstract is pleasant. Pleasure only arises in action: therefore the truly happy man will also live most pleasantly—and that this should be so is no idle claim of men.

Since the doctor has a standard by reference to which he assesses what is healthy for the body and what is not, and up to what point each thing ought to be done and, if[1] well done, is healthy,[2] while if less or more it is not, so too in regard to actions and choices of what is naturally good but not praiseworthy, the virtuous man should have a standard both of disposition and of choice and avoidance with regard to the amount, whether great or small, of wealth and of good fortune. This—as was said earlier—is as reasoning directs; but that is as if one said in regard to diet that the standard should be as medicine and its reasoning direct. And this, though true, is not illuminating.

One must, here as elsewhere, live with reference to the ruling element and to the state that corresponds to the exercise of the ruling element, as the slave must live with reference to that of the master, and each of us by the rule proper to him. Since man is by nature composed of a ruler and a ruled, each of us should live according to his own ruling element. But this is of two kinds; for medicine rules in one way, health in another, and the former is for the sake of latter.

20

1249b

5

10

---

1 Adding εἰ before εὖ (Collingwood).

2 Reading ὑγιεινόν (after the Latin translation) for ὑγιαῖνον.

And so it is with the contemplative faculty; for god is not a
ruler who commands: rather, he is that for the sake of which
wisdom commands (that for the sake of which has two
forms, and has been distinguished elsewhere); for god needs
nothing. What choice, then, or possession of the natural
goods—whether bodily goods, wealth, friends, or other
things—will most produce the contemplation of god, that is
best, and this is the noblest standard. Any choice that
through lack or excess hinders one from serving and contemplating god is base. This a man possesses in his soul, and
this is the best standard for the soul—to perceive the irrational part of the soul, as such, as little as possible.

So much, then, for the standard of gentlemanliness and
the aim of things good in the abstract.

NICOMACHEAN ETHICS

FIRST OXFORD TRANSLATION:
W. D. Ross

GREEK TEXT:
I. Bywater, OCT

CONTENTS

INTRODUCTION

1094a

EVERY CRAFT AND EVERY INQUIRY, AND SIMILARLY AC-
tions and choices, are thought to aim at some good; that is
why the good has rightly been declared to be that at which all
things aim. But a certain difference is found among ends:
some are activities, others are products apart from the activities that produce them. Where there are ends apart from the
actions, it is the nature of the products to be better than the
activities. Now, as there are many actions, crafts, and sciences, their ends also are many: the end of medicine is
health, that of shipbuilding a vessel, that of generalship victory, that of economics riches. But where crafts fall under a
single capacity—as bridle-making and the other crafts concerned with the equipment of horses fall under horse-riding,
and this and every military action under generalship, and in
the same way other crafts under yet others—in all of these
the ends of the master-crafts are more desirable than all the
subordinate ends; for it is for the sake of the former that the
latter are pursued. It makes no difference whether the activities themselves are the ends of the actions, or something else
apart from the activities, as in the case of the sciences just
mentioned.

   If, then, there is some end in matters of action which we
desire for its own sake (everything else being desired for the
sake of this), and if we do not choose everything for the sake
of something else (for in this way the process goes on to infinity, so that the desire is empty and vain), plainly this must
be the good and the chief good. Will not the knowledge of it,
then, have a great influence on life? Shall we not, like archers
who have a mark to aim at, be more likely to hit upon what
we should? If so, we must try to determine, in outline at
least, what it is, and of which of the sciences or capacities it is

the business. It would seem to belong to the most authoritative craft and that which is most truly the master craft. Politics appears to be of this nature. For it is this that ordains
1094b   which of the sciences should be studied in a State, and which
each class of citizens should learn and up to what point they
should learn them; and we see even the most highly esteemed of capacities to fall under this—for instance generalship, economics, rhetoric. Since politics uses the rest of the
5   sciences, and since, again, it legislates as to what we are to do
and what we are to abstain from, the end of this science must
include those of the others, so that this end must be the
human good. For even if the end is the same for an individual and for a State, that of the State seems at all events something greater and more complete both to attain and to preserve; for though we should be content to attain the end for a
10   single individual, it is more noble and more divine to attain it
for a nation or for States. These, then, are the ends at which
our inquiry, being a sort of political science, aims.

Our discussion will be adequate if it is as illuminating as
the subject-matter allows; for precision is not to be looked
for alike in all discussions, any more than in the products of
15   the crafts. Now noble and just actions, which political science investigates, exhibit much variety and fluctuation, so
that they are thought to exist only by convention and not by
nature. And goods also exhibit a similar fluctuation because
they bring harm to many people: before now men have been
undone by their riches, and others by their courage. We must
20   be content, then, in speaking about such things and setting
out from such things to indicate the truth roughly and in
outline, and in speaking about things which hold only for
the most part and setting out from such things to reach conclusions of that kind. In the same spirit, therefore, should
each of our statements be received; for it is the mark of an
educated man to look for precision in each class of things
25   just so far as the nature of the subject admits: it is evidently
similar to accept probable reasoning from a mathematician
and to demand demonstrations from a rhetorician.

Each man assesses rightly the things he knows, and of these he is a good assessor. And so the man who has been educated in a subject is a good assessor of that subject, and the man who has received an all-round education is a good assessor *tout court*. That is why a young man is not an appropriate student of political science; for he is inexperienced in the actions that occur in life, but its discussions start from these and are about these; and, further, since he tends to follow his emotions, his study will be vain and unprofitable, 5 because the end aimed at is not knowledge but action. And it makes no difference whether he is young in years or youthful in character: the deficiency does not depend on time, but on his living and pursuing things as his emotions direct. For to such persons, as to the incontinent, knowledge brings no profit; but to those who desire and act in ac- 10 cordance with reason knowledge about such matters will be of great benefit.

These remarks about the student, the way in which our statements should be received, and the purpose of the inquiry, may be taken as our preface.

I

HAPPINESS AND THE
HUMAN GOOD

LET US TAKE UP OUR INQUIRY AND STATE, IN VIEW OF THE
fact that all knowledge and choice aims at some good, what
it is that we say political science aims at and what is the highest of all goods among matters of action. Verbally, pretty well
everyone agrees; for both the general run of people and the
refined say that it is happiness, and assume that living well
and faring well are the same thing as being happy; but with
regard to what happiness is they differ, and the general run
do not give the same account as men of understanding do.
For the former think it is some clear and evident thing, like
pleasure or riches or honour—some one thing and some another, and often the same man identifies it with different
things (with health when he is ill, with riches when he is
poor). But, conscious of their ignorance, they admire those
who talk about some great thing that is above their heads.
Now some thought that apart from these many goods there
is another which is good in itself and which causes the goodness of all these.

To examine all the beliefs that have been held would no
doubt be somewhat fruitless: it is enough to examine those
that are most prevalent or that seem to have some reason in
their favour.

Let us not fail to notice, however, that there is a difference
between arguments from the originating principles and
those to the principles. For Plato was right in raising this
problem and inquiring: 'Are we on the way from the principles or to the principles?'—as if in a race-course, from the
judges' stand to the end of the track or *vice versa*. For, while

we must begin with what is familiar, things are so in two ways—some to us, some in the abstract. Perhaps, then, we must begin with things familiar to us. That is why any ade- 5 quate student of what is noble and just and generally about political matters must have been brought up in good habits. For the facts are principles, and if they are sufficiently plain to him, he will not need the reason why as well; and someone who has been well brought up possesses or can easily grasp the principles. And as for him who neither posseses nor can grasp them, let him hear the words of Hesiod:[1]

Far best is he who knows all things himself;
Good, he that hearkens when men counsel right;   10
but he who neither knows, nor lays to heart
another's wisdom, is a useless wight.

LET US RESUME OUR DISCUSSION AT THE POINT AT WHICH we digressed. To judge from their lives, most men, and men 15 of the most vulgar type, assume (not without reason) that the good and happiness are pleasure—that is why they cherish the life of the voluptuary. For there are three prominent types of life: the one just mentioned, the political, and thirdly the contemplative life.

Now the mass of mankind are evidently quite slavish in 20 their tastes, choosing a life suitable to cattle; but they get some reason for their view from the fact that many of those in positions of power share the tastes of Sardanapallus.

Those who are refined and active identify happiness with honour; for this is pretty much the end of the political life. But it seems too superficial to be what we are looking for, since it is thought to depend on those who bestow honour 25 rather than on him who receives it, whereas the good we divine to be something of one's own and not easily taken away. Further, men seem to pursue honour in order that they may be convinced of their own goodness—at least, it is by men of

1 *Works and Days* 293–297.

wisdom that they look to be honoured, and among those
who know them, and on the ground of their virtue. Plainly,
30   then, according to them at any rate, virtue is better. And perhaps one might even assume this rather than honour to be
the end of the political life. But even this appears somewhat
incomplete; for possession of virtue seems compatible with
being asleep or inactive throughout one's life and, further,
1096a   with the greatest sufferings and misfortunes. But a man who
was living so no one would call happy, unless he were defending a thesis. But enough of this; for the subject has been
sufficiently treated in our popular discussions.

5   Third comes the contemplative life, which we shall consider later.

The life of money-making is one undertaken perforce, and
riches are plainly not the good we are looking for; for they are
useful and for the sake of something else. That is why one
might rather assume that the aforenamed objects are ends;
for they are cherished for themselves. But evidently not even
10   these are ends—although many arguments have been thrown
down in support of them. Let us then dismiss them.

WE HAD PERHAPS BETTER CONSIDER THE UNIVERSAL
good and consider the problem of what is meant by it, although such an inquiry is made an uphill one by the fact that
the Forms have been introduced by friends of ours. Yet it
might perhaps be thought that it is better, and we ought for
15   the sake of the truth to destroy even what is our own, especially as we are philosophers; for, while both are dear, piety
requires us to honour truth above our friends.

Those who introduced this belief did not posit Ideas of
things within which they recognized priority and posterior-
ity (which is the reason why they did not set up an Idea of
20   the numbers). But things are called good both in quiddity[2]
and in relation, and that which is *per se* and substance is
prior in nature to the relative (for the latter is like an off-

2 Deleting, with Spengel, καὶ ἐν τῷ πόσῳ ('and in quantity').

shoot and accident of what is); so that there will not be an Idea common to all these goods. Further, since things are said to be good in as many ways as they are said to be (for things are called good both in quiddity, as god and intelli- 25 gence, and in quality, as the virtues, and in quantity, as that which is the appropriate amount, and in relation, as the useful, and in time, as the right opportunity, and in place, as habitat, and so on), plainly the good cannot be something universal, common and single; for then it would not have been predicated in all the categories but in one only. Further, since of the things answering to one Idea there is one 30 science, there would have been one science of all the goods; but as it is there are many sciences even of the things that fall under one category—for instance opportunity (for opportunity in war is studied by generalship and in disease by medicine), and the appropriate amount in food is studied by medicine and in exertion by gymnastics. And one might raise the problem of what in the world they mean by 'a thing itself', if in man himself and in a particular man the account 1096b of man is one and the same. For in so far as they are men, they will in no respect differ; and if this is so, neither will there be a difference in so far as they are good. Again it will not be any the more good for being eternal, since that which lasts long is no whiter than that which perishes in a day. (The 5 Pythagoreans seem to give a more plausible account of the good, when they place the one in the column of goods; and it is they that Speusippus seems to have followed. But let us discuss these matters elsewhere.)

An objection to what we have said may be discerned in the fact that they have not been speaking about all goods, and 10 that the goods that are pursued and cherished for themselves are called good by reference to a single Form, while those which tend to produce or to preserve these somehow or to prevent their contraries are called so by reference to these, and in a different manner. Plainly, then, goods must be spoken of in two ways, and some must be good in themselves, the others by reason of these. Let us separate, then, things 15

good in themselves from things beneficial, and consider
whether the former are called good by reference to a single
Idea. What sort of goods would one call good in themselves?
Is it those that are pursued even when isolated from others,
such as intelligence, sight, and certain pleasures and honours? For even if we pursue these also for the sake of something else, yet one would place them among things good in
20   themselves. Or is nothing other than the Idea good in itself?
In that case the Form will be pointless. But if the things we
have named are also good in themselves, the description of
the good will have to appear as something identical in them
all, as that of whiteness is identical in snow and in white lead.
But the description of the goodness of honour, wisdom, and
25   pleasure, differs from case to case. The good, therefore, is
not something common answering to one Idea.

But then in what way are things called good? They are not
like the things that only chance to have the same name. Then
is it by being derived from one thing or by all contributing to
one thing? Or rather by analogy? For as sight is in the body,
30   so is intelligence in the soul, and so on in other cases. But
perhaps these subjects had better be dismissed for the present; for precision about them would be more appropriate to
another branch of philosophy. And similarly with regard to
the Idea: even if there is some one good which is predicated
in common of goods or is capable of separate and independent existence, plainly it could not be a matter of human action or acquisition; but we are now looking for something of
that sort. Perhaps, however, someone might think it worth-
1097a   while to have knowledge of it with a view to the goods that
are matters of action and acquisition; for having this as a sort
of pattern we shall know better the goods that are good for
us, and if we know them shall attain them. This argument
has some plausibility, but it seems to clash with the proce-
5   dure of the sciences; for all of these, though they aim at some
good and look to supply the deficiency of it, leave on one side
the knowledge of it. Yet that all craftsmen should be ignorant of, and should not even look for so great an aid is not

reasonable. It is problematic, too, to see how a weaver or a carpenter will be benefited in regard to his own craft by knowing this goodness itself, or how the man who has viewed the Idea itself will be a better doctor or general. For a doctor seems not even to consider health in this way, but the health of man—or perhaps rather of a particular man; for it is individuals that he is healing. But enough of these topics.

Let us again return to the good we are looking for and ask what it can be. It is evidently different in different actions and crafts: it is different in medicine, in generalship, and in the other crafts likewise. What then is the good of each of them? Surely that for whose sake everything else is done. In medicine this is health, in generalship victory, in building a house, elsewhere something else, and in every action and choice the end; for it is for the sake of this that all men do whatever else they do. Therefore, if there is an end for all that we do, this will be the good in matters of action, and if there are more than one, these will be the goods.

So the argument has by a different course reached the same point; but we must try to state this more illuminatingly. Since there are evidently several ends, and we choose some of them (for instance riches, flutes, and in general instruments) for the sake of something else, plainly not all ends are complete ends; but the chief good is evidently something complete. Therefore, if there is only one complete end, this will be what we are looking for, and if there are several, the most complete of them. Now we call that which is in itself worthy of pursuit more complete than that which is worthy of pursuit for the sake of something else, and that which is never desirable for the sake of something else more complete than the things that are desirable both in themselves and for the sake of that other thing, and we call complete *tout court* that which is always desirable in itself and never for the sake of something else.

Now such a thing happiness, above all else, is held to be; for this we choose always for itself and never for the sake of something else, whereas honour, pleasure, intelligence, and

223

every virtue we choose indeed for themselves (for if nothing
resulted from them we should still choose each of them), but
5   we choose them also for the sake of happiness, assuming
that through them we shall be happy. But happiness no one
chooses for the sake of these, nor, in general, for anything
other than itself.

From the point of view of self-sufficiency the same result
evidently follows; for the final good is thought to be self-
sufficient. Now by self-sufficient we do not mean that which
is sufficient for a man by himself living a solitary life, but also
10   for parents, children, wife, and in general for his friends and
fellow citizens, since man is political by nature. But some
limit must be set to this; for if we extend it to parents of parents[3] and descendants and friends' friends we are in for an
infinite series. Let us examine this question, however, on another occasion; the self-sufficient we now define as that
15   which when isolated makes life desirable and lacking in
nothing; and such we think happiness to be. Further we
think it most desirable of all things, without being counted
as one good thing among others—if so counted it is plainly
more desirable by the addition of even the least of goods; for
that which is added yields a superiority in goods, and of
20   goods the greater is always more desirable. Happiness, then,
is something complete and self-sufficient, and is the end in
matters of action.

Perhaps, however, to say that happiness is the chief good
seems a platitude, and a clearer account of what it is is still
desired. This might perhaps be given, if we could first grasp
25   what a man's task is. For just as for a flute-player, a sculptor,
or any craftsman, and, in general, for anyone who has a task
and an action, the good and the 'well' is thought to reside in
the task, so would it seem to be for man, if he has a task.
Have the carpenter, then, and the tanner certain tasks and
30   actions, and man none? Is man naturally idle? Or as eye,
hand, foot, and in general each of the parts evidently have a

3 Adding τῶν γονεῶν (Rassow).

task, may one lay it down that man similarly has a task apart from all these? What then can this be? Life is evidently common even to plants, but we are looking for what is proper to man. Let us exclude, therefore, the life of nutrition and growth. Next there would be a life of sense-perception, but it also is evidently common to the horse, the ox, and every animal. There remains, then, an active life of the element that has reason. (Of this element, one part has reason as being obedient to it, the other as possessing it and exercising thought.) Since this too can be taken in two ways, we must state that life in the sense of activity is what we mean; for this seems to be the stricter use of the term. Now if the task of man is an activity of soul in accordance with reason, or not without reason, and if we say a so-and-so and a virtuous so-and-so have a task which is the same in kind (for instance, a lyre-player and a good lyre-player, and so generally in all cases), superiority in respect of virtue being added to the task (for the task of a lyre-player is to play the lyre, and that of a good lyre-player is to do so well): if this is the case,[4] the human good turns out to be activity of soul in conformity with virtue, and if there are several virtues, in conformity with the best and most complete.

But we must add 'in a complete life'. For one swallow does not make a summer, nor does one day; and so too one day, or a short time, does not make a man blessed and happy.

Let this serve as an outline of the good; for we must presumably first sketch it, and then later fill in the details. But it would seem that anyone is capable of carrying on and articulating what has once been well outlined, and that time is a good discoverer or collaborator in such matters. That is how

4 At this point the manuscripts have the following passage, which Bywater deletes as a repetition:

> ... and if we state that the task of man is a certain kind of life, and that this is an activity of soul or actions involving reason, and that the task of a good man is the good and noble performance of these, and if any action is well performed when it is performed in accordance with the appropriate virtue: if this is the case ...

25   the advances of the crafts have been made; for anyone can
add what is lacking.

We must also remember what has been said before, and
not look for precision in all things alike but in each class of
things such precision as accords with the subject-matter and
so much as is appropriate to the inquiry. For a carpenter and
30   a geometer look for right angles in different ways: the former does so in so far as it is useful for his task, while the latter inquires what it is or what sort of thing it is; for he is a
spectator of the truth. We must act in the same way, then, in
other matters as well, so that our task may not be subordi-
1098b   nated to side-tasks. Nor must we demand the cause in all
matters alike: it is enough in some cases that the fact be well
established, as in the case of the originating principles—the
fact is primary and a principle. Now of principles we consider some by induction, some by sense-perception, some by
5   a certain habituation, and others in other ways. We must try
to investigate each sort in the natural way, and we must take
pains to determine them aright, since they have a great influence on what follows. For the origin is thought to be more
than half of the whole, and many of the questions we ask are
cleared up by it.

We must consider it, however, in the light not only of our
10   conclusion and our premises, but also of what is said about
it; for with a true view all the facts harmonize, but with a
false one they[5] soon clash. Now goods have been divided
into three classes, and some are described as external, others
as relating to soul or to body; and we call those that relate to
15   soul most especially and strictly goods. But we are considering actions and activities relating to soul.[6] Therefore our account must be sound, at least according to this belief, which
is an old one and agreed on by the philosophers. It is correct

5 Deleting τἀληθές (Rassow). The received text reads: 'The true soon
clashes with the false'.

6 Deleting ψυχικάς (Goebel). The received text reads: 'But we consider
that actions and activities of the soul are concerned with the soul'.

also in that we identify the end with certain actions and activity; for thus it falls among goods of the soul and not among external goods. 20

It also harmonizes with our account that the happy man lives well and fares well; for we have more or less defined happiness as a sort of living well and faring well. Also, the characteristics that are looked for in happiness all evidently hold of what we have said. For some people identify happiness with virtue, some with wisdom, others with a kind of understanding, others with these, or one of these, accompa- 25 nied by pleasure or not without pleasure; while others include also external prosperity. Now some of these views have been held by many men and men of old, others by a few reputable men; and it is not reasonable that either of these should be entirely mistaken, but rather that they should be right in at least some one respect or even in most respects.

With those who identify happiness with virtue or some 30 one virtue our account is in harmony; for virtue is expressed in the activity of virtue. But it makes, perhaps, no small difference whether we assume that the chief good lies in possession or in use, in state or in activity. For the state may exist without producing any good result, as in a man who is 1099a asleep or in some other way inactive, but the activity cannot; for it will of necessity be acting, and acting well. And just as in the Olympic Games it is not the most handsome and the strongest that are crowned but those who compete (for it is 5 some of these that are victorious), so those who act correctly win the noble and good things in life.

Their life is also in itself pleasant. For pleasure is a state of soul, and to each man that which he is said to be a lover of is pleasant—for instance a horse to a lover of horses, and a spectacle to a lover of shows—and in the same way just 10 things are pleasant to the lover of justice and in general virtuous things to the lover of virtue. Now for most men their pleasures are in conflict with one another because they are not by nature pleasant. But the lovers of what is noble find pleasant the things that are by nature pleasant; and virtuous

15 actions are such, so that these are pleasant both for such men and also *per se*. Their life, therefore, has no further need of pleasure as a sort of adventitious charm: it has its pleasure in itself. For, besides what we have said, the man who does not delight in noble actions is not even good: no one would call a man just who did not delight in acting justly, nor any
20 man liberal who did not enjoy liberal actions; and similarly in all other cases. If this is so, virtuous actions must be in themselves pleasant. But they are also good and noble, and have each of these attributes in the highest degree, since the virtuous man assesses them well and he assesses in the way we have described.

Happiness, then, is the best, noblest, and most pleasant
25 thing, and these attributes are not severed as in the inscription at Delos—

> Most noble is that which is justest, and best is health;
> But pleasantest is it to win what we love.

30 For all these attributes belong to the best activities; and these, or one—the best—of these, we identify with happiness.

Yet evidently, as we said, it needs the external goods as well; for it is impossible, or not easy, to perform noble acts
1099b without the proper equipment. In many actions we use friends and riches and political power as instruments; and there are some things the lack of which takes the lustre from blessedness, such as good birth, satisfactory children, beauty—for the man who is very ugly in appearance or ill-
5 born or solitary and childless is hardly happy, and perhaps a man would be still less so if he had thoroughly bad children or friends or had lost good children or friends by death. As we said, then, happiness seems to need this sort of prosperity in addition; for which reason some identify happiness with good fortune.[7]

7 Deleting, with Giphanius, the clause which follows in the received text: '... though others identify it with virtue'.

For this reason also the problem is raised, whether happiness is to be acquired by learning or by habituation or some   10
other sort of training, or comes from some divine provi-
dence or again by fortune. Now if there is any gift of the gods
to men, it is reasonable that happiness should be god-given,
and the most surely god-given of all human things inasmuch
as it is the best. But this question would perhaps be more appropriate to another inquiry: happiness, however, even if it
is not god-sent but comes as a result of virtue and some pro-   15
· cess of learning or training, is evidently among the most divine things; for that which is the prize and end of virtue
seems to be the chief good and something divine and blessed.

It will also be widely shared; for all who are not disabled
as regards virtue may win it by a certain kind of learning and   20
care. If it is better to be happy thus than by fortune, it is reasonable that things should be so, since everything that depends on the action of nature is by nature as good as it can
be, and similarly everything that depends on craftsmanship
or any cause, and especially if it depends on the best of all
causes. To entrust to fortune what is greatest and most noble
would be a very defective arrangement.   25

The answer to the question is evident also from the definition; for it has been said to be a certain kind of activity of
soul.[8] Of the remaining goods, some are necessary and others are naturally collaborative and useful as instruments.
And this will be found to agree with what we said at the out-
set; for we stated the end of political science to be the best   30
end, and political science spends most of its care on making
the citizens to be of a certain character, namely good and capable of noble acts.

It is reasonable, then, that we call neither ox nor horse
nor any other of the animals happy; for none of them is ca-   1100a
pable of sharing in such activity. For this reason also a boy is

8 Deleting κατ' ἀρετήν. The received text gives: '. . . a certain kind of activity of soul in accordance with virtue'.

not happy; for he is not yet capable of such acts, owing to his age; and boys who are called happy are being felicitated by reason of the hopes we have for them. For there is required,
5   as we said, not only complete virtue but also a complete life, since many changes occur in life, and all manner of fortunes, and the most prosperous may encounter great disasters in old age, as is told of Priam in the Trojan Cycle; and one who has experienced such fortunes and has ended wretchedly no one calls happy.

10   MUST NO ONE AT ALL, THEN, BE CALLED HAPPY WHILE HE lives? Must we, as Solon says, see the end? And if we are to lay this down, is it also the case that a man is happy when he is dead? Or is not this quite absurd, especially for us who say
15   that happiness is an activity? But if we do not call the dead happy, and if Solon means not this but that one can then safely call a man blessed as being at last beyond evils and misfortunes, this also affords matter for discussion; for both evil and good are thought to exist for a dead man, as much as
20   for one who is alive but does not perceive them—for instance honours and dishonours and the successes and misfortunes of children and in general of descendants. This also presents a problem; for though a man has lived blessedly up to old age and has had a death that befits his life, many re-
25   verses may befall his descendants—some of them may be good and attain a life they are worthy of, while with others the contrary may be the case; and plainly too the degrees of relationship between them and their ancestors may vary indefinitely. It would be absurd, then, if the dead man were to share in these changes and become at one time happy, at an-
30   other wretched; while it would also be absurd if the fortunes of the descendants did not for some time have some effect on their ancestors.

But we must return to our first problem; for perhaps the present question might be considered from that point of view. Now if we must see the end and only then call a man blessed, not as being blessed but as having been so before, surely it is absurd that when he is happy what holds of him will not be true of him because we do not want to call living men happy, on account of the changes that may befall them, and because we have supposed happiness to be something lasting and by no means easily changed, while one and the same man may suffer many turns of fortune's wheel. For plainly if we were to follow his fortunes, we should often call the same man happy and again wretched, making the happy man out to be a chameleon and insecurely based. Or is following his fortunes in this way quite incorrect? Doing well or badly does not depend on these, but human life, as we said, needs these as well, while virtuous activities or their contrary control happiness or the contrary.

The problem we have now discussed testifies in favour of our definition. For no human task has as much firmness as virtuous activities do (they are thought to be more lasting even than knowledge), and of these themselves the most valuable are more lasting because those who are blessed spend their life most readily and most continuously in them; for this seems to be the reason why we do not forget them. The attribute in question, then, will belong to the happy man, and he will be happy throughout his life; for always, or in preference to everything else, he will do and contemplate what is virtuous, and he will bear the fortunes of life most nobly and altogether decorously, if he is truly good and four-square beyond blame.

Now many things happen by fortune, things differing in importance: small pieces of good fortune or of its opposite plainly do not weigh down the scales of life one way or the other, but a multitude of great ones if they turn out well will make life more blessed (for not only are they themselves such as to add adornment to life, but the way a man deals with them may be noble and virtuous), while if they turn out ill they crush and maim blessedness (for they both bring pain with them and hinder many activities). Yet even in these

1100b

5

10

15

20

25

30

nobility shines through, when a man bears gracefully many great misfortunes, not through insensitivity but through breeding and pride.

If, as we said, it is activities that control life, no blessed man can become wretched; for he will never perform actions that are hateful and base. For the man who is truly good and wise, we think, bears all the fortunes of life becomingly and always acts as nobly as the circumstances allow, just as a good general makes the best military use of the army at his command and a shoemaker makes the best shoes out of the hides that are given him; and so with all other craftsmen. And if this is the case, the happy man can never become wretched—though he will not be blessed if he meets with fortunes like those of Priam.

Nor, again, is he many-coloured and changeable; for he will not be moved from his happy state easily or by any ordinary misadventures but only by many great ones—and in that case he will not recover his happiness in a short time but (if at all) only in a long and complete one in which he has attained great and noble successes.

What then prevents our saying that he is happy who exercises himself in conformity with complete virtue and is sufficiently equipped with external goods, not for some chance period but throughout a complete life? Or must we add 'and who will live thus and die as befits his life'? Certainly the future is obscure to us, while happiness, we claim, is an end and something in every way complete. If so, we shall call blessed those among living men in whom these conditions are, and are to be, fulfilled—but humanly blessed. So much for these questions.

THAT THE FORTUNES OF DESCENDANTS AND OF ALL A MAN'S friends should not affect his happiness at all seems a very unfriendly doctrine, and one contrary to the beliefs men hold; but since the events that happen are numerous and admit of all sorts of difference, and some come more near to us and others less so, it is evidently a long—indeed an endless—

task to discuss each in detail: a general outline will perhaps suffice. If, then, as some of a man's own misfortunes have a certain weight and influence on his life while others seem lighter, so too it is with those of all our friends, and if it makes a difference whether the various experiences are had by the living or by the dead (much more even than whether lawless and terrible deeds are presupposed in a tragedy or done on the stage), this difference also must be taken into account; or rather, perhaps, we must take into account that it is a problem whether the dead share in any good or evil. For it seems, from these considerations, that even if anything whether good or the contrary penetrates to them, it must be something dim and small, either in the abstract or for them, or if not, at least it must be such in degree and kind as not to make happy those who are not happy nor to take away their blessedness from those who are. The successes and misfortunes of friends, then, seem to have some effects on the dead, but effects of such a kind and degree as neither to make the happy unhappy nor to produce any other change of the kind.

THESE QUESTIONS HAVING BEEN ANSWERED, LET US CON-sider whether happiness is among the things that are praise-worthy or rather among the things that are valuable; for plainly it is not to be placed among capacities. Everything that is praiseworthy seems to be praiseworthy because it is of a certain character and is related somehow to something else; for we praise the just man and the courageous man and in general both the good man and virtue because of the actions and deeds involved, and we praise the strong man and the good runner, and so on, because he is of a certain kind and is related in a certain way to something good and virtuous. This is plain also from the praises of the gods; for although it is evidently ridiculous that the gods should be referred to our standard, this is done because praise involves a reference, as we said. But if praise is for things such as we have described, plainly what applies to the best things is not praise, but something greater and better, as is indeed evident; for what we do to the gods and the most divine of men is to call them blessed and happy. And so too with good things: no one praises happiness as he does justice, but rather calls it blessed, as being something more divine and better.

Eudoxus also seems to have been right in his method of advocating the supremacy of pleasure: he thought that the fact that, though a good, it is not praised indicated it to be better than the things that are praiseworthy, and that this is what god and the good are; for by reference to these all other things are judged. Praise is appropriate to virtue; for from virtue men perform noble actions. Encomia are bestowed on deeds, whether of the body or of the soul. Perhaps precision in these matters is more appropriate to those who have made a study of encomia; but to us it is plain from what has been said that happiness is among the things that are valuable and complete. It seems to be so also from the fact that it is an originating principle; for it is for the sake of this that we all do everything else, and the principle and cause of goods is, we claim, something valuable and divine.

2

VIRTUE

SINCE HAPPINESS IS AN ACTIVITY OF SOUL IN ACCORDANCE 5
with complete virtue, we must consider the nature of virtue;
for perhaps we shall thus see better the nature of happiness.
The true politician, too, is thought to have studied this above
all things; for he wants to make his fellow citizens good and
obedient to the laws. As an example of this we have the law- 10
givers of the Cretans and the Spartans, and any others of the
kind that there may have been. And if this inquiry belongs to
political science, plainly the pursuit of it will be in accordance with our original plan.

Plainly, the virtue we must study is human virtue; for the
good we were looking for was human good and the happi- 15
ness human happiness. By human virtue we mean not that
of the body but that of the soul; and happiness we call an activity of soul. But if this is so, plainly the student of politics
must know somehow the facts about soul, just as the man
who is to heal the eyes must know about the whole body 20
also—and all the more since politics is more valuable and better than medicine. (Among doctors the more refined spend
much labour on acquiring knowledge of the body.) The student of politics, then, must consider the soul, and must consider it with these objects in view, and do so just to the extent
which is sufficient for the questions we are discussing; for
further precision is perhaps something more laborious than 25
our purposes require.

Some things are said about it, adequately enough, even in
public discussions, and we must use these: for instance, that
one part of the soul is irrational and one has reason. Whether
these are separated as the parts of the body or of anything 30

divisible are, or are two in definition but by nature insepara-
ble, like convex and concave in the circumference of a circle,
does not affect the present question.

Of the irrational part one element seems to be common
to all and vegetative in its nature, I mean that which causes
nutrition and growth; for it is this kind of capacity of the
1102b soul that one must assign to all nurslings and to embryos,
and this same capacity to full-grown creatures (this is more
reasonable than to assign some different capacity to them).
Now the virtue of this seems to be common to all and not
5 specifically human; for this part or capacity seems to be exercised most in sleep, while the good and the bad are least
manifest in sleep (whence comes the saying that the happy
are not better off than the wretched for half their lives; and
this happens reasonably enough, since sleep is an idleness of
the soul in that respect in which it is called virtuous or base),
unless perhaps to a small extent some of the movements ac-
10 tually penetrate, and in this respect the dreams of upright
men are better than those of ordinary people. But enough of
this: let us leave the nutritive capacity alone, since it has by
its nature no share in human virtue.

There seems to be also another irrational element in the
soul—one which in a sense, however, shares in reason. For
15 we praise the reason of the continent man and of the incontinent, and the part of their soul that has reason, since it ex-
horts them correctly and towards the best objects; but there
is found in them also another natural element beside reason,
which conflicts with it and resists it. For exactly as paralysed
20 limbs when we choose to move them to the right turn on the
contrary to the left, so is it with the soul: the impulses of incontinent people move in contrary directions. Whereas in
the body we see what moves astray, in the soul we do not; but
perhaps we must nonetheless suppose that in the soul too
there is something beside reason, resisting and contrary to
25 it. (In what way it is distinct does not matter.) Now this too
seems to have a share in reason, as we said: at any rate in the
continent man it obeys reason—and presumably in the tem-

perate and courageous man it is still more obedient; for in them it speaks on all matters with the same voice as reason.

Therefore the irrational element appears to be twofold. For the vegetative element in no way shares in reason, but the appetitive and in general the desiderative element in a way shares in it, in so far as it listens to and obeys it: this is the way in which we speak of paying heed to one's father or one's friends, not that in which we speak of the rational in mathematics.[1] That the irrational element is in some way persuaded by reason is indicated also by the giving of advice and by all criticism and exhortation. And if this element also must be said to have reason, there will be two elements having reason, one having it strictly speaking and in itself, and the other having a tendency to obey as one does one's father.

Virtue too is distinguished into kinds in accordance with this difference; for we say that some virtues are intellectual and others moral—understanding and judgement and wisdom being intellectual, liberality and temperance moral. For in speaking about a man's character[2] we do not say that he is a man of understanding or judicious but that he is good-tempered or temperate; yet we praise the man of understanding with respect to his state, and of states we call those which are praiseworthy virtues.

Virtue, then, being of two kinds, intellectual and moral, intellectual virtue in the main owes both its birth and its growth to teaching (for which reason it requires experience and time), while moral virtue comes about as a result of habit (whence it gets its name 'êthikê', which comes with a slight variation from 'ethos' or 'habit'). From this it is plain that none of the moral virtues arises in us by nature; for nothing that exists by nature can form a habit contrary to its nature. For instance, a stone which by nature moves downwards cannot be habituated to move upwards, not even if one

30

1103a

5

10

Book B

15

20

---

1 The Greek phrase 'λόγον ἔχειν' means (i) 'possess reason', (ii) 'pay heed to', 'obey', (iii) 'be rational' (in the mathematical sense).

2 'Character' is ἦθος, and 'moral' is ἠθικός.

habituates it by throwing it up ten thousand times; nor can fire be habituated to move downwards, nor can anything else that by nature behaves in one way be habituated to behave in another. Neither by nature, then, nor against nature do vir-
25   tues arise in us: rather we are adapted by nature to receive them, and are made perfect by habit.

Again, of all the things that come to us by nature we first acquire the capacity and later exhibit the activity. This is
30   plain in the case of the senses; for it was not by often seeing or often hearing that we got these senses but the reverse: we had them before we used them, and did not come to have them by using them. But virtues we get by first exercising them, as happens in the case of the crafts as well. For the things we have to learn before we can do, we learn by doing: for instance, men become builders by building and lyre-
1103b   players by playing the lyre; so too we become just by doing just acts, temperate by doing temperate acts, courageous by doing courageous acts.

This is confirmed by what happens in States; for legisla-tors make the citizens good by forming habits in them, and
5   this is the wish of every legislator; and those who do not do so well miss their mark, and it is in this that a good constitu-tion differs from a base one.

Again, it is from the same sources and by the same means that every virtue is produced and destroyed, and similarly every craft; for it is from playing the lyre that both good and
10   bad lyre-players are produced. Similarly for builders and for all the rest: men will be good or bad builders as a result of building well or badly. For if this were not so, there would have been no need of a teacher but all men would have been born good or bad at their craft. This, then, is the case with the virtues also: by performing the acts that we do in our
15   transactions with other men we become just or unjust, and by performing the acts that we do in fearful circumstances and being habituated to feel fear or confidence, we become courageous or cowardly. The same is true of appetites and feelings of anger: some men become temperate and good-

tempered, others self-indulgent and irascible, by behaving 20
in one way or the other in the appropriate circumstances.
Thus, in a word, states arise out of like activities. This is why
the activities we exhibit must be of a certain kind: it is because the states correspond to the differences between
them. It makes no small difference, then, whether we form
habits of one kind or of another from our very youth—it
makes a very great difference, or rather all the difference. 25

SINCE, THEN, THE PRESENT INQUIRY DOES NOT AIM AT
contemplation like the others (for we are inquiring not in
order to know what virtue is, but in order to become good,
since otherwise our inquiry would have been of no advantage), we must examine the nature of actions, namely how
we ought to do them; for these also control the nature of the 30
states that are produced, as we have said. Now, that we
should[3] act according to correct reasoning is commonly
agreed and must be supposed. (It will be discussed later—
both what it is, and how it is related to the virtues.)

It must be agreed beforehand that the whole account of 1104a
matters of action ought to be given in outline and not precisely—just as we said at the beginning that the accounts we
demand must be in accordance with the subject-matter; and
matters of action and what is advantageous have no fixity,
any more than matters of health. The general account being 5
of this nature, the account of particular cases is yet more
lacking in precision; for they do not fall under any craft or
set of precepts—rather, the agents themselves must in each
case consider what is appropriate to the occasion, as happens also in the art of medicine or of navigation. 10

But though our present account is of this nature we must
try to give what help we can. First, then, let us consider this:
it is the nature of such things to be destroyed by lack and
excess, as we see in the cases of strength and of health (for
as testimony to the unevident we must take the evident):

3 Adding δεῖν after πράττειν.

15 both excessive and deficient physical training destroy the strength, and similarly too much and too little drink or food destroy the health, while that which is proportionate both produces and increases and preserves it. So too is it, then, in the case of temperance and courage and the other vir-
20 tues. For the man who flies from and fears everything and faces up to nothing becomes a coward, and the man who fears nothing at all but goes to meet every danger becomes over-confident; and similarly the man who enjoys every pleasure and abstains from none becomes self-indulgent, while the man who shuns every pleasure, as boors do, be-
25 comes in a way insensible: temperance and courage, then, are destroyed by excess and deficiency, and preserved by the mean.

Not only are the sources and causes of their birth and growth and destruction the same: their activities will be found in the same circumstances; for this is also true of the
30 things which are more evident: for instance, strength is pro-duced by taking much food and facing much exertion, and it is the strong man that will be most able to do these things. So too is it with the virtues: by abstaining from pleasures we become temperate, and it is when we have become so that we are most able to abstain from them; and similarly too in the
1104b case of courage: by being habituated to despise things that are frightening and to face up to them we become coura-geous, and it is when we have become so that we shall be most able to face up to frightening things.

WE MUST TAKE AS AN INDICATION OF STATES THE PLEA-
5 sure or pain that supervenes on the deeds; for the man who abstains from bodily pleasures and delights in this very fact is temperate, while the man who is annoyed at it is self-indulgent, and he who faces up to things that are fearful and delights in this, or at least is not pained, is courageous, while the man who is pained is a coward. For moral virtue is con-cerned with pleasures and pains: it is on account of pleasure
10 that we do base things, and on account of pain that we

abstain from noble ones. That is why we ought to have been
brought up in a particular way from our very youth, as Plato
says, so as both to delight in and to be pained by the things
that we ought; for this is the correct education.

Again, if the virtues are concerned with actions and emotions, and every emotion and every action is accompanied by
pleasure and pain, for this reason also virtue will be con-   15
cerned with pleasures and pains. This is indicated also by the
fact that punishment is inflicted by these means; for it is a
kind of therapy, and it is the nature of therapies to be effected
by contraries.

Again, as we said but lately, every state of soul has a nature
relative to and concerned with the kind of things by which it
tends to be made worse or better; but it is by reason of plea-   20
sures and pains that men become base, by pursuing and
avoiding them—either the pleasures and pains they ought
not or when they ought not or as they ought not, or by going
wrong in one of the other similar ways that reason distinguishes. That is why men actually define the virtues as certain states of impassivity and rest; not well, however, be-   25
cause they speak simply, and do not say 'as one ought' and 'as
one ought not' and 'when', and the other things that get
added. We suppose, then, that this kind of virtue tends to do
what is best with regard to pleasures and pains and that vice
does the contrary.

The following facts also may make it evident to us that
they are concerned with these same things. There being   30
three objects of choice and three of avoidance, the noble, the
advantageous, the pleasant, and their contraries, the ignoble, the injurious, the painful, about all of these the good
man tends to succeed and the bad man to err, and especially
about pleasure; for this is common to the animals, and it accompanies all objects of choice—for the noble and the ad-   1105a
vantageous appear pleasant.

Again, it has grown up with us all from our infancy: this
is why it is difficult to rub off this phenomenon, engrained
as it is in our life. And we estimate even our actions, some of

5 us more and others less, by pleasure and pain. For this reason, then, our whole inquiry must be about these; for to feel
delight and pain well or badly has no small effect on our
actions.

Again, it is harder to fight against pleasure than against
passion, to use Heraclitus' phrase, and both craftsmanship
and virtue are always concerned with what is harder; for
10 even the good is better when it is harder. Therefore for this
reason also the whole concern of both virtue and political
science is with pleasures and pains; for the man who uses
these well will be good, he who uses them badly bad.

That virtue, then, is concerned with pleasures and pains,
and that by the acts from which it arises it is both increased
15 and, if they are done differently, destroyed, and that the acts
from which it arose are those in which it exercises itself—let
this be taken as said.

THE PROBLEM MIGHT BE RAISED OF WHAT WE MEAN BY
saying that we must become just by doing just acts, and temperate by doing temperate acts; for if men do just and tem-
20 perate acts, they are thereby just and temperate, exactly as, if
they do what is grammatical or musical, they are proficient
in grammar and music. Or is this not true even of the crafts?
It is possible to do something grammatical either by fortune
or under the guidance of another. A man will be proficient in
grammar, then, only when he has both done something
25 grammatical and done it grammatically; and this means
doing it in accordance with the grammatical knowledge in
himself.

Again, the case of the crafts and that of the virtues are not
similar; for the products of the crafts have their goodness in
themselves, so that it is enough that they should have a certain character; but if the acts that are in accordance with the
virtues have themselves a certain character it does not follow
30 that they are done justly or temperately: the agent also must
be in a certain condition when he does them. In the first
place he must have knowledge, secondly he must choose the

acts, and choose them for their own sakes, and thirdly his action must proceed from a firm and unchangeable character. These are not numbered in as conditions for the possession of a craft—except the bare knowledge; but as a condition of the possession of the virtues, knowledge has little or no weight, while the other conditions count not for a little but for everything and they result from often doing just and temperate acts.

Acts, then, are called just and temperate when they are such as the just or the temperate man would do; but it is not the man who does these that is just and temperate, but the man who does them as just and temperate men do them. It is well said, then, that it is by doing just acts that the just man is produced, and by doing temperate acts the temperate man: without doing these no one would have even a prospect of becoming good.

But most people do not do these but take refuge in words and think they are being philosophers and will become virtuous in this way. They behave somewhat like patients who listen attentively to their doctors but do none of the things they are ordered to do. As the latter will not be made well in body by such a course of treatment, so the former will not be made well in soul by such a course of philosophy.

NEXT WE MUST CONSIDER WHAT VIRTUE IS. SINCE THINGS that are found in the soul are of three kinds—emotions, capacities, states—virtue must be one of these. By emotions I mean appetite, anger, fear, confidence, envy, joy, love, hatred, longing, emulation, pity, and in general the feelings that are accompanied by pleasure or pain; by capacities the things on account of which we are said to be capable of feeling these emotions—for instance of becoming angry or being pained or feeling pity; by states the things in virtue of which we stand well or badly with reference to the emotions—for instance, with reference to anger we stand badly if we feel it intensely or weakly, and well if we feel it moderately; and similarly with reference to the other emotions.

Now neither the virtues nor the vices are emotions, be-
30 cause we are not called virtuous or base on the ground of our
emotions, but are so called on the ground of our virtues and
our vices; and because we are neither praised nor blamed for
our emotions (for the man who feels fear or anger is not
praised, nor is the man who simply feels anger blamed but
1106a the man who feels it in a certain way), but for our virtues and
our vices we are praised or blamed. Again, we feel anger and
fear without choice, but the virtues are choices of a kind or
involve choice. Further, in respect of the emotions we are
5 said to be moved, but in respect of the virtues and the vices
we are said not to be moved but to be disposed in a particular
way.

For the following reasons they are not capacities. We are
neither called good nor bad, nor praised nor blamed, for
simply being capable of feeling. Again, we have the capaci-
10 ties by nature, but we are not made good or bad by nature
(we have spoken of this before).

If, then, the virtues are neither emotions nor capacities, it
remains that they are states.

Thus we have stated what virtue is in respect of its genus.

WE MUST, HOWEVER, NOT ONLY DESCRIBE IT AS A STATE
15 but also say what sort of state it is. We may remark, then,
that every virtue both brings into good condition the thing
of which it is the virtue and also makes it perform its task
well. For instance, the virtue of the eye makes both the eye
and its task good; for it is by the virtue of the eye that we see
well. Similarly the virtue of the horse makes a horse both
20 good in itself and good at running and at carrying its rider
and at awaiting the attack of the enemy. So if this holds in
every case, the virtue of man also will be the state which
makes a man good and which makes him perform his task
well.

25 How this is to happen we have stated already, but it will be
made evident also by the following consideration of the nature of virtue. In everything that is continuous and divisible

it is possible to take more, less, or an equal amount, and that either in terms of the object itself or relatively to us; and the equal is a mid-point between excess and deficiency. By the mid-point in the object I mean that which is equidistant from each of the extremes, which is one and the same for all; by the mid-point relatively to us that which is neither too much nor too little—and this is not one, nor the same for all. For instance, if ten is many and two is few, six is midway, in terms of the object; for it exceeds and is exceeded by an equal amount. It is midway according to arithmetical proportion. But the middle relatively to us is not to be taken so: if ten pounds are too much for someone to eat and two too little, it does not follow that the trainer will order six pounds; for this also is perhaps too much for the person who is to take it, or too little—too little for Milo, too much for one who is beginning his physical training. The same holds for running and wrestling. Thus an expert avoids excess and deficiency, but seeks the mid-point and chooses this—the mid-point not in the object but relatively to us.

If it is thus, then, that every branch of knowledge finishes its task well—by looking to the mid-point and referring its tasks to it (so that we often say of good works that it is not possible either to take away or to add anything, implying that excess and deficiency destroy the goodness, while the mean preserves it; and good craftsmen, as we say, look to this in their work), and if, further, virtue is more precise and better than any craftsmanship, as nature also is, then it must be such as to aim at the mid-point. I mean moral virtue; for it is this that is concerned with emotions and actions, and in these there is excess, deficiency, and the mid-point. For instance, both fear and confidence and appetite and anger and pity and in general pleasure and pain may be felt both too much and too little, and in both cases not well; but to feel them when you should, with reference to what you should, towards the people you should, with the end you should have, and how you should—this is what is both midway and best, and this is characteristic of virtue. Similarly with regard

to actions also there is excess, deficiency, and the mid-point.
25   Now virtue is concerned with emotions and actions, in
which excess is a form of error, and so is deficiency, while the
mid-point is praised and is a form of success; and both these
things are characteristics of virtue. Therefore virtue is a kind
of mean, since it is such as to aim at what is in the middle.

Again, it is possible to err in many ways (for the bad be-
30   longs to the class of the unlimited, as the Pythagoreans con-
jectured, and the good to that of the limited), while to succeed is possible only in one way (that is why one is easy and
the other difficult—to miss the mark easy, to hit it difficult):
for these reasons also, then, excess and deficiency are characteristic of vice, and the mean of virtue:

35   For men are good in but one way, but bad in many.

Virtue, then, is a state concerned with choice, lying in a
1107a   mean relative to us, this being determined by reason and in
the way in[4] which the wise man would determine it. It is a
mean between two vices, that which arises from excess and
that which arises from deficiency; and again it is a mean because the vices fall short of or exceed what should be the case
5   in both emotions and actions, while virtue both finds and
chooses that which is in the middle. That is why in respect of
its substance and the account which states its quiddity it is a
mean, with regard to what is best and well it is an extreme.

Not every action nor every emotion admits of a mean; for
10   some have names that already imply baseness—for instance
spite, shamelessness, envy, and in the case of actions adultery, theft, murder; for all of these and suchlike things imply
by their names that they are themselves base, and not the excesses or deficiencies of them. It is not possible, then, ever to
15   succeed with regard to them: one must always err. Nor does
goodness or badness with regard to such things depend on
committing adultery with whom you should, when you
should, and how you should—rather, simply to do any of

4 Reading ὡς (with the manuscripts) rather than ᾧ.

246

them is to err. It would be equally absurd, then, to claim that
in unjust, cowardly, and self-indulgent action there is a
mean, an excess, and a deficiency; for at that rate there   20
would be a mean of excess and of deficiency, an excess of excess, and a deficiency of deficiency. But as there is no excess
and deficiency of temperance and courage because what is in
the middle is in a sense an extreme, so too of the actions we
have mentioned there is no mean nor any excess and deficiency—rather, however they are done they are errors; for in   25
general there is neither a mean of excess and deficiency, nor
excess and deficiency of a mean.

WE MUST NOT ONLY MAKE THIS UNIVERSAL STATEMENT
but also apply it to the individual cases. For among statements about actions those which are universal apply more   30
widely, but those which are particular are more true, since
actions have to do with individual cases, and our statements
must harmonize with the facts in these cases. We may take
these cases from the table.

     With regard to feelings of fear and confidence courage is a
mean. Of the people who exceed, he who exceeds in fearless-   1107b
ness has no name (many of the states have no name), while
the man who exceeds in confidence is over-confident, and he
who exceeds in fear and falls short in confidence is a coward.
With regard to pleasures and pains—not all of them, and not   5
so much with regard to the pains—the mean is temperance,
the excess self-indulgence. Persons deficient with regard to
the pleasures are not often found; hence such persons also
have received no name. But let us call them insensible.

     With regard to giving and taking of wealth the mean is
liberality, the excess and the deficiency prodigality and illib-   10
erality. They exceed and fall short in contrary ways to one
another:⁵ the prodigal exceeds in spending and falls short in
taking, while the illiberal exceeds in taking and falls short in
spending. (At present we are giving an outline or summary,

5 Reading δὲ αὐταῖς (with most manuscripts) rather than δ᾽ ἐν αὐταῖς.

15 and are satisfied with this: later these states will be more precisely determined.) With regard to money there are also
other dispositions—a mean, magnificence (for the magnificent man differs from the liberal man: the former deals with
large sums, the latter with small ones), an excess, tasteless-
20 ness and vulgarity, and a deficiency, shabbiness: these differ
from the states opposed to liberality, and how they differ will
be stated later.

With regard to honour and dishonour the mean is pride,
the excess is called a sort of vanity, and the deficiency is diffidence; and as we said liberality was related to magnificence,
25 differing from it by dealing with small sums, so there is a
state similarly related to pride, being concerned with small
honours while that is concerned with great. For it is possible
to desire honours as one ought, and more than one ought,
and less, and the man who exceeds in his desires is called ambitious, the man who falls short unambitious, while the per-
30 son in the middle has no name. The dispositions also are
nameless, except that that of the ambitious man is called
ambition. Hence the people who are at the extremes lay
claim to the middle place; and we ourselves sometimes call
the person in the middle ambitious and sometimes unambi-
1108a tious, and sometimes praise the ambitious man and sometimes the unambitious. The reason for our doing this will be
stated in what follows. Now let us speak of the remaining
states according to the method which has been indicated.

With regard to anger also there is an excess, a deficiency,
5 and a mean. Although they can scarcely be said to have
names, yet since we call the person in the middle good-
tempered let us call the mean good temper; and of the persons at the extremes let the one who exceeds be called irascible, and his vice irascibility, and the man who falls short an
inirascible sort of person, and the deficiency inirascibility.

10 There are also three other means, which have a certain
likeness to one another but differ from one another; for they
are all concerned with a sharing in words and actions, but

differ in that one is concerned with truth in this sphere, the other two with pleasantness; and of this one kind is exhibited in amusement, the other in all the circumstances of life. We must therefore speak of these too, that we may the better see that in all things the mean is praiseworthy, and the extremes neither praiseworthy nor correct but blameworthy. Now most of these states also have no names, but we must try, as in the other cases, to invent names ourselves so that we may be clear and easy to follow.

With regard to truth, then, the person in the middle is a candid sort of person and the mean may be called candour, while the pretence which exaggerates is boastfulness and the person characterized by it a boaster, and that which understates is self-deprecation and the person characterized by it a self-deprecator. With regard to pleasantness in amusement the person in the middle is convivial and the disposition conviviality, the excess is buffoonery and the person characterized by it a buffoon, while the man who falls short is a sort of boor and his state is boorishness. With regard to the remaining kind of pleasantness, that which is exhibited in life in general, the man who is pleasant in the way one should be is friendly and the mean is friendliness, while the man who exceeds is obsequious if he has no end in view and a flatterer if he is aiming at his own advantage, and the man who falls short and is unpleasant in all circumstances is quarrelsome and grumpy.

There are also means in the feelings and concerned with the emotions; for although modesty is not a virtue, praise is extended to the modest man. For in these matters too one man is said to be in the middle, and another to exceed, as for instance the bashful man who is ashamed of everything; while he who falls short or is not ashamed of anything at all is shameless, and the person in the middle is modest. Indignation is a mean between envy and spite, and these states are concerned with the pain and pleasure that are felt at the fortunes of our neighbours: the indignant man is pained at

undeserved good fortune, the envious man exceeds him and
5   is pained at all good fortune, and the spiteful man falls so far
short of being pained that he even feels delight. But these
states there will be an opportunity of describing elsewhere.
With regard to justice, since it is not spoken of in only one
way, we shall, after describing the other states, distinguish
its two kinds and say how each of them is a mean; and simi-
10 larly for the rational virtues.

THERE ARE THREE KINDS OF DISPOSITION, THEN, TWO OF
them vices, involving excess and deficiency, and one a virtue,
the mean, and all are in a sense opposed to all; for the extreme states are contrary both to the middle state and to
15 each other, and the middle to the extremes: as the equal is
greater relatively to the less, less relatively to the greater, so
the middle states are excessive relatively to the deficiencies
and deficient relatively to the excesses, both in emotions and
in actions. For the courageous man appears over-confident
20 relatively to the coward, and cowardly relatively to the over-
confident man; and similarly the temperate man appears
self-indulgent relatively to the insensible man and insensible
relatively to the self-indulgent, and the liberal man prodigal
relatively to the illiberal man and illiberal relatively to the
prodigal. That is why the people at the extremes each push
25 the person in the middle over to the other, and the courageous man is called over-confident by the coward and cowardly by the over-confident man, and correspondingly in the
other cases.
    These states being thus opposed to one another, the
greatest contrariety is that of the extremes to each other
rather than to the middle; for these are further from each
other than from the middle, as the great is further from the
30 small and the small from the great than both are from the
equal. Again, to the middle some extremes show a certain
likeness, as that of over-confidence to courage and that of
prodigality to liberality; but the extremes show the greatest

unlikeness to each other. Now contraries are defined as the things that are furthest from each other, so that things that are further apart are more contrary. 35

To the middle point in some cases the deficiency, in some the excess is more opposed: for instance, it is not over-confidence, which is an excess, but cowardice, which is a deficiency, that is more opposed to courage, and it is not insensibility, which is a lack, but self-indulgence, which is an excess, that is more opposed to temperance. This happens 5 for two reasons, one being drawn from the thing itself: because one extreme is nearer to and more like the middle, we oppose not this but rather its contrary to the middle. For instance, since over-confidence is thought more like and nearer to courage, and cowardice more unlike, we oppose 10 rather the latter to courage; for things that are further from the middle are thought more contrary to it. This, then, is one reason, drawn from the thing itself. Another is drawn from ourselves; for the things to which we ourselves naturally tend more seem more contrary to the middle. For instance, we ourselves naturally tend more to pleasures—that 15 is why we are more easily carried away towards self-indulgence than towards propriety. We describe as contrary to the mean, then, the states to which we are more inclined; and therefore self-indulgence, which is an excess, is more contrary to temperance. 20

THAT MORAL VIRTUE IS A MEAN, THEN, AND HOW IT IS SO, and that it is a mean between two vices, the one involving excess and the other deficiency, and that it is so because it is such as to aim at what is midway in emotions and in actions, has been sufficiently stated. That is why it is no easy task to be virtuous. For in everything it is no easy task to find the 25 middle: for instance, to find the middle of a circle is not for everyone but for him who knows; so, too, anyone can get angry—that is easy—or give or spend money; but to do this to the person you should, to the extent you should, when

1109a

251

you should, with the end you should have, and how you should, *that* is not for everyone, nor is it easy. That is why
30   goodness is both rare and praiseworthy and noble.

That is why he who aims at the middle must first depart from what is the more contrary to it, as Calypso advises—

Hold the ship out beyond that surf and spray.[6]

For of the extremes one is more erroneous, one less so. Therefore, since to hit the middle point is extremely diffi-cult, we must as a second best, as people say, take the least of
1109b   the evils; and this will be done best in the way we describe.

We must consider the things towards which we ourselves are easily carried away; for some of us tend to one thing, some to another; and this will be recognizable from the plea-
5   sure and the pain we feel. We must drag ourselves away to the contrary extreme; for we shall get into the middle state by drawing well away from error, as people do in straighten-ing sticks that are bent.

Now in everything the pleasant or pleasure is most to be guarded against; for we do not assess it impartially. We ought, then, to feel towards pleasure as the elders of the peo-
10   ple felt towards Helen, and in all circumstances repeat their saying;[7] for if we dismiss pleasure thus we are less likely to err. It is by doing this, then, (to sum the matter up) that we shall best be able to hit the middle point.

This is no doubt difficult, and especially in individual
15   cases. For it is not easy to determine how and with whom and on what provocation and how long one should be angry; for sometimes we praise those who fall short and call them good-tempered and sometimes those who are angry, calling them manly. But it is not the man who deviates little from goodness who is blamed, whether he do so in the direction
20   of the more or of the less, but the man who deviates more widely—for he does not fail to be noticed. But up to what

6 Homer, *Odyssey* XII 219.
7 See Homer, *Iliad* III 156–160.

point and to what extent a man must deviate before he becomes blameworthy it is not easy to determine by reason, any more than anything else that is perceived by the senses: such things depend on particular facts, and the assessment depends on sense-perception. So much, then, makes it plain that the middle state is in all things praiseworthy, but that we must incline sometimes towards the excess, sometimes towards the deficiency—for so shall we most easily hit the middle point and what is well.   25

3

ACTION

SINCE VIRTUE IS CONCERNED WITH EMOTIONS AND AC-
tions, and in voluntary cases praise and blame are bestowed,
in those that are involuntary sympathy and sometimes also
pity, to determine the voluntary and the involuntary is presumably necessary for those who are studying virtue and
useful also for legislators with a view to both honours and
punishments.

Those things, then, are thought involuntary, which take
1110a   place by force or owing to ignorance; and that is enforced of
which the originating principle is outside and nothing is
contributed by the person who acts or is acted upon—for instance, if he were to be carried somewhere by a wind, or by
men who had him under their control.

With regard to the things that are done from fear of
5   greater evils or for some noble object (for instance, if a tyrant
were to order one to do something ignoble, having one's parents and children under his control, and if one did the action
they would be saved but otherwise put to death), it is debated
whether such actions are involuntary or voluntary. Something of the sort happens also with regard to the throwing of
goods overboard in a storm; for in the abstract no one
10   throws goods away voluntarily, but on condition of its secur-
ing the safety of himself and his crew any intelligent man
does so. Such actions, then, are mixed, but are more like voluntary actions; for they are desirable at the time when they
are done, and the end of an action is relative to the occasion.
Both the terms, then, 'voluntary' and 'involuntary', must be
15   used with reference to the moment of action. Now the man
acts voluntarily; for the originating principle that moves the

instrumental parts of the body in such actions is in him, and the things of which the origin is in a man himself are in his power to do or not to do. Such actions, therefore, are voluntary, but in the abstract perhaps involuntary; for no one would choose any such act in itself.

For such actions men are sometimes even praised when 20 they face up to something ignoble or painful in return for great and noble objects; in the opposite case they are blamed, since to face up to the most ignoble treatment for no noble end or for a trifling end is the mark of a base man. On some actions praise indeed is not bestowed but sympathy is, when one does what he ought not under pressure which over- 25 strains human nature and which no one would face up to. Some actions, perhaps, we cannot be compelled to do, but ought rather to die after the most fearful sufferings; for the things that compelled Euripides' Alcmaeon to slay his mother seem ridiculous. It is difficult sometimes to decide what is desirable at what cost, and what should be faced in 30 return for what gain, and yet more difficult to abide by our decisions; for as a rule what is expected is painful and what we are compelled to do is ignoble, whence praise and blame are bestowed on those who have been compelled or have not. 1110b

What sort of things, then, should be called enforced? Shall we answer simply that actions are so when the cause is in the external circumstances and the agent contributes nothing? But the things that in themselves are involuntary, but now and in return for these gains are desirable, and whose origin is in the agent, are in themselves involuntary, 5 but now and in return for these gains voluntary. They are more like voluntary acts; for actions are in the class of particulars, and the particular acts here are voluntary. What sort of things are to be chosen in return for what, it is not easy to state; for there are many differences in the particular cases.

If someone were to say that pleasant and noble objects have a force, compelling us from without, then all acts 10 would be for him enforced; for it is for these ends that all men do everything they do. And those who act perforce and involuntarily act with pain, but those who do acts for their pleasantness and nobility do them with pleasure: it is ridiculous to make external circumstances responsible, and not oneself, as being easily caught by such attractions, and to make oneself responsible for noble acts but the pleasant objects responsible for ignoble acts. The enforced, then, seems to be that whose origin is outside, the person enforced contributing nothing.

Everything that is done owing to ignorance is nonvoluntary: what produces pain and regret is involuntary. For the man who has done something owing to ignorance, and feels not the least vexation at his action, has not acted voluntarily, since he did not know what he was doing, nor yet involuntarily, since he is not pained. Of people, then, who act owing to ignorance he who regrets is thought an involuntary agent, and the man who does not regret may, since he is different, be called a non-voluntary agent; for, since he differs, it is better that he should have a name of his own.

Acting owing to ignorance seems also to be different from acting in ignorance; for the man who is drunk or in a rage is thought to act owing not to ignorance but to one of the causes mentioned, yet not knowingly but in ignorance.

Now every depraved man is ignorant of what he ought to do and what he should abstain from, and error of this kind makes men unjust and in general bad; but the term 'involuntary' tends to be used not if a man is ignorant of what is to his advantage—for ignorance in choice is a cause not of involuntariness but of depravity, nor is ignorance of the universal (for *that* men are blamed), but rather ignorance of the particular circumstances in which the action is found and with which it is concerned (for it is on these that both pity and sympathy depend). For the person who is ignorant of any of these acts involuntarily.

Perhaps it is well, therefore, to determine their nature and number. A man may be ignorant, then, of who he is, what he is doing, what or whom he is acting on, and sometimes also what (for instance, what instrument) he is doing it

256

with, and to what end (for instance, for safety), and how he is   5
doing it (for instance gently or intensely). Now no one could
be ignorant of all of these unless he were mad, and plainly
too he could not be ignorant of the agent; for how could he
not know himself? But of what he is doing a man might be
ignorant, as for instance people say 'it slipped out of their
mouths as they were speaking',[1] or 'they did not know it was
a secret', as Aeschylus said of the mysteries, or a man might   10
say he let it off when he merely wanted to show it, as the man
did with the catapult. Again, one might think one's son was
an enemy, as Merope did, or that a pointed spear had a but-
ton on it, or that a stone was pumice-stone; or one might
give a man a draught to save him, and kill him; or one might
want to touch a man, as people do in sparring, and strike   15
him. The ignorance may relate, then, to any of these things,
i.e., of the circumstances of the action, and the man who was
ignorant of any of these is thought to have acted involuntarily, and especially if he was ignorant on the most authoritative points—which are thought to be what[2] he is doing and
to what end. Further,[3] the doing of an act that is called involuntary in virtue of ignorance of this sort must be painful and   20
involve regret.

Since that which is done by force or owing to ignorance is
involuntary, the voluntary would seem to be that of which
the originating principle is in the agent himself, he being
aware of the particular circumstances of the action. Presumably acts done by reason of passion or appetite are not rightly   25
called involuntary. For in the first place, on that showing
none of the other animals will act voluntarily, nor will children; and secondly, is it meant that we do not do voluntarily
any of the acts that are due to appetite or passion, or that we

1 Reading λέγοντας (Aspasius) for λέγοντες, and αὐτοῖς (Lambinus) for
αὐτούς. Bywater prints the manuscript text between obeli.

2 Reading ὅ for ἐν οἷς ἡ πρᾶξις ('. . . thought to be the circumstances of the
action and the end').

3 Reading δέ (Thurot) for δή ('So, the doing . . .').

do the noble acts voluntarily and the ignoble acts involuntarily? Is not the latter ridiculous given that one and the same
thing is the cause? But it would surely be absurd to describe
30 as involuntary the things one ought to desire; and we ought
both to be angry at certain things and to have an appetite for
certain things, for instance for health and for learning. Also
what is involuntary is thought to be painful, but what is in
accordance with appetite is thought to be pleasant. Again,
what is the difference in respect of involuntariness between
errors committed upon calculation and those committed in
1111b passion? Both are to be avoided, but the irrational emotions
are thought no less human, and therefore also the actions
which proceed from passion or appetite are the man's actions. It would be absurd, then, to treat them as involuntary.

BOTH THE VOLUNTARY AND THE INVOLUNTARY HAVING
5 been determined, we must next discuss choice; for it is
thought to be most closely related to virtue and to discrimi-
nate characters better than actions do.
    Choice, then, is evidently voluntary, but it is not the same
thing as the voluntary: the voluntary extends more widely.
For both children and the other animals share in voluntary
action but not in choice, and acts done on the spur of the
10 moment we describe as voluntary but not as chosen.
    Those who say it is appetite or temper or will or a kind of
belief do not seem to be correct. For choice is not common
to irrational creatures as well, but appetite and passion are.
Again, the incontinent man acts with appetite but not with
15 choice; while the continent man does the reverse—he acts
with choice but not with appetite. Again, appetite is contrary
to choice, but not appetite to appetite. Again, appetite relates to the pleasant and the painful, choice neither to the
painful nor to the pleasant.
    Still less is it passion; for acts due to passion least of all
are thought to be chosen.
20   But neither is it will or wanting, though it seems near to
it; for choice cannot relate to impossibles, and if anyone said

he chose them he would be thought a fool; but you may want what is impossible, for instance immortality. And wanting may relate to things that could in no way be brought about by one's own efforts, for instance that a particular actor or athlete should win; but no one chooses such things, but   25 rather the things that he thinks could be brought about by his own efforts. Again, will relates rather to the end, choice to what contributes to the end: for instance, we want to be healthy but we choose the acts which will make us healthy, and we want to be happy and say we do but we cannot well say we choose to be so; for, in general, choice seems to relate   30 to the things that are in our own power.

Nor can it be belief; for belief is thought to relate to all kinds of things, no less to eternal things and impossible things than to things in our own power; and it is distinguished by its falsity or truth, not by its badness or goodness, while choice is distinguished rather by these.

Now with belief in general perhaps no one says it is iden-   1112a tical. But it is not identical even with any kind of belief; for by choosing what is good or bad we are men of a certain character, which we are not by holding certain beliefs. And we choose to get or avoid something good or bad, but we have beliefs about what a thing is or whom it is good for or how it is good for him: we can hardly be said to believe to get   5 or avoid anything. And choice is praised for being of the object it ought to be of rather than for being correctly related to it, belief for being truly related to its object. And we choose what we best know to be good, but we have beliefs about what we do not know at all. And it is not the same people that are thought to make the best choices and to have the best beliefs, but some are thought to have fairly good beliefs   10 but by reason of vice to choose what they should not. If belief precedes choice or accompanies it, that makes no difference; for it is not this that we are considering, but whether it is identical with some kind of belief.

What, then, or what kind of thing is it, since it is none of the things we have mentioned? It is evidently voluntary, but

15   not all that is voluntary is an object of choice. Is it, then, what has been decided on by previous deliberation? For choice involves reason and thought. Even the name seems to intimate that it is what is chosen before other things.[4]

DO WE DELIBERATE ABOUT EVERYTHING, AND IS EVERY-thing an object of deliberation, or are there some things about which there is no deliberation? We ought presumably

20   to call an object of deliberation not what a fool or a madman would deliberate about but what an intelligent man would. Now about eternal things no one deliberates, for instance about the universe or the incommensurability of the diagonal and the side. But no more do we deliberate about the things that involve movement but always happen in the same

25   way, whether of necessity or by nature or from any other cause, for instance the solstices and the risings of the stars; nor about things that happen now in one way, now in another, for instance droughts and rains; nor about matters of fortune, for instance the finding of treasure. Nor do we deliberate about all human affairs—for instance, no Spartan deliberates about the best constitution for the Scythians.

30   For none of these things can be brought about by our own efforts.

   We deliberate about things that are in our power and are matters of action; and these are in fact what is left. For nature, necessity, and fortune are thought to be causes, and also intelligence and everything that is brought about by man. Now every class of men deliberates about what are mat-

1112b   ters for their own action. And in the case of precise and self-sufficient sciences there is no deliberation, for instance about the letters of the alphabet (for we are not in two minds about how they should be written). Rather, the things that are brought about by our own efforts but not always in the same way are the things about which we deliberate, for

4 'Choice' is προαίρεσις, 'chosen before other things' is πρὸ ἑτέρων αἱρετόν.

instance questions of medicine or business matters. And we
do so more in the case of the art of navigation than in that of
gymnastics, inasmuch as it has been less precisely worked
out, and again about the others in the same way; and more
also in the case of the crafts than in that of the sciences—for
we are more in two minds about them. Deliberation is concerned with things that happen in a certain way for the most
part, but in which the outcome is obscure, and with things in
which it is indeterminate. We call in others to aid us in deliberation on important questions, distrusting ourselves as not
being equal to deciding.

We deliberate not about ends but about what contributes
to ends. For a doctor does not deliberate whether he shall
heal, nor an orator whether he shall convince, nor a states-
man whether he shall produce law and order, nor does anyone else deliberate about his end. Rather, having set the end
they consider how and by what means it is to be attained;
and if it seems to be produced by several means they consider by which it is most easily and best produced, while if it
is achieved by one only they consider how it will be achieved
by this and by what means *this* will be achieved, till they come
to the first cause, which in the order of discovery is last. For
the person who deliberates seems to inquire and analyse in
the way described as though he were analysing a geometrical
construction (evidently not all inquiry is deliberation—for
instance mathematical inquiries—but all deliberation is inquiry), and what is last in the order of analysis seems to be
first in the order of becoming. And if we come on an impossibility, we give up, for instance if we need wealth and this
cannot be got; but if a thing appears possible we try to do it.
Possible are things that might be brought about by our own
efforts; and these in a sense include things that can be
brought about by the efforts of our friends, since the originating principle is in ourselves. The subject of inquiry is
sometimes the instruments, sometimes the use of them; and
similarly in the other cases—sometimes the means, sometimes the mode of using it or the means of bringing it about.

It seems, then, as has been said, that man is an origin of actions, that deliberation is about things which are matters of action for the agent himself, and that actions are for the sake of things other than themselves. For the end cannot be an object of deliberation but only what contributes to the ends. Nor indeed can the particular facts be objects of delib-
1113a   eration, as whether this is bread or has been baked as it should; for these are matters of sense-perception. If we are to be always deliberating, we shall have to go on to infinity.

The same thing is deliberated upon and is chosen, except that the object of choice is already determinate, since it is that which has been decided upon as a result of deliberation
5   that is the object of choice. For everyone ceases to inquire how he is to act when he has brought the origin back to himself and to the ruling part of himself; for this is what chooses. This is plain also from the ancient constitutions, which Homer represented; for the kings announced their choices
10   to the people. The object of choice being one of the things in our own power which is desired after deliberation, choice will be deliberate desire of things in our own power; for when we have made an assessment as a result of delibera-tion, we desire in accordance with our deliberation.

We may take it, then, that we have described choice in outline, and stated the nature of its objects and the fact that it is concerned with what contributes to the ends.

15   THAT WILL OR WANTING IS FOR THE END HAS ALREADY been stated; but some think it is for the good, others for the apparent good. Now those who say that the good is the ob-ject of wanting must admit in consequence that that which the man who does not choose correctly wants is not an object of wanting (for if it is to be an object of wanting, it must also
20   be good; but it was, if it so happened, bad); while those who say the apparent good is the object of wanting must admit that there is no natural object of wanting, but only what seems so to each man. Now different things appear so to dif-ferent people, and, if it so happens, even contrary things.

If these consequences are not approved of, are we to say that in the abstract and in truth the good is the object of wanting, but for each person the apparent good? That which is in truth an object of wanting is an object of wanting to the virtuous man, while any chance thing may be so to the base man, just as in the case of bodies also the things that are in truth healthy are healthy for bodies which are in good condition, while for those that are diseased other things are healthy (or bitter or sweet or hot or heavy, and so on); since the virtuous man assesses each class of things correctly, and in each the truth appears to him. For each state of character has its own ideas of the noble and the pleasant, and perhaps the virtuous man differs from others most by seeing the truth in each class of things, being as it were the norm and measure of them. In most things the error seems to be due to pleasure; for it appears a good when it is not. We therefore choose the pleasant as a good, and avoid pain as an evil.

The end, then, being what we want, and the things contributing to the end being what we deliberate about and choose, actions concerning the latter will be according to choice and voluntary. Now the activity of the virtues is concerned with these. Therefore virtue also is in our own power, and so too vice. For where it is in our power to act it is also in our power not to act, and *vice versa*; so that, if to act, where this is noble, is in our power, not to act, which will be ignoble, will also be in our power, and if not to act, where this is noble, is in our power, to act, which will be ignoble, will also be in our power. Now if it is in our power to do noble or ignoble acts, and likewise in our power not to do them, and this was what being good or bad meant, then it is in our power to be upright or base.

To say that no one is voluntarily vicious nor involuntarily blessed seems to be part false and part true; for no one is involuntarily blessed but depravity is voluntary. Or should we dispute what has just been said and deny that a man is an origin or begetter of his actions as he is of his children? But if these facts are evident and we cannot refer actions to origins other than those in ourselves, the acts whose origins are in us must themselves also be in our power and voluntary.

Witness seems to be borne to this both by individuals in their private capacity and by the legislators themselves; for these punish and take vengeance on those who do depraved acts (unless they have acted perforce or owing to ignorance
25   for which they are not themselves responsible), while they honour those who do noble acts, as though they meant to encourage the latter and restrain the former. But no one is encouraged to do the things that are neither in our power nor voluntary: it is supposed that there is no gain in being persuaded not to be hot or in pain or hungry or the like, since
30   we shall experience these feelings nonetheless. Indeed, we punish a man for his very ignorance, if he is thought the cause of the ignorance, as when penalties are doubled in the case of drunkenness; for the origin is in the man himself, since it was in his control not to get drunk and his getting drunk was the cause of his ignorance. And we punish those who are ignorant of anything in the laws that they ought to
1114a   know and that is not difficult, and so too in the case of anything else that they are thought to be ignorant of through carelessness: we suppose that it is in their power not to be ignorant, since it was in their control to take care.

But perhaps a man is the kind of man not to take care?
5   Still they are themselves by their slack lives the cause of their becoming men of that kind and of their being unjust or self-indulgent, in that they cheat or spend their time in drinking bouts and the like; for it is activities exercised on particular objects that make people so. This is plain from the case of people training for any contest or action: they practise the activity the whole time. Now not to know that it is from the
10   exercise of activities on particular objects that states of character are produced is the mark of a thoroughly insensible person.

Again, it is irrational to suppose that a man who acts unjustly does not want to be unjust or a man who acts self-indulgently to be self-indulgent. But if without being ignorant a man does the things which will make him unjust, he will be unjust voluntarily. Yet it does not follow that if he wants he will cease to be unjust and will be just. For neither does the man who is ill become well on those terms— although[5] he may, perhaps, be ill voluntarily, through living incontinently and disobeying his doctors. In that case it was *then* open to him not to be ill, but not now, when he has thrown away his chance. In the same way, once you have thrown a stone it is too late to recover it; but nevertheless it was in your power to throw it, since the originating principle was in you. So, too, to the unjust and to the self-indulgent man it was open at the beginning not to become men of this kind (that is why they are such voluntarily); but now that they have become so it is not possible for them not to be so.

Not only are the vices of the soul voluntary, but so also are those of the body for some men, whom we accordingly criticize: while no one criticizes those who are ugly by nature, we criticize those who are so owing to want of exercise and care. So it is, too, with respect to weakness and infirmity: no one would reproach a man blind from birth or by disease or from a blow, but rather pity him, while everyone would blame a man who was blind from alcoholism or some other form of self-indulgence. Of vices of the body, then, those in our own power are blamed, those not in our power are not. And if this be so, in the other cases also the vices that are blamed must be in our own power.

Now someone may say that all men aim at the apparent good but do not control how things appear to them: rather, the end appears to each man in a form answering to his character. If each man is somehow the cause of the state he is in, he will also be himself somehow the cause of how things appear; but if not, no one is the cause of his own bad actions but everyone acts badly owing to ignorance of the end, thinking that by these he will get what is best for him, and the aiming at the end is not self-chosen—rather, one must

5 Reading καίτοι (Rassow) for καί.

be born with an eye, as it were, by which to assess things nobly and choose what is truly good, and he is well endowed by nature who is nobly endowed with this. For it is what is greatest and most noble, and what we cannot get or learn from another, but must have just such as it was at birth, and to be well and nobly endowed with this will be complete and true natural endowment. If this is true, then, how will virtue be more voluntary than vice? To both men alike, the good and the bad, the end appears and is fixed by nature or however it may be, and it is by referring everything else to this that men do whatever they do.

Whether, then, it is not by nature that the end appears to each man such as it does appear but something also depends on him, or the end is natural but because the virtuous man does the rest voluntarily virtue is voluntary, vice also will be nonetheless voluntary; for in the case of the bad man there is equally present that which is brought about by himself—in his actions even if not in his end. If, then, as is asserted, the virtues are voluntary (for we are ourselves somehow co-causes of our states of character, and it is by being persons of a certain kind that we suppose the end to be so and so), the vices also will be voluntary; for the same is true of them.

With regard to the virtues in general we have stated their genus in outline, namely that they are means and that they are states, and that they tend by their own nature to the doing of the acts by which they are produced, and that they are in our power and voluntary, and act as correct reasoning prescribes. But actions and states are not voluntary in the same way: we control our actions from the beginning to the end if we know the particular facts; but as for states, though we control their origin, the particular way in which they develop is not known (any more than it is in illnesses), and yet because it was in our power to act in this way or not in this way, the states are voluntary.

4

THE MORAL VIRTUES

LET US TAKE UP THE SEVERAL VIRTUES AND SAY WHICH
they are and what sort of things they are concerned with and
how they are concerned with them; at the same time it will
become plain how many they are. And first let us speak of
courage.

That it is a mean with regard to fear and confidence has
already been made evident; and plainly the things we fear are
frightening things, and these are, broadly speaking bad
things—that is why people even define fear as expectation of
something bad. Now we fear all bad things (for instance disgrace, poverty, disease, friendlessness, death); but the courageous man is not thought to be concerned with all; for some
things one ought to fear and it is noble to do so, and ignoble
not to fear them—for instance, disgrace: he who fears it is
upright and modest, and he who does not is shameless. But
some people call him courageous by an extension of the
word; for he has in him something which is like the courageous man, since the courageous man also is a fearless person. Poverty and disease we perhaps ought not to fear, nor in
general the things that do not proceed from vice and are not
brought about by the man himself. The man who is fearless
of these is not courageous either. Yet we apply the word to
him too in virtue of a similarity; for some who in the dangers
of war are cowards are liberal and are confident in face of the
loss of wealth. Nor is a man a coward if he fears an outrage to
his wife and children or envy or anything of the kind; nor
courageous if he is confident when he is about to be flogged.

With what sort of frightening things, then, is the courageous man concerned? Surely with the greatest; for no one is

more likely than he to face up to what is fearful. Now death is the most frightening of all things; for it is the end, and nothing is thought to be any longer either good or bad for the dead. But the courageous man would not seem to be concerned even with death in all circumstances, for instance at sea or by disease. In what circumstances, then? Surely in the noblest. Now such deaths are those in battle; for these take place in the greatest and noblest danger. And this agrees with the ways in which honours are bestowed in States and at the courts of monarchs. Strictly speaking, then, he will be called courageous who is fearless in face of a noble death, and of all emergencies that involve death; and the emergencies of war are in the highest degree of this kind. Yet at sea also, and in disease, the courageous man is fearless, but not in the same way as the seamen; for he has given up hope for safety, and is vexed at the thought of death in this shape, while they are sanguine because of their experience. At the same time, we show courage in situations where there is the opportunity of showing prowess or where death is noble; but in these forms of death neither of these conditions is fulfilled.

What is frightening is not the same for all men; but we say there are things frightening even beyond human strength. These, then, are frightening to everyone—at least to every intelligent man; but the frightening things that are not beyond human strength differ in magnitude and degree, and so too do the things that inspire confidence. Now the courageous man is as dauntless as a man may be. Therefore, while he will fear even the things that are not beyond human strength, he will fear them as he ought and as reason directs, and[1] he will face them for the sake of what is noble; for this is the end of virtue. It is possible to fear these more, or less, and again to fear things that are not frightening as if they were. Of the errors that are committed one consists in fearing what one should not, another in fearing as one should

---

1 Adding τε after ὑπομενεῖ.

not, another in fearing when one should not, and so on; and so too with respect to the things that inspire confidence. The man, then, who faces and who fears what he should and with the end he should have and how he should and when he should, and who feels confidence under the corresponding conditions, is courageous; for the courageous man feels and acts worthily and as reason directs. The end of every activity is conformity to the corresponding state. This is true, therefore, of the courageous man. But courage is noble.[2] Therefore the end also is noble; for each thing is defined by its end. Therefore it is for a noble end that the courageous man faces things and acts as courage directs.

Of those who go to excess he who exceeds in fearlessness has no name (we have said previously that many states have no names), but he would be a sort of madman or insensate person if he feared nothing, neither earthquakes nor the waves, as they say the Celts do not; while the man who exceeds in confidence about what is frightening is over-confident. The over-confident man is also thought to be boastful and a pretender to courage: thus[3] as the courageous man *is* with regard to what is frightening, so the over-confident man wants to *appear*; and so he imitates him where he can. That is why most of them are a mixture of over-confidence and cowardice; for, while in these situations they display confidence, they do not face what is frightening.

The man who exceeds in fear is a coward; for he fears both what he ought not and as he ought not, and all the similar characterizations attach to him. He is lacking also in confidence; but he is more conspicuous for his excess of fear in painful situations. The coward, then, is a pessimistic sort of person; for he fears everything. The courageous man has the contrary disposition; for confidence is the mark of an optimistic disposition. The coward, the over-confident man, and

20

25

30

1116a

5

2 Reading δή · ἡ δ' ἀνδρεία for δὲ ἡ ἀνδρεία (which Bywater prints between obeli).

3 ´Reading οὖν (Bywater changes to γοῦν).

the courageous man, then, are concerned with the same things but are differently disposed towards them; for the first two exceed and fall short, while the third is in a middling state and as he should be; and over-confident men are impetuous, and are willing before the dangers arrive but draw back when they are in them, while courageous men are keen in the moment of action but quiet beforehand.

10 As we have said, then, courage is a mean with respect to things that inspire confidence or fear, in the circumstances that have been stated; and it chooses or faces up to things because it is noble to do so, or because it is ignoble not to do so. But to die to escape from poverty or love or anything painful is not the mark of a courageous man, but rather of a coward; for it is softness to fly from what demands exertion, and such 15 a man faces death not because it is noble but rather to avoid something bad.

COURAGE, THEN, IS SOMETHING OF THIS SORT; BUT THE name is also applied to five other kinds. First comes the political kind; for this is most like it. Citizens seem to face dangers because of penalties imposed by the laws and re- 20 proaches, and because of honours; and therefore those peoples seem to be most courageous among whom cowards are held in dishonour and courageous men in honour. This is the kind of courage that Homer depicts, for instance in Diomedes and in Hector:

Polydamas will be the first to taunt me;

and

25 For Hector one day 'mid the Trojans shall utter his vaulting harangue:
'Afraid was Tydeides, and fled from my face'.[4]

This kind of courage is most like that which we described earlier because it is due to virtue; for it is due to modesty and to desire of a noble object (honour) and to avoidance of

4 *Iliad* XXII 100 and VII 148–149.

reproach, which is ignoble. One might rank in the same class even those who are compelled by their rulers; but they are inferior, inasmuch as they act not from modesty but from fear, and to avoid not what is ignoble but what is painful; for those who control them compel them, as Hector does: 30

But if I shall spy any dastard that cowers far from the fight,

and

Vainly will such a one hope to escape from the dogs.[5]

And those who give them their orders and beat them if they retreat do the same, and so do those who draw them up with trenches or something of the sort behind them: all of these apply compulsion. But one ought to be courageous not under compulsion but because it is noble to be so. 1116b

Experience with regard to particular facts is also thought to be courage—this is why Socrates thought courage was knowledge. Other people exhibit this quality in other dangers, and soldiers exhibit it in the dangers of war; for there seem to be many empty alarms in war, of which these have had the most comprehensive experience: so they seem courageous because the others do not know the nature of the facts. Again, their experience makes them most capable of doing without being done to, since they can use their arms and have the kind that are likely to be best both for doing and for not being done to: so they fight like armed men against unarmed or like trained athletes against amateurs—for in such contests too it is not the most courageous men that fight best but those who are strongest and have their bodies in the best condition. Soldiers turn cowards, however, when the danger puts too great a strain on them and they are inferior in numbers and equipment; for they are the first to fly, while citizen-forces die at their posts, as in fact happened at the temple of Hermes. For to the latter flight is ignoble and death is more desirable than safety on those terms; while the 5 10 15 20

5 *Iliad* II 391 and XV 348.

former from the beginning faced the danger on the supposition that they were stronger, and when they know the facts they fly, fearing death more than what is ignoble. The courageous man is not that sort of person.

Passion also is sometimes reckoned as courage: those who act from passion, like brutes rushing at those who have wounded them, are thought to be courageous, because courageous men also are given to passion. For passion above all things is eager to rush on danger, and hence Homer's 'He put strength in his passion' and 'He aroused their spirit and passion' and 'bitter spirit in his nostrils' and 'his blood boiled'.[6] For all such expressions seem to indicate the stirring and onrush of passion. Now courageous men act because of the noble, and passion collaborates with them; but brutes act because of pain—they attack because they have been wounded or because they are afraid, since if they are in a forest they do not come near one. Thus they are not courageous because, driven by pain and passion, they rush on danger without foreseeing anything fearful. At that rate even asses would be courageous when they are hungry—for blows will not drive them from their food; and their appetites make adulterers do many daring things.[7] The courage that is due to passion seems to be the most natural, and to be courage if choice and aim be added.

Men suffer pain when they are angry, and are pleased when they exact their revenge. Those who fight for these reasons, however, are pugnacious but not courageous; for they do not act for the sake of the noble nor as reason directs, but from emotion. They have, however, something akin to courage.

Nor are optimists courageous; for they are confident in danger only because they have conquered often and against

6 *Iliad* V 470; XI 11; XVI 529; *Odyssey* XXIV 318.

7 Most manuscripts here add a sentence which Bywater deletes: 'Those things are not courageous, then, which are driven on to danger by pain or passion'.

many foes. Yet they closely resemble courageous men, because both are confident; but courageous men are confident
for the reasons stated earlier, while these are so because they
think they are the strongest and will suffer nothing. (Drunks
also behave in this way: they become optimistic.) When their   15
adventures do not succeed, however, they run away; but it is
the mark of a courageous man to face things that are, and
seem, frightening for a man, because it is noble to do so and
ignoble not to. That is why it is thought the mark of a more
courageous man to be fearless and undisturbed in sudden
alarms than to be so in those that are foreseen; for it must
have proceeded more from a state of character, because less   20
from preparation; for acts that are foreseen may be chosen
by calculation and reason, but sudden actions in accordance
with one's state of character.

   People who are ignorant also appear courageous, and they
are not far removed from the optimists, but are inferior inasmuch as they have no self-confidence while these have. That
is why the optimists hold their ground for a time; but those   25
who have been deceived fly if they know or suspect that
things are different—as happened to the Argives when they
fell in with the Spartans and took them for Sicyonians.

   We have, then, described the character both of courageous men and of those who are thought to be courageous.

THOUGH COURAGE IS CONCERNED WITH CONFIDENCE
and fear, it is not concerned with both alike, but more with   30
frightening things; for he who is undisturbed in face of these
and bears himself as he should towards them is more courageous than the man who does so towards the things that inspire confidence. It is for facing what is painful, then, as has
been said, that men are called courageous. That is why courage involves pain, and is justly praised; for it is harder to face
what is painful than to abstain from what is pleasant. Yet the
end which courage sets before it would seem to be pleasant,   1117b
but to be concealed by the attending circumstances, as happens also in athletic contests; for the end at which boxers

aim is pleasant—the crown and the honours—but the blows they take are distressing to flesh and blood, and painful, and so is their whole exertion; and because the blows and the exertions are many, the aim, which is but small, appears to have nothing pleasant in it. And so, if the case of courage is similar, death and wounds will be painful to the courageous man and he will receive them involuntarily, but he will face them because it is noble to do so or because it is ignoble not to. And the more he is possessed of virtue in its entirety and the happier he is, the more he will be pained at the thought of death; for life is best worth living for such a man, and he is knowingly losing the greatest goods, and this is painful. But he is nonetheless courageous, and perhaps all the more so, because he chooses noble deeds of war at that cost. It is not the case, then, with all the virtues that the exercise of them is pleasant, except in so far as it reaches its end. But perhaps nothing prevents it from being the case that the best soldiers are not men of this sort but rather those who are less courageous but have no other good; for these are ready to face danger, and they sell their life for trifling profits.

So much, then, for courage; it is not difficult to grasp its nature in outline, at any rate, from what has been said.

AFTER COURAGE LET US SPEAK OF TEMPERANCE; FOR these seem to be the virtues of the irrational parts. We have said that temperance is a mean with regard to pleasures (for it is less, and not in the same way, concerned with pains); and self-indulgence also is manifested in the same circumstances. Now, therefore, let us determine with what sort of pleasures they are concerned. We may take for granted the distinction between bodily pleasures and those of the soul, such as love of honour and love of learning. The lover of each of these things delights in that of which he is a lover, his body being in no way affected but rather his mind; but men who are concerned with such pleasures are called neither temperate nor self-indulgent. Nor, again, are those who are concerned with the other pleasures that are not bodily; for those

who are fond of hearing and telling stories and who spend
their days on anything that turns up are called gossips but
not self-indulgent, nor are those who are pained at the loss
of wealth or of friends.

Temperance must be concerned with bodily pleasures—
but not with all of them. For those who delight in objects of
sight, such as colours and shapes and painting, are called
neither temperate nor self-indulgent; yet it would seem pos-   5
sible to delight even in these either as one should or to excess
or deficiency. And so too is it with objects of hearing: no one
calls those who delight excessively in music or acting self-
indulgent, nor those who do so as they ought temperate.
Nor do we apply these names to those who delight in smells,
unless it be coincidentally: we call self-indulgent not those   10
who delight in the smell of apples or roses or incense, but
rather of unguents or of dainty dishes; for self-indulgent
people delight in these because these remind them of the objects of their appetite. And one may see other people, when
they are hungry, delighting in the smell of food; but to de-   15
light in this kind of thing is the mark of the self-indulgent
man; for these are objects of appetite to him.

Nor is there in animals other than man any pleasure connected with these senses except coincidentally. For dogs do
not delight in the scent of hares but in eating them—but the
scent lets them perceive them; nor does the lion delight in   20
the lowing of the ox but in eating it—but he perceived by the
lowing that it was near, and therefore appears to delight in
the lowing; and similarly he does not delight because he sees
'a stag or a wild goat'[8] but because he is going to make a meal
of it. Temperance and self-indulgence, however, are concerned with the kind of pleasures that the other animals   25
share in, which therefore appear slavish and brutish: these
are touch and taste. But of taste they appear to make little or
no use; for the business of taste is the discriminating of fla-
vours, which is done by wine-tasters and people who season

8 Homer, *Iliad* III 24.

30 dishes. They hardly take delight in these things—or at least self-indulgent people do not—but rather in the enjoyment, which in all cases comes through touch, both in the case of food and in that of drink and in that of sexual intercourse. This is why a certain gourmand prayed that his throat might become longer than a crane's, implying that it was the con-

1118b tact that he took pleasure in. Thus self-indulgence is connected with what is the most widely shared of the senses; and it would seem to be justly a matter of reproach because it attaches to us not as men but as animals. To delight in such things, then, and to cherish them above all others, is brutish.

5 For the most liberal of the pleasures of touch have been eliminated—for instance, those produced in the gymnasium by rubbing and by the consequent heat; for the contact characteristic of the self-indulgent man does not affect the whole body but certain parts.

Of the appetites some seem to be common, others to be peculiar to individuals and acquired: for instance, the appe-

10 tite for nourishment is natural, since everyone who is without it craves for food or drink, and sometimes for both—and for a bed too (as Homer says) if he is young and lusty; but not everyone craves for this or that kind, nor for the same things. That is why such craving appears to be our very own. Yet it has of course something natural about it; for different things are pleasant to different kinds of people, and some things

15 are more pleasant to everyone than chance objects. Now in the natural appetites few err, and only in one direction, that of excess; for to eat or drink whatever offers itself till one is surfeited is to exceed the natural amount, since natural appetite is the replenishment of a lack. That is why these peo-

20 ple are called belly-gods, this implying that they fill their belly beyond what they should. It is people of entirely slavish character that become like this. But with regard to the pleasures peculiar to individuals many people err and in many ways. For while the people who are fond of so and so are so called because they delight either in what they should not, or more than most people do, or not how they should, the self-

indulgent exceed in every way: they delight in some things   25
that they ought not to delight in (since they are are hateful),
and if one ought to delight in some of the things they delight
in, they do so more than one ought and than most men do.

Plainly, then, excess with regard to pleasures is self-
indulgence and is blameworthy. With regard to pains one is
not, as in the case of courage, called temperate for facing   30
them or self-indulgent for not doing so—rather the self-
indulgent man is so called because he is pained more than he
ought to be at not getting pleasant things (even his pain being
caused by pleasure), and the temperate man is so called because he is not pained at the absence of what is pleasant and
at his abstinence from it.

The self-indulgent man, then, craves for all pleasant things   1119a
or those that are most pleasant, and is led by his appetite to
choose these at the cost of other things. That is why he is
pained both when he fails to get them and when he is craving for them (for appetite involves pain); but it seems absurd to be pained because of pleasure. People who fall short   5
with regard to pleasures and delight in them less than they
should are hardly found; for such insensibility is not human.
Even the other animals distinguish different kinds of food
and delight in some and not in others; and if there is anyone
who finds nothing pleasant and nothing more attractive
than anything else, he must be something quite different   10
from a man. This sort of person has not received a name because he is hardly found. The temperate man occupies a
middle position with regard to these objects. For he neither
takes pleasure in the things that the self-indulgent man
takes most pleasure in—but rather is vexed by them—nor in
general in the things that he should not, nor in anything of
this sort intensely; nor again does he feel pain or appetite
when they are absent, or does so only to an appropriate degree, and not more than he should, nor when he should not,   15
and so on. But the things that, being pleasant, make for
health or for good condition, he will desire appropriately
and as he should, and also other pleasant things if they are

not hindrances to these ends, or contrary to what is noble, or beyond his means. For he who neglects these conditions

20 cherishes such pleasures for more than they are worth, whereas the temperate man is not that sort of person but the sort of person that correct reasoning prescribes.

Self-indulgence is more like a voluntary state than cowardice is. For the former is actuated by pleasure, the latter by pain, of which the one is desirable and the other to be avoided; and pain upsets and destroys the nature of the person who feels it, while pleasure does nothing of the sort. So

25 self-indulgence is more voluntary. That is why also it is more a matter of reproach; for it is easier to become habituated to its objects, since there are many things of this sort in life, and the process of habituation is free from danger, while with frightening things the reverse is the case. But cowardice would seem to be voluntary in a different degree from its particular acts; for it is itself painless, whereas in acting we

30 are upset by pain, so that we even throw down our arms and disgrace ourselves in other ways—that is why our acts are even thought to be done perforce. For the self-indulgent man, on the other hand, the particular acts are voluntary (for he does them with appetite and desire), but the whole state is less so; for no one craves to be self-indulgent.

The name self-indulgence is applied also to childish er-

1119b rors; for they bear a certain resemblance to it. Which is called after which, makes no difference to our present purpose: plainly, however, the later is called after the earlier. The extension of the name seems not a bad one; for that which desires what is ignoble and which develops quickly ought to

5 have been chastised,⁹ and these characteristics belong above all to appetite and to the child, since children in fact live at the beck and call of appetite, and it is in them that the desire for what is pleasant is strongest. If, then, it is not obedient and subject to the ruling principle, it will go to great lengths;

9 'Self-indulgent' is ἀκόλαστος, 'to have been chastised' is κεκολάσθαι, the perfect passive infinitive of κολάζειν.

for in an unintelligent being the desire for pleasure is insatiable and tries every source of gratification, the exercise of appetite increases its innate force, and if appetites are strong and intense they even expel the power of calculation. That is why they should be appropriate and few, and should in no way be contrary to reason (this is what we call an obedient and chastened state); and as the child should live according to the direction of his tutor, so the appetitive element should live according to reason. That is why the appetitive element in a temperate man should harmonize with reason; for the noble is the mark at which both aim, and the temperate man craves for the things he ought, as he ought, and when he ought; and this is what reason directs.

Here we conclude our account of temperance.

LET US SPEAK NEXT OF LIBERALITY. IT SEEMS TO BE THE mean with regard to wealth; for the liberal man is praised not in respect of military matters, nor of those in respect of which the temperate man is praised, nor of assessments, but with regard to the giving and taking of wealth, and especially in respect of giving. Now by wealth we mean all the things whose worth is measured by money. Prodigality and illiberality are excesses and deficiencies with regard to wealth. Illiberality we always impute to those who busy themselves more than they ought about wealth, but we sometimes apply the word 'prodigality' in a complex sense; for we call those men prodigals who are incontinent and spend on self-indulgence. That is why they are thought the basest characters; for they have more vices than one. The application of the word to them is not appropriate; for 'prodigal' means a man who has a single bad quality, that of wasting his substance; for a prodigal is one who is being ruined by his own doing, and the wasting of substance is thought to be a sort of ruining of oneself, life being held to depend on possession of substance. This, then, is how we understand prodigality.

The things that have a use may be used either well or badly; riches are a useful thing; and everything is used best

Book Δ

by the man who has the virtue concerned with it: riches, therefore, will be used best by the man who has the virtue concerned with wealth, and this is the liberal man. Spending and giving seem to be the using of wealth; taking and keeping rather the possessing of it. That is why it is more the
10   mark of the liberal man to give to whom he should to than to take whence he should and not to take whence he should not. For it is more characteristic of virtue to do good than to have good done to one, and to do what is noble than not to do what is ignoble; and it is not hard to see that giving implies doing good and doing what is noble, and taking implies
15   having good done to one or not acting ignobly. Gratitude is felt towards him who gives, not towards him who does not take, and praise also is bestowed more on him. It is easier too not to take than to give; for men are apter to give away their own too little than to take what is another's. Givers,
20   too, are called liberal whereas those who do not take are not praised for liberality but rather for justice, and those who take are not praised at all. The liberal are practically the most loved of all virtuous characters, since they are beneficial; and this depends on their giving.

Virtuous actions are noble and done for the sake of the noble. Therefore the liberal man will give for the sake of the
25   noble and correctly: he will give to whom he should, as much as he should, and when he should, with all the other qualifications that accompany correct giving. And that with pleasure or without pain; for that which is virtuous is pleasant or painless—least of all will it be painful. He who gives to those he should not or not for the sake of the noble but for some other cause, will be called not liberal but by some other
30   name. Nor is he liberal who gives with pain; for he would prefer the wealth to the noble action, and this is not characteristic of a liberal man. No more will he take whence he should not; for such taking is not characteristic of the man who sets no value on wealth. Nor will he be a ready asker; for it is not characteristic of a benefactor to accept gifts lightly. But he will take from where he should, for instance from his

own possessions—not as something noble but as a necessity,
so that he may have something to give. Nor will he neglect
his own property, since he wants by means of this to help
others. And he will refrain from giving to all and sundry so
that he may have something to give to whom he should,
when he should, and where it is noble to do so. It is highly
characteristic of a liberal man also to go to excess in giving, 5
so that he leaves less for himself; for it is the nature of a liberal man not to look to himself.

The term 'liberality' is used relatively to a man's substance; for liberality resides not in the multitude of the gifts
but in the state of the giver, and this is relative to the giver's
substance.[10] There is therefore nothing to prevent the man 10
who gives less from being the more liberal man, if he has less
to give. Those are thought to be more liberal who have not
acquired their wealth but inherited it; for they have no experience of want, and all men cherish their own products more,
as parents and poets do. It is not easy for the liberal man to
be rich, since he is not apt either at taking or at keeping but 15
rather at giving away, and he does not value wealth for its
own sake but for the sake of giving. That is why the charge is
brought against fortune that those who are most worthy of
riches get least. But it is not unreasonable that it should turn
out so; for you cannot have wealth, any more than anything 20
else, if you do not take care to have it. He will not give to
those he ought not, when he ought not, and so on; for he
would no longer be acting in accordance with liberality, and
if he spent on these objects he would have nothing to spend
on what he should. For, as has been said, he is liberal who
spends according to his substance and on what he should.
He who exceeds is prodigal. That is why we do not call des- 25
pots prodigal; for it is thought not easy for them to give and
spend beyond the amount of their possessions.

Liberality, then, being a mean with regard to the giving
and taking of wealth, the liberal man will both give and

---

10 Omitting δίδωσιν (as Bywater suggests).

spend as much as he should on what he should, alike in small
30   things and in great, and that with pleasure; he will also take
as much as he should whence he should. For, the virtue being
a mean with regard to both, he will do both as he should. For
an upright sort of taking goes with an upright sort of giving,
and a taking that is not upright is contrary: accordingly
those that accompany each other are present together in the
1121a   same man, while the contrary kinds plainly are not. If he
happens to spend not what he should or not what is noble,
he will be pained—but appropriately and as he should; for it
is the mark of virtue both to be pleased and to be pained at
what one should be and how one should be. Further, the lib-
5   eral man is an easy associate in business matters; for he can
be treated unjustly since he sets no value on wealth, and is
more annoyed if he has not spent something that he ought
than pained if he has spent something that he ought not, and
he wins the approval of Simonides.[11] The prodigal errs in
these respects also; for he is neither pleased nor pained at
what he should be nor how he should be—this will be more
evident as we go on.
10   We have said that prodigality and illiberality are excesses
and deficiencies, and in two things, in giving and in taking;
for we include spending under giving. Now prodigality exceeds in giving and not taking, and falls short in taking, while
15   illiberality falls short in giving and exceeds in taking, except
in small things. The characteristics of prodigality are not
often combined; for it is not easy to give to all if you take from
none. Private persons soon exhaust their substance with
giving, and it is they that are thought to be prodigal—though
a man of this sort would seem to be in no small degree better
20   than an illiberal man. For he is easily cured both by age and by
poverty, and thus he may come to the middle state. For he
has the characteristics of the liberal man, since he both gives
and refrains from taking, though he does neither of these

11 See the anecdote in *Rhet* B, 1391a8–12, according to which Simonides
said that it is better to be rich than to be wise.

as he should or well. So if he were habituated to do so or changed in some other way, he would be liberal; for he would then give to whom he should, and would not take whence he should not. This is why he is thought not to have a base character: it is the mark not of a depraved or ill-bred man to go to excess in giving and not taking, but of a fool. The man who is prodigal in this way is thought much better than the illiberal man both for the aforesaid reasons and because he benefits many while the other benefits no one, not even himself.

But most prodigal people, as has been said, also take whence they should not, and are in this respect illiberal. They become apt to take because they want to spend and cannot do this readily; for their possessions soon run short. Thus they are compelled to provide means from some other source. At the same time, because they care nothing for the noble, they take disdainfully and from any source; for they crave to give, and they do not mind how or whence. Hence also their giving is not liberal; for it is not noble, nor does it aim at nobility, nor is it done as it should be: sometimes they make rich those who should be poor, and they will give nothing to people of respectable character, and much to flatterers or to those who provide them with some other pleasure. That is why most of them are self-indulgent; for they spend readily and waste money on their indulgences, and they incline towards pleasures because they do not live with a view to what is noble.

The prodigal man, then, turns into what we have described if he is left untutored, but if he is cared for he will arrive at the middle state and where he should be. But illiberality is both incurable (for old age and every incapacity is thought to make men illiberal) and more innate in men than prodigality; for most men are fonder of wealth than of giving. It also extends widely, and is multiform—for there seem to be many kinds of illiberality.

It consists in two things, deficiency in giving and excess in taking, and is not found complete in all cases but is some-

20 times divided, some men being excessive in taking and others falling short in giving. Those who are called by such names as 'miserly', 'close', 'stingy', are all deficient in giving, but they do not aim for the possessions of others nor want to get them. In some this is due to a sort of uprightness and

25 avoidance of what is ignoble (for some seem, or at least profess, to hoard their money so that they may not some day be compelled to do something ignoble: to this class belong the cheeseparer and everyone of the sort, who are so called from their excess in not giving). Others again keep their hands off other people's goods from fear, on the ground that it is not

30 easy, if one takes the property of others oneself, to avoid having one's own taken by them—they approve, therefore, neither of taking nor of giving.

Others again exceed in respect of taking by taking anything and from any source, for instance those who ply sordid trades, pimps and all such people, and those who lend small

1122a sums and at high rates. For all of these take more than they ought and whence they ought not. What is common to them is evidently avarice: they all face up to reproaches for the sake of profit, and little profit at that. For those who make great profits whence they should not and which they should not—for instance, despots when they sack cities and spoil

5 temples—we do not call illiberal but rather vicious, impious, and unjust. But the gamester and the footpad[12] belong to the class of the illiberal, since they are avaricious. For it is for gain that both of them ply their craft and face up to reproaches, and the one faces the greatest dangers for the sake

10 of the takings, while the other profits from his friends, to whom he ought to be giving. Both, then, since they are willing to profit whence they ought not, are avaricious; and all such forms of taking are illiberal.

It is reasonable that illiberality is described as the contrary of liberality; for it is a greater evil than prodigality, and

15

12 Omitting (perhaps with Aspasius) καὶ ὁ λῃστής ('and the brigand').

men err more often in this direction than in the way of the prodigality we have described.

So much, then, for liberality and the opposed vices.

IT WOULD SEEM COHERENT TO DISCUSS MAGNIFICENCE next. For this also seems to be a virtue concerned with wealth; but it does not like liberality extend to all the actions 20 that are concerned with wealth but only to those that involve expenditure; and in these it surpasses liberality in scale. For, as the name itself intimates, it is a fitting expenditure involving largeness of scale.[13] The largeness is relative; for the expense of equipping a trireme is not the same as that of heading a sacred embassy. It is what is fitting, then, in relation to 25 the agent, and to the circumstances and the object. The man who in small or moderate matters spends worthily is not called magnificent (for instance, the man who can say 'many a gift I gave the wanderer'[14]), but only the man who does so in great things. For the magnificent man is liberal, but the liberal man is not necessarily magnificent.

The deficiency of this state is called shabbiness, the excess 30 vulgarity, tastelessness, and the like. They do not go to excess by spending largely on what they should but by showy expenditure where it should not be made and as it should not be made. We shall speak of these vices later.

The magnificent man is like a connoisseur; for he can contemplate what is fitting and spend large sums tastefully. For, as we said at the beginning, a state is determined by its 1122b activities and by its objects. Now the expenses of the magnificent man are great and fitting. Such, therefore, are also his deeds; for thus there will be a great expenditure and one that is fitting for the deed. Therefore the deed should be worthy 5 of the expense, and the expense should be worthy of the

13 'Magnificence' is μεγαλοπρέπεια, a compound deriving from μέγας ('great') and πρέπειν ('to be fitting').
14 Homer, *Odyssey* XVII 420.

deed, or should even exceed it. The magnificent man will spend such sums for the sake of the noble; for this is common to the virtues. Further, he will do so gladly and lavishly; for precise calculation is a shabby thing. And he will consider how the result can be made most noble and most becoming 10 rather than for how much and in what way most cheaply. It is necessary, then, that the magnificent man be also liberal. For the liberal man will spend what he ought and as he ought; and it is in these matters that the greatness implied in the name of the magnificent man—his magnitude, as it were— is found, since liberality is concerned with these matters; and at an equal expense he will do a more magnificent deed. 15 For a possession and a deed have not the same virtue. The possession worth most is that which is most valuable (for instance, gold), but the deed worth most is that which is great and noble (for the contemplation of such a thing inspires admiration, and so does magnificence); and the virtue of a deed[15] involves magnitude.

It concerns expenditures of the kind we call honourable, 20 for instance those connected with the gods—offerings, buildings, sacrifices—and similarly with anything to do with religion, and all those that are proper objects of public-spirited ambition, as when people think they ought to equip a chorus or a trireme, or entertain the city in a brilliant way. But in all cases, as has been said, we have regard to the agent 25 as well and ask who he is and what means he has; for the expenditure should be worthy of his means, and suit not only the deed but also the doer. That is why a poor man cannot be magnificent, since he has not the means with which to spend large sums fittingly; and he who tries is a fool, since he spends unworthily and not as he should, and it is correct ex- 30 penditure that is virtuous. It is fitting for those who have suitable means to start with, acquired by their own efforts or from ancestors or connexions, and for people of high birth

15 Omitting ἡ μεγαλοπρέπεια (Muretus).

or reputation, and so on; for all these things bring with them greatness and prestige.

Primarily, then, the magnificent man is of this sort, and magnificence is found in expenditures of this sort, as has been said; for these are the greatest and most honourable. Of private occasions they are those that take place once for all, for instance a wedding or anything of the kind, or anything about which the whole State or the people of prestige in it busy themselves, and the receiving of foreign guests and the sending of them on their way, and gifts and countergifts. For the magnificent man spends not on himself but on public objects, and gifts bear some resemblance to offerings. A magnificent man will also furnish his house fittingly to his riches (for a house is a sort of adornment), he will spend by preference on those deeds that are lasting (for they are the noblest), and on every class of things he will spend what is fitting—for the same things are not suitable for gods and for men, nor in a temple and a tomb. And since each expenditure may be great of its kind, and what is most magnificent in the abstract is great expenditure on a great object, but what is magnificent *here* is what is great in *these* circumstances, and greatness in the deed differs from greatness in the expense (for the most beautiful ball or bottle is magnificent as a gift to a child, but its value is small and ungenerous)—therefore it is characteristic of the magnificent man, whatever kind of thing he is doing, to do it magnificently (for that is not easily exceeded) and to make it worthy of the expenditure.

Such, then, is the magnificent man. The man who goes to excess and is vulgar exceeds, as has been said, by spending beyond what he should. For on small objects of expenditure he spends much and displays a tasteless showiness: for instance, he gives a club dinner on the scale of a wedding banquet, and when he provides the chorus for a comedy he brings them on to the stage in purple, as they do at Megara. And all such things he will do not for the sake of the noble

1123a

5

10

15

20

25

287

but to show off his riches, and because he thinks he is admired for these things; and where he ought to spend much he spends little and where little, much. The shabby man on the other hand will be deficient in everything, and after spending the greatest sums will spoil the nobility of it for a trifle, and whatever he is doing he will hesitate and consider how he may spend least, and lament even that, and think he is doing everything on a bigger scale than he ought.

These states, then, are vices; yet they do not incur reproach because they are neither harmful to one's neighbour nor very unseemly.

PRIDE SEEMS EVEN FROM ITS NAME TO BE CONCERNED with great things:[16] with what sort of great things, is the first question we must try to answer. It makes no difference whether we consider the state of character or the man characterized by it. Now the man is thought to be proud who thinks himself worthy of great things, being worthy of them; for he who does so beyond his worth is a fool, but no virtuous man is foolish or unintelligent. The proud man, then, is the man we have described. For he who is worthy of little and thinks himself worthy of little is temperate but not proud; for pride implies greatness, as beauty implies a big body—little people may be neat and well-proportioned but cannot be beautiful. He who thinks himself worthy of great things, being unworthy of them, is vain; though not everyone who thinks himself worthy of more than he is is vain. The man who thinks himself worthy of less than he is, is diffident, whether his worth be great or moderate, or his worth small but his claims yet smaller. And the man whose worth is great would seem most diffident; for what would he have done if it had been less? The proud man, then, is extreme in respect of greatness, but midway in respect of what he should be; for he

16 'Pride' is μεγαλοψυχία, a compound from μέγας ('great') and ψυχή ('soul').

claims what is in accordance with his worth, while the others   15
are excessive or deficient.

If, then, he is worthy of great things and claims them (and
above all the greatest things), he will be concerned with one
thing in particular. Worth is relative to external goods; and
the greatest of these, we should say, is that which we render
to the gods, and which people of prestige most aim at, and
which is the prize appointed for the noblest deeds; and this   20
is honour: that is the greatest of external goods. Honours
and dishonours, therefore, are the objects with respect to
which the proud man is as he should be. And even apart from
argument it is evident that proud men are concerned with
honour; for it is honour that they chiefly claim—but in accordance with their worth. The diffident man is deficient
both in comparison with his own worth and in comparison   25
with the proud man's claims. The vain man goes to excess in
comparison with his own worth but does not exceed the
proud man's claims.

The proud man, since he is worthy of the greatest things,
must be good in the highest degree; for the better man is always worthy of the greater things, and the best man of the
greatest. Therefore the truly proud man must be good. And
greatness in every virtue would seem to be characteristic of a   30
proud man. It would be most unsuitable for a proud man to
fly from danger, swinging his arms by his sides, or to treat
anyone unjustly; for to what end will he do ignoble acts, he
to whom nothing is great? If we consider him point by point
we shall see that a proud man who is not good would be utterly ridiculous. Nor, again, would he be worthy of honour if
he were base; for honour is the prize of virtue and it is to the   1124a
good that it is rendered. Pride, then, seems to be a sort of ornament of the virtues; for it makes them greater, and it is not
found without them. That is why it is hard to be truly proud;
for it is impossible without gentlemanliness.

It is chiefly with honours and dishonours, then, that the   5
proud man is concerned; and at honours that are great and

conferred by virtuous men he will be moderately pleased, thinking that he is coming by his own or even less than his own. For there can be no honour that is worthy of perfect virtue, yet he will at any rate accept it since they have nothing

10   greater to bestow on him. Honour from all and sundry and on trifling grounds he will utterly disdain, since it is not this of which he is worthy, and dishonour too, since in his case it cannot be just. In the first place, then, as has been said, the proud man is concerned with honours; yet he will also bear himself appropriately towards riches and power and all good

15   or bad fortune, whatever may befall him, and will be neither over-joyed by good fortune nor over-pained by bad. For not even about honour does he care much, although it is the greatest thing[17] (for power and riches are desirable for the sake of honour—at least those who have them want to get honour by means of them); and for him to whom even hon-

20   our is a little thing the other things must be so too. Hence proud men are thought to be supercilious.

The goods of fortune also are thought to contribute towards pride. For men who are well-born are thought worthy of honour, and so are those who enjoy power or riches; for they are in a superior position, and everything that has a superiority in something good is held in greater honour. That is why even such things make men prouder; for they are hon-

25   oured by some. In truth the good man alone is to be honoured; but he who has both advantages is thought the more worthy of honour. But those who without virtue have such goods are neither justified in making great claims nor correctly called proud; for these things imply perfect virtue. Su-

30   percilious and insolent, however, even those who have such goods become. For without virtue it is not easy to bear grace-

1124b fully the goods of fortune; and, being unable to bear them, and thinking themselves superior to others, they despise others and themselves do what they please. They imitate the proud man without being like him, and this they do where

17 Omitting ὡς.

they can. They do not act virtuously, but they do despise   5
others. For the proud man despises justly (since he has true
beliefs), but the many do so at random.

He does not run into trifling dangers, nor is he fond of
danger, because he honours few things; but he will face great
dangers, and when he is in danger he is unsparing of his life,
knowing that there are conditions on which life is not worth
having. And he is the sort of man to be a benefactor, but he is
ashamed of being a beneficiary; for the one is the mark of a   10
superior, the other of an inferior. And he is apt to confer
greater benefactions in return; for thus the original benefactor will incur a debt to him, and will have been done well by.
They seem also to remember any service they have done, but
not those they have received (for he who receives a service is
inferior to him who has done it, and the proud man wants to
be superior), and to hear of the former with pleasure, of the   15
latter with displeasure. That, it seems, is why Thetis did not
mention to Zeus the benefactions she had showered on him,
and why the Spartans did not recount their services to the
Athenians but those they had received from them.[18]

It is a mark of the proud man also to ask for nothing or
scarcely anything, but to give help eagerly, and to be haughty
towards people who enjoy prestige and good fortune, and
unassuming towards those of the middle class—for it is a dif-   20
ficult and dignified thing to be superior to the former, but
easy to be so to the latter, and a dignified bearing over the
former is no mark of ill-breeding, but among humble people
it is as vulgar as a display of strength against the weak.

Again, it is characteristic of the proud man not to aim at
the things held in honour, or the things in which others
excel; to be idle and to hold back except where there are
great honours and great deeds; and to be a man of few deeds   25
but of great and notable ones. He must also be open in his
hate and in his love (for to conceal one's feelings is a mark of

18 See Homer, *Iliad* I 503–504 (Thetis), and Xenophon, *Hell* VI v 33–34
(the Spartans)—though neither text supports what Aristotle says.

fear), and must care[19] more for the truth than for his reputation, and must speak and act openly; for he is free of speech
30 because he is supercilious, and candid, except when he speaks in self-deprecation to the vulgar. He must be unable
1125a to make his life revolve round another unless it be a friend; for this is slavish—that is why all flatterers are servile and the humble are flatterers. Nor is he given to admiration; for nothing to him is great. Nor is he mindful of wrongs; for it is not the part of a proud man to have a long memory, espe-
5 cially for wrongs, but rather to overlook them. Nor is he a gossip; for he will speak neither about himself nor about another, since he cares not to be praised nor for others to be blamed; nor again is he given to praise; and for the same reason he is not an evil-speaker, even about his enemies, except from insolence. With regard to necessary or small matters he
10 is least of all men given to lamentation or the asking of favours; for it is the part of one who busies himself about such matters to behave so with respect to them. He is one who will possess beautiful and fruitless things rather than fruitful and beneficial ones; for this is rather a mark of the self-sufficient man.

A slow step is thought characteristic of the proud man, a deep voice, and a level utterance; for the man who busies
15 himself about few things is not likely to be hurried, nor the man who thinks nothing great to be excited, while a shrill voice and a rapid gait are the results of hurry and excitement.

Such, then, is the proud man: the man who is deficient is diffident, and the man who exceeds is vain. These are not thought to be bad (for they are not evil-doers) but mistaken.
20 For the diffident man, being worthy of good things, robs himself of what he is worthy of, and seems to have something bad about him from the fact that he does not think himself worthy of good things. He seems also not to know himself: else he would have desired the things he was worthy

19 Reading μέλειν with most manuscripts for ἀμελεῖν ('and must not care').

of, since these were good. Yet such people are not thought to be fools, but rather retiring. Such a belief, however, seems actually to make them worse; for each class of people aims at what corresponds to its worth, and these people stand back even from noble actions and undertakings, deeming themselves unworthy, and from external goods no less. Vain people, on the other hand, are fools and ignorant of themselves, and that manifestly; for, not being worthy of them, they attempt honourable undertakings, and then are found out; and they adorn themselves with clothing and outward show and such things, and want their strokes of good fortune to be evident, and speak about them as if they would be honoured for them. Diffidence is more opposed to pride than vanity is; for it is both commoner and worse.

PRIDE, THEN, IS CONCERNED WITH HONOUR ON THE grand scale, as has been said. There appears to be a virtue concerned with it, as was said in our first remarks, which would seem to be related to pride as liberality is to magnificence. For neither of these has anything to do with the grand scale, but both dispose us as we should be with regard to moderate and small matters: just as in getting and giving of wealth there is a mean and an excess and deficiency, so too honour may be desired more than it should be, or less, or whence it should be and as it should be. We blame both the ambitious man as aiming at more honour than he should and whence he should not, and the unambitious man as not choosing to be honoured even for noble reasons. But sometimes we praise the ambitious man as being manly and a lover of what is noble, and the unambitious man as being moderate and temperate as we said in our first remarks on the subject. Plainly, since people are said to love such and such in more than one way, we do not assign the term 'ambition'[20] always to the same thing: rather, when we praise the

20 'Ambition' is φιλοτιμία, a compound in φιλο-: a φιλο-such-and-such is someone who φιλεῖ or loves such-and-such.

quality we think of the man who loves honour more than most people, and when we blame it we think of him who loves it more than he should. The mean being without a name, the extremes seem to dispute for its place as though that were vacant. But where there is excess and deficiency, there is also a middle state: men desire honour both more
20   than they should and less, and so it is possible also to do so as one should; and this is the state that is praised, being an unnamed mean in respect of honour. Relatively to ambition it seems to be unambitiousness, and relatively to unambitiousness it seems to be ambition, while relatively to both it seems in a sense to be both. This appears to be true of the other vir-
25   tues also. But in this case the men at the extremes seem to be opposed because the man in the middle state has not received a name.

GOOD TEMPER IS A MEAN WITH RESPECT TO ANGER: THE middle state being unnamed, and the extremes practically without a name as well, we place good temper in the middle position, though it inclines towards the deficiency, which is without a name. The excess might be called a sort of irasci-
30   bility. For the emotion is anger, while its causes are many and diverse.

The man who is angry at what he should be and with whom he should be, and, further, as he should, when he should, and for as long as he should, is praised. This will be the good-tempered man, then, since good temper is praised. For the good-tempered man tends to be undisturbed and not to be led by emotion, but rather to be angry in the manner, at the things, and for the length of time, that reason dic-
1126a   tates. He is thought to err rather in the direction of deficiency; for the good-tempered man is not revengeful, but rather tends to sympathize.

The deficiency, whether it is a sort of inirascibility or whatever it is, is blamed. For those who are not angry at the things
5   they should be are thought to be fools, and so are those who are not angry as they should be, when they should be, or with

whom they should be; for such a man is thought not to perceive things nor to be pained by them, and since he does not get angry, he is thought unlikely to defend himself; and to endure being insulted and to overlook insults to one's associates is slavish.

The excess can be manifested in all the points (for one can be angry with whom one should not be, at what one should not be, more than one should be, too quickly, or too long); yet all are not found in the same person. Indeed they could not be; for the bad destroys even itself, and if it is complete becomes unbearable. Hot-tempered people get angry quickly and with whom they should not and at what they should not and more than they should, but their anger ceases quickly—which is the best point about them. This happens to them because they do not repress their anger but retaliate openly owing to their quickness of temper, and then their anger ceases. By reason of excess choleric people are quick-tempered and ready to be angry with everything and on every occasion; whence their name.[21] Bitter people are hard to appease, and retain their anger long; for they repress their passion. But it ceases when they retaliate; for revenge ends their anger, producing in them pleasure instead of pain. If this does not happen they retain their burden; for owing to its not being manifest no one even tries to persuade them, and to digest one's anger in oneself needs time. Such people are most troublesome to themselves and to their closest friends. We call bad-tempered those who are angry at what they should not be, more than they should be, and longer, and cannot be appeased until they inflict vengeance or punishment.

To good temper we oppose the excess rather than the deficiency; for not only is it commoner (since revenge is the more human), but bad-tempered people are worse to live with.

---

21 'Choleric' is ἀκρόχολος, which Aristotle seems to construe as 'having bile near the surface'.

What we have said before is plain also from what is said; for it is not easy to define how, with whom, at what, and how long one should be angry, and up to what point one acts cor-

35   rectly or errs. For the man who strays a little from the path, either towards the more or towards the less, is not blamed; for sometimes we praise those who exhibit the deficiency,

1126b   and call them good-tempered, and sometimes we call angry people manly, as being capable of ruling. How far, therefore, and how a man must stray before he becomes blameworthy, it is not easy to determine by reason; for the assessment depends on the particular facts and on perception. But this

5   much at least is plain: the middle state is praiseworthy—that in virtue of which we are angry with whom we should be, at what we should, as we should, and so on; and the excesses and deficiencies are blameworthy—slightly so if they are present in a low degree, more if in a higher degree, and very much if they are intense. Plainly, then, we must cling to the middle state.

10   Enough of the states relative to anger.

IN COMPANY, IN LIVING TOGETHER AND IN THE SHARING of words and actions, some men are thought to be obsequious, namely those who to give pleasure praise everything and oppose nothing but think they should give no pain to the people they meet; while those who, on the contrary, op-

15   pose everything and care not a whit about giving pain are called grumpy and contentious. That the states we have named are blameworthy is plain enough, and that the middle state is praiseworthy—that in virtue of which a man will put up with, and will be vexed at, what he should and as he

20   should. No name has been assigned to it, though it most resembles friendship. For the man who corresponds to this middle state is the sort whom, with affection added, we tend to call an upright friend. But it differs from friendship in that it implies no emotion or affection for one's companions; for it is not by reason of loving or hating that such a man takes

things as he should, but by being a man of a certain kind. For he will behave so alike towards those he knows and those he does not know, towards intimates and those who are not so, except that in each of these cases he will behave as is befitting; for it is not proper to have the same care for intimates and for strangers, nor again to pain them in the same ways.

Now we have said generally that he will behave in company as he should; but it is by reference to what is noble and what is advantageous that he will aim at either[22] giving pain or contributing pleasure. For he seems to be concerned with the pleasures and pains of being in company with people; and wherever it is not noble, or is harmful, for him to contribute pleasure, he will be vexed, and will choose rather to give pain. If his acquiescence in another's action would bring disgrace, and that in a high degree, or harm, on the agent, while his being contrary to it brings a little pain, he will not acquiesce but will be vexed. He will behave differently in the company of people of prestige and with ordinary people, with closer and more distant acquaintances, and so too with regard to all other differences, rendering to each class what is fitting. And while for its own sake he chooses to contribute pleasure, and avoids the giving of pain, he will be guided by the consequences if these are greater—I mean by the noble and the advantageous. For the sake of a great future pleasure, too, he will inflict small pains.

The man in the middle state, then, is such as we have described, but has not received a name. Of those who contribute pleasure, the man who aims at being pleasant with no other aim is obsequious, and the man who does so in order that he may get some advantage in the way of money or the things that money buys is a flatterer; while the man who is vexed at everything is, as has been said, grumpy and contentious. The extremes seem to be opposed to each other because the middle is without a name.

22 Reading ἢ λυπεῖν (Imelmann) for μὴ λυπεῖν ('not giving pain').

THE MEAN FOR BOASTFULNESS[23] CONCERNS PRETTY WELL
the same things. It too is without a name. It will be no bad
plan to describe these states as well; for we shall both know
the facts about character better if we go through them in detail, and we shall be convinced that the virtues are means if
we see this to be so in all cases. In the matter of living together those who make the giving of pleasure or pain their
object in seeking the company of others have been described:
let us now describe those who pursue truth or falsehood
alike in words and deeds and in their pretentions. The boastful man, then, is thought to be apt to pretend to the things
that bring reputation, when he has not got them, or to pretend to more of them than he has, and the self-deprecator,
conversely, to disclaim what he has or belittle it, while the
man in the middle state is one who calls a thing by its own
name, being candid both in life and in word, owning to what
he has, and neither more nor less. Each of these courses may
be adopted either with or without an aim. Each man speaks
and acts and lives in accordance with his character if he is not
acting for some aim. And falsehood is in itself base and
blameworthy, and truth noble and praiseworthy. Thus the
candid man, being in the middle, is praiseworthy, and false
men of both sorts are blameworthy, but more so the boastful
man.

Let us discuss them both—but first the candid man. We
are not speaking of the man who is true to his agreements
and in the things that pertain to justice or injustice (for this
would belong to another virtue), but rather of him who in
the matters in which nothing of this sort is at stake is true
both in word and in life because his character is such. Such a
man would seem to be upright. For the man who loves truth,
and is truthful where nothing is at stake, will still more be
truthful where something is at stake: he will avoid falsehood
as something ignoble, seeing that he avoided it even for its

23 Omitting καὶ εἰρωνείας (which Bywater inserts).

own sake; and such a man is praiseworthy. He inclines rather to understate the truth; for this seems in better taste because exaggerations are wearisome.

He who pretends to more than he has with no end in view   10
is a base sort of fellow (otherwise he would not delight in falsehood), but seems futile rather than bad. If it is done with an end in view, he who does it for the sake of reputation or honour is (for a boaster[24]) not very much to be blamed, but he who does it for money, or the things that lead to money, is an uglier character (it is not the capacity that makes the boaster, but the choice; for it is in virtue of his   15
state and by being a man of a certain kind that he is a boaster). In the same way, one man is a liar because he delights in the lie itself, and another because he desires reputation or profit. Now those who boast for the sake of reputation pretend to such qualities as win praise or felicitation, while those whose end is profit pretend to qualities which are enjoyed by his neighbours and the absence of which is   20
not easily detected—for instance, the powers of a seer, a sage, or a doctor. For this reason it is such things as these that most people pretend to and boast about; for in them the above-mentioned qualities are found.

Self-deprecators, who understate things, seem more refined in character; for they are thought to speak not for profit but to avoid parade; and it is especially qualities which   25
bring reputation that they disclaim, as Socrates did. Those who disclaim trifling and evident qualities are called humbugs and are more despicable; and sometimes this seems to be boastfulness, like the Spartan dress; for both excess and great deficiency are boastful. But those who use understate-   30
ment appropriately and understate about matters that are not too obtrusive or evident seem refined. It is the boaster that seems to be opposed to the candid man; for he is the worse character.

24 Reading ὡς γ᾽ ἀλαζών (Imelmann) for ὡς ὁ ἀλαζών ('like the boaster').

SINCE LIFE INCLUDES REST AS WELL, AND IN THIS IS IN-
cluded leisure and amusement, there seems here also to be a
tasteful kind of behaviour in company: there is such a thing
as saying—and again listening to—what one should and as
one should. The kind of people one is speaking or listening to
will also make a difference. Plainly, here also there is both an
excess and a deficiency with regard to the middle. Those who
carry humour to excess are thought to be vulgar buffoons,
striving after humour at all costs, and aiming rather at raising
a laugh than at saying what is becoming and at avoiding pain
to the object of their mockery; while those who cannot say
anything funny themselves and are vexed with those who do
are thought to be boorish and unpolished. Those who joke in
a tasteful way are called convivial, which implies a sort of
readiness to turn this way and that;[25] for such things are
thought to be movements of the character, and as bodies are
assessed by their movements, so too are characters. The ridiculous side of things is not far to seek, however, and most people delight more than they should in amusement and in
mockery, and so even buffoons are called convivial because
they are found refined; but that they differ from the convivial
man, and to no small extent, is plain from what has been said.

Tact is related to the middle state, and it is the mark of a
tactful man to say and listen to such things as befit an upright and liberal man; for there are some things that it befits
such a man to say and to hear by way of amusement, and the
liberal man's amusements differ from those of a slavish man,
and those of an educated man from those of an uneducated.
One may see this even from the old and the new comedies:
to the authors of the former ignoble language was funny, to
those of the latter innuendo is more so; and these differ in no
small degree in respect of gracefulness.

Should we define the man who mocks well by his saying
what is not unbecoming to a liberal man, or by his not giving

25 'Conviviality' is εὐτραπελία, which Aristotle connects to εὔτροπος ('easily turning').

pain, or even giving delight, to the hearer? Or is the latter, at any rate, itself indefinite, since different things are hateful or pleasant to different people? The kind of things he will listen to will be the same; for the kind he can face up to are also the kind he seems to make. There are, then, things he will not do; for mockery is a sort of abuse, and there are things that lawgivers restrain us from abusing; and they should, perhaps, have restrained us even from mocking them. The refined and liberal man, therefore, will be as we have described, being as it were a law to himself.

Such, then, is the man in the middle state, whether he be called tactful or convivial. The buffoon is the slave of his sense of humour: he spares neither himself nor others if he can raise a laugh, and says things none of which a man of refinement would say, and to some of which he would not even listen. The boor is useless in company; for he contributes nothing and is vexed at everything. But relaxation and amusement are thought to be a necessary element in life.

The means in life that have been described, then, are three in number, and are all concerned with the sharing of words and actions of some kind. They differ, however, in that one is concerned with truth, and the others with pleasantness. Of those concerned with pleasure, one is displayed in amusements, the other in the rest of life's companionships.

MODESTY SHOULD NOT BE DESCRIBED AS A VIRTUE; FOR IT is more like an emotion than a state of character. It is defined, at any rate, as a kind of fear of disrepute and produces an effect similar to that[26] produced by fear of danger; for people who feel disgraced blush, and those who fear death turn pale. Both seem to be in a way bodily conditions, which is thought to be characteristic of emotions rather than of states of character.

The emotion is not becoming to every age but only to youth. For we think young people should be prone to mod-

26 Reading ἀποτελεῖ τι for ἀποτελεῖται.

esty because they live by emotion and therefore commit
many errors, but are restrained by modesty; and we praise
young people who are modestly inclined, but an older person no one would praise for being prone to shame, since we
think he should not do anything of which he should feel
ashamed. For shame is not even characteristic of an upright
man, since it is consequent on base actions (for such actions
should not be done; and if some actions are ignoble in very
truth and others only according to belief, this makes no difference; for neither sort should be done, so that no shame
should be felt); and it is a mark of a base man even to be such
as to do any ignoble action. To be so constituted such as to
feel ashamed if one does such an action, and for this reason
to think oneself upright, is absurd; for it is for voluntary actions that modesty is felt, and the upright man will never voluntarily do base actions. Modesty may indeed be said to be
conditionally an upright thing: if a good man did such actions, he would feel ashamed; but the virtues are not like
that. And if shamelessness—not to be ashamed of doing ignoble actions—is base, that does not make it upright to be
ashamed of doing such actions. Continence too is not virtue
but rather a mixed sort of state; this will be shown later.

Now let us discuss justice.

5

FRIENDSHIP *

AFTER WHAT WE HAVE SAID, A DISCUSSION OF FRIENDSHIP would naturally follow, since it is a virtue or implies virtue, and is besides most necessary with a view to living. For without friends no one would choose to live, though he had all other goods: indeed, rich men and those in possession of office and of power are thought to need friends most of all; for what is the use of such prosperity without the opportunity of beneficence, which happens chiefly and in its most praiseworthy form towards friends? Or how can prosperity be guarded and preserved without friends? The greater it is, the more exposed is it to risk. And in poverty and in other misfortunes men think friends are the only refuge. It helps the young, too, to keep from error. It aids older people by ministering to their needs and supplementing the activities that are failing from weakness. Those in the prime of life it stimulates to noble actions: 'two men together'[1]—for with friends men are more able both to think and to act. Again, parent seems by nature to feel it for offspring and offspring for parent, not only among men but among birds and most animals. It is felt mutually by members of the same kind, and especially by men—whence we praise philanthropy. We may see even in our travels how near and dear every man is to every other. Friendship seems too to hold States together, and lawgivers to busy themselves more about friendship

---

* Chapters 5–8 of EE have usually been printed as Books EZH of NE (see pp. 5 and 20): hence the gap in the Bekker numbers here.

1 'Two men together see things that one would miss': Homer, *Iliad* X 224.

than about justice; for concord seems to be something like friendship, and this they aim at most of all, and expel faction as their worst enemy; and when men are friends they have no need of justice, while when they are just they need friendship as well, and the truest form of justice is thought to be a friendly quality.

It is not only necessary but also noble; for we praise those who love their friends, and it is thought to be a noble thing to have many friends; and again we think it is the same people that are good men and are friends.

Not a few things about friendship are matters of debate. Some set it down as a kind of likeness and say like people are friends, whence come the sayings 'Like to like', 'Birds of a feather', and so on; others on the contrary say 'Two of a trade never agree'. On this very question they inquire more deeply and in a more scientific fashion, Euripides saying that

> The parched earth longs for the rain, and heaven
> when filled with rain longs to fall to earth;

and Heraclitus that 'It is what opposes that helps' and 'From different tones comes the fairest harmony' and 'All things are produced through strife'; while Empedocles, as well as others, expresses the contrary view that like aims at like. The scientific problems we may leave alone (for they are not appropriate to the present inquiry); but let us examine those which are human and involve character and emotion—for instance, whether friendship can arise between any two people or people cannot be friends if they are depraved, and whether there is one species of friendship or more than one. Those who think there is only one because it admits of degrees have relied on an inadequate indication; for even things different in species admit of degree. We have discussed this matter previously.[2]

2 But not in the surviving parts of NE: Aspasius suggests that the reference is to a lost part; other commentators delete the sentence.

PERHAPS IT WILL BECOME EVIDENT IF WE COME TO KNOW
what is lovable. For not everything seems to be loved but
only the lovable, and this is good, pleasant, or useful. Since it
would seem to be that by which some good or pleasure is   20
produced that is useful, it is the good and the pleasant that
are lovable as ends. Do men love, then, the good, or what is
good for them? These sometimes clash. So too with regard to
the pleasant. It is thought that each loves what is good for
himself, and that while the good is in the abstract lovable,
what is good for each man is lovable for him. (Each man   25
loves not what is actually good for him but what seems good.
This however will make no difference: we shall say that this
is that which seems lovable.)

    There are three grounds on which people love. Of the love
of inanimate things we do not use the word 'friendship'; for
it is not mutual love, nor is there a wanting of good to the
other (for it would surely be ridiculous to want wine to do
well—if one wants anything for it, it is that it may keep, so   30
that one may have it oneself). To a friend they say we ought
to want what is good for his sake. But to those who thus want
good we ascribe only benevolence unless the same comes
from the other side—for benevolence when it is reciprocal is
friendship. Or must we add 'when it is recognized'? For
many people feel benevolence towards those whom they
have not seen but assess to be upright or useful; and one of   1156a
these might return this feeling. These people seem to bear
benevolence to each other; but how could one call them
friends when they do not know each other's feelings? They
must, then, recognize one another as bearing benevolence
and wanting good things for each other for one of the afore-   5
said reasons.

THESE DIFFER FROM EACH OTHER IN KIND: SO THERE-
fore, do the forms of loving and friendship. So there are
three kinds of friendship, equal in number to the things that
are lovable; for with respect to each there is a mutual and

recognized love, and those who love each other wish each
other well in that respect in which they love. Those who love
each other for their utility do not love each other for themselves but in virtue of some good which they get from each
other. So too with those who love for the sake of pleasure: it
is not for their character that men cherish convivial people
but because they find them pleasant. So those who love for
the sake of utility feel affection for the sake of what is good
for themselves, and those who love for the sake of pleasure
do so for the sake of what is pleasant to themselves, and not
in so far as the person loved is who he is[3] but in so far as he is
useful or pleasant. So these friendships are only coincidental; for it is not as being the man he is that the loved person is
loved but as providing some good or pleasure. Such friendships, then, are easily dissolved, if the parties do not remain
like themselves; for if they are no longer pleasant or useful
they cease to love. The useful is not permanent but is always
changing. Thus when the ground of the friendship is done
away, the friendship too is dissolved, inasmuch as it existed
only for the ends in question.

This kind of friendship seems to exist chiefly between old
people (for at that age people pursue not the pleasant but the
beneficial) and, of those who are in their prime or young, between those who pursue what is advantageous. Such people
do not live much with each other either; for sometimes they
do not even find each other pleasant. Nor do they need such
companionship unless they are beneficial to each other; for
they are pleasant to each other only in so far as they have
hopes of something good to come. Among such friendships
people also class the friendship of host and guest.

The friendship of young people seems to aim at pleasure;
for they live by their emotions, and pursue above all what is
pleasant to themselves and what is immediately before
them; (but with increasing age their pleasures become different). This is why they quickly become friends and quickly

3 Reading ἐστιν <ὅσπερ ἐστίν> (Bonitz).

cease to be so: their friendship changes with the object that
pleases, and such pleasure alters quickly. Young people are   1156b
amorous too; for the greater part of being in love depends
on emotion and is grounded in pleasure. This is why they
love and quickly cease to love, changing often within a single
day. But they do want to spend their days and lives together;   5
for it is thus that they attain the purpose of their friendship.

Perfect friendship is the friendship of men who are good
and alike in virtue; for these alike want good things for each
other *qua* good, and they are good in themselves. Those who
want good things for their friends for their sake are most   10
truly friends; for they do this by reason of their own nature
and not coincidentally; therefore their friendship lasts as
long as they are good—and virtue is an enduring thing. And
each is good in the abstract and to his friend; for the good are
both good in the abstract and beneficial to each other. So too
they are pleasant; for the good are pleasant both in the ab-   15
stract and to each other, since to each his own actions and
others like them are pleasurable, and the actions of the good
are the same or like. Such a friendship is, as might be expected, lasting, since there meet in it all the qualities that
friends should have. For all friendship is grounded on good
or on pleasure—either in the abstract or for him who has the   20
friendly feeling—and is based on a certain resemblance. To a
friendship of good men all the qualities we have named belong in virtue of their nature; for in the case of this kind of
friendship the other qualities also are alike, and that which is
good in the abstract is also in the abstract pleasant, and these
are the most lovable qualities. Love and friendship therefore
are found most and in their best form between such men.

It is likely that such friendships should be infrequent; for   25
such men are few. Further, such friendship requires time
and familiarity: as the proverb says, men cannot know each
other till they have 'eaten salt together'; nor can they admit
each other to friendship or be friends till each has been
found lovable and been trusted by the other. Those who
quickly show the marks of friendship to each other want to   30

307

be friends, but are not friends unless they both are lovable and know the fact; for a will for friendship may arise quickly but friendship does not.

THIS KIND OF FRIENDSHIP, THEN, IS PERFECT BOTH IN RE-spect of duration and in all other respects, and in it each gets from the other in all respects the same or something similar, which is what ought to happen between friends. Friendship grounded in pleasure bears a resemblance to this kind; for good people too are pleasant to each other. So too does friendship grounded in utility; for the good are useful to each other. Among men of these sorts too, friendships are most permanent when the friends get the same thing from each other (for instance, pleasure), and not only that but also from the same source, as happens between convivial people, not as happens between lover and beloved. For these do not take pleasure in the same things, but the one in seeing the beloved and the other in receiving attentions from his lover; and when the bloom of youth passes the friendship some-times passes too (for the one finds no pleasure in the sight of the other, and the other gets no attentions). But many lovers on the other hand are constant, if familiarity has led them to feel affection for each other's characters, these being alike. But those who exchange not pleasure but utility in their love are both less truly friends and less constant. Those who are friends for the sake of utility part when the advantage is at an end; for they were friends not of each other but of what is expedient.

On the ground of pleasure or utility, then, even base men may be friends of each other, or upright men of base, or one who is neither of any sort of person. But for their own sake plainly only good men can be friends; for bad men do not de-light in each other unless some benefit accrues.

The friendship of the good too alone is proof against slan-der; for it is not easy to trust anyone about someone who has long been tested by oneself; and it is among good men that are found trust and the absence of unjust acts and all the other things that are claimed of true friendship. In the other kinds of friendship there is nothing to prevent such things from arising. 25

Men apply the name of friends even where the ground is utility (like States—for the alliances of States are thought to aim at advantage), and to those who feel affection for each other on the ground of pleasure (as children are called friends). So we too ought perhaps to call such people friends, and say that there are several kinds of friendship—first and 30 strictly speaking that of good men *qua* good, and by similarity the other kinds; for it is in virtue of something good and something similar that they are friends, since the pleasant is good for the lovers of pleasure. But these two kinds of friendship are not often united, nor do the same people become friends because of utility and because of pleasure; for things 35 that are coincidentally connected are not often coupled together.

Friendship being divided into these kinds, base men will 1157b be friends because of pleasure or utility, being in this respect like each other, whereas good men will be friends for their own sake and *qua* good. These, then, are friends in the abstract: the others are friends coincidentally and through a 5 resemblance to these.

JUST AS IN REGARD TO THE VIRTUES SOME MEN ARE CALLED good in respect of a state, others in respect of an activity, so too in the case of friendship; for those who live together delight in each other and confer good things on each other, whereas those who are asleep or apart at a distance are not exercising but are disposed to exercise their friendship— 10 distance does not break off the friendship *tout court* but its exercise. But if the absence is lasting, it seems to make men forget their friendship: hence the saying 'Out of sight, out of mind'. Neither old people nor sour people seem to make friends easily; for there is little that is pleasant in them, and 15 no one can spend his days with one whose company is painful, or not pleasant, since nature seems above all to avoid the

painful and to aim at the pleasant. Those who approve of
each other but do not live together seem to be benevolent
rather than friends. For there is nothing so characteristic of
20   friends as living together (since while it is people who are in
need that desire benefits, even those who are blessed desire
to spend their days together; for solitude suits such people
least of all); but people cannot live together if they are not
pleasant and do not delight in the same things, as comrades
seem to do.

25   The truest friendship, then, is that of the good, as we have
frequently said; for that which is in the abstract good or
pleasant seems to be lovable and desirable, and for each person that which is so to him; and the good man is lovable and
desirable to the good man for both these reasons. It looks as
if loving were an emotion, friendship a state; for there is
30   such a thing as loving inanimate things as well, but mutual
love involves choice and choice springs from a state; and
men want good things for those whom they love, for their
sake, not as a result of emotion but as a result of a state. In
loving a friend men love what is good for themselves; for the
good man in becoming a friend becomes a good to his friend.
35   Each, then, both loves what is good for himself, and makes
an equal return in good will and in pleasantness; for friend-
1158a   ship is said to be equality, and these things are found most in
the friendship of the good.

BETWEEN SOUR AND ELDERLY PEOPLE FRIENDSHIP ARISES
less readily inasmuch as they have less grace and take less delight in company; for these are thought to be the greatest
marks of friendship and most productive of it. This is why,
5   while young men become friends quickly, old men do not;
for men do not become friends with those in whom they do
not delight. Similarly for sour people. But such men may feel
benevolence towards each other; for they want good things
for each other and aid one another in need; but they are
hardly friends because they do not spend their days together

nor delight in each other, and these are thought the greatest 10
marks of friendship.

One cannot be a friend to many people in the way of perfect friendship, just as one cannot be in love with many people at once (for it is like an excess, and it is the nature of such
only to be felt towards one person); and it is not easy for
many people at the same time to win intense approval from
the same person, or perhaps even to be good. One must, too, 15
acquire some experience of the other person and become familiar with him, and that is very hard. But it is possible for
many people[4] to win the approval of many people on the
ground of utility or pleasure; for many people are useful or
pleasant, and these services take little time.

Of them, the one which is grounded on pleasure is the
more like friendship, when both parties get the same things
from each other and delight in each other or in the same
things, as in the friendships of the young; for liberality is 20
more found in such friendships. Friendship grounded on
utility is for the commercially minded. People who are
blessed have no need of useful friends but of pleasant
friends; for they want to live with others, and, though they
can bear for a short time what is painful, no one could face it
continuously, nor even with goodness itself if it were painful 25
to him: this is why they look for friends who are pleasant.
Perhaps they should look for friends who, being pleasant,
are also good, and good for them too; for so they will have all
the characteristics that friends should have.

People in positions of authority evidently have different
classes of friends: some are useful to them and others are
pleasant, but the same are rarely both; for they look neither 30
for those whose pleasantness is accompanied by virtue nor
for those whose utility is with a view to noble objects. Rather,
they look for convivial people in their desire for pleasure,
and for men who are clever at doing what they are told—and

4 Reading πολλούς (Ramsauer) for πολλοῖς.

311

these characteristics are rarely combined. We have said that
the virtuous man is at the same time pleasant and useful; but
such a man does not become the friend of one who is his su-
35   perior, unless the latter is inferior in virtue; if this is not so,
then being inferior he cannot establish proportionate equality. But such men are not so easy to find.

1158b   The aforesaid friendships involve equality; for the friends
get the same things from one another and want the same
things for one another, or else exchange one thing for another—for instance, pleasure for utility. We have said, however, that they are both less truly friendships and less perma-
5   nent. It is from their likeness and their unlikeness to the
same thing that they are thought both to be and not to be
friendships. It is by their likeness to the friendship based on
virtue that they seem to be friendships (for one of them involves pleasure and the other utility, and these characteristics belong to the friendship based on virtue as well); while it
is because the friendship based on virtue is proof against
10   slander and is lasting, while they quickly change (besides differing in many other respects), that they appear not to be
friendships because of their unlikeness to it.

THERE IS ANOTHER KIND OF FRIENDSHIP, WHICH IN-
volves a superiority—for instance, that of father to son and
in general of elder to younger, that of man to wife and in general that of ruler to ruled. These differ from each other; for it
15   is not the same that holds between parents and children and
between rulers and ruled, nor is even that of father to son the
same as that of son to father, nor that of husband to wife the
same as that of wife to husband. For the virtue and the role
of each of these is different, and so are the reasons for which
they love: the love and the friendship are therefore different
20   also. The one party, then, neither gets the same from the
other nor ought to look for it; but when children render to
parents what they ought to render to those who brought
them into the world, and parents render what they should to
their children, the friendship of such persons will be lasting

and upright. In all friendships involving superiority the love also should be proportional: the better should be more loved 25 than he loves, and so should the more beneficial, and similarly in each of the other cases; for when the love is in proportion to worth, then in a way there is equality, and that is held to be characteristic of friendship.

Equality does not seem to take the same form in matters of justice and in friendship; for in matters of justice what is 30 equal in the primary way is that which is in proportion to worth, while quantitative equality is secondary; but in friendship quantitative equality is primary and proportion to worth secondary. This becomes plain if there is a great interval in respect of virtue or vice or affluence or anything else; for then they are no longer friends, and do not even 35 claim to be so. This is most obvious in the case of the gods; for they surpass us most in all good things. But it is clear also in the case of kings; for with them, too, men who are much 1159a their inferiors do not claim to be friends; nor do men of no worth claim to be friends with the best men or with men of great understanding. In such cases it is not possible to define exactly up to what point they can be friends; for much can be taken away and friendship remain, but not when one party is 5 removed to a great distance, as a god is.

This is the origin of the problem of whether men really want the greatest goods for their friends—for instance, that of being gods; for in that case their friends will no longer be friends to them, and therefore will not be good things for them (for friends are good things). So if we were right in saying that a friend wants good things for his friend for his sake, 10 his friend must remain the sort of being he is: it is for him as a man that he will want the greatest goods. But perhaps not all the greatest goods; for it is for himself most of all that each man wants what is good.

MOST PEOPLE SEEM, OWING TO AMBITION, TO WANT TO BE loved rather than to love. That is why most men love flattery; for the flatterer is a friend in an inferior position, or pretends 15 to be such and to love more than he is loved; and being loved seems to be akin to being honoured, and this is what most people aim at. But it seems to be not for its own sake that they choose honour, but coincidentally. For most people delight in being honoured by those in positions of authority because of their hopes (for they think that if they want anything they will get it from them; and therefore they delight in honour as an indication of favour to come); while those who desire honour from upright men, and learned men, are aiming at confirming their own belief about themselves: they delight in honour because they are convinced of their own goodness by the assessment of those who speak about them. In being loved, on the other hand, people delight for its own sake—that is why it would seem to be better than being honoured, and friendship to be desirable in itself. But it seems to lie in loving rather than in being loved, as is indicated by the delight mothers take in loving; for some mothers hand over their children to be brought up, and know and love them but do not look to be loved in return (if they cannot have both): it is enough for them if they see them prospering; and they themselves love their children even if these owing to their ignorance give them nothing of a mother's due. Since friendship lies more in loving, and it is those who love their friends that are praised, loving seems to be the characteristic virtue of friends, so that it is those in whom this is found in proportion to worth that are lasting friends in a lasting friendship.

It is in this way more than any other that unequals can be friends: they can be equalized. Equality and likeness are friendship, and especially the likeness of those who are like in virtue; for being steadfast in themselves they hold fast to each other, and neither ask nor give base services, but rather (one may say) prevent them; for it is characteristic of good men neither to err themselves nor to let their friends do so. Depraved men have no firmness (for they do not even stay similar to themselves). They become friends for a short time because they delight in each other's depravity. Friends who are useful or pleasant last longer—as long as they provide each other with pleasures or benefits. Friendship grounded on utility seems to be that which most easily exists between contraries—for instance between poor and rich, between ignorant and learned; for what a man lacks he aims at, and he gives something else in return. Under this head, too, one might bring lover and beloved, beautiful and ugly. This is why lovers sometimes seem ridiculous, when they claim to be loved as they love: if they are equally lovable then perhaps they ought so to claim; but when things are nothing like that it is ridiculous. Perhaps, however, contrary does not even aim at contrary in itself but only coincidentally, the desire being for what is in the middle; for that is what is good—for instance, it is good for the dry not to become wet but to come to the middle state, and similarly with the hot and in all other cases. These subjects we may dismiss; for they are foreign to our inquiry.

FRIENDSHIP AND JUSTICE SEEM, AS WE HAVE SAID AT THE start, to be concerned with the same things and to be found in the same places. For in every association there is thought to be some form of justice, and friendship too: men address as friends their fellow-voyagers and fellow-soldiers, and so too those joined with them in any other kind of association. And the extent of their association is the extent of their friendship, and also of justice. The proverb 'What friends have is common property' is correct; for friendship depends on sharing. Brothers and comrades have all things in common, but the others have definite things in common—some more, others fewer; for of friendships, too, some are more and others less truly friendships. And matters of justice differ too: those between parents and their children and those among brothers are not the same, nor those among comrades and those among fellow-citizens; and so, too, with the other kinds of friendship. So there is a difference also between what counts as unjust in each of these cases; and the injustice increases by being exhibited towards those who are

5 more truly friends—for instance, it is a more terrible thing
to defraud a comrade than a fellow-citizen, more terrible not
to help a brother than a stranger, and more terrible to strike
your father than anyone else. The claims of justice also naturally increase with the friendship, which implies that friendship and justice are found in the same places and have an
equal extension.

All forms of association are like parts of political associa-
10 tion: men journey together with a view to some particular
advantage, and to provide something that they need for the
purposes of life; and it is for the sake of advantage that political association too seems both to have come about originally and to endure—for this is what legislators aim at, and
they call just that which is to the common advantage. The
15 other associations aim at some particular advantage—for
instance, sailors at what is advantageous on a voyage with a
view to gaining wealth or something of the kind, fellow-
soldiers at what is advantageous in war, whether it is wealth
or victory or the taking of a city that they seek, and members
of tribes and demes act similarly. All these seem to fall under
the political partnership; for it aims not at present advantage but at what is advantageous for life as a whole. Some associations seem to arise for the sake of pleasure—religious
20 guilds and social clubs; for these exist for the sake of offering
25 sacrifice and of companionship[5]—they sacrifice and arrange
gatherings for the purpose, and assign honours to the gods,
and provide pleasant relaxations for themselves. For the ancient sacrifices and gatherings seem to take place after the
harvest as a sort of first fruits, because it was at these seasons
that people had most leisure. All the associations, then, seem
to be parts of the political association; and the particular

5 The words 'Some associations seem . . . and of companionship' appear
in the manuscripts immediately after '. . . and demes act similarly' in
1160a18: following a suggestion of Bywater, we transpose them to follow '. . .
life as a whole'. (Bywater himself deletes the words and marks a lacuna after
'. . . life as a whole'.)

kinds of friendship will correspond to the particular kinds   30
of association.

THERE ARE THREE KINDS OF CONSTITUTION, AND AN
equal number of deviations—perversions, as it were, of
them. The constitutions are monarchy and aristocracy, and
thirdly that which is based on a property qualification, which
it seems appropriate to call timocratic,[6] though most people   35
usually call it polity. The best of these is monarchy, the worst
timocracy. The deviation from monarchy is tyranny (for both   1160b
are forms of one-man rule); but there is the greatest difference between them: the tyrant looks to his own advantage,
the monarch to that of the ruled. For a man is not a monarch
unless he is self-sufficient and superior in all good things;
and such a man needs nothing further; therefore he will not   5
look to his own interests but to those of his subjects—one
not like that would be a sort of monarch chosen by lot. Tyranny is the contrary of this: the tyrant pursues his own good.
And it is more evident in the case of tyranny that it is the
worst deviation, and it is the contrary of the best that is
worst.

Monarchy changes into tyranny; for tyranny is the base   10
form of monarchy and a depraved monarch becomes a tyrant. Aristocracy changes into oligarchy by the vice of the
rulers, who distribute contrary to worth what belongs to the
city—all or most of the good things to themselves, and office
always to the same people, paying most regard to riches;   15
thus the rulers are few and are depraved men instead of the
most upright. Timocracy changes into democracy; for these
are coterminous, since timocracy too tends to involve a mass
of people, and all who have the property qualification are
equal. Democracy is the least depraved; for its form of con-   20
stitution is but a slight deviation. These then are the transi-
tions to which constitutions are most subject; for these are
the smallest and easiest changes.

6 'Timocratic' is τιμοκρατικός and 'property qualification' is τίμημα.

One may find resemblances to the constitutions and, as it were, patterns of them even in households. For the asso-
25 ciation of a father with his sons bears the form of monarchy, since the father cares for his children; and this is why Homer calls Zeus father: monarchy is supposed to be paternal rule. But among the Persians the rule of the father is tyrannical: they use their sons as slaves. Tyrannical too is the
30 rule of a master over slaves; for it is the advantage of the master that is brought about in it. Now this seems to be a correct form of government but the Persian type is an error; for the modes of rule appropriate to different relations are diverse. The relationship of man and wife seems to be aristocratic; for the man rules in accordance with worth, and in those matters in which a man should rule, but
35 the matters that befit a woman he hands over to her. If the man has authority in everything it changes into oligarchy;
1161a for he does this contrary to worth and not *qua* better. Sometimes, however, women rule, because they are heiresses: they rule not because of virtue but because of riches and power, as in oligarchies. The relationship among brothers is like timocracy; for they are equal, except in so far as they
5 differ in age; hence if they differ much in age, the friendship is no longer of the fraternal type. Democracy is found chiefly in masterless dwellings (for here everyone is on an equality), and in those in which the ruler is weak and everyone is in authority.

10 To each of the constitutions may be seen to correspond a type of friendship, just in so far as there corresponds a type of justice. The friendship between a monarch and his subjects depends on a superiority in benefaction; for he does well by his subjects if being a good man he cares for them with a view to their well-being, as a shepherd does for his
15 sheep (whence Homer called Agamemnon shepherd of the people). Such too is the friendship of a father, though this exceeds in the greatness of its benefaction; for he is responsible for the existence of his children, which is thought the greatest good, and for their nurture and upbringing. These

318

things are ascribed to ancestors as well. By nature a father tends to rule over his sons, ancestors over descendants, a monarch over his subjects. These friendships imply superiority: that is why parents are honoured. The justice between persons so related is not the same but in proportion to worth; for that is true of the friendship as well. The friendship of man and wife is the same that is found in an aristocracy; for it is in accordance with virtue—the better gets more of what is good, and each gets what is fitting; and so, too, with the justice. The friendship of brothers is like that of comrades; for they are equal and of like age, and such persons are for the most part like in their emotions and their character. Like this is the friendship appropriate to timocratic government; for the citizens tend to be equal and upright, and so rule is taken in turn and on equal terms; and so too the friendship.

In the deviations, just as justice hardly exists, so too with friendship. And least in the worst form: in tyranny there is little or no friendship. For where there is nothing common to ruler and ruled, there is no friendship either, since there is no justice—for instance, between craftsman and tool, soul and body, master and slave. The latter in each case is benefited by that which uses it. But there is no friendship or justice towards inanimate things. Nor towards a horse or an ox, nor to a slave *qua* slave. For there is nothing common to the two parties: the slave is an animate tool and the tool an inanimate slave. *Qua* slave then, one cannot be friends with him. But *qua* man one can; for there seems to be some justice between any man and any other who can share in a system of law or be a party to a compact: so there can also be friendship with him in so far as he is a man. So while in tyrannies friendship and justice hardly exist, in democracies they exist more fully; for where the citizens are equal they have much in common.

Every form of friendship, then, involves association, as has been said. One might, however, mark off both the friendship of relations and that of comrades. Those of fellow-

319

15 citizens, fellow-tribesmen, fellow-voyagers, and the like are more like friendships of association; for they seem to rest on a sort of agreement. With them one might class the friendship of host and guest.

The friendship of relations, while it seems to be of many kinds, appears to depend in every case on paternal friendship; for parents feel affection for their children as being a part of themselves, and children their parents as as originat-
20 ing from them.[7] Now parents know their offspring better than their offspring know that they are their children, and the begetter is more attached to his offspring than the offspring to their begetter; for what comes from something is close to what it comes from (for instance, a tooth or hair or anything else to him whose it is), but the reverse is not so, or less so. Length of time produces the same result: parents feel
25 affection for their children as soon as these are born, but children love their parents after some time has elapsed and they have acquired judgement or perception. From this it is also plain why mothers love more. Parents, then, love their children as themselves (for their issue are by virtue of their separate existence a sort of other selves), while children love
30 their parents as being born of them, and brothers love each other as being born of the same parents; for their identity with them makes them identical with each other (which is the reason why people talk of the same blood, the same stock, and so on). They are, therefore, in a way the same thing, though in separate individuals. Two things that contribute greatly to friendship are a common upbringing and similarity of age; for 'two of an age take to each other', and familiarity makes for comradeship—that is why the friend-
1162a ship of brothers is akin to that of comrades. Cousins and other relations are attached by derivation from brothers—by being derived from the same stock. They come to be nearer or farther apart by virtue of the nearness or distance of their common ancestor.

7 Omitting τι (with the Laurentian manuscript).

The friendship of children to parents, and of men to gods,   5
is as to something good and superior; for they have conferred the greatest benefits, since they are the causes of their
being and of their nourishment, and of their education from
their birth. This kind of friendship possesses pleasantness
and utility also, more than that of strangers, inasmuch as
their life is lived more in common. The friendship of broth-   10
ers has the characteristics found in that of comrades (and especially when these are upright), and in general between
people who are like each other, inasmuch as they are nearer
to each other and have an affection for each other from birth,
and inasmuch as those born of the same parents and brought
up together and similarly educated are more akin in character; and the test of time has been applied most fully and
firmly in their case.   15

Between other relations friendship is found in due proportion. Between man and wife friendship seems to exist by
nature; for man is naturally inclined to form couples more
than to form States, inasmuch as the household is earlier
and more necessary than the State, and reproduction is common to animals. With the other animals the association ex-   20
tends to this point, but human beings live together not only
for the sake of reproduction but also for the various purposes of life. For from the start the tasks are divided, and
those of man and woman are different; and so they help each
other by throwing their special gifts into the common stock.
It is for these reasons that both utility and pleasure seem to   25
be found in this kind of friendship. It may be grounded also
on virtue, if the parties are upright; for each has its own virtue and they will delight in the fact. Children seem to be a
bond (that is why childless people part more easily); for children are a good common to both and what is common holds
them together.

How man and wife and in general friend and friend ought   30
to live seems to be the same question as how it is just for
them to do so; for it does not seem to be the same for a
friend, a stranger, a comrade, and a schoolfellow.

THERE ARE THREE KINDS OF FRIENDSHIP, AS WE SAID AT
35   the start, and in respect of each some are friends on an equality and others by virtue of a superiority (for not only can
1162b   equally good men become friends but a better man can make
friends with a worse, and similarly in friendships of pleasure
or utility they may be equal or different in the benefits they
confer). Equals must equalize on a basis of equality in love
and in all other respects, while unequals must render what is
in proportion to their superiority.

5   Complaint and grumbling arise either only or chiefly in
the friendship of utility, and this is only to be expected. For
those who are friends on the ground of virtue are eager to do
well by each other (since that is a mark of virtue and of
friendship), and between men who are emulating each other
in this there cannot be complaints or quarrels: no one is
10   vexed at a man who loves him and does well by him—rather,
if he is a person of refinement he takes his revenge by doing
well in return. The man who exceeds will not complain of his
friend, since he gets what he aims at; for each man desires
what is good. Nor do complaints arise much even in friendships of pleasure; for both get at the same time what they desire, if they take delight in spending their time together; and
15   a man who complained of another for not affording him
pleasure would seem ridiculous, since it is in his power not
to spend his days with him.

The friendship of utility is given to complaint; for as they
use each other for their own benefit they always ask for
more, and think they have got less than is fitting, and grum-
ble at their partners because they do not get all they ask for
20   although they are worthy of it; and those who do well by others cannot help them as much as those whom they benefit
ask for.

It seems that, as justice is of two kinds, one unwritten and
the other legal, one kind of friendship of utility is moral and
the other legal. And so complaints arise most of all when
25   men do not dissolve the relation in the spirit in which they
contracted it. The legal type is that which is on fixed terms:

322

its purely commercial variety is on the basis of immediate payment, while the more liberal variety allows time but agrees on a *quid pro quo*. Here the debt is plain and not ambiguous, but in the postponement it contains an element of friendliness; and so for some there are no lawsuits about the matter—rather, they think that men who have bargained on a basis of trust ought to put up with it. The moral type is not on fixed terms: it makes a gift, or does whatever it does, as to a friend. But one claims to receive as much or more, as having not given but lent; and if a man is worse off when the relation is dissolved than he was when it was contracted he will complain. This happens because all or most men, while they want what is noble, choose what is beneficial; and while it is noble to do well by another without a view to repayment, it is the receiving of benefactions that is advantageous.

If we can we should return in proportion to the worth of what we have received; for we must not make a man our friend against his will: we must recognize that we were mistaken at the start and were well treated by a person by whom we should not have been—since it was not by a friend, nor by one who did it for the sake of doing so—and the relation must be dissolved as if we had received benefactions on fixed terms. Indeed, one would agree to repay if one could (if one could not, not even the giver would claim it); and so if it is possible we must repay. But at the start we must consider who our benefactor is and on what terms he is acting, in order that we may stand by the terms, or else decline.

It is disputed whether we ought to measure a service by its benefit to the receiver and make the return with a view to that, or by the beneficence of the giver. For those who have received say they have received from their benefactors what meant little to the latter and what they might have got from others—minimizing the service; while the givers conversely say it was the biggest thing they had, and what could not have been got from others, and that it was given in times of danger or similar need. Now if the friendship is one grounded on utility, is not the benefit to the receiver the

measure? For it is he that asks for the service, and the other man helps him on the supposition that he will receive an equal benefit; so the assistance has been as great as the ben-
20   efit to the receiver, and therefore he must return as much as he has received, or even more (for that would be nobler).

In friendships of virtue complaints do not arise, and the choice of the doer is a sort of measure; for in choice lies the element which controls virtue and character.

Differences arise also in friendship based on superiority;
25   for each claims more, and when this happens the friendship is dissolved. Not only does the better man think it is fitting for him to get more (since more should be assigned to a good man), but the more useful man similarly expects so (for they say a useless man should not get as much, since it becomes
30   an act of public service and not a friendship if the proceeds of the friendship do not answer to the worth of the deeds). For they think that, just as in a business association those who put more in get more out, so it should be in friendship. But the man who is in a state of need and is worse makes the opposite claim: it is the part of a good friend to help those who are in need; for what, they say, is the use of being the friend of a virtuous man or a powerful man if one is to get no
1163b   enjoyment from it? It seems that each makes a correct claim, and that each should get more out of the friendship—but not more of the same thing: rather, the superior more hon-our and the needy more profit. For honour is the prize of vir-tue and of beneficence, while profit is the assistance given to
5   need.

It seems to be so in constitutions also: the man who con-tributes nothing good to the common stock is not hon-oured; for what is common is given to the man who is a com-mon benefactor, and honour is something common. For it is not possible to get wealth from the public stock and at the same time honour. For no one puts up with the smaller share
10   in all things; and so to the man who loses in wealth they as-sign honour and to the man who is willing to be paid, wealth,

since proportion to worth equalizes and preserves the friendship, as we have said.

This then is also the way in which we should keep company with unequals: the man who is benefited in respect of wealth or virtue must give honour in return, repaying what he can. For friendship requires a man to do what he can, not   15
what is consonant with the other's worth, since that cannot always be done: for instance, in honours paid to the gods or to parents—no one could ever return to them what they are worth, but the man who serves them to the utmost of his power is thought to be an upright man.

This is why it would not seem open to a man to disown his father (though a father may disown his son): being in debt,   20
he should repay, but there is nothing a son can give that has the worth of what he has received, so that he is always in debt. Creditors can waive a debt and so a father can do so. At the same time it is thought that no one perhaps would repudiate a son who was not excessively depraved; for apart from the natural friendship it is human nature not to reject assistance.   25
But the son, if he is depraved, will avoid aiding his father, or not busy himself about it; for most people want to be well treated but avoid treating others well, as a thing inexpedient.

So much for these questions.

IN ALL FRIENDSHIPS BETWEEN DISSIMILARS IT IS, AS WE   Book I
have said, proportion that equalizes and preserves the friendship: for instance, in political friendship the shoemaker gets a return for his shoes in proportion to his worth, and the weaver and the rest do the same. Now here a com-   1164a
mon measure has been provided in the form of money, and everything is referred to this and measured by this; but in the friendship of lovers sometimes the lover complains that his excess of love is not met by love in return (though perhaps there is nothing lovable about him), while often the beloved   5
complains that the lover who formerly promised everything now performs nothing. Such incidents happen when the

lover loves the beloved for the sake of pleasure while the beloved loves the lover for the sake of utility, and they do not
both possess the qualities expected of them. If these be the
objects of the friendship it is dissolved when they do not get
the things for the sake of which they loved; for each did not
feel affection for the other person himself but for the qualities he had, and these were not enduring: that is why the
friendships also are transient. But the love of characters, as
has been said, endures because it is self-dependent. Differences arise when what they get is something different and
not what they desire; for it is like getting nothing when we
do not get what we aim at—for instance, the person who
made promises to a lyre-player, promising him the more
the better he sang, but on the morrow, when the other de-
manded the fulfilment of his promises, said that he had
given pleasure for pleasure. If this had been what each
wanted, all would have been well; but if the one wanted enjoyment and the other profit, and the one has what he
wanted while the other has not, the terms of the association
will not have been kept; for each fixes his mind on what he
asks for, and it is for the sake of that that he will give what he
has.

Who is to fix the worth of the service, he who makes the
offer or he who takes it up? The one who offers seems to leave
it to the other. This is what they say Protagoras used to do:
whenever he taught anything, he bade the learner value the
worth of the knowledge, and accepted the amount so fixed.
But in such matters some men approve of the saying 'Let a
man have his fixed reward'.[8]

Those who take the cash and then do none of the things
they said they would, owing to the excesses of their promises, reasonably find themselves the objects of complaint; for
they do not fulfil what they agreed to. The sophists are perhaps compelled to do this because no one would give cash
for the things they know. These people, then, who do not do

8 Hesiod, *Works and Days* 370.

what they have been paid for, are reasonably made the objects of complaint.

Where there is no agreement about the service, those who offer something for the sake of the other party cannot (as we have said) be complained of (for that is the nature of the friendship of virtue), and the return to them must be made on the basis of their choice (for choice is characteristic of a friend and of virtue). And so too, it seems, for those who have shared their philosophizing; for its worth cannot be measured against wealth, and no honour would balance their services—but it is perhaps enough, as it is with the gods and with one's parents, to give what one can.

If the giving was not of this sort but was made on conditions, then perhaps the return made ought (if it is at all possible) to be one that seems to both to be in accordance with worth; but if this is not done, it would seem not only necessary that the person who gets the first service should fix the value, but also just; for the second will get what it was worth to the first if he takes the amount by which the first was benefitted or which he would have given for the pleasure.

We see this happening too with things put up for sale, and in some places there are laws providing that no lawsuits shall arise out of voluntary contracts, on the supposition that one should settle with a person whom one has trusted in the spirit in which one associated with him. The law holds that it is more just that the person to whom credit was given should fix the terms than that the person who gave credit should do so. For most things are not given an equal value by those who have them and those who want to get them: each class sets a high worth on what is its own and what it is offering; yet the return is made on the terms fixed by the receiver. Perhaps the receiver should value a thing not at what it seems worth when he has it, but at what he valued it at before he had it.

A FURTHER PROBLEM IS SET BY SUCH QUESTIONS AS whether one should in all things give the preference to one's father and obey him, or whether when one is ill one should

trust a doctor, and when one has to elect a general should
25   elect a man of military skill; and similarly whether one
should render a service by preference to a friend or to a virtuous man, and should show gratitude to a benefactor or
oblige a comrade, if one cannot do both.

Are not all such questions hard to decide with precision?
For they admit of many variations of all sorts in respect both
of the magnitude of the service and of its nobility and neces-
30   sity. But that we should not give the preference in all things
to the same person is plain enough; and we must for the
most part return benefactions rather than give to comrades,
as we should pay back a loan to a creditor rather than make
one to a friend. But perhaps even this is not always true: for
instance, should a man who has been ransomed out of the
hands of brigands ransom his ransomer in return, whoever
he may be (or pay him if he has not been captured but re-
1165a   quests payment), or should he ransom his father? It would
seem that he should ransom his father in preference even to
himself.

As we have said, then, generally the debt should be paid,
but if the gift is exceedingly noble or exceedingly necessary,
5   one should defer to these considerations. For sometimes it
is not even fair to return what one has received, when the
one man has done a service to one he knows to be virtuous,
while the other makes a return to one he believes to be depraved—nor, sometimes, lend in return to one who has lent
to oneself; for the one person lent to an upright man, ex-
pecting to recover his loan, while the other has no hope of
10   recovering from one who is vicious. So if the facts really are
so, the claim is not fair; and if they are not but people think
they are, they would be held to be doing nothing absurd. As
we have often said, then, discussions about emotions and actions have as much definiteness as their subject-matter.

That we should not make the same return to everyone,
15   nor give a father the preference in everything, as one does
not sacrifice everything to Zeus, is plain enough; and since
we ought to render different things to parents, brothers,

comrades, and benefactors, we ought to render to each class what is appropriate and fitting. And this is what people seem in fact to do. To marriages they invite their kinsfolk, for these have a part in the family and therefore in the actions that affect the family; and at funerals also they think that kinsfolk, before all others, should meet, for the same reason. And it would be thought that in the matter of food we should help our parents before all others, since we owe our own nourishment to them, and it is more noble to help in this respect the authors of our being even before ourselves. Honour too one should give to one's parents as one does to the gods, but not any and every honour; for one should not give the same honour to one's father and one's mother, nor again should one give them the honour due to a man of understanding or to a general, but rather the honour due to a father, or again to a mother. To all older persons, too, one should give honour appropriate to their age, by rising to receive them and finding seats for them and so on. To comrades and brothers one should allow freedom of speech and common use of all things. To kinsmen and fellow-tribesmen and fellow-citizens and to every other class one should always try to assign what is appropriate, and to compare the claims of each class with respect to nearness of relation and to virtue or usefulness. The comparison is easier when the persons belong to the same class, and more of a task when they are different. Yet we must not on that account shrink from it but decide the question as best we can.

ANOTHER PROBLEM THAT ARISES IS WHETHER FRIENDSHIPS should or should not be broken off when the other party does not remain the same. Perhaps there is nothing absurd in breaking off a friendship based on utility or pleasure, when our friends no longer have these attributes? For it was of these attributes that we were the friends; and when they have failed it is reasonable to love no longer. But one might complain if someone who cherished us for our utility or pleasantness pretended to love us for our character. For, as

329

we said at the start, most differences arise between friends
when they are not friends in the way they think they are. So
when a man has been mistaken and has assumed he was
being loved for his character when the other person was
doing nothing of the kind, he must hold himself responsible; but when he has been deceived by the pretences of the
other person, it is just that he should complain against his
deceiver—and with more justice than one does against people who counterfeit the currency inasmuch as the cheating is
concerned with something more valuable.

If one accepts another man as good, and he becomes depraved and is believed to become so, must one still love him?
Surely it is impossible, since not everything can be loved but
only what is good. What is vicious neither can nor should be
loved; for one should not be a lover of viciousness nor become like what is base (and we have said that like is dear to
like). Must the friendship, then, be forthwith broken off? Or
not in all cases but only when they are incurable in their depravity? If they are capable of being reformed one should
rather come to the assistance of their character than to their
property, inasmuch as this is better and more appropriate to
friendship. But a man who breaks off such a friendship
would seem to be doing nothing absurd; for it was not to a
man of this sort that he was a friend: when his friend has
changed, therefore, and he is unable to save him, he gives
him up.

If one friend remained the same while the other became
more upright and far outstripped him in virtue, should he
treat him as a friend? Surely he cannot. When the interval is
great this becomes most plain—for instance, in the case of
childhood friendships: if one friend remained a child in intellect while the other became a fully developed man, how
could they be friends when they neither approved of the
same things nor delighted in and were pained by the same
things? For not even with regard to each other will their
tastes agree, and without this (as we saw) they cannot be
friends; for they cannot live together. But we have discussed

these matters. Should he, then, behave no otherwise towards him than he would if he had never been his friend? Surely he should keep a remembrance of their former intimacy, and as we think we ought to oblige friends rather than strangers, so to those who have been our friends we ought to make some allowance for our former friendship, when the breach has not been due to excess of depravity.

FRIENDLY RELATIONS WITH ONE'S NEIGHBOURS AND THE marks by which friendships are defined seem to have proceeded from a man's relations to himself. For men think a friend is one who wants and does what is good, or seems so, for the sake of his friend, or one who wants his friend to exist and live, for his sake—as mothers do for their children, and friends do who have come into conflict. Some think a friend is one who lives with and has the same tastes as another, or one who grieves and feels delight with his friend; and this too is found in mothers most of all. It is by some one of these characteristics that friendship is defined.

Each of these holds of the upright man's relation to himself (and of all other men in so far as they assume that they are good; and virtue and the virtuous man seem, as has been said, to be the measure of every class of things). For he has the same views as himself, and he desires the same things with his whole soul; and so he wants for himself what is good and what seems so, and does it (for it is characteristic of the good man to exert himself for the good), and does so for his own sake (for he does it for the sake of the thinking element in him, which is thought to be the man himself); and he wants to live himself and to be preserved, and especially the element by virtue of which he thinks. For existence is good to the virtuous man, and each man wants for himself what is good, while no one chooses to possess the whole world on condition of becoming someone else (for even now God possesses the good) but rather on condition of being whatever he is. And the element that thinks would seem to be the man himself, or to be so more than any other element in

him. And such a man wants to live with himself; for he does
25 so with pleasure, since the memories of his past acts are de-
lightful and his hopes for the future are good and such hopes
are pleasant. His mind is well stored too with subjects of
contemplation. And he grieves and takes pleasure, more
than any other, with himself; for the same things are always
painful and pleasant, and not one thing at one time and another at another; and he has, so to speak, nothing to regret.

30   Since each of these characteristics belongs to the upright
man in relation to himself, and he is related to his friend as
to himself (for his friend is another self), friendship too is
thought to be one of these attributes, and those who have
these attributes to be friends. Whether there is or is not
friendship between a man and himself is a question we may
dismiss for the present; but there would seem to be friendship in so far as he is two or more, to judge from what has
1166b been said, and from the fact that the excess of friendship is
like one's love for oneself.

The attributes named evidently belong even to the majority of men, base though they are. Are we to say then that in so
far as they approve of themselves and assume that they are
5 good, they share in these attributes? Certainly no one who is
thoroughly base and impious has these attributes, nor even
seems to do so. They scarcely belong even to base people; for
such people are at variance with themselves, and have appetites for some things and wants for others—for instance, incontinent people: they choose, instead of the things they
themselves think good, things that are pleasant but harmful.
10 Others again, through cowardice and idleness, shrink from
doing what they think best for themselves. Those who have
done many terrible deeds and are hated for their depravity
even flee from life and destroy themselves. Depraved men
look for people with whom to spend their days, and flee them-
15 selves; for they remember many a vexatious deed and antici-
pate others like them when they are by themselves, but when
they are with others they forget. And having nothing lovable
in them they have no feeling of love towards themselves. So

such men do not feel delight or grieve with themselves; for
their soul is rent by faction, and one element in it by reason of   20
its depravity grieves when it abstains from certain acts, while
the other is pleased, and one draws them this way and the
other that, as if they were pulling them in pieces. If a man cannot at the same time be pained and pleased, at all events after
a short time he is pained because he was pleased, and he could
have wished that these things had not been pleasant to him—
for base men are laden with regrets.   25

Thus the base man does not seem to be lovingly disposed
even towards himself, because there is nothing in him to
love. So that if to be thus is the height of wretchedness, we
should strain every nerve to avoid depravity and should endeavour to be upright; for so one may be both friendly to
oneself and a friend to another.

BENEVOLENCE IS LIKE FRIENDSHIP BUT IS NOT THE SAME   30
as friendship; for one may feel benevolence both towards
people whom one does not know and without their knowing
it, but not have such a friendship. This has been said already.
But benevolence is not even friendly feeling. For it does not
involve intensity or desire, whereas these accompany
friendly feeling; and friendly feeling implies intimacy while
benevolence may arise of a sudden: for instance, towards
competitors in a contest: we come to feel benevolence for   1167a
them and to share in their wishes, but we would not do anything with them. For, as we said, we feel benevolence suddenly and affection superficially.

Benevolence seems to be an origin of friendship, as the
pleasure of the eye is an origin of love. For no one loves if he   5
has not first been delighted by the form of the beloved, but
he who delights in the form of another does not, for all that,
love him: rather, he does so when he also longs for him when
absent and craves for his presence. So too it is not possible
for people to be friends if they have not come to feel benevolence, but those who feel benevolence are not for all that
friends; for they only wish well to those for whom they feel

10 benevolence, and would not do anything with them nor take trouble for them. That is why one might by an extension of the term say that benevolence is an idle friendship, which when it is prolonged and reaches the point of intimacy becomes friendship—not the friendship based on utility nor that based on pleasure; for benevolence does not arise on
15 those terms. A beneficiary bestows benevolence in return for what has been done to him, and in doing so does what is just; while he who wants someone to prosper because he hopes for affluence through him seems to have benevolence not to him but rather to himself, just as a man is not a friend to another if he serves him for the sake of some use to be made of him. In general, benevolence arises on account of some vir-
20 tue and uprightness, when one man seems to another noble or brave or something of the sort, as we said in the case of competitors in a contest.

CONCORD ALSO SEEMS TO BE A FRIENDLY RELATION. FOR this reason it is not sameness of belief; for that might occur even with people who do not know each other; nor does one say that people who have the same views on any and every
25 subject are in concord—for instance, those who agree about the heavenly bodies (for concord about these is not a friendly relation); rather, one says that a State is in concord when men have the same views about what is to their interest, and choose the same things, and act on what they have resolved in common. It is about matters of action, therefore, that people are said to be in concord, and, among these, about
30 matters of consequence and in which it is possible for both or all parties to get what they want—for instance, a State is in concord when all its citizens think that the offices in it should be elective, or that they should form an alliance with Sparta, or that Pittacus should be their ruler at a time when he himself was also willing to rule. But when each of two people wants it for himself, like the captains in the *Phoenissae*, they are in a state of faction: it is not concord when each of the two thinks the same thing, whatever that may be,

but rather when they think the same thing in relation to the same person—for instance, when both the common people and the upright men want the best men to rule; for thus do all get what they aim at. Concord seems, then, to be political friendship, as indeed it is said to be; for it is concerned with things that are to our advantage and have an influence on our life.

Such concord is found among upright men; for they are in concord both with themselves and with one another, being, so to say, of one mind (for the wishes of such men are constant and do not flow this way and that like a race in a strait), and they want what is just and what is advantageous, and they aim at these things in common. Base men cannot be in concord except to a small extent, any more than they can be friends, since they covet more in matters of benefit and undertake less in matters of exertion and public service; and each man wanting things for himself quizzes his neighbour and stands in his way. For if people do not watch it carefully the common interest is soon destroyed. The result is that they are in a state of faction, putting compulsion on each other but unwilling themselves to do what is just.

BENEFACTORS ARE THOUGHT TO LOVE THE OBJECTS OF their benefaction more than those who have been well treated love those that have treated them well, and this is inquired into as being paradoxical. Most people think it is because the latter are in the position of debtors and the former of creditors; and therefore as in the case of loans debtors wish their creditors did not exist while creditors actually take care of the safety of their debtors, so it is thought that benefactors want the objects of their action to exist since they will then get their gratitude, whereas beneficiaries take no interest in making this return. Epicharmus would perhaps declare that they say this because they look at things on their vicious side, but it is like human nature; for most people are forgetful, and aim rather to be well treated than to treat others well.

335

But the cause would seem to be more natural, and the
30 case of those who have lent money not to be similar. For they
have no friendly feeling to their debtors, but only a wish that
they may be kept safe with a view to what is to be got from
them; while those who have done a service to others cherish
and love those they have served even if these are not of any
use to them and never will be. This is what happens with
craftsmen too: every man cherishes his own product better
1168a than he would be cherished by it if it came alive. This happens perhaps most of all with poets; for they cherish their
own poems excessively, showing an affection for them as if
they were their children. This is what the position of benefactors is like; for that which they have treated well is their
5 product, and therefore they cherish it more than the product
does its maker. The cause of this is that existence is to all
men a thing to be chosen and loved, and that we exist by activity—by living and acting—and that the product is in a way
the maker in activity. So he feels affection for his product because he does so for his own existence. And this is natural;
for what he is in capacity, his product manifests in activity.
10 At the same time, to the benefactor that which depends
on his action is noble, so that he delights in the object of his
action, whereas to the patient there is nothing noble in the
agent but at most something advantageous, and this is less
pleasant and lovable. What is pleasant is activity in the present, expectation for the future, and memory of the past; but
15 most pleasant is that which is active, and similarly this is
most lovable. If a man has made something, his product remains (for the noble is lasting); but for the person acted on
the utility passes away. And the memory of noble things is
pleasant, but that of useful things is not at all so, or less so.
The reverse seems true of expectation.
20 Further, loving is like producing, being loved like being
acted upon; and loving and its concomitants are attributes
of those who are superior in action.
Again, all men have more affection for what they have
won by exertion: for instance, those who have made their

wealth love it more than those who have inherited it; and to be well treated seems to involve no exertion, while to treat others well is a task. These are the reasons, too, why mothers   25
are fonder of their children: bringing them into the world costs them more exertions, and they know better that the children are their own. This last point, too, would seem to apply to benefactors.

THE PROBLEM IS ALSO RAISED OF WHETHER A MAN should love himself most, or someone else. People criticize those who cherish themselves most, and call them self-   30
lovers, using this as an epithet of ignobility; and a base man seems to do everything for his own sake, and the more so the more depraved he is—and so men complain that, for instance, he does nothing which does not touch on himself—while the upright man acts for the sake of the noble, and the better he is the more so; and he acts for his friend's sake, and sacrifices his own interest.

But the facts clash with these arguments, and this is not   1168b
unreasonable. For men say that one ought to love best one's best friend, and a man's best friend is one who wishes well to the object of his wish for his sake, even if no one is to know of it; and these attributes are found most of all in a man's attitude towards himself. And so are all the other attributes by which a friend is defined; for, as we have said, it is from this   5
relation that all the characteristics of friendship have extended to others. All the proverbs take the same view: for instance, 'A single soul', and 'What friends have is common property', and 'Friendship is equality', and 'Charity begins at home'. All this will be found most in a man's relation to himself: he is his own best friend and therefore ought to love   10
himself best. It is therefore reasonably a problem which of the two views we should follow; for both are credible.

Perhaps we ought to mark off such arguments from each other and determine how far and in what respects each is true. If we grasp the sense in which each party uses the expression 'self-lover', the truth may become plain. Those who   15

337

use the term as one of reproach ascribe self-love to people who assign to themselves the greater share of wealth, honours, and bodily pleasures; for these are what most people desire and busy themselves about as though they were the best of all things—that is why they are fought over. So those who are covetous with regard to these things gratify their appetites and in general their emotions and the irrational element of the soul; and most men are of this nature. That is why the epithet has taken its meaning from the prevailing type of self-love, which is a base one. It is just, therefore, that men who are self-lovers in this way are reproached for being so. That it is those who assign such things to themselves that most people usually call self-lovers is plain; for if a man were always busy that he himself, above all things, should act justly, temperately, or in accordance with any other of the virtues, and in general were always to try to secure for himself the noble course, no one would call such a man a self-lover or blame him.

But such a man would seem rather to be a self-lover; at all events he assigns to himself the things that are noblest and best, and gratifies the most authoritative element in himself and in all things obeys this. Just as a State or any other organization is most properly identified with the most authoritative element in it, so is a man; and therefore the man who cherishes this and gratifies it is most of all a self-lover. Besides, a man is said to be continent or incontinent according as his intelligence has or has not the mastery,[9] on the assumption that this is the individual himself; and the acts men have done from reason are thought most properly their own and voluntary. That this is the individual himself, then, or is so more than anything else, is plain, and also that the upright man cherishes most this part of him. That is why he is most truly a self-lover, of another type than that which is a matter of reproach, and as different from that as living

---

9 'Continent' and 'incontinent' are ἐγκρατής and ἀκρατής, each of them cognate with κρατεῖν or 'to master'.

according to reason is from living according to emotion, and desiring what is noble from desiring what seems advantageous. Those, then, who busy themselves in an exceptional degree with noble actions all men approve and praise; and if all were to strive towards what is noble and strain every nerve to do the noblest deeds, everything would be as it should be for the common good and everyone would secure for himself the goods that are greatest, since virtue is the greatest of goods.

So the good man should be a self-lover (for he will both himself profit by doing noble acts and benefit his fellows), but the depraved man should not; for he will harm both himself and his neighbours, following as he does base emotions. For the depraved man, what he does clashes with what he ought to do, but what the virtuous man ought to do he does; for the intellect always chooses what is best for itself, and the good man obeys his intellect. It is true of the virtuous man too that he does many acts for the sake of his friends and his country, and dies for them if he ought to; for he will surrender wealth and honours and in general the goods that are fought over, gaining for himself nobility, since he would prefer a short period of intense pleasure to a long one of mild enjoyment, a twelvemonth of noble life to many years of humdrum existence, and one great and noble action to many trivial ones. Those who die for others doubtless attain this result; it is therefore something great and noble that they choose for themselves. They will surrender wealth too on condition that their friends will gain more; for while a man's friend gains wealth he himself achieves nobility; he is therefore assigning the greater good to himself. The same too is true of honour and office: all these things he will surrender to his friend; for this is noble and praiseworthy for himself. Reasonably enough, then, he is thought to be virtuous, since he chooses nobility before all else. He may even surrender up actions to his friend, and it may be nobler to become the cause of his friend's acting than to act himself. In all things praiseworthy, therefore, the virtuous man is seen to assign

1169b   to himself the greater share in what is noble. In this way, then, as has been said, a man should be a self-lover; but in the way in which most men are so, he ought not.

IT IS ALSO DISPUTED WHETHER THE HAPPY MAN WILL need friends or not. It is said that those who are blessed and
5   self-sufficient have no need of friends; for they have the things that are good, and therefore being self-sufficient they need nothing further while a friend, being another self, furnishes what a man cannot provide by his own effort—whence the line: 'When fortune is kind, what need of friends?'[10] But it seems absurd, when one assigns all good things to the happy man, not to assign friends, who are
10   thought the greatest of external goods. And if it is more characteristic of a friend to treat well than to be well treated, and to be a benefactor is characteristic of the good man and of virtue, and it is nobler to treat friends well than strangers, then the virtuous man will need people to treat well. This is why the question is asked whether we need friends more in
15   good fortune or in bad, on the supposition that a man in bad fortune needs benefactors and that those in good fortune need people to treat well. Perhaps it is absurd, too, to make the blessed man a solitary; for no one would choose to possess all good things on condition of being alone, since man is a political creature and one whose nature is to live with oth-
20   ers. So this holds of the happy man; for he has the things that are by nature good. And plainly it is better to spend his days with friends and upright men than with strangers or any chance persons. Therefore the happy man needs friends.

What then is it that the first party means, and in what respect is it true? Is it that most men think that it is useful people who are their friends? Of such friends indeed the blessed
25   man will have no need, since he already has the things that are good; nor will he need those whom one makes one's friends because of their pleasantness, or he will need them

10 Euripides, *Orestes* 667.

only to a small extent (for his life, being pleasant, has no need of adventitious pleasure); and because he does not need such friends he is thought not to need friends.

But that is surely not true. For we said at the start that happiness is a certain activity, and activity plainly comes into being and is not present like a piece of property. If happiness lies in living and being active, and the good man's activity is good and pleasant in itself, as we said at the start, and if a thing's being one's own is one of the attributes that make it pleasant, and if we can contemplate our neighbours better than ourselves and their actions better than our own, and if the actions of virtuous men who are their friends are pleasant to good men (since both have the attributes that are naturally pleasant)—if this be so, the blessed man will need friends of this sort, since he chooses to contemplate upright actions and actions that are his own, and the actions of a good man who is his friend are such.

Men think that the happy man ought to live pleasantly. If he were a solitary, life would be hard for him; for by oneself it is not easy to be continuously active, but with others and towards others it is easier. So his activity will be more continuous, being in itself pleasant, as it ought to be for the man who is blessed; for a virtuous man *qua* virtuous delights in virtuous actions and is vexed at vicious ones, just as a musical man takes pleasure in beautiful tunes but is pained at base ones. A certain training in virtue arises also from living together with the good, as Theognis remarks.[11]

If we look deeper into the nature of things, a virtuous friend seems to be naturally desirable for a virtuous man. For that which is virtuous by nature, we have said, is for the virtuous man good and pleasant in itself. Now life is defined in the case of animals by the capacity of sense-perception, in that of man by the capacity for perception or for thought. A capacity is referred to its activity, and the authoritative

11 'From good men you will learn good things; but if you mix with the bad, you will lose what sense you have': Theognis, lines 35–36.

element is in the activity. So life seems strictly speaking to be
perceiving or thinking. Life is among the things that are
good and pleasant in themselves, since it is determinate and
the determinate is of the nature of the good. That which is
good by nature is also good for the upright man. (That is why
life seems pleasant to all men.) But we must not apply this to
a depraved and corrupt life nor to a life spent in pain; for
such a life is indeterminate, as are its attributes. (The nature
of pain will become more evident in what follows.) If life itself is good and pleasant (which it seems to be, from the very
fact that all men desire it, and particularly those who are upright and blessed; for to them life is most desirable, and their
life is the most blessed); and if he who sees perceives that he
sees, and he who hears, that he hears, and he who walks, that
he walks, and in similarly all other cases there is something
which perceives that we are active, so that if we perceive, we
perceive that we perceive, and if we think, that we think; and
if to perceive that we perceive or think is to perceive that we
exist (for existence is perceiving or thinking); and if perceiving that one lives is one of the things that are pleasant in
themselves (for life is by nature good, and to perceive what is
good present in oneself is pleasant); and if life is desirable,
and particularly so for good men, because to them existence
is good and pleasant (for they are pleased at the consciousness of what is in itself good); and if as the virtuous man is to
himself, so is he to his friend also (for his friend is another
self)—then just as his own existence is desirable for each
man, so, or almost so, is that of his friend. Now his existence
was seen to be desirable because he perceived his own goodness, and such perception is pleasant in itself. He ought,
therefore, to be conscious of the existence of his friend as
well, and this will come about in their living together and
sharing in discussion and thought—for this is what living together would seem to mean in the case of man, and not, as in
the case of cattle, feeding in the same place.

If, then, existence is in itself desirable for the blessed man
(since it is by its nature good and pleasant), and that of his

friend is very much the same, a friend will be one of the things that are desirable. Now that which is desirable for him he must have, or he will be lacking in this respect. The man who is to be happy will therefore need virtuous friends.

SHOULD WE, THEN, MAKE AS MANY FRIENDS AS POSSIBLE,   20
or—as in the case of hospitality it is thought to be gracefully said that one should be 'neither a man of many guests nor a man of none'[12]—will it apply to friendship as well so that one should neither be friendless nor have an excessive number of friends?

To friends made with a view to utility this saying would seem thoroughly applicable; for to do services to many peo-   25
ple in return is a laborious task and life is not long enough for its performance. Therefore friends in excess of those who are sufficient for our own life are superfluous, and hindrances to the noble life; so that we have no need of them. Of friends made with a view to pleasure, also, few are enough, as a little seasoning in food is enough.

But as regards virtuous friends, should we have as many   30
as possible, or is there a limit to the number of one's friends, as there is to the size of a city-state? You cannot make a State of ten men, and if there are a hundred thousand it is a State no longer: the proper quantity is presumably not a single number but anything that falls between certain fixed points. So for friends too there is a fixed number—perhaps the larg-   1171a
est number with whom one can live together (for that is thought to be most characteristic of friendship); and that one cannot live with many people and distribute oneself among them is plain. Further, they too must be friends of one another, if they are all to spend their days together; and   5
it is a hard business for this condition to be fulfilled with a large number. It is found difficult, too, to feel delight and to grieve appropriately with many people; for it is likely to happen that one has at once to be pleased in the company of one

12 Hesiod, *Works and Days* 715.

friend and to mourn with another. Presumably, then, it is well to look to have not as many friends as possible but as many as are enough for the purpose of living together; for it would seem impossible to have an intense friendship with many people. This is why one cannot be in love with several people: being in love tends to be a sort of excess friendship, and that can only be felt towards one person; therefore intense friendship too can only be felt towards a few people. This seems to be confirmed in practice; for we do not find many people who are friends in the comradely way of friendship, and the famous friendships of this sort are always between two people. Those who have many friends and mix appropriately with them all are thought to be no one's friend (except in the way proper to fellow-citizens) and such people are called obsequious. In the way proper to fellow-citizens, indeed, it is possible to be the friend of many and yet not be obsequious but a truly upright man; but one cannot have with many people the friendship based on virtue and on the character of our friends themselves, and we must be content if we find even a few such.

DO WE NEED FRIENDS MORE IN GOOD FORTUNE OR IN BAD? They are looked for in both; for while men in times of bad fortune need help, in times of good fortune they need people to live with and to treat well—for they want to do good. Friendship is more necessary in bad fortune, and that is why it is useful friends that one needs in this case; but it is more noble in good fortune, and that is why we also look for upright men, since it is more desirable to be their benefactor and to live with them. For the very presence of friends is pleasant both in good fortune and also in bad, since pain is lightened when friends grieve with us. That is why one might raise the problem of whether they share as it were our burden, or—without that happening—their presence by its pleasantness, and the thought of their grieving with us, makes our pain less. Whether it is for these reasons or for some other that our pain is lightened, is a question that may be dismissed: at all events what we have described evidently takes place.

But their presence seems to contain a mixture of various factors. For on the one hand, just to see one's friends is pleas- 1171b ant, especially in times of bad fortune, and becomes a certain help against pain (for a friend tends to comfort us both by the sight of him and by his words, if he is tactful, since he knows our character and the things that please or pain us); and on the other hand, to perceive that a friend is pained at our misfortunes is painful; for everyone shuns being a cause 5 of pain to his friends. For this reason people of a manly nature guard against making their friends share their pain, and, unless he be exceptionally insensible to pain, such a man cannot face the pain that ensues for his friends, and in general does not admit fellow-mourners because he is not himself given to mourning—women and effeminate men 10 delight in those who lament with them, and they love them as friends and companions in grief. But in all things one plainly ought to imitate the better type of person.

The presence of friends in times of good fortune implies both a pleasant passing of our time and the thought of their pleasure at our own good things. That is why it would seem 15 that we ought to summon our friends eagerly to share our good fortunes (for it is noble to be beneficent), but summon them to our bad fortunes with hesitation; for we ought to give them as little a share as possible in our evils—whence the saying 'Enough is my own misfortune'. We should invite friends most of all when they are likely by suffering a few inconveniences to do us a great benefit.

Conversely, it is fitting to go unasked and eagerly to those 20 in bad fortune (for it is characteristic of a friend to do good, and especially to those who are in need and have not claimed anything: such action is nobler and pleasanter for both); but when our friends are enjoying good fortune we should join eagerly in their activities (for they need friends for these too), but be tardy in coming forward to be the objects of their kindness; for it is not noble to be eager to receive benefits. 25

But we must no doubt avoid getting the reputation of kill-joys by repulsing them; for that sometimes happens.

The presence of friends, then, seems desirable in all circumstances.

30   IS IT THE CASE THAT, JUST AS FOR THOSE IN LOVE IT IS SEE-ing which most contents them, and they prefer this sense to the others because it is this above all which gives rise to being in love and which keeps it in existence, so for friends the most desirable thing is living together? For friendship is an association, and as a man is to himself, so is he to his friend: now in his own case the perception of his existence is desir-able, and so therefore is that of his friend's, and the exercise
1172a   of this perception occurs when they live together, so that it is reasonable that they aim at this. And whatever existence means for each class of men, or whatever it is for the sake of which they choose life, in that they want to occupy them-selves with their friends: so some drink together, others dice together, others train together and hunt together or philo-
5   sophize together, each spending their days together in what-ever most contents them in life. For since they want to live with their friends, they do and share in those things as far as they can.[13] Thus the friendship of base men is depraved (for because of their lack of firmness they share in base pursuits,
10   and they become depraved by becoming like each other), while the friendship of upright men is upright, being aug-mented by their companionship; and they are thought to be-come better too by their activities and by correcting each other; for from each other they take the mould of the charac-teristics they approve—whence the saying: 'From good men, good things'.[14]

So much, then, for friendship: our next task must be to discuss pleasure.

---

13 Reading ὡς οἷόν τε (with the Laurentian manuscript) for οἷς οἴονται, and deleting συζῆν.

14 Theognis: above, 1170a12 and note.

6

PLEASURE

AFTER THESE MATTERS WE OUGHT PERHAPS NEXT TO DIS-
cuss pleasure. For it is thought to be most intimately connected with our human kind: that is why in educating the
young we steer them by the rudders of pleasure and pain. It
is thought, too, that to delight in the things we ought and to
hate the things we ought has the greatest bearing on virtue
of character. For these things extend right through life, with
a weight and power of their own in respect both to virtue and
to the happy life, since men choose what is pleasant and
avoid what is painful. Such things, it will be thought, we
should least of all omit to discuss, especially since they admit
of much dispute.

For some say pleasure is the good, while others, on the
contrary, say it is thoroughly base—some no doubt being
convinced that the facts are actually so, and others thinking
it has a better effect on our life to exhibit pleasure as a base
thing even if it is not; for most people (they think) incline towards it and are the slaves of their pleasures—that is why
they ought to lead them in the contrary direction, since thus
they will reach the middle state. But surely this is not correct. For arguments about matters concerned with emotions
and actions are less reliable than facts; and so when they
clash with the facts of perception they are despised, and dis-
credit the truth as well. For if a man who heaps blame on
pleasure is once seen to be aiming at it, his inclining towards
it is thought to imply that it is all like that—for most people
are not good at drawing distinctions. True arguments seem,
then, most useful not only with a view to knowledge but also
with a view to life; for since they harmonize with the facts

they are found convincing, and that is why they encourage those who grasp them to live according to them. But enough of such matters: let us proceed to review the opinions that have been expressed about pleasure.

10   Eudoxus thought pleasure was the good because he saw all things, both rational and irrational, aiming at it, and because in all things what is desirable is upright, and what is most desirable is best. Thus the fact that all things moved towards the same object indicated that this was for all things the chief good (for each thing, he argued, finds its own good, as it finds its own nourishment); and that which is good for 15 all things and at which all aim was the good. His arguments convinced because of the virtue of his character rather than for their own sake: he was thought to be remarkably temperate, and so it was thought that he was not saying what he did say as a friend of pleasure but that the facts really were so. He thought that the same conclusion followed no less evidently from a study of the contrary of pleasure: pain was in itself an 20 object of aversion to all things, and so its contrary must be similarly an object of desire. And again, that is most desirable which we choose not because of something else or for the sake of something else, and pleasure is admittedly of this nature; for no one asks to what end he is pleased, thus implying that pleasure is in itself desirable. Further, he argued that 25 pleasure when added to any good (for instance, to just or temperate action) makes it more desirable, and that it is by itself that the good is increased.

    This argument seems to show it to be one of the goods, and no more a good than any other; for every good is more desirable along with another good than taken alone. And so it is by an argument of this kind that Plato proves the good 30 not to be pleasure: he argues that the pleasant life is more desirable with wisdom than without, and that if the mixture is better, pleasure is not the good; for the good cannot become more desirable by the addition of anything to it.[1] Now

1 See Plato, *Philebus* 60BE.

it is plain that nothing else can be the good if it is made more desirable by the addition of any of the things that are good in themselves. What, then, is there that satisfies this criterion, which at the same time we can share in? It is something of this sort that we are looking for.

Those who object that that at which all things aim is not good are talking nonsense. For we say that that which everyone thinks really is so; and the man who attacks this conviction will hardly have anything more convincing to maintain. If it is unintelligent beings that desire the things, there would be something in what they say; but if wise beings do so as well, how can there be? And perhaps even in base beings there is some natural good stronger than themselves which aims at their own good.

Nor does the argument about the contrary of pleasure seem to be right. They say that if pain is bad it does not follow that pleasure is good; for bad is opposed to bad, and both are opposed to the neutral state—which is right but is not true of the things in question. For if both were bad they ought both to be objects of aversion, while if neutral neither should be or both equally. But in fact people evidently avoid the one as bad and choose the other as good; that then must be the nature of the opposition between them.

Nor again, if pleasure is not a quality, does it follow that it is not a good; for the activities of virtue are not qualities either, nor is happiness.

They say, however, that the good is determinate, while pleasure is indeterminate, because it admits of degrees. Now if it is from being pleased that they make this assessment, the same will be true of justice and the other virtues in respect of which we say that people of a certain character are manifestly so more or less, and act more or less in accordance with these virtues; for people may be more just or brave, and it is possible to act more or less justly or temperately. But if their assessment is based on the pleasures, surely they are not stating the cause, if some pleasures are unmixed and others mixed. Again, just as health admits of degrees

25 without being indeterminate, why should not pleasure? The
    same proportion is not found in all things, nor a single pro-
    portion always in the same thing: rather, it may be relaxed
    and yet persist up to a point, and it may differ in degree. The
    case of pleasure also may therefore be of this kind.

        Supposing that the good is complete while movements
30 and processes are incomplete, they try to exhibit pleasure as
    being a movement and a process. But they do not seem to be
    right, nor does it seem to be a movement.[2] For speed and
    slowness are thought to be appropriate to every movement,
    if not in itself (for instance, that of the heavens), then in rela-
    tion to something else; but of pleasure neither of these
1173b things holds. For while we may become pleased quickly as we
    may become angry quickly, we cannot be pleased quickly, not
    even in relation to someone else, while we can walk or grow
    or the like quickly. While, then, we can change quickly or
    slowly into a state of pleasure, we cannot quickly be active
    with regard to it—I mean, feel pleasure. Again, how can it be
5   a process? It is not thought that any chance thing can pro-
    ceed from any chance thing, but that a thing is dissolved into
    that out of which it proceeds; and pain would be the destruc-
    tion of that of which pleasure is the process.

        They say, too, that pain is the lack of that which is accord-
    ing to nature, and pleasure is replenishment. But these phe-
    nomena are bodily. So if pleasure is replenishment with that
10 which is according to nature, that which feels pleasure will
    be that in which the replenishment takes place—therefore in
    the body. But that is not thought to be the case. Therefore the
    replenishment is not pleasure, though one might feel plea-
    sure while replenishment was taking place, just as[3] one
    might feel pain while one was being operated on. This belief
    seems to be based on the pains and pleasures connected with
15 nutrition: when people have lacked food and have felt pain

    2 Reading κίνησις for κίνησιν.

    3 Reading ὥσπερ for καί (Bywater obelizes the participle 'being operated
    on').

beforehand they feel pleasure at the replenishment. But this does not happen with all pleasures; for the pleasures of learning are painless, and so too, among the pleasures of the senses, are those of smell, and also many sounds and sights, and memories and hopes. Of what then will these be the processes? There has not been lack of anything of which they could be the replenishment.   20

In reply to those who bring forward the pleasures that deserve reproach one may say that these are not pleasant: if things are pleasant to people of vicious constitution, we must not suppose that they are also pleasant to others than these, just as we do not reason so about the things that are healthy or sweet or bitter to sick people, or ascribe whiteness   25 to the things that seem white to those suffering from a disease of the eye. Or one might answer thus—that the pleasures are desirable but not from *these* sources, as riches are desirable but not as the reward of betrayal, and health but not at the cost of eating anything and everything. Or perhaps pleasures differ in kind; for those derived from noble sources are different from those derived from ignoble ones, and one cannot get the pleasure of the just man without   30 being just, nor that of the musical man without being musical, and so on.

˙ The fact, too, that a friend is different from a flatterer seems to make it evident that pleasure is not a good or that pleasures are different in kind; for the one is thought to seek our company with a view to the good, the other with a view to pleasure, and the one is reproached while the other is praised, thus implying that he seeks our company for a dif-   1174a ferent end. No one would choose to live with the intellect of a child throughout his life, however much he were to take pleasure in the things that children take pleasure in, nor to delight in doing some most ignoble deed, though he were never to feel any pain in consequence. There are many things we should be keen about even if they brought no pleasure—   5 for instance, seeing, remembering, knowing, possessing the virtues. If pleasures necessarily do accompany these, that

makes no difference: we should choose them even if no pleasure resulted from them.

It seems to be plain, then, that neither is pleasure the
good nor is all pleasure desirable, and that some pleasures
are desirable in themselves, differing in kind or in their
sources. So much for the things that are said about pleasure
and pain.

What pleasure is, or what kind of thing, will become more
evident if we take up the question again from the beginning.
Seeing seems to be at any moment complete; for it does not
lack anything which, coming into being later, will complete
its form; and pleasure also seems to be of this nature. For it
is a whole, and at no time can one find a pleasure whose form
will be completed if the pleasure lasts longer. For this reason, too, it is not a movement. For every movement (for instance that of building) takes time and is for the sake of an
end, and it is complete when it has made what it aims at. So
it is complete either in the whole time or at the final moment. In their parts and during the time they occupy, all
movements are incomplete, and they are different in kind
from the whole movement and from each other. For the fitting together of the stones is different from the fluting of the
column, and these are different from the making of the temple; and the making of the temple is complete (for it lacks
nothing with a view to the end proposed), whereas the making of the base or of the triglyph is incomplete (for each is the
making of a part). They differ in kind, then, and it is not possible to find at any and every time a movement complete in
form but if at all, in the whole time. So too in the case of
walking and all other movements. For if locomotion is a
movement from here to there, it, too, has differences in
kind—flying, walking, jumping, and so on. And not only so,
but in walking itself there are differences; for the whence
and whither are not the same in the whole racecourse and in
a part of it, nor in one part and in another, nor is it the same
thing to traverse this line and that—for one traverses not
only a line but one which is in a place, and this one is in a

different place from that. Elsewhere we have discussed movement with precision: it seems that it is not complete at any and every time, but that most movements are incomplete and different in kind, since the whence and whither give them their form. But of pleasure the form is complete at any and every time. Plainly, then, pleasure and movement must be different from each other, and pleasure must be one of the things that are whole and complete. This would seem to be the case, too, from the fact that it is not possible to move otherwise than in time, but it is possible so to be pleased; for that which takes place in a moment is a whole.

From these considerations it is clear, too, that these thinkers are not right in saying there is a movement or a process of pleasure.[4] For these cannot be ascribed to all things but to those that are divisible and not wholes: there is no process of seeing nor of a point nor of a unit, nor is any of these a movement or process: therefore there is none of pleasure either; for it is a whole.

Since every sense is exercised in relation to an object of sense-perception, and one which is in good condition exercises completely in relation to the noblest of its objects (for complete exercise or activity seems to be especially of this nature—it may be taken to make no difference whether we say that it is itself that is active or rather that in which it resides), it follows that in the case of each sense the best exercised is that of what is best-conditioned in relation to the finest of its objects. And this activity will be the most complete and most pleasant. For while there is pleasure in respect of any sense, and in respect of thought and contemplation no less, the most complete is pleasantest, and that of something well-conditioned in relation to the best of its objects is the most complete; and the pleasure completes the activity. But the pleasure does not complete it in the same way as the object perceived and the faculty of perception, if they are good,

4 Reading τῆς ἡδονῆς (Ramsauer) for τὴν ἡδονήν ('saying that pleasure is a movement or a process').

do—just as health and the doctor are not in the same way the cause of a man's being healthy. (That pleasure is produced in respect to each sense is plain; for we speak of sights and sounds as pleasant. It is also plain that it arises most of all when the sense is at its best and is active about an object of that sort: if both the object of perception and the perceiver are of the best there will always be pleasure, since the agent and patient are both present.) Pleasure completes the activity not as the inherent state does but as an end which supervenes—as the bloom of youth does on those in the flower of their age. So long, then, as both the object of thought or perception and also the assessing or contemplative element are as they should be, pleasure[5] will be involved in the activity; for when both the passive and the active elements are unchanged and are related to each other in the same way, the same result naturally follows.

How then is it that no one is pleased continuously? Is it that we grow weary? Certainly all human things are incapable of continuous activity. Therefore pleasure also is not continuous; for it accompanies activity. Some things delight us when they are new but later do so less, for the same reason: at first the intellect is in a state of stimulation and exercises itself strenuously about them, as people are with respect to their vision when they look hard at a thing; but afterwards the activity is not of this kind but has grown relaxed—that is why the pleasure also is dulled.

One might think that all men desire pleasure because they all aim at life. Life is an activity, and each man is active about those things and with those faculties that he cherishes most: for instance, the musician is active with his hearing in reference to tunes, the student with his intellect in reference to objects of contemplation, and so on in each case. Now pleasure completes the activities, and therefore life, which they desire. It is with good reason, then, that they aim at pleasure, since for everyone it completes life, which is desirable. (Whether

5 Omitting ἡ before ἡδονή as Bywater suggests.

we choose life for the sake of pleasure or pleasure for the sake of life is a question we may dismiss for the present. For they seem to be bound up together and not to admit of separation, since without activity pleasure does not arise, and every activity is completed by pleasure.)

For this reason pleasures seem to differ in kind. For things different in kind are, we think, completed by different things (we see this to be true both of natural objects and of things produced by the crafts—for instance, animals, trees, a painting, a sculpture, a house, an implement); and, similarly, we think that activities differing in kind are completed by things differing in kind. Now the exercises of thought differ from those of the senses, and among themselves, in kind; so, therefore, do the pleasures that complete them.

This may be seen, too, from the fact that each of the pleasures is appropriate to the activity it completes. For an activity is increased by its own pleasure, since each class of things is better assessed and brought to precision by those who exercise it with pleasure: for example, it is those who take delight in geometry that become geometers and grasp the various propositions better, and similarly those who love music or architecture and so on make progress in their task by taking delight in it; and the pleasures increase the exercises, and what increases a thing is appropriate to it, and what is appropriate to things different in kind itself differs in kind.

This will be even more apparent from the fact that activities are hindered by pleasures arising from other sources. For people who love the flute cannot attend to arguments if they overhear someone playing the flute, since they enjoy flute-playing more than the activity in hand; so the pleasure connected with flute-playing destroys the activity concerned with argument. This happens, similarly, in all other cases when one is active about two things at once: the more pleasant activity drives out the other, and if it is much more pleasant does so all the more, so that one even ceases from the other. This is why when we feel intense delight in something we do not throw ourselves into anything else, and do one thing when we do not greatly approve of another: for instance, in the theatre the people who eat sweets do so most when the actors are poor. Now since activities are made precise and more enduring and better by their own pleasures and injured by alien pleasures, plainly the two kinds of pleasure are far apart. For alien pleasures do pretty much what appropriate pains do, since activities are destroyed by their own pains: for instance, if a man finds writing or calculating unpleasant and painful, he does not write or does not calculate because the activity is painful. So an activity suffers contrary effects from its own pleasures and pains, and its own pleasures are those that occur in virtue of its own nature. Alien pleasures have been stated to do much the same as pain: they destroy the activity—but not in the same way.

Since activities differ in respect of virtuousness and baseness, and some are desirable, others to be avoided, and others neutral, so too are the pleasures; for to each activity there is its own pleasure. The pleasure of a serious activity is virtuous and that of a base activity depraved—just as the appetites for noble objects are praiseworthy and those for ignoble objects blameworthy. But the pleasures involved in activities are nearer to them than the desires; for the latter are separated both in time and in nature, while the former are close to the exercises, and so hard to distinguish from them that it admits of dispute whether the activity is not the same as the pleasure. (Still, pleasure does not seem to be thought or perception—that would be absurd; but because they are not separated they appear to some people the same.) As the activities are different, then, so are the pleasures. Sight is superior to touch in purity, and hearing and smell to taste: the pleasures, therefore, are similarly superior, and those of thought superior to these, and within each of the two kinds some are superior to others.

Each animal is thought to have its own pleasure, as it has its own task: that which corresponds to its activity. If we consider them one by one this will be evident: horses, dogs, and men have different pleasures—as Heraclitus says, asses would prefer chaff to gold; for food is pleasanter than gold to asses. So the pleasures of those different in kind differ in kind, and it is reasonable to suppose that those of a single species do not differ. But they vary to no small extent, in the case of men at least: the same things delight some people and pain others, and are painful and hateful to some, and pleasant to and loved by others. This happens, too, in the case of sweet things: the same things do not seem sweet to a man in a fever and a healthy man—nor hot to a weak man and one in good condition. The same happens in other cases. But in all such matters that which appears to the virtuous man is thought to be really so. If this is right, as it seems to be, and virtue and the good man as such are the measure of each thing, those also will be pleasures which appear so to him, and those things pleasant which he takes delight in. If the things he finds vexing seem pleasant to someone, that is not remarkable; for men may be destroyed and injured in many ways—but the things are not pleasant, except to these people and to people in this condition. Those which are admittedly ignoble plainly should not be said to be pleasures, except to a depraved taste; but of those that are thought to be virtuous what kind of pleasure or what pleasure should be said to be that proper to man? Is it not plain from the activity? For the pleasures follow these. Whether, then, the complete and blessed man has one or more activities, the pleasures that complete these will be said strictly speaking to be pleasures proper to man, and the rest will be so in a secondary and fractional way, as are the activities.

7

HAPPINESS

NOW THAT WE HAVE SPOKEN OF THE VIRTUES, THE FORMS of friendship, and the varieties of pleasure, it remains to discuss in outline happiness, since this is what we state the end of human nature to be. Our discussion will be the more concise if we take up what we have said already. We said, then, that it is not a state; for if it were it might belong to someone who was asleep throughout his life, living the life of a plant, or, again, to someone who was suffering the greatest misfortunes. If these implications do not meet with approval, and we must rather class happiness as an activity, as we have said before, and if some activities are necessary and desirable for the sake of something else while others are so in themselves, plainly happiness must be placed among those desirable in themselves, not among those desirable for the sake of something else; for happiness does not lack anything but is self-sufficient. Now those activities are desirable in themselves from which nothing is looked for apart from the activity. And virtuous actions are thought to be such; for to do noble and virtuous deeds is a thing desirable for its own sake.

Pleasant amusements also are thought to be of this nature: we choose them not for the sake of other things; for we are harmed rather than benefited by them, since we are led to neglect our bodies and our possessions. But most of the people who are deemed happy resort to such pastimes. That is why those who are convivial on such occasions are highly esteemed at the courts of tyrants: they make themselves pleasant in the tyrant's favourite pursuits, and that is the sort of man they want. These things are thought to be of the nature of happiness because people in power spend their leisure in them. But perhaps such people are no indication; for virtue and intelligence, from which virtuous activities come, do not depend on power. Nor if these people, who have never tasted pure and generous pleasure, resort to the bodily pleasures, should these for that reason be thought more desirable; for boys, too, think the things that are valued among themselves are the best. It is reasonable, then, that, as different things seem valuable to boys and to men, so they should to base men and to upright men. Now, as we have often maintained, those things are both valuable and pleasant which are such to the virtuous man; and to each man the activity in accordance with his own state is most desirable, and so to the virtuous man that which is in accordance with virtue. Happiness, therefore, does not lie in amusement: it would, indeed, be absurd if the end were amusement, and one were to take trouble and suffer hardship all one's life in order to amuse oneself. For, in a word, everything that we choose we choose for the sake of something else—except happiness, which is an end. Now to be busy and to exert oneself for the sake of amusement seems silly and utterly childish. But to amuse oneself in order that one may be busy, as Anacharsis puts it, seems correct; for amusement is a sort of relaxation, and we need relaxation because we cannot exert ourselves continuously. Relaxation is not an end; for it is taken for the sake of activity.

The happy life is thought to be one of virtue, and it requires seriousness and does not consist in amusement. We say that serious things are better than laughable things and those connected with amusement, and that the activity of the better —whether it be a part or a man—is the more virtuous; but the activity of the better is superior and thereby more of the nature of happiness. And any chance person— even a slave—can enjoy the bodily pleasures no less than the best man; but no one assigns to a slave a share in happiness—unless he assigns to him also a share in life. For happiness does not lie in such pastimes but, as we have said before, in virtuous activities.

IF HAPPINESS IS AN ACTIVITY IN ACCORDANCE WITH VIR-
tue, it is reasonable that it should be in accordance with the
highest virtue; and this will be that of the best. Whether it be
intelligence or something else that is thought to be our natural ruler and guide and to take thought of things noble and
divine (whether it be itself also divine or the most divine element in us), the activity of this in accordance with its own
virtue will be complete happiness. That this activity is contemplative we have already said.

This would seem to be in agreement both with what we
have said before and with the truth. For this activity is the
best (since intelligence is the best thing in us and the objects
of intelligence are the best of knowable objects). Again, it is
the most continuous, since we can contemplate more continuously than we can perform any action. And we think
happiness must have pleasure mingled with it, and the activity of understanding is admittedly the pleasantest of virtuous activities: at all events philosophy is thought to offer
pleasures marvellous for their purity and their firmness,
and it is reasonable that those who know will pass their
time more pleasantly than those who inquire. And the self-
sufficiency that is spoken of must belong most to contemplative exercise. For while a man of understanding, as well
as a just man and the rest, needs the necessaries of life,
when they are sufficiently equipped with things of that sort
the just man needs people towards whom and with whom
he shall act justly, and the temperate man, the brave man,
and each of the others is in the same case, but the man of
understanding, even when by himself, can contemplate,
and the more so the greater his understanding: he can perhaps do so better if he has collaborators—but still he is the
most self-sufficient. And this activity alone would seem to
be cherished for its own sake; for nothing arises from it
apart from the contemplating, while from practical activities we gain more or less apart from the action. And happiness is thought to depend on leisure; for we are busy that we
may have leisure, and make war that we may live in peace.

Now the activity of the practical virtues is exhibited in political or military affairs, but the actions concerned with these seem to be unleisurely. Warlike actions are completely so; for no one chooses to be at war, or prepares for war, for the sake of being at war: a man would seem absolutely murderous if he were to make enemies of his friends in order to bring about battles and slaughter. But the action of the politician is also unleisurely, and (apart from the political action itself) aims at power and honours, or at all events happiness, for himself and his fellow citizens—a happiness different from political action, and plainly sought as being different. So if among virtuous actions political and military actions are distinguished by nobility and greatness, and these are unleisurely and aim at an end and are not desirable for their own sake, whereas the exercise of intelligence, which is contemplative, seems both to be superior in seriousness and to aim at no end beyond itself, and to have its own pleasure (and this increases the activity), and if the self-sufficiency, leisureliness, unweariedness (so far as this is possible for man), and all the other attributes ascribed to the blessed man are evidently those connected with this activity, it follows that this will be the complete happiness for man, if it be allowed a complete term of life (for none of the attributes of happiness is incomplete).

Such a life would be too high for man; for it is not in so far as he is man that he will live so but in so far as something divine is present in him; and by so much as this is superior to our composite nature is its activity superior to that of the other kind of virtue. If the intelligence is divine, then, in comparison with man, the life according to it is divine in comparison with human life. But we must not follow those who advise us being men to think of human things, and being mortal of mortal things. Rather, we must, so far as we can, make ourselves immortal, and do everything to live in accordance with the highest thing in us; for even if it be small in bulk, much more does it in power and value surpass everything. This would seem, too, to be each man himself, since it

is the authoritative and better part of him. It would be absurd, then, if he were to choose the life not of himself but of
5   something else. And what we said before will apply now:
that which is appropriate to each thing is by nature best and
most pleasant for each thing, and so for man the life of the
intelligence is best and pleasantest, since intelligence more
than anything else is the man. This life therefore is also the
happiest.

But in a secondary degree the life in accordance with the
10   other kind of virtue is happy; for the activities in accordance
with this are human. Just and brave acts, and other virtuous
acts, we do in relation to each other, observing what is fitting
to each with regard to contracts and services and all manner
of actions and with regard to the emotions, and all of these
are evidently human. Some of them seem even to arise from
15   the body, and virtue of character to be in many ways bound
up with the emotions. Wisdom, too, is coupled with virtue of
character, and this with wisdom, since the originating principles of wisdom are in accordance with the moral virtues
and correctness in the moral virtues is in accordance with
20   wisdom. Being connected with the emotions, the moral virtues will concern our composite nature; and the virtues of
our composite nature are human: so, therefore, are the life
and the happiness which correspond to these. The virtue of
the intelligence is separate: let this much be said about it; for
to describe it precisely is more than our purpose requires. It
25   would seem to need external equipment little, or less than
moral virtue does. Grant that both need the necessaries, and
do so equally, even if the politician's exertions have more
concern with the body and things of that sort; for there will
be little difference there. But in what they need for the exercise of their activities there will be much difference. The lib-
30   eral man will need wealth for his liberal actions; the just man
will need it for the returning of services (for wants are obscure, and even people who are not just pretend to want to
act justly); the brave man will need power if he is to accom-
plish any of the acts that correspond to his virtue; and the

temperate man will need opportunity—for how else is either
he or any of the others to be recognized? It is debated, too,
whether choice or action is more authoritative over virtue,
which is taken to involve both. It is surely plain that its
completion involves both; but for actions many things are   1178b
needed, and more the greater and nobler they are. But the
man who is contemplating needs no such things, at least
with a view to the exercise of his activity. Rather, they are,
one may say, even hindrances, at all events to his contempla-   5
tion; but in so far as he is a man and lives with a number of
people, he chooses to act virtuously: he will therefore need
such aids to living a human life.

That complete happiness is a contemplative activity will
appear from the following consideration as well. We suppose the gods to be above all other beings blessed and happy.
But what sort of actions must we assign to them? Acts of jus-   10
tice? Will not the gods seem ridiculous if they make contracts and return deposits, and so on? Acts of a brave man,
then, facing up to what is frightening and confronting dangers because it is noble to do so?[1] Or liberal acts? To whom
will they give? It will be absurd if they are to have money or   15
anything of the kind. And what would their temperate acts
be? Is not such praise vulgar, since they have no base appetites? If we were to run through them all, the circumstances
of action would be found trivial and unworthy of gods. Still,
everyone assumes that they live and therefore that they are
active themselves: we cannot suppose them to sleep like En-
dymion. Now if you take away from a living being action,   20
and still more production, what is left but contemplation?
Therefore the activity of god, which is especially blessed, will
be contemplative; and so of human activities that which is
most akin to this must be most of the nature of happiness.

This is indicated, too, by the fact that the other animals
have no share in happiness, being completely deprived of   25
such activity. For while the whole life of the gods is blessed,

1 The text of this sentence is uncertain.

and that of men too in so far as some likeness of such activity belongs to them, none of the other animals is happy, since they in no way share in contemplation. Happiness extends, then, just so far as contemplation does, and those to whom
30 contemplation more fully belongs are more truly happy, not coincidentally but in virtue of the contemplation; for this is in itself valuable. Happiness, therefore, must be a kind of contemplation.

Being a man, one will also need external prosperity; for our nature is not self-sufficient for contemplation—rather, our body also must be healthy and must have food and other
1179a attention. Still, we must not think that the man who is to be happy will need many things or great things if he cannot be blessed without external goods. For self-sufficiency and action do not depend on excess, and we can do noble acts with-
5 out ruling earth and sea; for even with moderate resources one can act virtuously (this is manifest enough; for private persons are thought to do upright acts no less than the powerful—indeed even more); and it is enough that we should have so much as that; for the life of the man who is active in
10 accordance with virtue will be happy. Solon perhaps described happy men well when he said that they are moderately equipped with externals but have done (as he thought) the noblest acts and have lived temperately. For one can with but moderate possessions do what one ought. Anaxagoras also seems to have assumed that the happy man is not rich or
15 powerful when he said that he would not be surprised if the happy man were to seem absurd to most people; for they assess things by externals, since these are all they perceive.

The beliefs of men of understanding seem, then, to harmonize with our arguments. But while such things carry some conviction, the truth in practical matters is assessed
20 from the facts of life; for these are in control. We must therefore survey what we have already said, bringing it to the test of the facts of life, and if it harmonizes with the facts we must accept it, but if it clashes with them we must assume it to be mere words. Now he who exercises his intelligence and

cultivates it seems to be both in the best state and most dear to the gods. For if the gods have any care for human affairs, as they are thought to have, it would be reasonable both that   25 they should delight in that which is best and most akin to them (and this is intelligence) and that they should reward those who cherish and honour this most, as caring for the things that are dear to them and acting both correctly and nobly. And that all these attributes belong most of all to the   30 man of understanding is plain. He, therefore, is the dearest to the gods. And the same man will presumably also be the happiest, so that in this way too the man of understanding will be especially happy.

8

CONCLUDING REMARKS

IF THESE MATTERS AND THE VIRTUES, AND ALSO FRIEND-
ship and pleasure, have been dealt with sufficiently in outline, are we to suppose that our programme has reached its
end? Surely, as is said, in matters of action the end is not to
contemplate and recognize each of them but rather to do
them. With regard to virtue, then, it is not enough to know:
we must try to have and to use it, or try any other way there
may be of becoming good.

If arguments were in themselves enough to make men
upright, they would justly (in Theognis' words) have won
many great rewards, and such rewards should have been
provided; but as things are, while they seem to have power to
encourage and stimulate the generous-minded among the
young, and to make a character which is gently born and a
true lover of what is noble, ready to be possessed by virtue,
they are not able to encourage the many to gentlemanliness.
For these by nature obey not modesty but fear, and do not
abstain from base acts because of their ignobility but because of punishments: living by their emotions they pursue
their own pleasures and the means to them, and avoid the
opposite pains, and have not even a conception of what is
noble and truly pleasant, since they have never tasted it.
What argument would remould such people? It is impossible, or not easy, to remove by argument the traits that have
long since been fixed in the character; and perhaps we must
be content if, when everything by which we are thought to
become upright is present, we get some hold on virtue.

Some think that we are made good by nature, others by
habituation, others by teaching. Nature's part plainly is not

in our power: rather, as a result of some divine causes it is present in those who are truly fortunate. Argument and teaching are perhaps not powerful with all men: the soul of the pupil must first have been worked on by means of habits for noble delight and hatred, like earth which is to nourish the seed. For he who lives by his emotions will not hear argument that discourages him, nor grasp it if he does; and how can we persuade one in such a state to change? In general emotion seems to yield not to argument but to force. The character, then, must somehow already be related to virtue, loving what is noble and being vexed at what is ignoble.

It is difficult to get from youth up a correct training for virtue if one has not been brought up under correct laws; for to live temperately and with endurance is not pleasant to most people, especially when they are young. That is why their nurture and occupations should be fixed by law; for they will not be painful when they have become customary. But perhaps it is not enough that when they are young they should get the correct nurture and attention: since they must, even when they are grown up, practise and be habituated to them, we shall need laws for this as well, and generally speaking for the whole of life; for most people obey necessity rather than argument, and punishments rather than what is noble.

This is why some think that legislators ought to invite men to virtue and encourage them to act for the sake of the noble, on the supposition that those who have been uprightly moulded by the formation of habits will listen to such things; and that punishments and penalties should be imposed on those who disobey and are less well endowed by nature, and that the incurable should be completely banished. An upright man (they think), since he lives for what is noble, will obey reason, while a base man, whose desire is for pleasure, is corrected by pain like a beast of burden. This is why they say the pains should be those that are most contrary to the pleasures such men cherish.

15   If (as we have said) the man who is to be good must be
nobly trained and habituated, and go on to spend his time in
upright occupations and neither voluntarily nor involuntarily perform base actions, and if this can be brought about
if men live in accordance with a sort of intelligence and correct order, provided this has strength—if this be so, the pa-
20   ternal command has not the required strength or compulsive power, nor in general has the command of one man,
unless he be a king or something similar; but the law has
compulsive power, while it is at the same time an account
proceeding from a sort of wisdom and intelligence. And
while people hate men who set themselves contrary to their
impulses even if they do so correctly, the law when it commands what is upright is not burdensome.

25   In the Spartan State alone, or almost alone, the legislator
seems to have taken care of nurture and occupations: in
most States such matters have been neglected, and each man
lives as he wants to, Cyclops-fashion, 'to his own wife and
children dealing law'.[1] Now it is best that there should be a
30   common and correct care for such matters; but if they are
neglected by the community it would seem fitting for each
man to help his own children and friends towards virtue,
and that they should be able to do this or at least to choose
to.[2]

It would seem from what has been said that one can do this
better if he makes himself capable of legislating. For common
care plainly is effected by laws, and upright care by virtuous
1180b   laws—whether written or unwritten would seem to make no
difference, nor whether they are laws providing for the education of individuals or of groups—any more than it does in the
case of music or gymnastics and other such occupations. For

1 Homer, *Odyssey* IX 114.

2 In the manuscripts the words 'and . . . do this' appear immediately after
'. . . for such matters' in 1180a30: following a suggestion of Bywater, we
transpose them to follow '. . . towards virtue' in 1180a32. (Bywater himself
deletes the words and marks a lacuna after '. . . towards virtue'.)

as in States laws and character have force, so in households do   5
the words and the habits of the father, and the more so because of their kinship and his benefactions; for children start
with a natural affection and disposition to obey. Further, individual education has an advantage over education in common, as individual medical treatment has; for while in general rest and abstinence from food are good for a man in a
fever, for a particular man they may not be; and a boxing   10
instructor presumably does not prescribe the same style of
fighting to all his pupils. It would seem, then, that the detail
is worked out with more precision if the care is particular
to individuals; for each person is more likely to get what suits
his case.

But individuals³ can be best cared for by a doctor or gymnastic instructor or anyone else who has the universal
knowledge of what is good for everyone or for people of a   15
certain kind (for the sciences both are said to be and are concerned with what is common); but there is perhaps no reason why some individual may be well cared for by an unsci-
entific person who has studied precisely in the light of
experience what happens in each case, just as some people
seem to be their own best doctors, though they could give no
help to anyone else. Nonetheless, it will perhaps be agreed   20
that if a man does want to become master of a craft or of a
contemplative science he must go to the universal, and come
to know it as well as possible; for, as we have said, it is with
this that the sciences are concerned.

And surely he who wants to make men, whether many or
few, better by his care must try to become capable of legislating, if it is through laws that we can become good. For to get   25
anyone whatever—anyone who is put before us—into the
right condition is not for the first chance comer: if anyone
can do it, it is the man who knows, just as in medicine and all
other matters which give scope for care and wisdom.

3 Reading καθ᾽ ἕνα for καθ᾽ ἕν.

Must we not, then, next examine whence or how one can
learn how to legislate? Is it, as in other cases, from politicians? After all, it was thought to be a part of the political
art. Or is a difference apparent between the political art and
the other sciences and skills? In the others the same people
are found offering to teach the skills and exercising them—
for instance, doctors or painters; but while the sophists profess to teach politics, it is practised not by any of them but
by the politicians, who would seem to do so by a certain capacity and experience rather than by thought; for they are
not found either writing or speaking about such matters
(though it were a nobler occupation perhaps than composing speeches for the law-courts and the assembly), nor again
are they found to have made politicians of their own sons or
any other of their friends. But it was reasonable that they
should if they could; for there is nothing better than such a
capacity that they could leave to their States or could choose
to have for themselves or, therefore, for those dearest to
them. Still, experience seems to contribute not a little; for
otherwise they would not have become politicians by familiarity with politics—that is why it seems that those who aim
at knowing about the art of politics need experience as well.

Those of the sophists who profess the art seem to be
very far from teaching it. For, to put the matter generally,
they do not even know what kind of thing it is nor what
kinds of things it is about—otherwise they would not have
made it identical with rhetoric or even inferior to it, nor
have thought it easy to legislate by collecting the laws that
are thought well of. They say it is possible to select the best
laws, as though even the selection did not demand judgement and as though correct assessment were not the greatest thing, as in matters of music. For while people experienced in any discipline assess its products correctly and can
judge by what means or how they are achieved and what
harmonizes with what, the inexperienced must be content
if they manage to see whether the product has been well or
ill made—as in the case of painting. Now laws are as it were

the product of politics: how then can one learn from them to be a legislator, or assess which are best? Even medical men do not seem to be made by a study of text-books. Yet people try, at any rate, to state not only the treatments but also how particular classes of people can be cured and should be treated, distinguishing the various states; but while this seems beneficial to experienced people, to the ignorant it is useless. Perhaps, then, while collections of laws and of constitutions may be serviceable to those who can consider them and assess what is done rightly or the contrary and what fits with what, those who go through such collections without knowledge will not assess them rightly (unless it be spontaneously), though they may perhaps become more judicious in such matters.

Since our predecessors have left the subject of legislation unexamined, it is perhaps best that we should ourselves consider it, and in general the question of the constitution, in order to complete to the best of our ability the philosophy of human nature. First, then, if any part has been discussed by earlier thinkers, let us try to review it; then in the light of the constitutions that have been collected let us consider what sorts of thing preserve and destroy States, and what sorts the particular kinds of constitution, and to what causes it is due that some are rightly administered and others the contrary. When these things have been considered we shall perhaps be more likely to see which constitution is best, and how each must be ordered, and what laws and customs it must use. Let us make a beginning of our discussion.

MAGNA MORALIA

FIRST OXFORD TRANSLATION:
St G. Stock

GREEK TEXT:
F. Susemihl, Teubner

CONTENTS

INTRODUCTION

SINCE OUR PURPOSE IS TO SPEAK ABOUT MORAL MATTERS,
we must first inquire of what moral character is a part. To
speak concisely, then, it would seem to be a part of nothing
else than the art of politics. For it is not possible to act at all
in political affairs unless one is of a certain kind—I mean,
virtuous. Now to be virtuous is to possess the virtues. If   1181b25
therefore one is to act in political affairs, one must have a virtuous character. The study of character then is, as it seems, a
part and an origin or principle of the craft of politics. And as
a whole it seems to me that the study ought rightly to be
called, not moral, but political.

We must therefore, as it seems, speak first about virtue,   1182a
both what it is and from what it arises. For it is perhaps of no
use to know virtue without realizing how or from what it will
arise. We should inquire not only in order to know what it is:
we must also consider from what it will arise. For we want   5
not only to know but also ourselves to be such; and this will
be impossible for us unless we also know from what and how
it will arise. Of course, it is indispensable to know what virtue is (for it is not easy to know from what and how it is to
arise, if one does not know what it is, any more than in the   10
sciences).

We ought to be aware of what others have said before us
on this subject. Pythagoras was the first to attempt to speak
about virtue—but not correctly. For by referring the virtues
to numbers he submitted the virtues to a treatment which
was not appropriate to them: justice is not a square number.
After him came Socrates, who spoke better and more fully   15
about this subject—but even he did not do so correctly. For
he made the virtues sciences, and this cannot possibly be.
For the sciences all involve reason, and reason is to be found

in the calculative part of the soul. So that all the virtues,
20 according to him, are to be found in the rational part of the
soul. The result is that in making the virtues sciences he is
doing away with the irrational part of the soul, and is thereby
doing away also both with emotion and with character. That
is why he has not been correct in this respect in his treatment
of the virtues.

After this Plato divided the soul into the rational and the
25 irrational part—and correctly so—and he assigned pertinent virtues to each. So far so good. But after this he went
astray. For he mixed up virtue with the treatment of the
good, which is not correct. For it is not appropriate: in
speaking about the truth of things he ought not to have dis-
30 coursed upon virtue; for there is nothing common to the
two.

These people then, have touched upon the subject so far
and in the way above described. The next thing will be to
consider what we ought to say ourselves upon the subject.

I

THE GOOD

FIRST OF ALL, THEN, WE MUST SEE THAT EVERY SCIENCE and skill has an end, and that too a good one; for no science or skill exists for the sake of the bad. Since then in every skill the end is good, it is plain that the end of the best will be best. But politics is the best skill, so that the end of this will be the good.[1] It is about good, then, as it seems, that we must speak—and about good not in the abstract but relatively to ourselves. For we have not to do with the good of the gods: to speak about that is a different matter, and the inquiry is foreign to our present purpose. It is therefore about the political good that we must speak.

We must make a distinction here: about what sort of good have we to speak? For goodness is not simple: we call good either what is best in the case of each being, that is, what is desirable because of its own nature, or that by partaking in which other things are good, that is, the Idea of good. Are we, then, to speak of the Idea of good? Or not of that, but of good as the element common to all goods? For this would seem to be different from the Idea. For the Idea is separate and by itself, whereas the common element exists in all: it therefore is not identical with what is separate. For that which is apart and whose nature it is to be by itself cannot exist in all. Are we then to speak about this inherent good or not? And why?

What is common is what is shown by definition or by induction. Now the aim of defining is to state the substance of

---

1 Reading τὸ ἀγαθόν (Casaubon) for ἀγαθόν.

each thing, either what good is or what bad is,[2] or whatever
20   else it may be. But the definition states that whatever is of
such a kind as to be desirable for its own sake is good universally. And what is inherent in all goods is similar to the definition. And the definition says what is good,[3] whereas no science or skill states of its own end that it is good: rather, it is
25   the business of another skill to consider this (for neither the
doctor nor the housebuilder says that health or a house is
good, but rather that one thing produces health, and how it
produces it, and another thing a house). It is evident then
that neither has the art of politics to do with the common element of good. For it is itself one science among the rest,
and we have seen that it is not the business of any skill or sci-
30   ence to talk of this as its end. It is not therefore the business
of the art of politics to speak of the common element of good
corresponding to the definition.

    Nor of the common element as arrived at by induction.
Why not? Because when we want to prove some particular
good,[4] we either prove by the definition that the same ac-
35   count applies to the good and to the thing which we want to
prove to be good, or else we use induction. For instance,
1183a   when we want to prove that pride is a good, we say that justice is a good and courage is a good, and so of the virtues generally, and that pride is a virtue, so that pride also is a good.
So the art of politics will not have to speak of the common
good arrived at by induction, because the same impossible
5   consequences will ensue in this case as in that of the common good corresponding to the definition. For here also one
will be saying what is good.[5] It is clear therefore that what it
has to speak about is the best good, and the best in the sense
of the best for us.

---

2 Reading ὅ τι twice (Stock) for ὅτι.

3 Reading ὅ τι (Stock) for ὅτι.

4 Adding κατά before μέρος (Stock).

5 Reading ὅ τι (Stock) for ὅτι.

In general, one can see that it is not the business of any one science or skill to consider every good. Why not? Because good occurs in all the categories—in quiddity, quality, quantity, time, relation, and generally in all. But what is good at a given time is known in medicine by the doctor, in navigation by the pilot, and in each craft by each craftsman. For it is the doctor who knows when one ought to operate, and the pilot when one ought to sail. And in each craft each craftsman will know the good time which concerns himself. For neither will the doctor know the good time in navigation nor the pilot that in medicine. For this reason too, then, we have not to speak about the common good; for time is common to all the crafts. Similarly the relative good and the good which corresponds to other categories is common to all, and it does not belong to any skill or science to speak of what is good in each at a given time, nor is it the business of politics to speak about the common element of good. Our subject then is the good, in the sense of the best, and the best for us.

Perhaps when one wants to prove something, one ought not to employ examples that are not evident, but rather illustrate the obscure by the evident, and the objects of thought by the objects of sense-perception (which are more evident). When, therefore, one undertakes to speak about the good, one ought not to speak about the Idea. And yet they think that when they speak about the good they ought to speak about the Idea. For they say that they ought to speak about what is most good, and the thing-itself in each kind has the quality of that kind in the highest degree, so that the Idea will be the most good, as they think. Perhaps there is truth in such a contention; but all the same the science or skill of politics, about which we are now speaking, does not inquire about this good but about that which is good for us.[6] That is why it does not speak about the Ideal good.

6 The received text continues with the following sentence (which Cook Wilson excised): 'For no science or skill pronounces its end to be good, so that politics does not do so.'

But perhaps (you say)[7] one may employ this good as an
origin or principle to set out from in speaking about particu-
1183b lar goods? Even this is not correct. For the principles that are
assumed must be appropriate. How absurd it would be if,
when one wanted to prove that the three angles of a triangle
are equal to two right angles, one were to assume, as a principle, that the soul is immortal. For it is not appropriate, and
a principle must be appropriate and connected: as a matter
5 of fact, one can prove that the three angles of a triangle are
equal to two right angles quite as well without the immortality of the soul. In the same way in the case of goods, one can
speculate about the rest without the Ideal good. That is why
such a good is not an appropriate origin or principle.[8]

Neither was Socrates correct in making the virtues sci-
10 ences. For he thought that nothing ought to be in vain, but
from the virtues being sciences he met with the result that
the virtues were in vain. Why so? Because in the case of the
sciences, as soon as one knows what the science is, it results
that one is a scientist (for anyone who knows what medicine
is, is thereby a doctor, and so with the other sciences). But
15 this result does not follow in the case of the virtues. For one
who knows what justice is, is not thereby just, and similarly
in the case of the rest. It follows then that either[9] the virtues
are actually in vain or they are not sciences.

NOW THAT WE HAVE SETTLED THESE POINTS, LET US TRY TO
20 say in how many ways we talk about good things. Goods may
be divided into the valuable, the praiseworthy, and the potential. By the valuable I mean such a thing as the divine, the
better (for instance, soul, intelligence), the more ancient, the
origin, and so on. For those things are valuable to which
value is accorded, and to all such things as these value is ac-
25 corded. Virtue then also is something valuable, at least when

7. Retaining φησι (read by half the manuscripts).
8 Reading τοῦτο τὸ ἀγαθόν (Bonitz) for τούτου τοῦ ἀγαθοῦ.
9 Reading ἤ...ἤ... for καὶ...καί.

someone has become a virtuous man in consequence of it; for already such a one has come into the pattern of virtue. Other goods are praiseworthy—for example, virtues; for praise is bestowed in consequence of the actions that express them. Others goods are potential—for instance, office, riches, strength, beauty; for these are things which the virtuous man can use well and the base man ill. That is why such   30 goods are called potential. Goods indeed they are (for everything is judged by the use made of it by the virtuous man, not by that of the base); but in the case of these same goods fortune is the cause of their production (for from fortune come riches, and also office, and generally all the things which   35 rank as potential). The fourth and last class of goods is that which is preservative and productive of good, as exercise is of health, and other things of that sort.

But goods admit of another division too: some goods are everywhere and absolutely desirable, and some are not. For instance, justice and the other virtues are everywhere and   1184a absolutely desirable, but strength, and riches, and power, and the like, are not so everywhere nor absolutely.

Again, there is another division: some goods are ends and some are not. For instance, health is an end, but the things done for the sake of health are not ends. Wherever things   5 stand in this relation, the end is always better: for instance, health is better than the means to health, and quite generally that for the sake of which the other things are done is, always and universally, better. Moreover, among ends themselves the complete is always better than the incomplete. A complete thing is one the presence of which leaves us in need of nothing: an incomplete thing is one despite the presence of which we need something further—for instance, although justice is   10 present, we need many things besides, but when happiness is present we need nothing more. This then is what we are looking for, viz. the chief good for us, which is a complete end. The complete end, then, is the good and end of goods.

The next point is how we are to consider the chief good. Is   15 it itself to be reckoned in with other goods? Surely that is

absurd. For the chief good is the complete end, and the complete end, broadly speaking, would seem to be nothing else than happiness, and happiness we regard as made up of
20   many goods. So that if, in considering the chief good, you reckon in itself also, it will be better than itself, because it is itself best. For instance, take the means to health, and health, and consider which is the best of all these. Health is the best. If then this is the best of all, it is also better than itself; so that an absurdity results. Perhaps then this is not the
25   way in which we ought to consider the chief good. Then how? As separate?[10] Is not this also absurd? For happiness is composed of certain goods. But to consider whether a given thing is better than its own components is absurd. For happiness is not something else apart from these, but just these.
30   But perhaps the right method of inquiry may be by a comparison of the chief good, i.e., by comparing happiness itself, which is made up of these goods, with others which are not contained in it—would this be the right way of considering the chief good? But the chief good which we are now looking for is not of a simple nature. For instance, one might say that
35   wisdom is the best of all goods when they are compared one by one. But perhaps this is not the way in which we ought to look for the chief good. For it is the complete good we are looking for, and wisdom by itself is not complete. So the chief good which we are looking for is not this nor what is in this way best.

1184b   Next, goods admit of another division: some goods are in the soul—for instance, the virtues; some in the body—for instance, health, beauty; and some external—riches, office,
5   honour, and suchlike. Of these those in the soul are best. But the goods in the soul are divided into three—wisdom, virtue, and pleasure.

    Now we come to happiness, which we all declare to be, and which seems in fact to be, the end of goods and the most

10 Reading αὐτό (after Spengel) for αὐτοῦ ('separate from it').

complete, and which we maintain to be identical with[11]
doing well and living well. But the end is not single but two-   10
fold. For the end of some things is the activity and use itself
(for instance, of sight); and the use is more desirable than
the possession; for the use is the end. For no one would want
to have sight, if he were never to see but always to have his
eyes shut. And the same with hearing and the like. When,
then, a thing may be both used and possessed, the use is al-   15
ways better and more desirable than the possession. For use
and activity are the end, whereas possession is for the sake of
use. Next, if one examines this point in the case of all the sciences, he will see that it is not one science that makes a house
and another that makes a good house, but rather the science
of housebuilding makes both; and what the housebuilder   20
makes, that same thing his virtue enables him to make well.
Similarly in all other cases.

11 Reading τῷ for τό.

2

HAPPINESS

NEXT, WE SEE THAT IT IS BY NOTHING ELSE THAN SOUL
that we live. Virtue is in the soul. We maintain that the soul
and the virtue of the soul do the same thing. But virtue in
each thing makes good that of which it is the virtue; and the
soul is (among other things) that which makes us live: it is
therefore owing to the virtue of the soul that we shall live
well. But to live well and do well, we say, is nothing else than
to be happy. Being happy, then, and happiness, consist in living well, and living well is living in accordance with the virtues. This, then, is the end and happiness and the chief good.
Happiness therefore will consist in a kind of use and activity.
For we found that where there was possession and use, the
use and activity are the end. Now virtue is a state of the soul.
And there is such a thing as the activity and use of it;[1] so that
the end will be its activity and use. Happiness therefore will
consist in living in accordance with the virtues. Since then
the chief good is happiness, and this is the end, and a complete end is an activity,[2] it follows that it is by living in accordance with the virtues that we shall be happy and shall have
the chief good.

Happiness, then, is a complete good and an end; and we
must not fail to observe that it will be found in that which is
complete. For it will not be found in a child (for a child is not
happy), but in a man (for he is complete). Nor will it be found
in an incomplete period of time but in a complete one. And a

---

1 Omitting τῶν ἀρετῶν—'. . . of the virtues' (Spengel).

2 Reading ἐνέργεια for the received ἐνεργείᾳ.

complete period will be as long as a man lives. For it is correctly said among the many that one ought to assess the
happy man in the longest time of his life, supposing that
what is complete ought to be in a complete period and a
complete man. That it is an activity can be seen also from the
following consideration about sleep: supposing someone to   10
be asleep all his life, we should hardly want to call such a man
happy. Life indeed he has, but life in accordance with the virtues he has not, and it was in this that we made the activity to
consist.

The topic that is next to be treated might seem to be neither very appropriate nor yet quite foreign. Since there is, as   15
it seems, a part of the soul whereby we are nourished, which
we call nutritive (for it is reasonable to suppose that this exists; at all events we see that stones are incapable of being
nourished, so that it is evident that to be nourished is a
property of animate things; and, if so, the soul will be the
cause of it; but none of these parts of the soul will be the   20
cause of nourishment—I mean the calculative or the passionate or the appetitive—but another besides these, to
which we can apply no more appropriate name than 'nutritive'), one might say, 'Very well, has this part of the soul also
a virtue? For if it has, it is plain that we ought to exercise   25
this also. For happiness is the activity of complete virtue'.
Now, whether there is or is not a virtue of this part is another question; but, if there is, it has no activity. For those
things which have no impulse will not have any activity either; and there does not seem to be any impulse in this
part—rather, it seems to be similar to fire. For that also will   30
consume whatever you throw in, but if you do not throw
anything in, it has no impulse to get it. So it is also with this
part of the soul; for, if you throw in food, it nourishes, but if
you fail to throw in food, it has no impulse to nourish. That
is why it has no activity, being devoid of impulse. So that
this part in no way cooperates towards happiness.

3

VIRTUE

AFTER THIS, THEN, WE MUST SAY WHAT VIRTUE IS, SINCE IT is the activity of this which is happiness. Broadly speaking, then, virtue is the best state. But perhaps it is not sufficient to speak broadly—rather, we should give a more illuminating account.

1185b First, then, we ought to speak about the soul in which it resides, not to say what the soul is (for to speak about that is another matter), but to divide it in outline. Now the soul is, as we say, divided into two parts, the rational and the irrational. In the rational part, then, there reside wisdom, astuteness, understanding, aptitude to learn, memory, and so on; and in the irrational the following items, which are called the virtues: temperance, justice, courage, and such other states of character as are held to be praiseworthy. For it is in respect of these that we are called praiseworthy; and no one is praised for the virtues of the rational part—no one is praised for understanding things or for being wise, or generally on the ground of anything of that sort. Nor indeed is the irrational part praised, except in so far as it is capable of subserving or actually subserves the rational part.

Moral virtue is destroyed by lack and excess. That lack and excess destroy can be seen from perceptible instances,[1] and we must use the evident as witness to the obscure. For one can see this at once in the case of gymnastic exercises: if too much is done, the strength is destroyed, while if too little, it is so also. And the same is the case with food and drink.

---

1 Reading αἰσθητῶν (a suggestion of Susemihl) for ἠθικῶν (which has been taken to mean 'from the *Ethics*').

For if too much is taken health is destroyed, and also if too   20
little, but by the right proportion strength and health are
preserved. The same is the case with temperance and courage and the rest of the virtues. For if you make a man too
fearless, so as not even to fear the gods, he is not courageous
but mad: if you make him afraid of everything, he is a cow-   25
ard. To be courageous, then, a man must fear neither everything nor nothing. The same things, then, both increase and
destroy virtue. For undue and indiscriminate fears destroy,
and so does total lack of fear. And courage has to do with
fears, so that moderate fears increase courage. Courage,   30
then, is both increased and destroyed by the same things.
For men are liable to this effect owing to fears. And the same
holds true of the other virtues.

   In addition, virtue may be determined not only by such
things but also by pleasure and pain. For it is owing to pleasure that we commit base actions, and owing to pain that we   35
abstain from noble ones. And generally it is not possible to
achieve virtue or vice without pain and pleasure. Virtue then
has to do with pleasures and pains.

   Moral virtue gets its name as follows, if we may consider
the truth by changing a letter[2] (as perhaps we should). Char-   1186a
acter gets its name from custom; for it is called moral virtue
because it is the result of accustoming.[3] Whereby it is evident
that no one of the virtues of the irrational part arises in us by
nature. For nothing that is by nature becomes other by custom. For instance, a stone, and heavy things in general, nat-   5
urally go downwards. If anyone, then, threw them up repeat-
edly and tried to accustom them to go up, all the same they
never would go up, but always down. Similarly in all other
such cases.

   After this, then, as we want to say what virtue is, we must   10
know what are the things that there are in the soul. They are

---

 2 Reading παραγραμματεύοντα for παρὰ γράμμα λέγοντα.

 3 'Moral' is ἠθικός, which derives from ἦθος ('character'): Aristotle connects ἦθος with ἔθος ('custom').

these—emotions, capacities, states; so that it is evident that
virtue will be some one of these. Now emotions are anger,
fear, hate, regret, emulation, pity, and the like, which are usually attended by pain or pleasure. Capacities are those things
in virtue of which we are said to be capable of these emotions:
15   for instance, those things in virtue of which we are capable of
feeling anger or pain or pity, and so on. States are those
things in virtue of which we stand in a good or bad relation to
these emotions: for instance, towards being angered—if we
are angry overmuch, we stand in a bad relation towards
anger, whereas if we are not angry at all where we ought to
be, in that case also we stand in a bad relation towards anger.
20   To be in a middling way, then, is neither to be pained overmuch nor to be absolutely insensate. When, then, we stand
thus, we are in a good condition. And similarly as regards
other like things. For even temper and good temper are in a
mean between anger and insensibility to anger. Similarly in
25   the case of boastfulness and self-deprecation. For to pretend
to more than one has shows boastfulness, while to pretend to
less shows self-deprecation. The mean, then, between these
is candour.

Similarly in all other cases. For this is what marks the
state: to stand in a good or bad relation towards these emotions, and to stand in a good relation towards them is to in-
30   cline neither towards the excess nor towards the lack. The
state, then, which implies a good relation is directed towards
the mean of such things in respect of which we are called
praiseworthy, whereas that which implies a bad relation inclines towards excess or lack.

Since, then, virtue is a mean of these emotions, and the
emotions are either pains or pleasures or not without pain
35   or pleasure, it is evident from this that virtue has to do with
pains and pleasures.[4]

But there are other cases, as one might think, where the
vice does not lie in any excess or deficiency: for instance,

4 Reading ὅτι (Bonitz) for ἐστι.

adultery and the adulterer. The adulterer is not the man who
corrupts free women too much: rather, both this and anything else of the kind which is comprised under the pleasure
of self-indulgence, whether[5] it be something in the way of
deficiency or of excess, is blameworthy.

After this, then, it is perhaps necessary to say what is opposed to the mean—whether it is the excess or the lack.   5
For to some means the lack is contrary and to some the excess; for instance, to courage it is not over-confidence,
which is the excess, that is contrary, but cowardice, which
is the lack; and to temperance, which is a mean between
self-indulgence and insensibility to pleasures, it does not
seem that insensibility, which is the lack, is contrary, but
rather self-indulgence, which is the excess. But both are   10
contrary to the mean—both excess and lack. For the mean
is lacking compared to the excess and excessive compared
to the lack. Hence it is that prodigals call the liberal illiberal,
while the illiberal call the liberal prodigals, and the over-   15
confident and impetuous call the courageous cowards,
while cowards call the courageous impetuous and mad.

There would seem to be two reasons for our opposing the
excess or the lack to the mean. Either people look at the matter from the point of view of the thing itself, to see which is
nearer to, or further from, the middle: for instance, in the   20
case of liberality, whether prodigality or illiberality is further
from it. For prodigality would seem more to be liberality
than illiberality is. Illiberality, then, is further off. But things
which are further distant from the middle would seem to be
more contrary to it. From the point of view, then, of the
thing itself the lack presents itself as more contrary. But   25
there is also another way: those things are more contrary to
the middle to which we have a greater natural inclination.
For instance, we have a greater natural inclination to be self-
indulgent than to be proper. The tendency, therefore, occurs
rather towards the things to which nature inclines us; the

5 Omitting ἤ (after Spengel).

things to which we have a greater tendency are more contrary; and our tendency is towards self-indulgence rather
than towards propriety: so the excess of the mean will be the
more contrary; for self-indulgence is the excess in the case of
temperance.

What virtue is, then, has been considered. It seems to be a
mean of the emotions, so that it will be necessary for the
man who is to obtain credit for his character to observe the
mean with regard to each of the emotions. That is why it is a
task to be virtuous; for to hit on the mid-point in anything is
a task. For instance, anyone can draw a circle, but to fix upon
the middle point in it is hard; and in the same way to be
angry is easy, and so is the contrary of this, but to be in the
middle state is hard; and quite generally, in the case of each
of the emotions one can see that what surrounds the middle
is easy but the middle hard, and this is the point for which we
are praised. That is why virtuousness is rare.

Since, then, virtue has been discussed,[6] we must next inquire whether it is possible of attainment or is not but rather,
as Socrates said, it is not in our power to become virtuous or
bad. For if, he says, one were to ask anyone whatever whether
he wanted to be just or unjust, no one would choose injustice. Similarly in the case of courage and cowardice, and so
on always with the rest of the virtues. And it is evident that
any who are bad will not be bad voluntarily; so that it is evident that neither will they be voluntarily virtuous.

Such a statement is not true. For why does the lawgiver
forbid the doing of bad acts, and bid the doing of noble and
virtuous ones? And why does he appoint a penalty for bad
acts, if one does them, and for noble acts, if one fails to do
them? Yet it would be absurd to legislate about those things
which are not in our power to do. But, as it seems, it is in our
power to be virtuous or bad.

Again, we have evidence in the praise and blame that are
accorded. For there is praise for virtue and blame for vice.

6 Susemihl marks a lacuna here.

But praise and blame are not bestowed upon things involuntary. So it is evident that it is equally in our power to do virtuous acts and to do bad.

They used also to employ some such comparison as this when they wanted to show that it is not voluntary: why, they say, when we are ill or ugly, does no one blame us for things of this sort? But this is not true. For we do blame people for things of this sort when we think that they themselves are the causes of being ill or of their having their body in a bad state, supposing that there is voluntariness even there. It seems, then, that there is voluntariness in being virtuous and vicious. 25

4

ACTIONS

30 ONE CAN SEE THIS STILL MORE CLEARLY FROM THE FOL-
lowing consideration. Every natural kind is given to generating a being like itself, i.e. plants and animals; for both are apt
to generate. And they are given to generating from their
originating principles—for instance, the tree from the seed;
for this is a kind of originating principle. And what follows
35 the principles stands thus: as are the principles, so are what
come from the principles. This can be seen more clearly in
matters of geometry. For there also, when certain principles
are taken, as are the principles so are what come from the
principles: for instance, if the triangle has its angles equal to
1187b two right angles, and the quadrilateral to four, then according as the triangle changes, so does the quadrilateral share in
its changes; and it converts: if the quadrilateral has not its
angles equal to four right angles, neither will the triangle
have its angles equal to two right angles.

So, then, and in the like way with this, is it in the case of
5 man. For since man is apt to generate substances from certain originating principles, he also generates the actions that
he performs. How else could it be? For we do not say that
anything inanimate acts, nor anything animate other than
men. It is evident, then, that a man is a generator of actions.

10 Since, then, we see that the actions change, and we never
do the same things, and the actions have been generated
from certain origins or principles, it is evident that, since the
actions change, the origins from which the actions proceed
also change, as we said in our comparison was the case in
geometry.

Now the origin of an action, whether virtuous or base, is   15
choice and will and everything that accords with reason. It is
plain, then, that these also change. But we change in our actions voluntarily. So that the origin also, choice, changes voluntarily. So that it is plain that it is in our power to be either
virtuous or base.   20

Perhaps, then, someone may say: 'Since it is in my power
to be just and virtuous, if I want I shall be the most virtuous
of all men'. This is not possible. Why not? Because in the case
of the body it is not so either. For if one wants to bestow attention upon his body, it does not follow that he will have the   25
best body that anyone has. For it is necessary not merely for
attention to be bestowed, but also for the body to be beautiful and good by nature. So he will have a better body but not
the best body of all. And so we must assume it to be also in
the case of soul. For he who chooses to be most virtuous will
not be so, unless nature also be present; better, however, he   30
will be.

Since, then, it appears that to be virtuous is in our power,
it is necessary next to say what the voluntary is. For this is
what is most authoritative over virtue, to wit, the voluntary.
The voluntary, broadly speaking, is that which we do when   35
not under compulsion. But perhaps we ought to speak about
it in a more illuminating manner.

What prompts us to action is desire; and desire has three
forms—appetite, passion, will or wanting.

First of all, then, we must inquire into the action which is
in accordance with appetite. Is that voluntary or involuntary? That it is involuntary would not seem to be the case.   1188a
Why not, and on what ground? Because wherever we do not
act voluntarily, we act under compulsion, and all actions
done under compulsion are attended with pain, whereas actions due to appetite are attended with pleasure, so that on
this way of looking at the matter actions due to appetite will
not be involuntary but voluntary.   5

But, again, there is another argument contrary to this,
which appeals to incontinence. No one (you say) performs

bad actions voluntarily, knowing them to be bad. But yet (you say) the incontinent, knowing that what he does is base, nevertheless does it, and does it in accordance with appetite. He is not therefore acting voluntarily. Therefore he is under compulsion. There again the same answer will meet this argument. For if the action is in accordance with appetite, it is not by compulsion; for appetite is attended with pleasure, and actions due to pleasure are not by compulsion.

There is another way in which it may be made plain that the incontinent acts voluntarily. For those who commit injustice do so voluntarily, and the incontinent are unjust and act unjustly. So that the incontinent man will voluntarily perform his actions of incontinence.

But, again, there is another argument contrary to this, which maintains that it is not voluntary. For the continent man voluntarily performs his actions of continence. For he is praised, and people are praised for voluntary actions. But if that which is in accordance with appetite is voluntary, that which runs counter to appetite is involuntary. But the continent man acts counter to his appetite. So that the continent man will not be continent voluntarily. But this does not seem to be so. Therefore the action which is in accordance with appetite is not voluntary.

Again, the same thing holds of actions prompted by passion. For the same arguments apply as to appetite, so that they will cause the problem. For it is possible to be incontinent or continent with respect to anger.

Among the desires in our division we have still to inquire about will or wanting, whether it is voluntary. Now the incontinent want for the time being the things to which their impulse is directed. Therefore the incontinent perform their base actions wanting to do so. But no one voluntarily performs bad actions, knowing them to be bad. But the incontinent man, knowing the bad things to be bad, does them and wants to do them. Therefore he is not a voluntary agent, and wanting therefore is not a voluntary thing. But this argument annuls incontinence and the incontinent man. For if he is not a voluntary agent, he is not blameworthy. But the incontinent is blameworthy. Therefore he is a voluntary agent. Therefore wanting is voluntary.

Since, then, there are arguments plainly contrary to one another, we must speak about the voluntary in a more illuminating manner.

Before doing so, however, we must speak about force and about compulsion. Force may occur even in the case of inanimate things. For inanimate things have each their proper place assigned to them—to fire the upper region and to earth the lower. It is, however, possible to force a stone to go up and fire to go down. It is also possible to apply force to an animate thing: for instance, when a horse is galloping straight ahead, one may take hold of him and divert his course. Now whenever the cause of men's doing something against their nature or against what they want is outside of them, we will say that they are forced to do what they do. But when the cause is in themselves, we will not in that case say that they are forced. Otherwise the incontinent man will have his answer ready, in denying that he is base. For he will say that he is forced by his appetite to perform the base actions.

Let this, then, be our definition of what is due to force: those things of which the cause by which men are forced to do them is external (but where the cause is internal and in themselves there is no force).

Now we must speak about compulsion and the compulsory. The term 'compulsory' must not be used in all circumstances or in every case—for instance, of what we do for the sake of pleasure. For if one were to say 'I was compelled by pleasure to corrupt my friend's wife', he would be absurd. For 'compulsory' does not apply to everything, but only to externals: for instance, whenever a man receives some harm by way of alternative to some other greater, when compelled by circumstances. For instance, 'I was compelled to hurry my steps to the country; otherwise I should have found my stock destroyed'. Such, then, are the cases in which we have the compulsory.

25   Since the voluntary lies in no impulse, it remains that it is what proceeds from thought. For the involuntary is what is done from compulsion or from force, and, thirdly, what is not accompanied by thought. This is plain from what happens. For whenever a man has struck or killed a man, or has

30   done something of that sort without having thought about it beforehand, we say that he has acted involuntarily, implying that the voluntariness lies in the having thought about it. For instance, they say that once a woman gave a philtre to somebody; then the man died from the effects of the philtre, and the woman was put on trial before the Areopagus; on her ap-

35   pearance she was acquitted, just for the reason that it was not done with forethought. For she gave the philtre from love, but missed her mark: that is why it was not held to be voluntary, because in giving the philtre she did not give it with the thought of killing. In that case, therefore, the voluntary falls under the head of what is accompanied with thought.

1189a   It now remains for us to inquire into choice. Is choice desire or is it not? Now desire is found in the other animals, but not choice; for choice is attended with reason, and none of

5   the other animals has reason. Therefore it will not be desire.

Is it then will or wanting? Or is it not this either? For wanting is concerned even with the impossible: for instance, we want to be immortal, but we do not choose to be. Again, choice is not concerned with the end but with what contributes to the end: for instance, no one chooses to be in health.

10   Rather, we choose what leads to health (walking, running), but we want the ends (we want to be in health). So that it is plain in this way also that will and choice are not the same thing.

Rather, choice seems to be what its name suggests: I mean, we choose one thing instead of another; for instance,

the better instead of the worse.[1] Whenever, then, we take the better in exchange for the worse as a matter of choice, there   15 the term 'to choose' would seem to be appropriate.

Since, then, choice is none of these things, can it be thought that constitutes choice? Or is this not so either? For we have many thoughts and beliefs in our minds. Do we then choose whatever we think or not? Often we think about   20 things in India, but we do not choose them. Choice therefore is not thought either.

Since, then, choice is not any of these singly, and these are the things that there are in the soul, choice must result from the pairing of some of them.

Since, then, choice, as was said before, is concerned with   25 the goods that contribute to the end and not with the end, and with the things that are possible to us, and with such as afford ground for controversy as to whether this or that is desirable, it is evident that one must have thought and deliberated about them beforehand; then when a thing appears best to us after having thought it over, there ensues an im-   30 pulse to act, and it is when we act in this way that we are held to act on choice.

If, then, choice is a deliberate desire attended with thought, the voluntary is not what is chosen. For there are many actions which we do voluntarily before thinking and deliberating about them (for instance, we sit down and stand up, and do many other things of the same sort voluntarily   35 but without having thought about them) whereas every action done by choice was found to be attended with thought. What is voluntary, therefore, is not chosen, but what is cho-   1189b sen is voluntary; for if we choose to do anything after deliberation, we act voluntarily. And a few legislators, even, appear to distinguish what is voluntary from what is chosen as being something different, in making the penalties that they   5

1 'Choose' is προαιρεῖσθαι, compounded from αἱρεῖσθαι ('choose') and πρό ('before', 'in preference to').

appoint for voluntary actions less than for those that are done by choice.

Choice, then, lies in matters of action, and in those in which it is in our power to do or not to do, and to act in this way or not in this way, and where we can grasp the reason why. But the reason why is not something simple. For in geometry, when you say that the quadrilateral has its angles equal to four right angles, and one asks the reason why, you say: 'Because the triangle has its angles equal to two right angles'. Now in such cases they grasped the reason why from a determinate origin or principle; but in matters of action, with which choice has to do, it is not so (for there is no determinate principle laid down). Rather, if one asks, 'Why did you do this?' the answer is, 'Because it was the only thing possible', or 'Because it was better so'. It is from the consequences themselves, according as they appear to be better, that one chooses, and these are the reason why.

That is why in such matters the deliberation is as to the how, but not so in the sciences. For no one deliberates about how he ought to write the name Archicles, because it is a determinate matter how one ought to write the name Archicles. The error, then, does not arise in the thought, but in the activity of writing. For where the error is not in the thought, neither do people deliberate about those things. But wherever there is an indeterminacy about the how, there error comes in.

Now there is the element of indeterminacy in matters of action, and in those matters in which the errors are twofold. We err, then, in matters of action and in what pertains to the virtues in the same way. For in aiming at virtue we err in the natural directions. For there is error both in deficiency and in excess, and we are carried in both these directions through pleasure and pain. For it is owing to pleasure that we perform base actions, and owing to pain that we abstain from noble ones.

Again, thought is not like the senses: for instance, with sight one could not do anything else than see, nor with hear-

ing anything else than hear. So also we do not deliberate   35
whether we ought to hear with hearing or rather see. But
thought is not like this: rather, it is able to do one thing and
others also. That is why deliberation comes in there.   1190a

Error, then, in the choice of goods is not about the ends
(for as to these all are of one mind—for instance, that health
is a good), but only about what is pertinent to the ends—for
instance, whether a particular food is good for health or not.   5
The chief cause of our going wrong in these matters is pleasure and pain; for we avoid the one and choose the other.

Since, then, it has been settled where error is found and
how it occurs, it remains to ask what it is that virtue aims at.
Does it aim at the end or at what contributes to the end? for   10
instance, at the noble or at what contributes to the noble?

How, then, is it with science? Does it belong to the science of housebuilding to propose the end rightly, or to see
what contributes to it? For if the proposal is right—I mean,
to make a beautiful house—it is no other than the housebuilder who will discover and provide what contributes to it.
And similarly in the case of all the other sciences. Then   15
would it seem that things hold similarly in the case of virtue
too? Or[2] that the aim of virtue is the end, which it must propose rightly, rather than what contributes to the end? (And
no one else will provide the materials for this or discover
what is needed to contribute to it.) It is reasonable to suppose that virtue should propose this. For both proposal and   20
execution always belong to that with which the originating
principle of the best lies. Now there is nothing better than
virtue; for it is for its sake that all other things are, and the
principle is relative to it, and the contributory factors are
rather for the sake of it. Now the end seems to be a kind of
principle, and everything is for the sake of it. And this will be   25
as it ought to be. So that it is plain also in the case of virtue,
since it is the best cause, that it aims at the end rather than at
what contributes to the end.

2 Adding ἢ before μᾶλλόν and repunctuating.

Now the end of virtue is the noble. This, then, is what virtue aims at rather than the things from which it will be produced. It has to do also with these; but to make these its whole concern is manifestly absurd. For perhaps in painting one might be good at representation and yet not be praised if one does not make it his aim to represent the best subjects. This, therefore, is quite the business of virtue, to propose what is noble.

Why, then, someone may say, did we say before that the activity was better than the corresponding state, whereas now it is not that from which the activity derives that we are assigning to virtue as being nobler, but rather something in which there is no activity? Yes, but now also we assert just the same that the activity is better than the state. For his fellow men when they consider the virtuous man assess him from his actions, owing to its not being possible to make clear the choice which each has, since if it were possible to know how the mind of each man stands towards the noble, he would have been thought virtuous even without acting.

5

THE MORAL VIRTUES

SINCE WE HAVE ENUMERATED SOME MEAN STATES OF THE
emotions, we must say with what sort of emotions we are
concerned.[1] Since, then, courage has to do with confidence
and fear, we must examine with what sort of fears and confi-   10
dences it has to do. If, then, someone is afraid of losing his
property, is he a coward? And if someone is confident about
these matters, is he courageous or not? And in the same way
if someone is afraid of or confident about illness, one ought
not to say that the man who fears is a coward or that the man
who does not fear is courageous. It is not, therefore, in such   15
fears and confidences as these that courage is found. Nor yet
in such as follow: for instance, if someone is not afraid of
thunder or of lightning or of anything else that is super-
humanly frightening, he is not courageous but a sort of madman. It is with human fears and confidences, then, that the
courageous man has to do; I mean to say that anyone who is   20
confident under circumstances in which most people or all
are afraid, is a courageous man.

These points having been settled, we must inquire, since
there are many ways in which men are courageous, which is
the courageous man. For you may have a man who is courageous from experience, like soldiers. For they know, owing
to experience, that in such a place or time or condition it is   25
impossible to suffer any harm. But the man who knows
these things and for this reason faces the enemy is not courageous; for if none of these things is the case, he does not

---

1 This sentence is excised by Susemihl (who supposes that it has sup-
planted something else—perhaps a table of the moral virtues).

face him. That is why one ought not to call those courageous whose courage is due to experience. Nor indeed was
Socrates correct in asserting that courage was knowledge.
30   For knowledge becomes knowledge by getting experience
from custom. But of those who face up to things because of
experience we do not say, nor will they say, that they are
courageous. Courage, therefore, will not be knowledge.

Again, and on the other hand, there are some who are
courageous from the contrary of experience. For those who
have no experience of what is going to happen are free from
35   fear owing to their inexperience. Neither, then, must we call
these courageous.

Again, there are others who appear courageous owing to
their emotions: for instance, those who are in love or are inspired by the gods. We must not call these courageous either.
1191a   For if their emotion is taken away, they are not courageous
any more, whereas the courageous man must always be courageous. That is why one would not call brutes such as boars
courageous, owing to their defending themselves when they
have been pained by a wound, nor ought the courageous
man to be courageous through emotion.

5   Again, there is another form of courage which is held to
be political: for instance, if men face up to dangers out of
shame before their fellow citizens, and so are thought to be
courageous. An indication of this is the way in which Homer
has represented Hector as saying

> Polydamas will be the first to taunt me.[2]

10   That is why he thinks that he ought to fight. We must not call
this sort of thing courage either. For the same distinction
will apply to each of these: he whose courage does not remain on the deprivation of something is not courageous; if,
then, I take away the shame owing to which he was courageous, he will no longer be courageous.

2 *Iliad* XXII 100.

There is yet another way of being thought courageous, namely, through hope and anticipation of good. We must not say that these are courageous either, since it appears absurd to call those courageous who are of such a character and in such circumstances. 15

No one, then, of the above kinds is to be put down as courageous.

We have then to ask who is to be so put down, and who is the courageous man. Broadly speaking, it is he who is courageous owing to none of the things above-mentioned, but owing to his thinking it to be noble, and who does so whether anyone is present or not. 20

Not, indeed, that courage arises entirely without emotion and impulse. But the impulse must proceed from reason and be directed to the noble. He, then, who is carried by a rational impulse to face danger for the sake of the noble, being fearless about these things, is courageous; and these are the things with which courage has to do. 25

He is fearless not in so far as it happens that a person is courageous for whom nothing at all is frightening—otherwise a stone and other inanimate things would be courageous. Rather, he must feel fear and yet face the danger; for if he faces it without feeling fear, he will not be courageous. 30

Further, according to the distinction that we made above, it is not concerned with all fears and dangers, but with those which threaten existence. Moreover, not at any and every time, but when the fears and the dangers are near. For if one is unafraid of a danger that is ten years off, it does not follow that he is courageous. For some are confident owing to its being far away, but if they come near it, die with fear. Such, then, are courage and the courageous man. 35

TEMPERANCE IS A MEAN BETWEEN SELF-INDULGENCE AND insensibility to pleasures. For temperance and quite generally every virtue is the best state, and the best state lies in the attainment of the best thing, and the best thing is the mid- 1191b

point between excess and lack; for people are blameworthy on both grounds, both on that of excess and on that of lack. So that, since the mid-point is best, temperance will be a cer-
5   tain mean between self-indulgence and insensibility. These, then, are the states between which it will be a mean.

Temperance is concerned with pleasures and pains, but not with all, nor with those that have to do with all objects. For one is not self-indulgent if one takes pleasure in con-templating a painting or a statue or something of that sort, and in the same way not so in the case of hearing or smell:
10   rather, in the pleasures which have to do with touch and taste. Nor yet with regard to these will a man be temperate who is in such a state as not to be affected at all by any plea-sures of this sort (for such a person is insensible), but rather he who feels them and yet does not let himself be led away into enjoying them to excess and regarding everything else
15   as a side-task; and we call[3] temperate the man who acts for the sake of the noble and nothing else. For whoever ab-stains from the excess of such pleasures either from fear or some other such motive is not temperate. For neither do we call the other animals temperate except man, because there
20   is not reason in them whereby they test and choose the noble. For every virtue is concerned with and aims at the noble. So temperance will be concerned with pleasures and pains, and with pleasures and pains that occur in touch and taste.

NEXT WE MUST SPEAK ABOUT GOOD TEMPER, SAYING WHAT it is and where it is found. Good temper, then, is midway be-
25   tween irascibility and inirascibility. And generally the virtues seem to be a kind of mean. One can show that they are means in this way as well: if the best is in the mean, and virtue is the best state, then virtue will be the middle point. But it will be
30   more plain as we inquire into them separately. For since he is irascible who gets angry with everybody and under all

---

3 Adding καλοῦμεν after σώφρονα (Rieckher)—Susemihl marks a lacuna.

circumstances and to too great an extent, and such a one is
blameworthy (for one ought not to be angry with everybody
nor at everything nor under all circumstances and always,
nor yet again ought one to be in such a state as never to be
angry with anybody; for this character also is blameworthy,
as being insensate)—since then both he who is excessive and
he who is deficient are blameworthy, the man who is in the   35
middle between them will be good-tempered and praiseworthy. For neither he who is deficient in anger nor he who is excessive is praiseworthy, but he who stands midway with regard to these things. He is good-tempered; and good temper
will be a mean state with regard to these emotions.

LIBERALITY IS A MEAN BETWEEN PRODIGALITY AND ILLIB-
erality. Emotions of this sort have to do with wealth. The   1192a
prodigal is he who spends on what he should not and more
than he should and when he should not, while the illiberal
man, in the contrary way to him, is he who does not spend
on what he should or as much as he should or when he
should. Both these are blameworthy. And one of them is   5
characterized by deficiency and the other by excess. The liberal man, therefore, since he is praiseworthy, will be midway
between them. Who, then, is he? He who spends on what he
should and as much as he should and when he should.

There are several forms of illiberality: for instance, we call
some people stingy and cheeseparers and avaricious and   10
petty. All these fall under the head of illiberality. For the bad
is multiform, but the good uniform: for instance, health is
single, but disease multiform. In the same way virtue is single, but vice multiform. For all these characters are blameworthy in relation to wealth.

Is it, then, the business of the liberal man also to acquire   15
and procure property or not? That sort of thing is not the
business of any virtue at all. It is not the business of courage
to make weapons, but of something else—it is its business
when it has got them to make a correct use of them; and
similarly in the case of temperance and the other virtues.

411

20 This, then, is not the business of liberality, but rather of
money-making.

PRIDE IS A MEAN BETWEEN VANITY AND DIFFIDENCE, AND
it has to do with honour and dishonour—not with honour
from the many but with that from the virtuous, or at any
25 rate[4] more with the latter. For the virtuous will bestow honour knowing and assessing things correctly. He will want
then rather to be honoured by those who know (as he does
himself) that he deserves honour. For he will not be concerned with every honour but with the best, and with the
honourable which is good and which ranks as an office.
30 Those, then, who are contemptible and base but claim great
things for themselves, and besides that think that they ought
to be honoured, are vain. Those who claim for themselves
less than befits them are diffident. The man, therefore, who
is midway between these is he who claims neither less honour than is befitting to him, nor greater honour than he is
35 worth, nor every honour. And he is the proud man. So that it
is evident that pride is a mean between vanity and diffidence.

MAGNIFICENCE IS A MEAN BETWEEN EXTRAVAGANCE AND
shabbiness. Magnificence has to do with expenses which are
1192b proper to be incurred by a man of eminence. Whoever therefore spends on what he should not is extravagant: for instance, one who feasts his dinner-club as though he were giving a wedding banquet is extravagant (for the extravagant
man is the sort of person who shows off his own means
5 where he should not). The shabby man is his contrary—
someone who fails to make a great expenditure when he
ought, or who, without going to that length, when, for instance, he is spending money on a wedding feast or the
mounting of a play, does it in an unworthy and deficient
way—such a person is shabby.[5] Magnificence from its very

---

4 Reading ἢ μᾶλλόν γε (a suggestion of Susemihl) for καὶ μᾶλλον δέ.
5 The text is uncertain.

name shows itself to be such as we are describing. For since it spends the great amount on the fitting occasion, it is rightly called magnificence.[6] Magnificence, then, since it is praiseworthy, is a mean between deficiency and excess with regard to proper expenses on the right occasions.

There are, as they think, more kinds of magnificence than one: for instance, people say 'His gait was magnificent', and other such things are said to be magnificent in an extended way, not strictly speaking. For it is not there that magnificence is found but where we have said.

INDIGNATION IS A MEAN BETWEEN ENVY AND SPITE. FOR both these states are blameworthy, but the man who shows indignation is praiseworthy. Now indignation is a kind of pain with regard to good things which are found to attach to the unworthy. The man, then, who feels indignation is he who is apt to feel pain at such things. And this same person again will feel pain if he sees a man faring ill who does not deserve it. Indignation, then, and the person who feels it, are perhaps of this sort, and the envious man is his contrary. For he will feel pain without distinction, whether one is worthy of doing well or not. In the same way the spiteful man will be pleased at failure, whether deserved or undeserved. Not so with the man who feels indignation: he is midway between these.

DIGNITY IS MIDWAY BETWEEN CHURLISHNESS AND OBSE-quiousness, and has to do with social relations. For the churlish man is inclined not to meet or talk to anybody (but his name seems to be given to him from his character; for a churlish man is self-pleasing—the name comes from his approving of himself[7]); but the obsequious man is ready to

6 'Magnificence' is μεγαλοπρέπεια, compounded from μέγας ('great') and πρεπεῖν ('to be fitting').

7 'Churlish' is αὐθάδης, which is here derived from αὐτός ('himself') and ἁνδάνειν ('to please').

keep company with anyone under any circumstances and anywhere. Neither of these is praiseworthy; but the dignified man, being midway between them, is praiseworthy. For he does not associate with everybody (but only with those who are worthy), nor yet with nobody (for he does associate with those who are worthy).

1193a MODESTY IS A MEAN BETWEEN SHAMELESSNESS AND bashfulness, and it has to do with actions and words. For the shameless man is he who says and does anything on any occasion and in front of anyone; and the bashful man is his

5   contrary, who is shy of saying or doing anything in front of anybody (for such a man is incapacitated for action, if he is bashful about everything). Modesty and the modest man are a mean between these. For he will not say and do just anything under just any circumstances, like the shameless man, nor, like the bashful man, be shy on every occasion and

10   under all circumstances: rather, he will say and do what he ought, where he ought, and when he ought.

CONVIVIALITY IS A MEAN BETWEEN BUFFOONERY AND boorishness, and it is concerned with jests. For the buffoon is he who thinks fit to mock at everyone and everything, and the boor is he who wants neither to mock[8] nor to be mocked,

15   but gets angry. The convivial man is midway between these: he neither mocks at all persons and under all circumstances, nor on the other hand is a boor. But conviviality is of two sorts. For both he who is able to mock in good taste and he who can stand being mocked may be called convivial. Such, then, is conviviality.

20   FRIENDLINESS IS A MEAN BETWEEN FLATTERY AND HOS-TILITY, and it has to do with actions and words. For the flatterer is he who adds more than is fitting and true, while the hostile man is an enemy and detracts from what the other

8 Omitting δεῖν (Bonitz).

man has. Neither of them, then, can correctly be praised. The friendly man is midway between the two. For he will not add more than what the other man has, nor praise what is   25 not fitting, nor on the other hand will he represent things as less than they are, nor oppose in all cases contrary to what he thinks. Such, then, is the friendly man.

CANDOUR IS BETWEEN SELF-DEPRECATION AND BOAST-fulness. It has to do with words, but not with all words. For the boaster is he who pretends to have more than he has, or   30 to know what he does not know; while the self-deprecator, his contrary, lays claim to less than he really has and does not declare what he knows, but tries to hide his knowledge. The candid man will do neither of these things: he will not pre-tend either to more than he has or to less, but will say that he   35 has and knows what he does have and does know.

Whether these are virtues or not is another question. But that they are means of the above-mentioned states is plain. For those who live according to them are praised.

6

JUSTICE

IT REMAINS TO SPEAK ABOUT JUSTICE—WHAT IT IS, WHERE it is found, and what it is concerned with.

First, then, if we could grasp what justice is. The just is twofold, of which one kind is legal. For people say that what the law commands is just. Now the law commands us to act
5 courageously and temperately, and quite generally to perform all the actions which come under the head of the virtues. That is why, they say, justice appears to be a kind of complete virtue. For if the things which the law commands us to do are just, and the law ordains what is in accordance with all virtues, it follows that he who abides by legal justice
10 will be completely virtuous, so that the just man and justice are a kind of complete virtue.

The just, then, of one kind is found here and is concerned with these things. But it is not the just of this kind, nor the justice concerned with these things, which we are investigating. For in respect of just conduct of this sort it is possible to be just when one is alone (for the temperate and the coura-
15 geous and the continent are each of them so when alone). But what is just in relation to someone else is different from the legal justice that has been spoken of. For in things just in relation to someone else it is not possible to be just when alone. But it is the just of this kind which we are investigating, and the justice concerned with these things.

The just, then, in relation to someone else is, abstractly
20 speaking, the equal. For the unjust is the unequal. For when people assign more of the good things to themselves and fewer of the bad, this is unequal, and in that case they think that injustice is done and suffered. It is evident, therefore,

that since injustice implies unequal things, justice and the
just will consist in an equality of contracts. So that it is evi-   25
dent that justice will be a mean between superiority and deficiency, between much and little. For the unjust man by being
unjust has more, and his victim by being treated unjustly has
less. The mid-point between these is just; and the mid-point
is equal: so the equal between more and less will be just, and
he will be just who wants to have what is equal. But the equal   30
implies two things at least. To be equal therefore in relation
to someone else is just, and a man of this sort will be just.

Since, then, justice consists in just and equal dealing and
in a mean, the just is said to be just for certain persons, the
equal to be equal among certain persons, and the mid-point   35
to be a mid-point for certain persons; so that justice and the
just will hold in relation to certain persons and among certain persons.

Since, then, the just is equal, the proportionally equal will
be just. Now proportion implies four terms at least; for as A
is to B, C is to D. For instance, it is proportional that he who
has much should contribute much, and that he who has little   1194a
should contribute little; again, in the same way, that he who
has made much exertion should receive much, and that he
who has made little exertion should receive little. As the man
who has exerted himself is to the man who has not exerted
himself, so is the much to the little; and as the man who has   5
exerted himself is to the much, so is the man who has not exerted himself to the little. Plato seems to employ this sort of
proportion[1] in his *Republic*.[2] For the farmer, he says, produces food, and the housebuilder a house, and the weaver a
cloak, and the shoemaker a shoe. Now the farmer gives the
housebuilder food, and the housebuilder gives the farmer a   10
house; and in the same way all the rest exchange their products for those of others. And this is the proportion: as the
farmer is to the housebuilder, so is the housebuilder to the

1 Omitting τοῦ δικαίου (Allan).
2 See *Rep* 369D.

farmer. In the same way with the shoemaker, the weaver, and
15 all the rest, the same proportion holds in relation to one another. And this proportion holds the constitution together.
So that the just seems to be the proportional. For the just
holds constitutions together, and the just is the same thing
as the proportional.

Since the housebuilder's product is of more worth than
20 the shoemaker's, and the shoemaker had to exchange his
product with the housebuilder, but it was not possible to get
a house for shoes, under these circumstances they had recourse to using something for which all these things are pur-
chasable, to wit silver, which they called money: they made
their mutual exchanges by each giving the worth of each
25 product, and thereby they held the political association
together.

Since, then, the just is found in those things which were
mentioned before, the justice which is concerned with these
things will be an habitual impulse[3] attended with choice concerned with and found in these things.

30 Reciprocity also is just—not, however, as the Pythagoreans maintained. For they thought that it was just that a man
should be done to as he had done. But this is not so in relation to all persons. For the same thing is not just for a servant as for a free man: if the servant has struck the free man,
it is not just that he should be struck in return—rather, he
should be struck many times. And reciprocal justice also
35 consists in proportion. For as the free man is to the slave in
being superior, so is being done to to doing. It will be the
same with one free man in relation to another. For it is not
just, if a man has knocked out somebody's eye, merely that
he should have his own knocked out: rather, he should suffer
more, if he is to observe the proportion. For he was the first
1194b to begin and he acted unjustly: he acts unjustly in both respects, so that the acts of injustice are proportional, and for
him to have more done to him than he did is just.

3 Reading τις ἕξις (Spengel) for τῇ ἕξει.

Since we speak of the just in more ways than one, we must determine what kind of just our inquiry is about.

There is, then, a sort of justice, they say, between servant and master, and between son and father. But the just in these cases would seem to be homonymous with political justice (for the justice about which we are inquiring is political justice); for this above all consists in equality (for citizens are a sort of associate, and tend to be similar by nature, though they differ in character). But a son and his father or a servant and his master would not seem to have any justice at all, any more than there is any justice between my foot and myself or my hand and myself (and in the same way with each of the parts). The same, then, would seem to be the case with a son and his father. For the son is, as it were, a part of his father, except that when he has already reached manhood and has been separated from him, he is then equal and similar to his father. Now citizens are supposed to be on that footing. And in the same way neither is there justice between a servant and his master for the same reason. For the servant is a part of his master. Or if there is justice between them, it is in the way of household justice. But this is not what we are in search of, but rather political justice; for political justice seems to lie in equality and similarity. Though, indeed, the justice that there is in the association of wife and husband comes near to political justice. For the wife is inferior to the husband, but closer to him, and partakes in a way more of equality, because their life is close to political association, so that justice between man and wife is more than any other like political justice. Since, then, the just is that which is found in political association, justice also and the just man will be concerned with the politically just.

Things are just either by nature or by law. But we must not regard them as things which cannot change; for even the things which are by nature partake of change. I mean, for instance, if we were all to practice always throwing with the left hand, we should become ambidextrous. But still by nature left is left, and the right hand is nonetheless naturally better than the left, even if we do everything with the left as we do with the right. Nor because things change does it follow that they are not by nature. But if for the most part and for the greater length of time the left continues thus to be left and 1195a the right right, this is by nature. The same is the case with things just by nature; nor[4] if things change owing to our use, is there for that reason no natural justice—rather, there is. For that which continues for the most part can plainly be seen to be naturally just. As to what we establish for our-

5 selves and practise, that is thereby just, and we call it legally just. Natural justice, then, is better than legal. But what we are investigating is political justice. Now the politically just is the legal, not the natural.

The unjust and an unjust act might seem to be the same, but they are not. For the unjust is that which is determined

10 by law (for instance, it is unjust to steal a deposit), but an unjust act is the actual doing of something unjustly. And in the same way the just is not the same as a just act; for the just is what is determined by law, but a just act is the doing of just deeds.

15 When, therefore, have we the just, and when not? Broadly speaking, it is when one acts in accordance with choice and voluntarily (what was meant by 'voluntarily' has been stated by us above), and when one does so knowing the person, the means, and the end, that one does something just. In the very same way the unjust man will be he who knows the person, the means, and the end. But when without knowing any

20 of these things one has done something unjust, one is not unjust but unfortunate. For if a man has killed his father thinking that he was killing an enemy, though he has done something that is unjust, still he is not treating anybody unjustly, but is unfortunate.

Not committing injustice when one does things that are unjust depends on being ignorant of what was mentioned a little above, viz. when one does not know whom one is

---

4 Reading μηδέ (Scaliger) for μή.

harming, nor with what, nor to what end. But we must now   25
define the ignorance, and say how the ignorance must arise
if a man is not to be doing an injustice to the person whom
he harms. Let this, then, be the definition: when the ignorance is the cause of his doing something, he does not do this
voluntarily, so that he does not commit injustice; but when
he is himself the cause of his ignorance and does something
in accordance with the ignorance of which he is himself the   30
cause, then he commits injustice, and such a person will
justly be called unjust. Take for instance people who are
drunk: those who are drunk and have done something bad
commit injustice. For they are themselves the causes of their
ignorance. For they need not have drunk so much as not to
know that they were beating their father. Similarly with the
other sorts of ignorance: when they are due to the agents   35
themselves, those who commit injustice from them are unjust; but where they are not themselves the causes, but their
ignorance is the cause of their doing what they do, they are
not unjust. This sort of ignorance is natural; for instance,
children strike their fathers in ignorance, but the ignorance   1195b
which is in them, being due to nature, does not make the
children be called unjust owing to this conduct. For it is ignorance which is the cause of their behaving thus, and they
are not themselves causes of their ignorance. That is why
they are not called unjust.

But how about being unjustly treated? Can a man be un-   5
justly treated voluntarily or not? We do indeed voluntarily
perform just and unjust acts, but are not unjustly treated voluntarily. For we try to avoid being punished, so that it is evident that we would not voluntarily be unjustly treated. For
no one voluntarily lets himself be harmed. Now to be unjustly treated is to be harmed.

Yes, but there are some who, when they ought to have an   10
equal share, give way to others, so that if, as we have seen,
to have the equal is just and to have less is to be unjustly
treated, then if a man voluntarily has less, then (you say)
he is unjustly treated voluntarily. But from the following

consideration it is evident, on the other hand, that this it is not voluntary. For all who accept less get in exchange honour or praise or glory or friendship or something of that sort. But he who gets something in exchange for what he forgoes is not unjustly treated; and if he is not unjustly treated, then he is not unjustly treated voluntarily.

Again, those who get less and are unjustly treated in so far as they do not get what is equal, plume and pride themselves on such things—they say, 'Though I might have taken an equal amount, I did not take it, but gave way to an elder' or 'to a friend'. But no one prides himself on being unjustly treated. But if they do not pride themselves upon being unjustly treated and do pride themselves upon such things, it follows generally that they will not be unjustly treated by thus getting less. And if they are not unjustly treated, then they will not be unjustly treated voluntarily.

But as against these and the like arguments[5] we have a contrary argument in the case of the incontinent man. For the incontinent man harms himself by doing base acts, and these acts he does voluntarily: he therefore harms himself knowingly, so that he is unjustly treated voluntarily by himself. But here if we add a distinction, it will block the argument. The distinction is this: no one wants to be unjustly treated. The incontinent man wants to do what he does from incontinence, so that he treats himself unjustly: he therefore wants to do what is base for himself. But no one wants to be unjustly treated, so that not even the incontinent man will voluntarily be treating himself unjustly.

But here again one might perhaps raise a problem: is it possible for a man to treat himself unjustly? If we consider the incontinent man it would seem possible. And, again, in this way: if it is just to do those things which the law ordains to be done, he who does not do these is committing injustice; and if when he does not do them to him to whom the

<hr>

5 Reading τοὺς τοιούτους λόγους with half the manuscripts (the others have the phrase in the dative).

law commands, he is treating that person unjustly; and if the law commands one to be temperate, to possess property, to take care of one's body, and all other such things, then he who does not do these things is treating himself unjustly. For it is not possible to refer such acts of injustice to anyone else. 5

But that can hardly be true, nor is it possible for a man to treat himself unjustly. For it is not possible for the same man at the same time to have more and less, nor at once to act voluntarily and involuntarily. But yet he who commits injustice, in so far as he does it, has more, and he who is unjustly 10 treated, in so far as he is unjustly treated, has less. If therefore a man treats himself unjustly, it is possible for the same man at the same time to have both more and less. But this is impossible. It is not therefore possible for a man to treat himself unjustly.

Again, he who commits injustice does it voluntarily, and he who is unjustly treated is unjustly treated involuntarily, so that if it is possible for a man to treat himself unjustly, it will 15 be possible at the same time to do something both involuntarily and voluntarily. But this is impossible. So in this way also it is not possible for a man to treat himself unjustly.

Again, one might look at the question from the point of view of particular acts of injustice. Whenever men commit injustice, it is either by not returning a deposit, or by committing adultery, or by thieving, or by doing some other particular act of injustice; but no one ever failed to return a deposit 20 to himself, or committed adultery with his own wife, or stole his own property; so that if the commission of injustice lies in such things, and it is not possible to do any of them to oneself, it will not be possible to treat oneself unjustly.

Or if so, it will not be an act of political injustice but rather 25 of household injustice. For the soul being divided into several parts has in itself a better and a worse, so that if there is any act of injustice within the soul, it will be done by the parts against one another. Now we distinguished acts of household injustice by their being directed against the worse 30 or better, so that a man may be unjust or just to himself. But this is not what we are investigating, but rather acts of political injustice. So that in such acts of injustice as form the subject of our inquiry, it is not possible for a man to treat himself unjustly.

Which of the two, again, commits injustice, and in which of the two does the act of injustice lie—in the man who has something unjustly or in him who has assessed and made the award, as in the games? For he who takes the palm from the president who has assessed the matter is not committing injustice, even if it be unjustly awarded to him: rather, it is he who has made a bad assessment and given the award who commits injustice. And he is in a way committing injustice, while in a way he is not. For in that he has not assessed what is truly and naturally just, he is committing an injustice, while in that he has assessed what appears to him to be just, he is not committing an injustice.

7

THE INTELLECTUAL VIRTUES

WE HAVE SPOKEN ABOUT THE VIRTUES, SAYING WHAT THEY
are and where they are found and what they are concerned   5
with, and also about each of them in particular, saying that
we must act for the best in accordance with correct reasoning. But to say 'to act in accordance with correct reasoning'
is much the same as if one were to say that health would be
best secured if one were to adopt the means of health. Such a
statement is unilluminating. I shall have it said to me: 'Ex-   10
plain what are the means of health'. So also in the case of reason: 'What is reasoning and which reasoning is correct?'
    Perhaps it is necessary first to discuss where reasoning or
reason is found. A distinction was made in outline about
soul before, how one part of it is possessed of reason and another is irrational.[1] But the part of the soul which is pos-   15
sessed of reason divides into two divisions, one concerned
with deliberation and the other with knowledge. That they
are different from one another will be evident from their
subject-matter. For as colour and flavour and sound and
smell are different from one another, so also nature has ren-   20
dered the senses whereby we perceive them different (for
sound we recognize by hearing, flavour by taste, and colour
by sight), and in like manner we must assume it to be the
same with all other things. When, then, the subject-matters
are different, we must assume that the parts of the soul
whereby we recognize these are also different. Now there is a   25
difference between objects of thought and objects of sense-
perception; and these we recognize by soul. The part of the

---

1 Omitting μόριον τῆς ψυχῆς (Allan).

soul, therefore, which is concerned with objects of perception will be different from that which is concerned with objects of thought. But the faculty of deliberation and choice
has to do with objects of perception that are liable to change,
and quite generally with all that is subject to generation and
destruction. For we deliberate about those things which it is
30   in our power both to do or not to do if we choose, about
which there is deliberation and choice as to whether to do
them or not. And these are objects of perception and are in
process of change. So that the part of the soul in which
choice resides will correspond to objects of perception.

THESE POINTS HAVING BEEN SETTLED, WE MUST GO ON AS
35   follows: the question is one of truth, and we are considering
how the truth stands; and there are knowledge, wisdom, intelligence, understanding, and assumption. What, then, is
the object of each of these?

Knowledge deals with the objects of knowledge, and does
1197a   so through demonstration and reasoning, but wisdom with
matters of action in which there is choice and avoidance and
it is in our power to act or not to act.

What produces a product and what performs an action
are not the same. For the productive crafts have some other
5   end apart from the producing: for instance, apart from
housebuilding, since that is the craft of producing a house,
there is a house as its end apart from the producing of it, and
similarly in the case of carpentry and the other productive
crafts. But in the practical crafts there is no other end apart
from the acting: for instance, apart from playing the harp
10   there is no other end, but the end simply is the activity and
the action. Wisdom, then, is concerned with action and with
matters of action, but craft with producing and with matters
of production; for crafting is found in matters of production
rather than in matters of action. So wisdom will be a state of
15   choosing and acting when it is in our own power to act or
not to act, so far as such acts contribute to our advantage.

426

Wisdom is a virtue, it would seem, not a science. For the wise are praiseworthy, and praise is bestowed on virtue. Again, every science has its virtue, but wisdom has no virtue, but, as it seems, is itself a virtue. 20

Intelligence has to do with the originating principles of whatever is intelligible and real. For knowledge has to do with things that can be demonstrated, but the principles are undemonstrable, so that it will not be knowledge that is concerned with the principles but intelligence.

Understanding is compounded of knowledge and intelligence. For understanding has to do both with the principles 25 and with what can be demonstrated from the principles, with which knowledge deals. In so far, then, as it deals with the principles, it itself partakes of intelligence, and in so far as it deals with demonstrations from the principles, it partakes of knowledge. So it is evident that understanding is compounded of intelligence and knowledge, so that it will deal with the same things as intelligence and knowledge. 30

Assumption is that whereby we are in two minds about all things as to whether they are in a particular way or not.

Are wisdom and understanding the same thing or not? Understanding has to do with things that can be proved and are always the same, but wisdom has not to do with these but with things that undergo change. I mean, for instance, 35 straight or crooked or convex and the like are always what they are, but what is advantageous is not such as never to change into anything else: rather, it does change, and a given thing is advantageous now but not to-morrow, to this man but not to that, and is advantageous in this way but not in 1197b that way. Now wisdom has to do with what is advantageous, but understanding does not. Therefore understanding and wisdom are not the same.

Is understanding a virtue or not? It might become plain that it is a virtue simply by looking at wisdom. For if wisdom 5 is, as we maintain, the virtue of one of the two rational parts, and wisdom is inferior to understanding (for its objects are inferior since understanding has to do with the eternal and the divine, as we maintain, but wisdom with what is advantageous for man)—if, then, the inferior is a virtue, it is reasonable that the better should be a virtue, so that it is plain that understanding is a virtue.

WHAT IS JUDGEMENT, AND WITH WHAT IS IT CONCERNED? Judgement is found where wisdom is—in matters of action. For the judicious man is presumably so called from his capacity for deliberation, and from his assessing and seeing things correctly. But his assessment concerns small things and is found among small things. Judgement, then, and the judicious man are a part of wisdom and the wise man, and are not found without them; for you cannot separate the judicious man from the wise man.

The case would seem to be the same with cleverness. For cleverness and the clever man are not wisdom and the wise man; the wise man, however, is clever. That is why cleverness co-operates in a way with wisdom. But the base man also is called clever: for instance, Mentor was thought to be clever, but he was not wise. For it is the business of the wise man and of wisdom to aim at the best things, and always to choose and do these, but it is the business of cleverness and the clever man to consider by what means any matter of action may be effected, and to provide these. It would seem then that the clever man is found here and is concerned with these things.

SOMEONE MIGHT RAISE A PROBLEM AND WONDER WHY, when speaking of character and dealing with political inquiry, we speak about understanding. Perhaps, first, because the inquiry about it will not seem foreign to our subject, if it is a virtue, as we maintain. Again, it is perhaps the business of the man of understanding to consider subjects in the same area. And it is necessary, when we are speaking about the contents of the soul, to speak about them all. Now

understanding is in the soul; so that it is not foreign to the   35
subject when we speak about understanding.[2]

AS CLEVERNESS IS TO WISDOM, SO IT WOULD SEEM TO BE
in the case of all the virtues. I mean, there are virtues which
arise by nature in different persons, a sort of impulse in the
individual, apart from reason, towards what is courageous
and just (and so in the case of each virtue); and there are also   1198a
virtues due to custom and choice. The virtues that are accompanied by reason, when they supervene, are completely
praiseworthy. Now this natural virtue which is unaccompanied by reason, is of little account so long as it remains apart
from reason, and falls short of being praised, but when   5
added to reason and choice, it makes complete virtue. That is
why the natural impulse to virtue collaborates with reason
and is not apart from reason. Nor are reason and choice
quite completed as virtue without the natural impulse. That   10
is why Socrates was not speaking correctly when he said that
virtue was reason, thinking that it was no use doing courageous and just acts unless one did them from knowledge and
rational choice. That is why he said that virtue was reason,
incorrectly. Our contemporaries do better; for they say that
virtue is doing what is noble in accordance with correct reasoning. Even they, indeed, are not right. For one might do   15
what is just without any choice at all and without knowledge
of the noble, but from an irrational impulse, and yet do this
correctly and in accordance with correct reasoning (I mean,
he may have acted in the way that right reason would command); but all the same, this sort of action is not praiseworthy. Rather, it is better to say, according to our definition,   20
that it is an impulse toward the noble accompanied by reason. For that is virtue and that is praiseworthy.

The problem might be raised whether wisdom is a virtue
or not. It will be plain, however, from the following consid-

2 Reading σοφίας (Victorius) for ψυχῆς ('. . . speaking about the soul').

eration that it is a virtue. If justice and courage and the rest
of the virtues, because they lead to the doing of what is noble,
are also praiseworthy, it is plain that wisdom will also be
among the things that are praiseworthy and that rank as virtues. For wisdom also has an impulse towards those acts towards which courage has an impulse. For, speaking generally, courage acts as wisdom ordains, so that if it is itself
praiseworthy for doing what wisdom ordains, wisdom will
be in a complete degree both praiseworthy and a virtue.

Whether wisdom is practical or not one might see by
looking at the sciences—for instance at housebuilding. For
there is, we say, in housebuilding one person who is called an
architect, and another who is subordinate to him and is a
housebuilder—and it is he who produces the house. But the
architect too, inasmuch as the builder made the house, produces the house. And the case is the same in all the other productive crafts in which there is a master-craftsman and his
subordinate. The master-craftsman too therefore will produce something, and the same thing as his subordinate. If,
then, it is similar in the case of the virtues, as is likely and
reasonable, wisdom also will be practical. For all the virtues
are practical, and wisdom is a kind of master-craftsman of
them; for as it shall ordain, so the virtues and those who have
them act. Since then the virtues are practical, wisdom also
will be practical.

Some hold that wisdom rules all things in the soul, and
some think it a problem whether it does or not. It would not
seem to rule what is better than itself: for instance, it does
not rule understanding. But (you say) this has charge of all,
and is authoritative in issuing commands. But perhaps it
holds the same position as the steward in the household. For
he has authority over all and manages everything. But it does
not follow that he rules all: rather, he procures leisure for the
master in order that he may not be hindered by necessary
cares and so shut out from doing something that is noble
and befitting. So and in like manner with him wisdom is, as
it were, a kind of steward of understanding, and procures

leisure for it and for the performance of its task by subduing
and tempering the emotions.   20

AFTER THIS WE MUST INQUIRE INTO EQUITY: WHAT IS IT,   Book B
where is it found, and what is it concerned with? Equity and
the equitable man is he who is inclined to take less than what
is legally just. There are matters in which it is impossible for
the lawgiver to define precisely, and where he speaks universally. When, then, a man gives way in these matters, and
chooses those things which the lawgiver wanted to define in   30
detail but was not able to, such a man is equitable. It is not
the way with him to take less than what is just *tout court*; for
he does not take less of what is naturally and truly just but
only of what is legally just in matters which the lawgiver
could but leave alone.

Good sense and the man of good sense have to do with the
same things as equity—with points of justice that have been   35
omitted by the lawgiver owing to the imprecision of his definitions. The man of good sense assesses the omissions of the
lawgiver, and knows that, though things have been omitted by
the lawgiver, they are nevertheless just. Such is the man of   1199a
good sense. Good sense is not found apart from equity; for to
the man of good sense it belongs to assess, and to the equitable man to act in accordance with the assessment.

SKILL IN DELIBERATION IS CONCERNED WITH THE SAME
things as wisdom (dealing with matters of action which con-   5
cern choice and avoidance), and it is not found apart from
wisdom. For wisdom leads to the doing of these things,
while skill in deliberation is a state or disposition or something of that sort which leads to the ascertainment of the
best and most expedient in matters of action. That is why
things that turn out as they should spontaneously do not
seem to be the business of skill in deliberation. For where   10
there is no reason which considers what is best, you would
not in that case say that a man to whom something turned
out as it should be was skilful in deliberation but rather that

he was fortunate. For successes that come along without the assessment of reason are due to good fortune.

IS IT IN THE PART OF THE JUST MAN TO PUT HIMSELF ON AN
15 equal footing with everybody he meets (I mean in the way of becoming all things to all men) or not? This would seem to be the part of a flatterer and obsequious person. But to suit his conversation to the worth of each would seem to be the part of the man who is both just and virtuous *tout court*.

HERE IS ANOTHER PROBLEM THAT MIGHT BE RAISED. IF
20 doing injustice is harming somebody voluntarily and with knowledge of the person and the manner and the end, and harm and injustice are found in good things and concerned with good things, then the doer of injustice and the unjust man will know what kind of things are good and what bad. But to know about these things is the business of the wise
25 man and of wisdom. The absurdity then follows that wisdom, which is the greatest good, is attendant upon the unjust man. Surely it will not be thought that wisdom is attendant upon the unjust man? For the unjust man does not consider and is not able to assess what is good in the abstract and what is good for him—rather, he errs. But the business
30 of wisdom is to be able to consider these things correctly— just as in matters of medicine we all know what is in the abstract healthy and what is productive of health—that hellebore and aperients and surgery and cautery are healthy and productive of health—and yet we do not possess the science
35 of medicine. For we do not yet know what is good in particular cases in the way in which the doctor knows for whom a given thing is good and when and in what condition; for herein the science of medicine displays itself. Thus we may know things that are in the abstract healthy, and yet not have
1199b the science of medicine attendant upon us. The same is the case with the unjust man: that in the abstract tyranny and government and power are good, he knows; but whether they are good for him or not, or when, or in what condition,

that he does not yet know. But this is just the business of wisdom, so that wisdom does not attend upon the unjust man. For the goods which he chooses and for which he commits injustice are what are good in the abstract, not what are good for him. For riches and office are good in the abstract, but for him perhaps they are not good; for by obtaining wealth and office he will do much harm to himself and his friends, for he will not be able to make a correct use of office.

Here also is a point which presents a problem and demands inquiry: can injustice be done to a base man or not? For if injustice consists in harm, and harm in the deprivation of good things, it would seem not to harm him. For the good things which he thinks to be good for him are not good. For office and wealth will harm the base man who is not able to make a correct use of them. If then they will harm him by their presence, he who deprives him of these would not seem to be treating him unjustly. This kind of argument will appear a paradox to the many. For all think that they are able to use office and power and riches. But their assumption is not correct. This is made plain by the lawgiver. For the lawgiver does not allow all to rule: rather, he determines the age and the wealth which must be possessed by him who is to rule, implying that it is not possible for everyone to rule. If then someone were to resent the fact that he does not hold office or that no one allows him to govern, the answer would be: 'You have nothing in your soul of a kind which will enable you to rule or to govern'. In the case of the body we see that those who apply to themselves things that are good in the abstract cannot become healthy: rather, if a man is to restore his ill body to health, he must first apply to it water and a low diet. And when a man has his soul in a base state, in order that he may not work any ill must he not be kept away from riches and office and power and things of that sort generally, the more so as soul is easier to move and more ready to change than body? For as the man whose body was ill was fit to be dieted in that way, so the man whose soul is base is fit to live thus, without having any things of this sort.

This also presents a problem: when it is not possible at the same time to do courageous and just acts, which is one to do? Now in the case of the natural virtues we said[3] that there existed only the impulse to the noble without reason; but he who has choice has it in reason and the rational part. So that as soon as choice is present, complete virtue will be there, which we said was accompanied by wisdom, but not without the natural impulse to the noble. Nor will one virtue run contrary to another; for its nature is to obey the dictates of reason, so that it inclines to that to which reason leads. For it is this which chooses the better. For the other virtues do not come into existence without wisdom, nor is wisdom complete without the other virtues, but they co-operate in a way with one another, attending upon wisdom.

No less will the following present itself as a problem: is it the same in the case of the virtues as in that of the other goods, whether external or bodily? For these when they run to excess make men worse; for instance, when riches become great they make men disdainful and unpleasant. And so also with the other goods—office, honour, beauty, stature. Is it, then, thus in the case of virtue too (so that, if one comes to have justice or courage to excess, he will be worse) or not? No, you say. But from virtue comes honour, and when honour becomes great, it makes men worse, so that it is plain (you say) that virtue when progressing to a great extent will make men worse. For virtue is a cause of honour, so that virtue also, if it becomes great, will make men worse. Surely this is not true? For virtue, if it has many other tasks, as indeed it has, has this among the most special: to be able to make a correct use of these and the like goods when they are present. If therefore the virtuous man, when there comes to him high honour or high office, does not make a correct use of these, he will no longer be virtuous. Therefore neither honour nor office will make the virtuous man worse, so that neither will virtue. Generally, since it was determined by us

3 The reference can only be to 1198a3–8.

at the start that the virtues are means, the more anything is a virtue, the more it is a mean; so that not only will virtue as it becomes great not make a man worse—it will make him better. For the mean was found to be a mean between lack and excess in the emotions.   35

So much then for these matters.

8

CONTINENCE AND INCONTINENCE

AFTER THIS WE MUST MAKE A NEW START AND SPEAK about continence and incontinence. But as the virtue and the vice are themselves of a strange nature, so the discussion which will ensue about them must necessarily be strange 1200b also. For this virtue is not like the others: in the others reason and the emotions have an impulse towards the same objects and are not contrary to one another, but in the case of this virtue reason and the emotions are contrary to one another.

5 There are three things in the soul in respect of which we are called base—vice, incontinence, brutishness. About virtue and vice—what they are and where they are found—we have spoken above: now we must speak about incontinence and brutishness.

Brutishness is a kind of excessive vice. For when we see 10 someone utterly base, we say that he is not even a man but a brute, implying that there is a vice of brutishness. The virtue opposed to this is without a name, but this sort of thing is beyond a man, a kind of heroic and divine virtue. This virtue is without a name, because virtue does not belong to god. For god is superior to virtue and it is not in virtue that his 15 goodness lies. For if it were, virtue would be better than god. That is why the virtue which is opposed to the vice of brutishness is without a name. But divine and superhuman virtue tend to be opposed to it. For as the vice of brutishness is beyond a man, so also is the virtue opposed to it.

20 With regard to incontinence and continence we must first state the problems and the arguments which run contrary to

people's perceptions, in order that, having considered the matter synoptically on the basis of the problems and the contrary arguments, and having examined these, we may see the truth about them so far as possible; for it will be more easy to see the truth in this way.

Now Socrates the elder rejected it outright and denied   25
that there was such a thing as incontinence, saying that no one would choose bad things if he knew them to be bad. But the incontinent man seems, while knowing things to be base, to choose them all the same, being led by his emotions. For that reason, he did not think that there was such a thing as incontinence—incorrectly. For it is absurd that one   30
should be convinced by this argument and reject what credibly occurs. For there are incontinent men, and they do things even though they themselves know them to be base.

Since, then, there is such a thing as incontinence, does the incontinent man possess some knowledge whereby he considers and examines base things? But, again, this would not seem so. For it would be absurd that the strongest and   35
firmest thing in us should be defeated by anything. For knowledge is of all things in us the most permanent and the most forceful. So that this argument again runs contrary to there being knowledge.[1]

Is it then not knowledge but belief? But if the incontinent man has a belief, he will not be blameworthy. For if he does   1201a
something base where he has no precise knowledge but a belief, one would sympathize with his siding with pleasure and doing what is base, if he does not know precisely that it is base but believes it is; and those with whom we sympathize we do not blame. So that the incontinent, if he has a belief,   5
will not be blameworthy. But he is blameworthy. Such arguments then raise problems. For some denied knowledge, making out that it had an absurd consequence; and others again denied belief, making out that it too had an absurd consequence.

1 Omitting μή (Spengel).

10   Here is another difficulty that might be raised: since it is
held that the temperate man is also continent, will this involve the temperate man's having intense appetites? If he is
to be continent, it will be necessary for him to have intense
15   appetites (for you would not speak of a man as continent
who masters moderate appetites); but if he is to have intense
appetites, in that case he will no longer be temperate (for the
temperate is he who does not crave or feel anything).

The following considerations again raise a problem. It results from the arguments that the incontinent man is sometimes praiseworthy and the continent man blameworthy.
For let it be supposed (you say) that someone has erred in his
calculation, and let it seem to him when he calculates that
20   noble things are base, and let appetite lead him to the noble:
then reason will forbid his doing it, but being led by appetite
he does it (for such was the incontinent man). He will therefore do what is noble, supposing that appetite leads him
thereto; but reason will restrain him, supposing that he errs
25   in his calculation about the noble), he will be incontinent
and yet praiseworthy; for in so far as he does what is noble,
he is praiseworthy. The result is absurd.

Again, on the other hand, let him err in his reason, and let
what is noble seem to him not to be noble, but let appetite
lead him to the noble. Now he is continent who, though he
30   craves a thing, yet does not act owing to reason. So if his reason errs[2] it will restrain him from doing the noble things
which he craves: therefore it restrains him from doing what
is noble (for to that his appetite led him). But he who fails to
do what is noble, when he ought to do it, is blameworthy.
Therefore the continent man will sometimes be blame-
35   worthy. In this way then also the result is absurd.

A problem might also be raised as to whether incontinence and the incontinent man are found everywhere and
are concerned with everything—for instance, with wealth
and honour and anger and reputation (for people seem to be

2 Reading λόγος (Bonitz) for τῷ λόγῳ.

incontinent with regard to all these things), or whether they do not, but incontinence has a certain definite concern.

These, then, are the points which raise problems; and it is necessary to solve the problems. First, then, that which is connected with knowledge. For it appeared to be an absurdity that one who possessed knowledge should cast it from him or fall away from it. But the same argument applies also to belief; for it makes no difference whether it is belief or knowledge. For if belief is intense by being firm and unalterable by persuasion, it will not differ from knowledge, belief carrying with it the conviction that things are as one believes them to be—for instance, Heraclitus of Ephesus has this sort of belief about the things that he holds.

But there is nothing absurd about the incontinent man's doing something base, whether he has knowledge or belief such as we describe. For there are two ways of knowing, one of which is the possessing of knowledge (for we say that one knows when he possesses knowledge), the other is exercising the knowledge. He then who possesses the knowledge of the noble but does not exercise it, is incontinent. When, then, he does not exercise this knowledge, it is not absurd that he should do what is bad though he possesses the knowledge. For the case is similar to that of sleepers. For they, though they possess the knowledge, nevertheless in their sleep both do and experience many vexatious things. For their knowledge is not exercised. So it is in the case of the incontinent. For he seems like one asleep and does not exercise his knowledge. Thus, then, is the problem solved. For the problem was whether the incontinent man expels his knowledge or falls away from it, both of which seem to be absurd.

Again, the thing may be made evident in this way: as we said in the *Analytics* a deduction depends on two propositions, and of these the first is universal, while the second falls under it and is particular. For instance, I know how to cure any man with a fever; this man has a fever: therefore I know how to cure this man. Now there are things which I know

5

10

15

20

25

30

with universal knowledge but not with particular. Here too then error is committed by the man who possesses the knowledge: for instance, I know how to cure anyone with a fever, but I do not know if this man has a fever. Similarly then in the case of the incontinent man who possesses the knowledge the same error will arise. For it is possible for the incontinent man to possess universal knowledge that such and such things are base and harmful, but yet not to know that these particular things are base, so that while possessing knowledge in this way he will err. For he has the universal knowledge, but not the particular. Neither, then, in this way is it at all absurd in the case of the incontinent man that he who has the knowledge should do something base.

For it is so in the case of persons who are drunk. For those who are drunk, when the intoxication has passed off, are themselves again. Reason was not expelled from them, nor was knowledge, but it was mastered by the intoxication; and when they have got rid of the intoxication, they are themselves again. So, then, it is with the incontinent. His emotion gained the mastery and brought his calculation to a standstill. But when the emotion, like the intoxication, has been got rid of, he is himself again.

There was another argument touching incontinence which presented a problem inasmuch as the incontinent man will sometimes be praiseworthy and the continent man blameworthy. But this does not result. For the man who is deceived in his reason is neither continent nor incontinent, but rather he whose reason is correct and who with it assesses the base and the noble: it is the man who disobeys this kind of reason who is incontinent, while he who obeys it and is not led by his appetites is continent. For if a man does not think it ignoble to strike his father and craves to strike him, but abstains from doing so, he is not continent. So that, since there is neither continence nor incontinence in such cases, neither will incontinence be praiseworthy nor continence blameworthy in the way that was thought.

There are forms of incontinence which are unhealthy and others which are due to nature. For instance, these are un- 20 healthy: there are some people who pull out their hair and others who bite their nails.[3] If one masters this pleasure, then, he is not praiseworthy, nor blameworthy if he fails to do so, or not very much. And natural incontinence: they say that a son who was brought to trial in court for beating his father defended himself by saying: 'Why, he did so to his own 25 father'—and he was acquitted; for the judges thought that his error was natural. If, then, such a one were to master the impulse to beat his father, he would not be praiseworthy. It is not, then, such forms of incontinence or continence as these which we are now investigating, but rather those for which we are called blameworthy or praiseworthy *tout court*.

Of goods some are external, such as riches, office, hon- 30 our, friends, reputation; others necessary and concerned with the body, for instance, touch and taste, and bodily plea- sures. He, then, who is incontinent with respect to these things would appear to be incontinent *tout court*; and the in- continence which we are investigating would seem to be concerned with just these things. There was a problem about what incontinence is concerned with. As regards honour, 35 then, a man is not incontinent *tout court*; for he who is incon- tinent with regard to honour is praised in a way, as being am- bitious. And generally when we call a man incontinent in the case of such things we do it with some addition, incontinent 'as regards honour or reputation or anger'. But when a man 1202b is incontinent *tout court*, we do not add anything, it being true and evident in his case what it concerns without the ad- dition. For he who is incontinent *tout court* has to do with the pleasures and pains of the body.

It is plain also from the following consideration that in- continence has to do with these things. Since the incon- 5 tinent man is blameworthy, the subject-matter of his incon-

3 Adding ἕτεροι δὲ ὄνυχας (as Susemihl suggests).

tinence ought also to be blameworthy. Now honour and reputation and office and wealth, and the other things concerning which people are called incontinent, are not blameworthy, whereas bodily pleasures are blameworthy. That is why the man who is⁴ concerned with these more than he ought is called (reasonably enough) completely incontinent.

10 Among what are called incontinences concerning other things, incontinence concerned with anger is the most blameworthy. But which is more blameworthy, incontinence concerning anger or incontinence concerning pleasures? Incontinence concerning anger resembles servants who are eager to minister to one's needs. For they, when the master

15 says 'Give me . . .', are carried away by their eagerness, and before they hear what they ought to give, give something, and err in what they give. For often, when they ought to give a book, they give a pen. Something like this is the case with the man who is incontinent concerning anger. For passion, as soon as it hears the first words 'He has unjustly treated . . .',

20 is impelled to take vengeance, without waiting to hear whether it ought or ought not, or not so intensely. This sort of impulse, then, to anger, which seems to be incontinence of anger, is not greatly to be criticized, but the impulse to pleasure is blameworthy. For it differs from the former because reason discourages action, and nevertheless it acts

25 against reason. That is why it is more blameworthy than incontinence due to anger. For incontinence due to anger is a pain (for no one feels anger without being pained), but that which is due to appetite is attended with pleasure. That is why it is more blameworthy. For incontinence due to pleasure seems to involve outrage.

30 Are continence and endurance the same thing or not? Continence has to do with pleasures and the continent man is he who masters pleasures, but endurance has to do with pains. For the man of endurance is he who endures and faces up to pains. Again, incontinence and softness are not the

4 Reading ὧν (Stock) for ἄν.

same thing. For softness and the soft person is he who does not face up to hardships—not all of them, but such as any- 35 one else would face up to if he had to; whereas the incontinent man is he who is not able to face up to pleasures, but is softened and led on by them.

Again, there is another character called self-indulgent. Is the self-indulgent, then, the same as the incontinent or not? 1203a The self-indulgent is the kind of man who thinks that what he does is best and most advantageous for himself, and who has no reason going contrary to the things which appear pleasant to him, whereas the incontinent does possess rea- 5 son which goes contrary to the things to which his appetite leads.

Which is the more easy to cure, the self-indulgent or the incontinent? It might perhaps seem that it is not the incontinent, for this reason: the self-indulgent is more easy to cure, since if reason were present in him to teach him that things are base, he will leave off doing them; but the incontinent man has reason, and nevertheless acts, so that such a person 10 would seem to be incurable. But which is in the worse condition, he who has no good at all, or he who has some good joined with these evils? Plainly the former, the more so inasmuch as it is the more valuable part that is in a bad condition. The incontinent man, then, does possess a good in his reason being correct, while the self-indulgent does not. 15 Again, reason is the originating principle in each. In the incontinent the principle, which is the most valuable thing, is in a good condition, but in the self-indulgent in a bad; so that the self-indulgent will be worse than the incontinent. Again, like the vice of brutishness of which we spoke, you cannot see it in a brute but in a man (for brutishness is a 20 name for excessive vice). Why so? Just because a brute has in it no base principle—the principle is reason. For which would do more bad things, a lion, or Dionysius or Phalaris or Clearchus or any one of those depraved men? Plainly the latter. For their having in them a base principle contributes 25 greatly, but in the brute there is no principle at all. In the self-indulgent, then, there is a base principle. For inasmuch as he does base acts and reason assents to these, and it seems to him that he ought to do these things, the principle in him is not healthy. That is why the incontinent would seem to be better than the self-indulgent.

30   There are two species of incontinence. One is impetuous[5] and without forethought and comes on suddenly (for instance, when we see a beautiful woman, we at once feel something, and from the emotion there ensues an impulse to do something which perhaps we ought not). The other is a sort of

35   weakness, but attended with reason which discourages. Now the former would not seem to be very blameworthy. For this kind occurs even in the virtuous, in those who are of warm

1203b   temperament and well endowed by nature; but the other in the cold and atrabilious, and such are blameworthy. Again, one may avoid the feeling by reasoning beforehand: 'There will come a pretty woman, so one must control oneself'. So that, if he has reasoned beforehand like that, he whose incon-

5   tinence is due to the suddenness of the impression will not feel anything, nor do anything ignoble. But he who knows from reason that he ought not, but gives in to pleasure and is softened by it, is more blameworthy. For the virtuous man would never become incontinent in that way, and reasoning

10   beforehand would be no cure for it. For this guide is present in him, and yet he does not obey it, but gives in to pleasure, and is softened and somehow becomes weak.

Whether the temperate man is continent was raised as a problem above: now let us speak of it. The temperate man is also continent. For the continent man is not merely he who,

15   when he has appetites in him, controls them owing to reason, but also he who is of such a kind that, though he has not appetites in him, he would control them if they did arise. But it is he who has no base appetites and who reasons correctly with respect to these things who is temperate, while the

---

5 Reading προπετής (Ramsauer) for προτρεπτική (προπετική, which Susemihl prints, is not Greek).

continent man is he who has base appetites and who reasons correctly with regard to these things. So continence will go along with temperance, and the temperate will be continent, but not the continent temperate. For while the temperate is he who has no feeling, the continent man is he who feels, or is capable of feeling, but masters his feelings. But neither of these is the case with the temperate. That is why the continent is not temperate.

Is the self-indulgent incontinent or the incontinent self-indulgent? Or does neither follow on the other? The incontinent is he whose reason fights with his emotions, but the self-indulgent is not of this sort, but rather he who in doing base deeds has the consent of his reason. Neither then is the self-indulgent like the incontinent nor the incontinent like the self-indulgent. Further, the self-indulgent is baser than the incontinent. For what comes by nature is harder to cure than what results from custom (for the reason why custom is held to be strong is that it turns things into nature). The self-indulgent, then, is in himself the kind of man who is base by nature, owing to which, and as a result of which, the reason in him is base. But not so the incontinent: it is not because he is in himself such a man that his reason is not virtuous (it would have to be base, if he were in himself by nature such as the base). The incontinent, then, seems to be base by custom, but the self-indulgent by nature. Therefore the self-indulgent is the harder to cure. For one custom is dislodged by another, but nothing will dislodge nature.

Seeing that the incontinent is the kind of man who knows and is not deceived in his reason, while the wise man also is of the same kind and considers everything by correct reasoning, is it possible for the wise man to be incontinent or not? One might raise the problems we have mentioned; yet if we follow our former statements, the wise man will not be incontinent. For we said that the wise man was not merely he in whom correct reasoning exists, but he who also does what appears in accordance with reasoning to be best. Now if the wise man does what is best, the wise man

will not be incontinent. Rather, an incontinent man is clever.
For we distinguished above between the clever and the wise
as being different. For though they are concerned with the
same things, yet the one does what he ought and the other
does not. It is possible, then, for the clever man to be incontinent (for he does not succeed in doing what he ought), but
it is not possible for the wise man to be incontinent.

9

PLEASURE

NEXT WE MUST SPEAK ABOUT PLEASURE, SINCE OUR DIS-
cussion is about happiness, and all think that happiness is ei-   20
ther pleasure and living pleasantly, or at any rate not without
pleasure. Even those who are vexed by pleasure, and think
that pleasure ought not to be numbered among goods, at
least add the absence of pain; now to be without pain is close
to pleasure. Therefore we must speak about pleasure, not   25
merely because other people think that we ought, but because it is actually necessary for us to do so. For since our
discussion is about happiness, and we have defined and declare happiness to be an activity of virtue in a complete life,
and virtue has to do with pleasure and pain, it is necessary to
speak about pleasure, since happiness is not found without   30
pleasure.

First, then, let us mention the reasons which some people
give for thinking that one ought not to regard pleasure as
part of good. First, they say that pleasure is a process, and
that a process is something incomplete, but that the good
never occupies the place of the incomplete. Secondly, that   35
there are some base pleasures, whereas the good is never to
be found in baseness. Again, that it is found in all—in the
base man and in the virtuous, and in brutes and in cattle; but
the good is unmixed with the base and not promiscuous. ***[1]   1204b
And that pleasure is not the best thing, whereas the good is
the best thing. And that it is an impediment to noble action,
and what tends to hinder the noble cannot be good.

---

1 Susemihl marks a lacuna, which he supposes to have contained a problem answering to the solution at 1206a26–30.

First, then, we must address ourselves to the first argument, that about process, and must endeavour to refute it on
the ground of its not being true. To begin with, not every
pleasure is a process. For the pleasure which results from
contemplation is not a process, nor that which comes from
hearing and seeing and smelling. For it does not arise from a
lack, as in the other cases—for instance, those of eating and
drinking. For these are the result of lack and excess, by replenishing a lack or by removing an excess: that is why they
are held to be processes. Now lack and excess are pains.
There is therefore pain wherever there is a process of pleasure. But in the case of seeing and hearing and smelling
there is no previous pain. For no one in taking pleasure in
seeing or smelling was in pain beforehand. Similarly in the
case of thought: one may contemplate something with pleasure without having felt any pain beforehand. So there are
pleasures which are not processes. If then pleasure, as their
argument maintained, is not a good because is a process, but
there is some pleasure which is not a process, this pleasure
may be good.

But generally no pleasure is a process. For even the pleasures of eating and drinking are not processes: rather, those
who say that these pleasures are processes err. For they think
that pleasure is a process because it ensues on the supplying
of something; but it is not. For there is a part of the soul with
which we feel pleasure, and this part of the soul is active and
moves simultaneously with the supplying of the things
which we lack, and its movement and activity are pleasure.
Owing, then, to that part of the soul being active simultaneously with the supplying, or owing to its activity, they think
that pleasure is a process since the supplying is plain but the
part of the soul obscure. It is like thinking that man is body,
because this is perceptible, while the soul is not—but the
soul also exists. So it is also in this case; for there is a part of
the soul with which we feel pleasure, which is active at the
same time as the supplying. That is why no pleasure is a
process.

It is, they say, a perceptible restoration to a natural state. But there is pleasure without such restoration to a natural state. For restoration is the replenishing of what by nature is lacking; but it is possible, as we maintain, to feel pleasure 1205a without any lack. For lack is pain, and we say that there is pleasure without pain and prior to pain. So that pleasure will not be a restoration of a lack. For in such pleasures there is no lack. So that if the reason for thinking that pleasure is not 5 a good was because it is a process, and no pleasure is a process, pleasure may be a good.

But next some pleasures, you say, are not good. One may look at it like this. Since we maintain that good is spoken of in all the categories (in that of substance and relation and 10 quantity and time and generally in all), this much is plain at once: every activity of something good is attended by a certain pleasure, so that, since good is in all the categories, pleasure also will be in all.[2] So since the goods and pleasure are found here, and the pleasure that comes from the goods is 15 pleasure, every pleasure will be good. At the same time it is plain from this that pleasures differ in kind. For the categories in which pleasure is found are different. For it is not as in the sciences, for instance grammar or any other science whatever. For if Lampros possesses the science of grammar, he as a grammarian will be disposed by this knowledge of 20 grammar in the same way as anyone else who possesses the science: there will not be two different sciences of grammar, that in Lampros and that in Neleus.[3] But in the case of pleasure it is not so. For the pleasure which comes from intoxication and that which comes from sex do not dispose in the same way. That is why pleasures would seem to differ in kind. 25

Another reason why pleasure was held by them not to be a good was because some pleasures are base. But this sort of thing and this kind of assessment are not proper to pleasure—they apply also to nature and to knowledge. For there

---

2 Reading ἐν ἁπάσαις (Rassow) for ἀγαθόν ('. . . will be good').

3 Reading Νηλεῖ, with half the manuscripts, for Ἰλεῖ.

30 is such a thing as a base nature (for example, that of worms and of beetles and of the lower animals generally), but it does not follow that nature is a base thing. In the same way there are base branches of knowledge, for instance the vulgar; nevertheless it does not follow that knowledge is a base thing. Rather, both knowledge and nature are good in kind. For

35 just as one must not consider the quality of a sculptor on the basis of his failures and bad workmanship but on that of his successes, so one must not consider the quality of knowledge or nature or of anything else on the basis of the base but

1205b on that of the virtuous. Similarly, pleasure is good in kind, though there are base pleasures—of that we ourselves are aware. For since the natures of animals differ in the way of base and virtuous, for instance that of man is virtuous, but

5 that of a wolf or some other brute base, and similarly a horse and a man and an ass and a dog have different natures, and since pleasure is a restoration of each to its own nature from that which runs counter to it, it follows that this will be most pleasant[4]—the base pleasure to the base nature. For it is not the same for a horse and a man, any more than for any of the

10 rest. But since their natures are different, their pleasures also are different. For pleasure, as we saw, is a restoration, and the restoration, they maintain, restores to nature, so that the restoration of the base nature is base, and that of the virtuous, virtuous.

Those who assert that pleasure is not virtuous are in much

15 the same case as those who, not knowing nectar, think that the gods drink wine, and that there is nothing more pleasant than this. But this is owing to their ignorance. In much the same case are all those who assert that all pleasures are processes, and not good. For owing to their not knowing other than bodily pleasures, and seeing these to be processes and

20 not good, they think in general that pleasure is not a good.

Since, then, there are pleasures both of a nature in the course of being restored and also of one already restored (for

---

4 Reading ἥδιστον (Aldine) for ἴδιον ('proper').

instance of the former the replenishments which follow upon lack, and of the latter the pleasures of sight, hearing, and so on), the activities of a restored nature will be better— for the pleasures of both kinds are activities. It is plain, then, that the pleasures of sight, hearing, and thought will be best, since the bodily pleasures result from a replenishment.

Again, this was also said by way of showing that it is not a good: what is found everywhere and is common to all is not good. Such an objection might seem appropriate rather to the case of an ambitious man and ambition. For the ambitious man is one who wants to be sole possessor of something and by some such means to surpass all others: so if pleasure is to be a good, it too must be something of this sort. Or is this not so? Rather, on the contrary, it would seem to be a good for this reason: all things aim at it. For it is the nature of all things to aim at the good, so that, if all things aim at pleasure, pleasure must be good in kind.

Again, they denied that pleasure is a good on the ground that it is an impediment. But their asserting it to be an impediment seems to arise from an incorrect view of the matter. For the pleasure that comes from the performance of the action is not an impediment: if it is a different pleasure, it is an impediment (for instance, the pleasure of intoxication is an impediment to action). But in this way one kind of knowledge will be a hindrance to another; for one cannot exercise both at once. But why is knowledge not good if it produces the pleasure that comes from knowledge? And will that pleasure be an impediment or not? Rather, it will intensify the action. For the pleasure is a stimulus to increased action, if it comes from the action itself. For suppose the virtuous man to be performing his acts of virtue, and to be performing them with pleasure: will he not be much more active in the action? And if he acts with pleasure, he will be virtuous; but if he does noble things with pain, he will not be virtuous. For pain attends upon what is due to compulsion, so that if one is pained at doing something noble, he is acting under compulsion; and he who so acts under compulsion is not virtuous.

But it is not possible to perform virtuous acts without pain or pleasure. The middle state does not exist. Why not? Because virtue implies emotion, and emotion pain or plea-
20   sure, and there is nothing in the middle. It is plain, then, that virtue is attended with pain or with pleasure. Now if one does what is noble with pain he is not virtuous. So that virtue will not be attended with pain. Therefore with pleasure. Not only, then, is pleasure not an impediment, but it is actually
25   an encouragement to action, and generally virtue cannot exist without the pleasure that comes from it.

There was another argument—that there is no science which produces pleasure. But this is not true either. For cooks and milliners and perfume-makers are engaged in the
30   production of pleasure. There is, therefore, a science pro-ductive of pleasure. The other sciences do not have pleasure as their end, but the end is with pleasure and not without it.

Again, there was another argument—that it is not the best thing. But in that way and by the like reasoning you will reject the particular virtues too. For courage is not the best thing. Is it, therefore, not a good? Surely this is absurd. And
35   the same with the rest. Neither, then, is pleasure not a good simply because it is not the best thing.

To pass on, a problem of the following kind might be raised in the case of the virtues. I mean, since the reason sometimes masters the emotions (for we say so in the case of the continent man), and the emotions again conversely mas-ter the reason (as happens in the case of the incontinent),
1206b since, then, the irrational part of the soul, if it is vicious, masters the reason, which is well-disposed (for the inconti-nent man is of this kind), the reason in like manner, if it is in a base condition, will master the emotions, which are well-disposed and have their appropriate virtue, and if this should
5   be the case, the result will be a bad use of virtue (for the rea-son being in a base condition and using virtue will use it badly): now such a result would seem to be absurd.

This problem it is easy to answer and resolve from what has been said by us before about virtue. For we assert that

452

there is virtue when the reason being in a good condition is   10
commensurate with the emotions, these possessing their
appropriate virtue, and the emotions with the reason; for in
such a condition they will accord with one another, so that
the reason will always ordain what is best, and the emotions
being well disposed find it easy to carry out what the reason
ordains. If, then, the reason is in a base condition and the   15
emotions in a good condition, there will not be virtue owing
to the failure of the reason (for virtue depends on both). So
that it is not possible to make a bad use of virtue.

Quite generally, it is not the case, as the others think, that
reason is the originating principle and guide of virtue:
rather, the emotions are. For there must first be produced in   20
us (as indeed is the case) an irrational impulse to the noble,
and then later on the reason must put the question to the
vote and decide it. One may see this from the case of children
and those who live without reason. For in these, apart from
reason, there spring up, first, impulses of the feelings towards the noble, and the reason, supervening later and giv-   25
ing its vote the same way, makes them perform noble actions. But if they have received from the reason the
originating principle of the noble, the feelings do not follow
and tell in the same sense but often are contrary to it. That is
why a right disposition of the emotions seems to be the originating principle of virtue rather than the reason.

10

GOOD FORTUNE

30 SINCE OUR DISCUSSION IS ABOUT HAPPINESS, IT WILL BE connected with the preceding to speak about good fortune. For the majority think that the happy life is the fortunate life, or at least not without good fortune, and perhaps correctly so. For it is not possible to be happy without external goods, which fortune controls. That is why we must speak

35 about good fortune, saying in the abstract who the fortunate man is, where he is found, and with what he is concerned.

First, then, one may raise problems by having recourse to the following considerations. One would not say of fortune that it is nature. For what is caused by nature comes about in

1207a the same way for the most part or always, but this is never the case with fortune where things are disorderly and as it may chance: this is why we speak of fortune in the case of such things. Neither would one identify it with any intelligence or correct reasoning. For here things are no less orderly and come about always in the same way—and there is no fortune. That is why where there is most of intelligence

5 and reason, there is least fortune, and where there is most fortune, there is least intelligence. Then is good fortune a sort of care on the part of the gods? Surely it will not be thought to be this? For we suppose that, if god controls things, he assigns both the good and the bad to those who are worthy of them, whereas fortune and matters of fortune

10 do truly occur as it may chance. But if we assign such a dispensation to god, we shall be making him a base assessor or else unjust. And this is not befitting to god.

And yet outside of these there is no other position which one can assign to fortune, so that it is plain that it must be one of these. Now intelligence and reason and knowledge seem to be utterly foreign to it. And yet neither would the care and benevolence of god seem to be good fortune, owing to its being found also in the base—for it is not likely that god would care for the base.

Nature, then, is left as being most akin to good fortune. And good fortune and fortune are found in things that are not in our own power and which we do not control and cannot bring about. That is why no one calls the just man, in so far as he is just, fortunate, nor yet the courageous man, nor any other virtuous character. For these things are in our power to have or not to have. Rather, we shall speak more appropriately of good fortune in cases like these: we call the well-born fortunate, and generally the man who possesses such kinds of goods of which he is not himself the controller.

All the same, even there it would not seem to be a matter of good fortune strictly speaking. We speak of the fortunate in several ways: we call a man fortunate to whom it has befallen to perform some good action against his own calculation, and him who has made a gain when he ought reasonably to have incurred a loss. Good fortune, then, consists in some good accruing against reason, and in escaping some evil that might reasonably have been expected. But good fortune would seem to consist to a greater extent and more appropriately in the obtaining of good. For the obtaining of good would seem to be in itself a piece of good fortune, while the escaping evil is a piece of good fortune coincidentally.

Good fortune, then, is nature without reason. For the fortunate man is he who apart from reason has an impulse to good things and obtains these, and this comes from nature. For there is in the soul by nature something of this sort whereby we are impelled, not under the guidance of reason, towards things for which we are well fitted. And if one were to ask a man in this state: 'Why do you approve of doing that?', he would say: 'I don't know, except that I do approve of it', being in the same condition as those who are inspired

by religious frenzy; for they also have an impulse to do something apart from reason.

5   We cannot call good fortune by a proper name of its own,
but we often say that it is a cause, though cause is not an appropriate name for it. For a cause and its effect are different,
and what is called a cause contains no reference to an impulse which attains good, in the way either of avoiding evil or
10   on the other hand of obtaining good when not thinking to
obtain it. Good fortune of this kind, then, is different from
the former, and this seems to result from the way in which
things fall out, and to be good fortune coincidentally. So if
this also is good fortune, at all events the sort more appro-
15   priate in relation to happiness is the sort wherein the origin
of the impulse towards the attainment of goods is in the man
himself.

Since, then, happiness cannot exist apart from external
goods, and these result from good fortune, as we said just
now, it will work together with happiness. So much then
about good fortune.

11

GENTLEMANLINESS

SINCE WE HAVE SPOKEN ABOUT EACH OF THE VIRTUES IN detail, it remains to sum up the particulars under one general statement. There is an expression, which is not badly used of the completely virtuous man: gentlemanliness. For he is gentlemanly, they say, when he is completely virtuous. For it is in the case of virtue that they use the expression 'gentlemanly': for instance, they say that the just man is gentlemanly, and the courageous man, and the temperate, and generally in the case of the virtues.

We make a dual division, and say that some things are noble and others good, and that some goods are good in the abstract and others not so, calling noble such things as the virtues and the actions which arise from them, and good such things as office, riches, reputation, honour, and the like: a gentleman is he to whom the things that are good in the abstract are good, and the things that are noble in the abstract are noble. For such a man is gentlemanly. But he to whom things good in the abstract are not good is not gentlemanly, just as a man to whom the things that are healthy in the abstract are not healthy would not be thought to be in good health. For if the accession of riches and office were to harm anybody, they would not be desirable—rather, he will want to have for himself such things as will not harm him. But he who is of such a nature as to shrink from having anything good would not seem to be gentlemanly. But he for whom the possession of all good things is good and who is not spoilt by them (as, for instance, by riches and office) is a gentleman.

5   ABOUT ACTING CORRECTLY IN ACCORDANCE WITH THE
virtues something indeed has been said, but not enough. For
we said that it was acting in accordance with correct reasoning. But possibly one might be ignorant as to this very point,
and might ask, 'What is acting in accordance with correct
reasoning? And where is correct reasoning?' To act, then, in

10   accordance with correct reasoning is when the irrational
part of the soul does not hinder the calculating part from exercising its own activity. For then the action will be in accordance with correct reasoning. For seeing that in the soul we
have a worse and a better part and the worse is always for the
sake of the better, as in the case of body and soul the body is

15   for the sake of the soul, and we shall say that we have our
body in a good state, when its state is such as not to hinder
but actually to help and take part in stimulating the soul to
perform its own task (for the worse is for the sake of the better, to work together with the better). When, then, the emotions do not hinder the intelligence from performing its own

20   task, then you will have what is done in accordance with correct reasoning.

Yes—but perhaps someone may say: 'In what state must
the emotions be so as not to act as a hindrance, and when are
they in this state? For I do not know'. This sort of thing is not
easy to state, any more than the doctor finds it so. When a
doctor has given orders that barley-gruel shall be administered to a patient in a fever, and you say to him, 'But how am
I to know when he has a fever?', he replies, 'When you see

25   him pale'. 'But how am I to know when he is pale'? There the
doctor says, 'Well, if you can't perceive that much yourself,
it's no good talking to you any more'.[1] The same thing applies in like manner to all such cases. And it is the same with
regard to recognizing the emotions. For one must contrib-

30   ute something oneself towards the perception.

Perhaps one might raise the following sort of question
also: If in fact I know these things, shall I then be happy'?

1 The text of this sentence is uncertain.

They think so—but it is not so. For none of the other sciences transmits to the learner the use and activity but only
the state. So in this case also the knowing of these things   35
does not transmit the use (for happiness is an activity, as we
maintain), but the state, nor does happiness consist in the
knowledge of what produces it—rather, it comes from the
use of these things. Now the use and activity of these it is not   1208b
the business of this treatise to impart; for no other science
imparts the use of anything but only the state.

12

FRIENDSHIP

IN ADDITION TO ALL THAT HAS GONE BEFORE, IT IS NECES-
sary to speak about friendship, saying what it is, where it is
found, and what it is concerned with. For since we see that it
5 is co-extensive with life and presents itself on every occasion, and that it is a good, we must embrace it also in our
view of happiness.

First, then, perhaps it will be as well to go through the
problems and questions. Does friendship hold among people who are alike, as is thought and said? For 'Jackdaw sits by
jackdaw', as they say, and

10   Unto the like God ever brings the like.[1]

There is a story also of a dog that used always to sleep upon
the same tile, and how Empedocles, on being asked: 'Why
does the dog sleep on the same tile'? said: 'Because the dog
has something that is like the tile', implying that it was owing
to the likeness that the dog resorted to it.

15   But again, on the other hand, some people think that
friendship is found rather among contraries. For, they say,

    Earth longs for rain when the plain is dry.[2]

It is contraries, they say, which love to be friends with contraries; for among the like there is no room for friendship.
20 For the like, they say, has no need of the like (and more to the
same effect).

---

1 Homer, *Odyssey* XVII 218.
2 A line from Euripides: cf. NE 1155b3–4.

Again, is it a task or easy to become a friend? Flatterers, at all events, readily become hangers-on but they are not friends though they appear to be.

Further, such problems as the following are raised. Will the virtuous man be a friend to the base or not? For friendship depends on trust and firmness, and the base man is not at all of this character. And will one base man be a friend to another? Or will this not be the case either?

First, then, we must determine what kind of friendship we are investigating. There is, people think, friendship towards god and towards inanimate things—incorrectly. For friendship, we maintain, exists only where there can be mutual love, but friendship towards god does not admit of love being mutual, nor of loving at all. For it would be absurd if one were to say that he loved Zeus. Neither is it possible to have mutual love with inanimate things, though there is a love of inanimate things (for instance wine or something else of that sort). That is why it is not friendship with god which we are investigating, nor friendship for inanimate things, but friendship with animate beings and with things where there can be mutual love.

If, then, one were to consider next what is the object of love, it is none other than the good. Now there is a difference between the object of love and what is to be loved, as between the object of wanting and what is to be wanted. For that the object of wanting is that which is good in the abstract, but for each person it is what is good for him which is to be wanted. So also that which is good in the abstract is the object of love, but what is to be loved is that which is good for oneself, so that what is an object of love is to be loved, but what is to be loved is not an object of love.[3]

Here, then, we see the source of the problem as to whether the virtuous man is a friend to the base man or not. For what

25

30

35

1209a

5

3 Reading (with one manuscript): φιλητὸν καὶ φιλητέον, τὸ δὲ φιλητέον οὐκ ἐστι φιλητόν. Susemihl's text translates: 'what is to be loved is an object of love, but what is an object of love is not to be loved'.

is good for oneself is in a way attached to the good, and so is
that which is to be loved to the lovable, and it depends on
and is implied by the good that it should be pleasant and
that it should be advantageous. Now friendship among the
virtuous lies in their loving one another; and they love one
another in so far as they are lovable; and they are lovable in
so far as they are good. The virtuous man, then (you say),
will not be a friend to the base. Yes he will. For since the
good implied the advantageous and the pleasant, in so far
as, though base, he is pleasant, so far he is a friend; again,
being advantageous, then so far as he is advantageous, so far
is he a friend. But this sort of friendship will not depend
upon lovableness. For the good, we saw, is lovable, but the
base man is not lovable. Rather such a friendship will depend on a man's being one who is to be loved. For deriving
from the perfect friendship which is found among the virtuous there are also these forms of friendship: that of the
pleasant and that of the advantageous. He, then, whose love
is based on the pleasant does not love with the love which is
based on the good, nor does he whose love is based upon the
advantageous.

These forms of friendship—of the good, of the pleasant,
and of the advantageous—are not the same, nor yet absolutely different from one another. Rather, they hang in a way
from the same point. For example, we call a knife medical, a
man medical, and knowledge medical, but they are not
called so in the same way—rather, the knife is called medical
from being useful in medicine, and the man from his being
able to produce health, and the knowledge from its being
cause and origin. Similarly, the forms of friendship are not
all called so in the same way—the friendship of the virtuous
which is based on the good, the friendship based on pleasure, and that based on advantage. Nor yet is it a case of
homonymy: rather, while they are not the same, they are in a
way concerned with the same things and originate from the
same things. If, therefore, someone says: 'He whose love is
prompted by pleasure is not a friend to so-and-so; for his

friendship is not based on the good', he is having recourse to the friendship of the virtuous, which is a compound of all these—of the good and the pleasant and the advantageous— 35 so that it is true that he is not a friend in respect of that friendship, but rather in respect of the friendship of the pleasant or the advantageous.

Will the virtuous man then be a friend to the virtuous or not? For the like (you say) has no need of the like. An argument of this sort investigates the friendship of advantage; for if they are friends in so far as the one has need of the 1209b other, they are in the friendship of advantage. But the friendship of advantage has been distinguished from that of virtue or of pleasure. It is likely, then, that the virtuous should be much more friends; for they have all the qualifications—the 5 good and the pleasant and the advantageous. But the virtuous may also be a friend to the base; for it may be that he is a friend in so far as he is pleasant. And the base also to the base; for it may be that they are friends in so far as the same things are advantageous to them. For we see as a matter of fact that, when the same things are advantageous, they are friends based on advantage, so that there will be nothing to 10 prevent the same things from being to some extent advantageous to the base.

Friendship among the virtuous, which is based on virtue and the good, is of course the firmest, the most abiding, and the noblest form. For virtue, to which the friendship is due, is unchangeable, so that it is reasonable that this form of friendship should be unchangeable. But advantage is never 15 the same. That is why the friendship which rests on advantage is never firm but changes along with the advantage; and the same with the friendship which rests on pleasure. The friendship, then, of the best men is that which arises from virtue, but that of the common run of men depends upon advantage, while that which rests on pleasure is found among vulgar and commonplace persons.

When people find their friends base, they are resentful 20 and surprised. But it is nothing absurd. For when friendship

463

has taken its start from pleasure, and this is why they are friends, or from advantage, so soon as these fail the friendship does not continue. Often the friendship does remain, but a man treats his friend badly: that is why there is resentment. But neither is absurd. For your friendship with this man was not based on virtue: that is why it is not absurd that he should do nothing of what virtue requires. Resentment, then, is not the correct attitude. Having formed their friendship with a view to pleasure, they think they ought to have the kind which is due to virtue; but that is not possible. For the friendship of pleasure and advantage does not depend on virtue. Having entered then into a partnership in pleasure, they look for virtue—incorrectly. For virtue does not follow upon pleasure and advantage: both these follow upon virtue. For it would be absurd not to think that the virtuous are the most pleasant to one another. For even the base, as Euripides says, are pleasant to one another: 'The bad man is fused into one with the bad'. For virtue does not follow upon pleasure, whereas pleasure does follow upon virtue.

Is it necessary that there should be pleasure in the friendship of the virtuous or not? It would be absurd to say that it should not. For if you deprive them of being pleasant to one another, they will procure other friends, who are pleasant, to live with; for in view of living together there is nothing more important than being pleasant. It would be absurd then not to think that the virtuous ought above all others to live with one another; and this cannot be without the element of pleasure. It will be necessary, then, as it seems, for them above all to be pleasant.

Friendships have been divided into three species, and in the case of these the problem was raised whether friendship takes place in equality or in inequality: it takes place in both. That which implies likeness is the friendship of the virtuous, and complete friendship, and that which implies unlikeness is the friendship of advantage. For the poor man is a friend to the rich owing to his own lack of what the wealthy man has in abundance, and the base man to the virtuous for the

same reason. For owing to his lack of virtue he is for this reason a friend to him from whom he thinks he will get it.
Among the unequal then there arises friendship based on
advantage. That is why Euripides says,

Earth longs for rain when the plain is dry,[4]   15

intimating that the friendship of advantage takes place between these as contraries. For if you like to set down fire and
water as most contrary, these are useful to one another. For
fire, they say, if it has not moisture, perishes, as this provides
it with a kind of nutriment, but only to such an extent as it
can master it; for if you make the moisture too great, it will   20
obtain the mastery, and will cause the fire to go out, but if
you supply it in due proportion, it will be of advantage to it.
It is plain, then, that friendship based on advantage occurs
among things most contrary.

All the forms of friendship, both those in equality and
those in inequality, are referred to the three in our division.
But in all the forms of friendship there is a difference that
arises between the partners when they do not love or benefit   25
or serve (or whatever else it may be) to the same degree. For
when one exerts himself energetically and the other is deficient, there is complaint and blame on the score of the deficiency. Now the deficiency on the part of the one is plain to
see in the case of such persons as have the same end in view in
their friendship (i.e., if both are friends to one another on the 30
ground of advantage or of pleasure or of virtue), and so if you
do me more good than I do you, I do not even dispute that
you ought to be loved more by me. But in a friendship where
we are not friends with the same object, there is more room   35
for differences. For the deficiency on one side or the other is
not plain. For instance, if one is a friend for pleasure and the
other for advantage, that is where the dispute will arise. For
he who offers a superior advantage does not think the pleasure a worthy exchange for the advantage, and he who is

4 See above, 1208b16–17.

465

1210b   more pleasant does not think that he receives in the advantageous a worthy return for the pleasure. That is why differences are more likely to arise in such kinds of friendship.

When men are friends on an unequal footing, those who
are superior in riches or anything of that sort do not think

5 that they themselves ought to love, but think that they ought
to be loved by those worse off. But it is better to love than to
be loved. For to love is an exercise of pleasure and a good,
whereas from being loved there results no exercise in the object of the love. Again, it is better to know than to be known;

10 for to be known and to be loved attach even to inanimate
things, but to know and to love to animate things. Again, to
be inclined to benefit is better than not; and he who loves is
inclined to benefit, just in so far as he loves, whereas this is
not the case with him who is loved, in so far as he is loved.

But owing to ambition men want rather to be loved than
to love, because of there being a certain superiority in being

15 loved. For he who is loved has always a superiority in pleasure or wealth or virtue, and the ambitious man desires superiority. And those who are in a position of superiority do
not think that they themselves ought to love, since they
make a return to those who love them in those things in
which they are superior. And again the others are inferior to
them—that is why the superiors do not think they them-

20 selves ought to love but to be loved. But he who is lacking in
wealth or pleasures or virtue admires him who has a superiority in these things, and loves him because he gets these
things or thinks that he will get them.

Such friendships arise from fellow-feeling, that is, from
wanting good for someone. But the friendship which takes

25 place in these cases has not all these features. For often we
want good for one person and want to live with another. But
ought we to say that these features are characteristics of
friendship or of the complete friendship which is founded
on virtue? For in that friendship all these things are contained; for there is none other with whom we should want to

30 live (for pleasantness and advantage and virtue are attributes

466

of the virtuous man), and it is for him that we should most want good, and to live and to live well for none other than him.

Whether a man can have friendship for and towards himself may be omitted for the present, but we shall speak of it later. But all the things that we want we want for ourselves— we want to live with ourselves (though that is perhaps unavoidable), and to live well, and to live, and to want the good for no one other than ourselves. Further, we have most fellow-feeling with ourselves; for if we stumble or meet with anything else of that sort, we are at once distressed. (That is why it would seem that there is friendship towards oneself.) In speaking then of such things as fellow-feeling and living well and so on we are referring either to friendship towards ourselves or to complete friendship. For all these things are found in both. For living together and wanting the existence and the well-being of someone and all the rest are found in these.

Further, it may perhaps be thought that wherever justice is, there friendship is too. That is why are as many species of friendship as there are of justice. Now there can be justice between a foreigner and a citizen, between a slave and his master, between one citizen and another, between son and father, between wife and husband, and quite generally every form of association has its separate form of friendship. But the firmest of friendships would seem to be that with a foreigner; for they have no common end about which to dispute, as is the case with fellow-citizens; for when these dispute with one another for the superiority, they do not remain friends.

It will be in place now to discuss whether there is friendship towards oneself or not. Since then we see, as we said a little earlier, that the act of loving is recognized from its particular features, and it is for ourselves that we should most want the particular features (good things, and existence, and well-being—and we have most fellow-feeling with ourselves, and we most want to live with ourselves); therefore, if friendship

is known from the particulars, and we should want the particulars to belong to ourselves, it is plain that there is friend-
25 ship towards ourselves—in the same way as we maintained that there is injustice towards oneself. For since it is one who acts unjustly and another who is treated unjustly, while each individual is one and the same, it seemed for that reason that there was no injustice towards oneself. It is possible, however, as we said on examining the parts of the soul, that since there are several such parts, when they are not in concord,
30 then there is injustice towards oneself. In the same way then there would seem to be friendship towards oneself. For a friend is, as we say when we want to describe a very close friend—we say 'My soul and his are one'. So since the parts of the soul are more than one, there will be a single soul when
35 the reason and the emotions are in accord with one another (for in this way it will be one), and when it has become one there will be friendship towards oneself. And this friendship towards oneself will be found in the virtuous man; for in him alone the parts of the soul are in proper relation to one another owing to their not being at variance—the base man is never a friend to himself, for he is always in conflict with himself. At all events the incontinent man, when he has done
1211b something to which pleasure prompts, not long afterwards has regrets and reviles himself. It is the same with the base man in other vices. For he is always in conflict and contrariety with himself.

There is also a friendship in equality: for instance, that of
5 comrades is on an equal footing in respect of number and capacity of good (for neither of them is worthy of a greater share of goods either in number or capacity or size, but of what is equal; for comrades are supposed to be a kind of equals). But that between father and son is on a footing of inequality, and that between ruler and ruled, between better
10 and worse, between wife and husband, and quite generally in all cases where there is one who occupies the position of worse or better in friendship. This friendship in inequality is proportional. For in giving of good no one would ever give

an equal share to the better and the worse, but always a
greater to the one who was superior. And this is the propor-   15
tionally equal. For the worse with a less good is in a kind of
way equal to the better with a greater.

Among all the above-mentioned forms of friendship love
is in a way strongest in that which is based on kinship, and
more particularly in the relation of father to son. Now why is   20
it that the father loves the son more than the son the father?
Is it, as some say—correctly enough as regards the many—
because the father has been a kind of benefactor to the son,
and the son owes him a return for the benefit? Now this
cause would seem to be present in the friendship of advantage. But as we see it to be in the sciences, so it is here also. I   25
mean, in some the end and the activity are the same, and
there is not any other end apart from the activity; for instance, to the flute-player the activity and end are the same
(for to play the flute is both his end and his activity); but not   30
to the art of housebuilding (for it has a different end apart
from the activity). Now friendship is a sort of activity, and
there is not any other end apart from the act of loving, but
just this. Now the father is always in a way more active owing
to the son being a kind of production of his. And this we see   35
to be so in the other cases also. For all feel a sort of benevolence towards what they have themselves produced. The father, then, feels a sort of benevolence towards the son as
being his own production, led on by memory and by hope.
This is why the father loves the son more than the son the
father.

There are other things which are called and are thought to
be forms of friendship, about which we must inquire
whether they are friendship. For instance, benevolence is   1212a
thought to be friendship. Now, in the abstract benevolence
would seem not to be friendship. For towards many persons
and often we feel benevolent either from seeing or hearing
some good about them. Are we friends or not? If someone
felt benevolence towards Darius, when he was among the   5
Persians, as someone may have done, it did not follow that

he had a friendship towards Darius. Rather, benevolence would seem to be sometimes an origin of friendship, and benevolence may become friendship if, where one has the power to do good, there be added the wish to do it for the sake of the person towards whom the benevolence is felt. Benevolence implies character and is relative to it. For no one is said to feel benevolent towards wine or towards any other inanimate thing that is good or pleasant. Rather, if anyone be of a virtuous character, benevolence is felt towards him. And benevolence is not separate from friendship, but is found in the same place. This is why it is thought to be friendship.

Concord is close to friendship, if the kind of concord that you take is that which is strictly so called. For if one makes the same assumptions as Empedocles and has the same views about the elements as he, is he in concord with Empedocles or not? Then the same thing would have to hold in any like case.[5] For first, concord is not found in matters of thought but in matters of action, and herein it is not in so far as they think the same, but in so far as in addition to thinking the same they choose to do the same about what they think. If both think to rule, but each of them thinks that he is to be ruler, are they therefore in concord or not? If I want to be ruler myself, and he wants me to be so, then we are in concord. Concord, then, is found in matters of action coupled with wanting the same thing. Concord in the strict sense, then, is concerned with the establishment of the same ruler.[6]

Since there is, as we maintain, such a thing as friendship towards oneself, will the virtuous man be a self-lover or not? Now the self-lover is he who does everything for his own sake in matters of expediency. The base man is a self-lover (for he does everything for his own sake), but not the virtuous man. For the reason why he is a virtuous man is that he

---

5 The text of this sentence is uncertain.

6 Omitting ἐν τοῖς πρακτοῖς (as Susemihl suggests).

does things for the sake of others: that is why he is not a self-lover. But all feel an impulse towards things that are good, and think that they themselves ought to have these in the highest degree. This is most apparent in the case of riches and office. Now the virtuous man will resign these to another, not on the ground that it does not become him in the highest degree to have them, but if he sees that another will be able to make more use of them than he. Other men will not do this owing to ignorance (for they do not think they might make a bad use of such goods) or else owing to an ambition to rule. But the virtuous man will not be affected in either of these ways. That is why he is not a self-lover as regards such goods at least; but, if at all, in respect of the noble. For this is the only thing which he will not resign to another, though he will resign things advantageous and pleasant. In the choice, then, of things in respect of nobility he will be a self-lover, but in the choice which we describe as being prompted by the advantageous and the pleasant it is not the virtuous man who will be so but the base man.

Will the virtuous man love himself most of all or not? In a way he will love himself most and in a way not. For since we say that the virtuous man will resign good in the way of advantage to his friend, he will love his friend more than himself. Yes; but he resigns such goods insofar as, by resigning them to his friend, he claims the noble for himself. In a way, therefore, he loves his friend more than himself, and in a way he loves himself most. In respect of the advantageous he loves his friend, but in respect of the noble and good he loves himself most; for he is claiming these for himself as being noblest. He is therefore a lover of good, not a self-lover. For, if he does love himself, it is only because he is good. But the base man is a self-lover. For he has nothing in the way of nobility for which he should love himself, and without any such thing he will love himself *qua* himself. That is why it is he who will be called a self-lover in the strict sense.

It will be in place to speak about self-sufficiency and the self-sufficient man. Will the self-sufficient man require friendship too or not? Rather, he will be sufficient to himself as regards that also. For the poets have such sayings as these—

What need of friends, when Heaven bestows the good?[7]

Whence also the problem arises of whether he who has all
30 the goods and is self-sufficient will need a friend. Or is it then that he will need him most? For to whom will he do good? Or with whom will he live? For surely he will not live alone. If, then, he will need these things, and these are not possible without friendship, the self-sufficient man will need friendship too. Now the comparison with god which is customar-
35 ily made in discussions is neither correct there nor useful here. For if god is self-sufficient and has need of nothing, it does not follow that we shall need nothing. We hear this kind of thing said about god: seeing that god (you say) possesses all goods and is self-sufficient, what will he do? We can hardly suppose that he will sleep. Well (you say), he will con-
1213a template something; for this is the noblest and the most appropriate thing to do. What, then, will he contemplate? For if he is to contemplate anything else, it must be something better than himself that he will contemplate. But it is absurd that there should be anything better than god. Therefore he will contemplate himself. But this also is absurd. For if a
5 man is absorbed in himself, we criticize him as insensible. It will be absurd therefore (you say) for god to contemplate himself. As to what god is to contemplate, then, we may let that pass. But the self-sufficiency about which we are inquiring is not that of god but of man, the question being whether
10 the self-sufficient man will require friendship or not. If, then, looking at a friend one saw the nature and attributes of a friend, ***[8] such as to be a second I, at least if you make a very close friend: as the saying has it, 'Here is another Heracles, a dear other I'. Now it is both a most difficult thing, as
15 some of the sages have said, to know oneself, and also a most

7 Euripides, *Orestes* 667
8 Susemihl marks a lacuna.

pleasant (for to know oneself is pleasant): we are not able to contemplate ourselves from ourselves (that we cannot do so is plain from the way in which we blame others without being aware that we do the same things ourselves; and this is the effect of benevolence or emotion, and there are many of us who are blinded by these things so that we do not assess   20 things correctly). So, just as when we want to see our own face we do so by looking into the mirror, in the same way when we want to know ourselves we can obtain that knowl- edge by looking at a friend. For a friend is, as we assert, an- other I. If, then, it is pleasant to know oneself, and it is not   25 possible to do so without having someone else for a friend, the self-sufficient man will require friendship in order to know himself.

Again, if it is a noble thing, as it is, to do good when one has the goods of fortune, to whom will he do good? And with whom will he live? For surely he will not spend his time alone; for to live with someone is pleasant and necessary. If, then, these things are noble and pleasant and necessary, and   1213b these things cannot be found without friendship, the self- sufficient man will need friendship.

Should one acquire many friends or few? Abstractly speak- ing, they ought neither to be many nor yet few. For if they are many, it is a task to apportion one's love to each. For in all   5 other things also the weakness of our nature incapacitates us from reaching far: we do not see far with our eyes—rather, if you distance the object further than is proportionate, the sight fails owing to the weakness of nature; and the case is the same with hearing, and similarly with all other things.   10 Failing, then, to show love through incapacity one would justly incur complaint, and one would not be a friend inas- much as one would be loving only in name—and this is not what friendship means. Again, if they are many, one can never be free from distress. For if they are many, it is always likely that some misfortune will strike one at least of them,   15 and when these things take place distress is unavoidable. Nor yet, on the other hand, should one have few—one or

two—but rather a number commensurate with one's circumstances and one's own impulse to love.

After this we must inquire how one ought to treat a friend.
This inquiry does not present itself in every friendship, but
20 in that in which friends are most liable to bring complaints
against one another. They do not do this so much in the
other cases: for instance, in the friendship between father
and son there is no complaint such as the claim they make in
some forms of friendship, 'As I to you, so you to me'—failing
which there is intense complaint. But between unequal
25 friends there is no equality, and the relation between father
and son is on a footing of inequality, as is also that between
wife and husband, or between servant and master, and generally between the worse and the better. They will therefore
not have complaints of this sort. But it is between equal
friends and in a friendship of that sort that a complaint of
this kind arises. So we must inquire how we ought to treat a
friend in the friendship between friends who are on a footing of equality.

VIRTUES AND VICES

FIRST OXFORD TRANSLATION:
J. Solomon

GREEK TEXT:
F. Susemihl, Teubner

CONTENTS

WHAT IS NOBLE IS PRAISEWORTHY, WHAT IS IGNOBLE blameworthy. At the head of what is noble stand the virtues, at the head of what is ignoble the vices.[1] Praiseworthy too are what cause the virtues and what accompany them and what they produce. The contraries are blameworthy.

If in agreement with Plato we take the soul to have three parts, then wisdom is the virtue of the calculative part, good temper and courage of the passionate part, temperance and continence of the appetitive part; and of the soul as a whole, justice, liberality, and pride. Folly is the vice of the calculative part, irascibility and cowardice of the passionate part, self-indulgence and incontinence of the appetitive part; and of the soul as a whole, injustice, illiberality, and diffidence.

WISDOM IS A VIRTUE OF THE CALCULATIVE PART WHICH provides what conduces to happiness. Good temper is a virtue of the passionate part through which men become difficult to stir to anger. Courage is a virtue of the passionate part through which men are undismayed by fears of death. Temperance is a virtue of the appetitive part through which men cease to desire the enjoyment of base pleasures. Continence is a virtue of the appetitive part through which men check by calculation the appetite that impels them to base pleasures. Justice is a virtue of the soul that distributes according to worth. Liberality is a virtue of the soul that spends freely on

1 Here Susemihl inserts a sentence: 'So that the virtues are praiseworthy'.

noble objects. Pride is a virtue of the soul through which men are able to bear good and bad fortune, honour and dishonour.

Folly is a vice of the calculative part causing evil living. Irascibility is a vice of the passionate part through which men are easily stirred to anger. Cowardice is a vice of the passionate part through which men are dismayed by fears, especially such as relate to death. Self-indulgence is a vice of the appetitive part through which men become desirous of the enjoyment of base pleasures. Incontinence is a vice of the appetitive part through which men prefer the enjoyment of base pleasures, though reason restrains them. Injustice is a vice of the soul through which men come to covet more than they are worth. Illiberality is a vice of the soul through which men aim at profit from every source. Diffidence is a vice of the soul through which men are unable to bear good and bad fortune, honour and dishonour.

TO WISDOM BELONG RIGHT DELIBERATION, RIGHT ASSESS-ment of what is good and bad and of everything in life that is desirable and to be avoided, noble use of all the goods that belong to us, correct social behaviour, spotting the right moments, the astute use of word and deed, the possession of experience of all that is useful. Memory, experience, tact, skill in deliberation, astuteness—each of these either arises from wisdom or accompanies it or else some of them are as it were side-causes of wisdom (such as experience and memory), while others are as it were parts (for instance skill in deliberation and astuteness).

To good temper belong the power to bear moderate[2] complaints and moderate disdain, not to rush hastily to vengeance, not to be easily stirred to anger, to be without bitterness or contentiousness in one's character, to have in one's soul tranquillity and steadfastness.

2 Reading μετρία (with most authorities) for μετρίως ('moderately').

To courage belong being undismayed by fears of death, confidence in fearful circumstances, boldness in the face of danger, preferring a noble death to an ignoble survival, and to be the cause of victory. Also to courage belong exertion, endurance, preferring danger.[3] Courage is accompanied by boldness, high spirits, and confidence; and further, by zeal and endurance.

To temperance belong not admiring the enjoyment of bodily pleasures, not desiring any ignoble voluptuous pleasure, fear of ill-repute, an ordered course of life alike in small things and in great. And temperance is accompanied by orderliness, propriety, modesty, caution.

To continence belong the power to repress appetite by calculation when it impels us to a base enjoyment of pleasures, and also endurance and the facing up to natural lack and pain.

To justice belong the capacity to distribute to each according to his worth, to preserve ancestral customs and practices, to preserve written laws, truthfulness in matters of importance, keeping agreements. The demands of justice are first to the gods, then to spirits, then to one's country and parents, then to the departed; among them is piety, which is either a part of justice or an accompaniment of it. Also justice is accompanied by reverence, candour, trust, and hatred of viciousness.

To liberality belong the expenditure of wealth on praiseworthy objects, lavishness in spending where one should, helpfulness with cash, philanthropy, not taking from where you should not. The liberal man is also clean in his dress and his house, ready to provide himself with those beautiful extras which make for a pleasant life and are not for

1250b

5

10

15

20

25

30

---

3 Reading αἱρεῖσθαι κινδυνεῦσαι (Bücheler): the received text is αἱρεῖσθαι καὶ δύνασθαι ('to prefer and to be able'); an indirect witness has αἱρεῖσθαι ἀνδραγαθίζεσθαι ('to prefer to play the man'—which Stock accepts); and Susemihl prints ἀνδραγαθίζεσθαι.

expediency, inclined to keep all animals that have anything peculiar or marvellous about them. Liberality is accompanied by a suppleness and ductility of character, by philanthropy, by pity, by love of friends, love of strangers, love of what is noble.

35 To pride belong bearing nobly good and bad fortune, honour and dishonour; not admiring either luxury or attention or power or victory in contests, but to have a sort of depth and greatness of soul. The proud man is one who nei-
40 ther sets much store on living nor loves life, but is in character simple and upright, one who can be treated unjustly without being prompt to avenge himself. Pride is accompanied by simplicity, uprightness and candour.

To FOLLY BELONG ASSESSING THINGS BADLY, DELIBERATing badly, bad social behaviour, bad use of what goods one
1251a has, false beliefs about what is good and noble as regards life. Folly is accompanied by ignorance, inexperience, poor assessment,[4] tactlessness, shortness of memory.

Of irascibility there are three species—choler, bitterness, sullenness. It is the mark of the irascible man to be unable to
5 bear mild disdain or minor defeats, to be ready to punish, prompt to avenge, easily stirred to anger by any chance word or deed. Irascibility is accompanied by excitability of charac-
10 ter, changeability, pettiness, distress at small things—and all these quickly and on slight occasion.

To cowardice belong being easily stirred by chance fears, especially if relating to death or maiming of the body, and asuming that it is better to survive no matter how than to die nobly. Cowardice is accompanied by softness, unmanliness,
15 despair, love of life. Beneath it is a sort of caution and an uncompetitiveness of character.

To self-indulgence belong choosing the enjoyment of harmful and ignoble pleasures, assuming that those living amid such pleasures are especially happy, love of laughter,

4 Reading ἀκρισία (Apelt) for ἀκρασία ('incontinence').

love of mockery, love of conviviality, and levity in word and   20
deed. Self-indulgence is accompanied by disorderliness,
shamelessness, impropriety, luxury, ease, negligence, con-
tempt, dissipation.

To incontinence belong preferring the enjoyment of pleasures though calculation restrains, partaking of them   25
though assuming it to be better not to partake of them, and,
while thinking one ought to do what is noble and advantageous, abstaining from these for the sake of pleasures. Incontinence is accompanied by softness, negligence, and
most of the things which accompany self-indulgence.

Of injustice there are three species—impiety, covetous-   30
ness, outrage. Impiety is wrong-doing towards gods, spirits,
the departed, one's parents, or one's country. Covetousness
is wrong-doing in regard to agreements, taking cash unworthily. Outrage occurs when in providing pleasure for oneself
one brings shame on others, whence Evenus says of it: 35

That which while gaining no profit, does injustice.

To injustice belong violation of ancestral customs and practices, disobedience of laws and rulers, lying, perjury, violation   1251b
of agreements and trust. Injustice is accompanied by chicanery, boasting, feigned philanthropy,[5] malignity, villainy.

Of illiberality there are three species—avarice, miserliness, stinginess: avarice through which they look for profit   5
from all sources and think more of the profit than of the
shame; miserliness through which they are unready to spend
wealth where they should; stinginess through which, while
spending, they spend in small sums and badly, and are more
harmed from not spending their cash in season. To illiberal-   10
ity belong setting most store by wealth, and thinking that no
shame can ever attach to what yields profit; a servile life,
suited to a slave, sordid, foreign to ambition and liberality.

---

5 Reading φιλανθρωπία προσποιητός (most authorities) for Susemihl's
ἀφιλανθρωπία, προσποίησις ('lack of philanthropy, pretence').

15 Illiberality is accompanied by pettiness, sullenness, diffidence, humbleness,[6] misanthropy.

To diffidence belong inability to bear either honour or dishonour, either good or bad fortune, but vanity when 20 honoured, elation at a little good fortune, inability to bear even the smallest dishonour, assessing any failure whatever as a great misfortune, lamenting and being impatient over everything. Further, the diffident man is such as to call every disdainful act an outrage and a dishonour, even such as are inflicted through ignorance or forgetfulness. Diffi- 25 dence is accompanied by pettiness, grumbling, pessimism, humbleness.

IN GENERAL, TO VIRTUE BELONGS MAKING THE CONDI- tion of the soul good, so that it uses tranquil and ordered motions and is in agreement with itself in all its parts—that is why the condition of a good soul seems a pattern for a 30 good political constitution. To virtue belong also benefi- cence towards the worthy, love for the good, hatred for the bad,[7] not being prompt either to punish or to avenge, but being gracious, kindly, and sympathetic. Virtue is accompa- nied by goodness, decency, good sense, optimism, and fur- 35 ther by such qualities as love of relations, love of friends, love of comrades, love of strangers, love of men, love of the noble: all these qualities are praiseworthy. To vice belong the con- trary qualities, and the contrary qualities accompany it; and all that belongs to vice and accompanies it is blamed.

6 Omitting ἀμετρία—'lack of proportion'—(Schuchhardt)

7 Retaining καὶ τὸ μισεῖν τοὺς φαύλους (which Susemihl excises).

GLOSSARIES

THE GLOSSARIES ARE IN THE MAIN LIMITED TO WORDS
which are part of Aristotle's ethical vocabulary. The translations hold, as Aristotle would have said, for the most part.
Generally speaking, translations of head-words apply *muta-
tis mutandis* to their cognates.

ENGLISH-GREEK

abstract, in the	ἁπλῶς
action	πρᾶξις
activity	ἐνέργεια
anger	ὀργή
appetite	ἐπιθυμία
assessment	κρίσις
association	κοινωνία
assumption	ὑπόληψις
astuteness	ἀγχίνοια
authoritative	κύριος
avarice	αἰσχροκέρδεια
bad	κακός
base	φαῦλος
bashfulness	κατάπληξις
belief	δόξα
benevolence	εὔνοια
blameworthy	ψεκτός
blessedness	μακαριότης
boastfulness	ἀλαζονεία
boorishness	ἀγροικία
brutishness	θηριότης
buffoonery	βωμολοχία

calculation	λογισμός
candour	ἀλήθεια
capacity	δύναμις
character	ἕξις, ἦθος
choice	προαίρεσις, αἵρεσις
churlishness	αὐθάδεια
cleverness	δεινότης
coincidentally	κατὰ συμβεβηκός
company	ὁμιλία
complete	τέλειος
compulsion	ἀνάγκη
comrade	ἑταῖρος
concord	ὁμονοία
confident	θρασύς
consider	θεωρεῖν
contemplate	θεωρεῖν
continence	ἐγκράτεια
contrary	ἐναντίος
controlling	κύριος
convention	νόμος
conviviality	εὐτραπελία
correctness	ὀρθότης
courage	ἀνδρεία
cowardice	δειλία
craft	τέχνη
craftsmanship	τέχνη
crave	ἐπιθυμεῖν
deed	ἔργον
deficiency	ἔλλειψις
deliberation	βουλή
delight in	χαίρειν
depraved	μοχθηρός
desirable	αἱρετός
desire	ὄρεξις
diffidence	μικροψυχία
dignity	σεμνότης
emotion	πάθος

end	τέλος
endurance	καρτερία
enjoy	ἀπολαύειν
envy	φθόνος
equality	ἰσότης
equity	ἐπιείκεια
excess	ὑπερβολή
exercise	ἐνέργεια
extravagance	δαπανηρία
extreme	ἄκρος
fact	ἔργον
fairness	ἰσότης
final	τέλειος
flattery	κολακεία
force	βία
fortune	τύχη
friendship	φιλία
gentlemanliness	καλοκἀγαθία
good	ἀγαθός
good temper	πραότης
grumpiness	δυσκολία
habit	ἔθος
happiness	εὐδαιμονία
harm	βλάβη
honour	τιμή
ignoble	αἰσχρός
illiberality	ἀνελευθερία
impetuousness	προπέτεια
incontinence	ἀκρασία
indignation	νέμεσις
in general	ἁπλῶς
insensibility	ἀναισθησία
insensitivity	ἀναλγησία
intellectual	διανοητικός
intelligence	νοῦς
involuntary	ἀκούσιος
irascibility	ὀργιλότης

judgement	σύνεσις
justice	δικαιοσύνη
knowledge	ἐπιστήμη
lack	ἔνδεια
law	νόμος
liberality	ἐλευθεριότης
loss	ζημία
love	φιλεῖν
luxuriousness	τρυφερότης
magnificence	μεγαλοπρέπεια
mean	μεσότης
middle	μέσος
modesty	αἰδώς
moral	ἠθικός
noble	καλός
obsequiousness	ἀρέσκεια
origin	ἀρχή
ostentatious	σαλακών
overconfidence	θρασύτης
pain	λύπη
passion	θυμός
people's perceptions	τὰ φαινόμενα
perception	αἴσθησις
perfect	τέλειος
pleasure	ἡδονή
political	πολιτικός
praiseworthy	ἐπαινετός
precision	ἀκρίβεια
pride	μεγαλοψυχία
principle	ἀρχή
process	γένεσις
prodigality	ἀσωτία
product	ἔργον
profit	κέρδος
rage	θυμός
regret	μεταμέλεια

rule	ἀρχή
science	ἐπιστήμη
self-deprecation	εἰρωνεία
self-indulgence	ἀκολασία
self-sufficiency	αὐτάρκεια
sense	γνώμη
sense-perception	αἴσθησις
shabbiness	μικροπρέπεια
shamelessness	ἀναισχυντία
share	κοινωνεῖν
softness	μαλακία
state	ἕξις
State	πόλις
surliness	ἀπέχθεια
sympathy	συγγνώμη
task	ἔργον
tastelessness	ἀπειροκαλία
temperance	σωφροσύνη
thought	διάνοια
tout court	ἁπλῶς
true	ἀληθής
understanding	σοφία
upright	ἐπιεικής
valuable	τίμιος
vanity	χαυνότης
vice	κακία
vicious	πονηρός
villainy	πανουργία
virtue	ἀρετή
virtuous	σπουδαῖος
voluntary	ἑκούσιος
voluptuary	ἀπολαυστικός
want	βούλεσθαι
will	βούλησις
wisdom	φρόνησις
worth	ἀξία

GREEK-ENGLISH

ἀγαθός	good
ἀγροικία	boorishness
ἀγχίνοια	astuteness
αἰδώς	modesty
αἵρεσις	choice
αἱρετός	desirable
αἴσθησις	(sense-)perception
αἰσχροκέρδεια	avarice
αἰσχρός	ignoble
ἀκολασία	self-indulgence
ἀκούσιος	involuntary
ἀκρασία	incontinence
ἀκρίβεια	precision
ἄκρος	extreme
ἀλαζονεία	boastfulness
ἀλήθεια	candour
ἀληθής	true
ἀνάγκη	compulsion
ἀναισθησία	insensibility
ἀναισχυντία	shamelessness
ἀναλγησία	insensitivity
ἀνδρεία	courage
ἀξία	worth
ἀπειροκαλία	tastelessness
ἀπέχθεια	surliness
ἁπλῶς	in the abstract, *tout court*
ἀπολαύειν	enjoy
ἀπολαυστικός	voluptuary
ἀρέσκεια	obsequiousness
ἀρετή	virtue
ἀρχή	origin, (originating) principle, rule
ἀσωτία	prodigality
αὐθάδεια	churlishness

αὐτάρκεια	self-sufficiency
βία	force
βλάβη	harm
βούλεσθαι	want
βουλή	deliberation
βούλησις	will
βωμολοχία	buffoonery
γένεσις	process
γνώμη	sense
δαπανηρία	extravagance
δειλία	cowardice
δεινότης	cleverness
διανοητικός	intellectual
διάνοια	thought
δικαιοσύνη	justice
δόξα	belief
δύναμις	capacity
δυσκολία	grumpiness
ἐγκράτεια	continence
ἔθος	habit
εἰρωνεία	self-deprecation
ἑκούσιος	voluntary
ἐλευθεριότης	liberality
ἔλλειψις	deficiency
ἐναντίος	contrary
ἔνδεια	lack
ἐνέργεια	activity, exercise
ἕξις	character, state
ἐπαινετός	praiseworthy
ἐπιεικής	upright, equitable
ἐπιθυμεῖν	crave
ἐπιθυμία	appetite
ἐπιστήμη	knowledge, science
ἐπιχαιρεκακία	spite
ἔργον	deed, fact, product, task
ἑταῖρος	comrade
εὐδαιμονία	happiness

εὔνοια	benevolence
εὐτραπελία	conviviality
ζημία	loss
ἡδονή	pleasure
ἠθικός	moral
ἦθος	character
θεωρεῖν	contemplate, consider
θηριότης	brutishness
θρασύς	confident
θρασύτης	overconfidence
θυμός	passion, rage
ἰσότης	equality, fairness
κακία	vice
κακός	bad
καλοκἀγαθία	gentlemanliness
καλός	noble
καρτερία	endurance
κατάπληξις	bashfulness
κατὰ συμβεβηκός	coincidentally
κέρδος	profit
κοινωνεῖν	share
κοινωνία	association
κολακεία	flattery
κρίσις	assessment
κύριος	authoritative, controlling
λογισμός	calculation
λύπη	pain
μακαριότης	blessedness
μαλακία	softness
μεγαλοπρέπεια	magnificence
μεγαλοψυχία	pride
μέσος	middle
μεσότης	mean
μεταμέλεια	regret
μικροπρέπεια	shabbiness
μικροψυχία	diffidence

μοχθηρός	depraved
νέμεσις	indignation
νόμος	convention, law
νοῦς	intelligence
ὁμιλία	company
ὁμονοία	concord
ὀργή	anger
ὀργιλότης	irascibility
ὄρεξις	desire
ὀρθότης	correctness
πάθος	emotion
πανουργία	villainy
πόλις	State
πολιτικός	political
πονηρότης	viciousness
πρᾶξις	action
πραότης	good temper
προαίρεσις	choice
προπέτεια	impetuousness
σαλακών	ostentatious
σεμνότης	dignity
σοφία	understanding
σπουδαῖος	virtuous
συγγνώμη	sympathy
σύνεσις	judgement
σωφροσύνη	temperance
τέλειος	complete, perfect
τέλος	end
τέχνη	craft, craftsmanship
τιμή	honour
τίμιος	valuable
τρυφερότης	luxuriousness
τύχη	fortune
ὑπερβολή	excess
ὑπόληψις	assumption
τὰ φαινόμενα	people's perceptions
φαῦλος	base

φθόνος	envy
φιλεῖν	love
φιλία	friendship
φρόνησις	wisdom
χαίρειν	delight in
χαυνότης	vanity
ψεκτός	blameworthy

INDEX OF NAMES

GENERAL INDEX

ability: *see* capacity
action [πρᾶξις]
    and choice, 117–118
    matters of, 41
    'mixed', 254–255
    not performed by animals, 61
    not performed by children, 61
    and particulars, 128
    see also origins; producing
activity [ἐνέργεια]
    vs capacity, 238
    vs movement, 352–353
    vs state, 46, 154, 156, 227, 239,
      309, 406, 459
actuality, vs potentiality [ἐνέργεια],
    7–8
adultery, 53, 93, 98, 104, 111, 246,
    272, 385, 423
ambiguity: *see* homonymy
ambition, 173, 248, 293–294, 451,
    466
amusement, 147, 300, 358–359
analogy, 164, 222
    see also homonymy
anger [ὀργή]
    objects of, 294–295
    and pain, 82, 272
    see also good temper; rage
animals
    cannot be happy, 229
    and courage, 70
    do not act, 61

do not choose, 68, 258, 402
and friendship, 165, 178, 319
and pleasure, 80–81, 153, 155,
    158, 275–276, 277, 356–357
and virtue, 131, 408
and the voluntary, 257–258
and wisdom, 123
see also brutishness
appetite [ἐπιθυμία]
    and choice, 66, 258
    and continence, 59–60
    kinds of, 141, 144, 276–277,
      278
    and the voluntary, 59–60, 257–
      258, 399–400
art: *see* crafts
associations [κοινωνία], 180–182,
    183, 315–317
assumption [ὑπόληψις], 134, 427
astuteness [ἀγχίνοια], 126
avarice [αἰσχροκέρδεια], 83, 284,
    411

bashfulness [κατάπληξις], 88, 249,
    414
belief [δόξα]
    and choice, 65–66, 259
    degrees of, 137
    and deliberation, 126
    and incontinence, 135–136, 137,
      149–150, 437, 439
    vs knowledge, 135